D1276908

Worlds of Difference

THE PINE FORGE PRESS SOCIAL SCIENCE LIBRARY

The Sociology of Work: Concepts and Cases by Carol J. Auster

Adventures in Social Research: Data Analysis Using SPSS® for Windows™ by Earl Babbie and Fred Halley

Critical Thinking for Social Workers: A Workbook by Leonard Gibbs and Eileen Gambrill

Race, Ethnicity, Gender, and Class: The Sociology of Group Conflict and Change by Joseph F. Healey

Race, Ethnicity, and Gender in the United States: Inequality, Group Conflict, and Power by Joseph F. Healey

Sociological Snapshots: Seeing Social Structure and Change in Everyday Life, 2nd Ed., by Jack Levin

Sociology: Snapshots and Portraits of Society by Jack Levin and Arnold Arluke

Aging: Concepts and Controversies by Harry R. Moody

Sociology: Exploring the Architecture of Everyday Life, 2nd Ed., by David M. Newman

Sociology: Exploring the Architecture of Everyday Life (Readings), 2nd Ed., by David M. Newman

Diversity in America by Vincent N. Parrillo

Expressing America: A Critique of the Global Credit Card Society by George Ritzer

The McDonaldization of Society, Rev. Ed., By George Ritzer

Shifts in the Social Contract: Understanding Change in American Society by Beth Rubin

The Pine Forge Press Series in Research Methods and Statistics
Edited by Kathleen S. Crittenden

Investigating the Social World: The Process and Practice of Research by Russell K. Schutt

A Guide to Field Research by Carol A. Bailey

Designing Surveys: A Guide to Decisions and Procedures by Ronald Czaja and Johnny Blair

How Sampling Works by Richard Maisel and Caroline Hodges Persell

Worlds of Difference

Inequality in the Aging Experience

Second Edition

ELEANOR PALO STOLLER

The University of Florida

ROSE CAMPBELL GIBSON

The University of Michigan

PINE FORGE PRESS

Thousand Oaks, California
London ▪ New Delhi

Copyright © 1997, 1994 by Pine Forge Press

All rights reserved. No part of this book may be reproduced or utilized in any form or by any means, electronic or mechanical, including photocopying, recording, or by any information storage and retrieval system, without permission in writing from the publisher.

For information address:

PINE FORGE PRESS
A Sage Publications Company
2455 Teller Road
Thousand Oaks, California 91320
(805) 499-4224
e-mail: sdr@pfp.sagepub.com

Sage Publications Ltd.
6 Bonhill Street
London EC2A 4PU
United Kingdom

Sage Publications India Pvt. Ltd.
M-32 Market
Greater Kailash I
New Delhi 110 048 India

Production Editor: Gillian Dickens
Book Designer: Lisa S. Mirski
Typesetter: Christina M. Hill
Cover Designer: Lee Fukui
Cover Photo: © Michael Orton/Tony Stone Images
Print Buyer: Anna Chin

Printed in the United States of America

97 98 99 10 9 8 7 6 5 4 3 2 1

Library of Congress Cataloging-in-Publication Data

Stoller, Eleanor Palo.
   Worlds of difference: Inequality in the aging experience/
Eleanor Palo Stoller, Rose Campbell Gibson. — 2nd ed.
      p.   cm.
   Includes bibliographical references and index.
   ISBN 0-8039-9099-5 (pbk.)
   1. Aging. 2. Gerontology. I. Gibson, Rose Campbell. II. Title.
HQ1061. S835 1996
305.26—dc20   96-15613

   This book is printed on acid-free paper that meets Environmental Protection Agency standards for recycled paper.

About the Authors

Eleanor Palo Stoller is Professor of Health Policy at the University of Florida. She was formerly Professor of Sociology and Chair of Women's Studies at the State University of New York—Plattsburgh, where she taught undergraduate courses in social gerontology and women's studies. She received her undergraduate degree in American studies from Grinnell College and her Ph.D. in sociology from Washington University. Her research on informal networks of older people and on lay care in illness has been funded by the National Institute of Aging and the Administration on Aging. Results of this research have appeared in a number of journals, including *Journal of Marriage and the Family, Journal of Gerontology, The Gerontologist, Journal of Health and Social Behavior, Research on Aging,* and *Medical Care.* She is a member of the editorial boards of *Journal of Gerontology: Social Sciences, The Gerontologist, Journal of Applied Gerontology,* and *Research on Aging.*

Rose Campbell Gibson is Faculty Associate at the Institute for Social Research and Professor in the School of Social Work at the University of Michigan, where she teaches Sociology of Aging and Research Methods. After receiving her Ph.D. from the University of Michigan, she was a Postdoctoral Fellow there in Statistics and Survey Research Design and Methodology on Minority Populations. She is the author of *Blacks in an Aging Society* and numerous articles and chapters that have appeared in volumes such as *Handbook of the Psychology of Aging, Journal of Gerontology, Milbank Quarterly,* the *Annals,* and the *Journal of Aging and Health.* She is Editor-in-Chief of *The Gerontologist* and serves on several other editorial boards in the field of aging. Her research on sociocultural factors in aging has been funded by the National Institute of Aging, the Administration on Aging, and private foundations.

About the Publisher

Pine Forge Press is a new educational publisher dedicated to publishing innovative books and software throughout the social sciences. On this and any other of our publications, we welcome your comments and suggestions.

Please call or write us at:

Pine Forge Press
A Sage Publications Company
2455 Teller Road
Thousand Oaks, CA 91320
(805) 499-4224
e-mail: sdr@pfp.sagepub.com

Contents

PART II

Social and Psychological Contexts of Aging

Cultural Images of Old Age

What are the images of old age in our society? How do individuals in interlocking hierarchies of gender, race, and class react differently to these controlling images?   75

PART III

Productive Activity: Paid and Unpaid

Expanding the Definition of Productivity in Old Age

PART V

Health and Mortality: Inequalities

Inequalities in Health and Mortality: Gender, Race, and Class

Disadvantaged positions in systems of inequality are associated with poor health, high mortality, poor health care, and different meanings of aging, health, illness, and dying. 263

Preface

Worlds of Difference is designed to enhance the inclusiveness of the undergraduate curriculum in social gerontology. We believe this is important for two reasons. First, undergraduate students today represent greater diversity in gender, race, and social class than did undergraduates in previous decades, and pedagogical research has demonstrated that students become engaged in curricula that "give voice" to their experiences. Second, projected increases in diversity within the elderly population over the coming decades demand that people working in the field of gerontology be knowledgeable about the experiences of people of different genders, races, ethnic groups, and social classes. Designing an inclusive curriculum is not just a matter of fairness or affirmative action; it is a central component of educating people to live and work in the twenty-first century (Moses, 1992).

In preparing the introductory essays and selecting the readings, we were guided by several principles. First, we believe it is essential to move beyond conceptions of gender, race, and class as attributes of individuals that must be controlled statistically or experimentally (J. S. Jackson, 1989). Instead, we conceptualize these categories as social constructs, as classifications based on social values that influence identity formation, opportunity structures, and adaptive resources. We visualize these social constructs as interlocking hierarchies that create systems of privilege as well as disadvantage. Too often, the experience of people who are disadvantaged along one or more hierarchies is contrasted with the experience of the dominant group, which is presented as the "norm." Supported by the ideology of a meritocracy, this approach masks the structural foundations of privilege. Too frequently, it is assumed that only people of color have "race," that only women have "gender," that only the poor have "social class," and that only recent immigrants have "ethnicity" (Higginbotham, 1989). Our emphasis on the intersections of these multiple systems of inequality is designed to help students understand that older people can experience disadvantage along one dimension but privilege along others. As Margaret Andersen and Patricia Hill Collins (1992) explain, "Race, class and gender are part of the whole fabric of experience for all groups, not just women and people of color" (p. xiii).

Second, we have attempted to supplement the "social problems" approach implicit in the multiple jeopardy perspective on gender, race, and class by emphasizing strengths as well as deficits. We selected readings that depict older people as active creators of culture rather than as merely passive victims. We emphasized the adaptive resources people develop across a lifetime of disadvantage and the ways in which these adaptive resources help people cope with the challenge of old age.

We minimized simple comparisons (e.g., female versus male, African American versus white) in which the dominant group is an implicit standard against which other groups are "compared" to see how they "differ" (Stanford & Yee, 1991). Instead, we explored diversity in the experience of aging along any one dimension. We selected readings to introduce students to African American women who are wealthy as well as others who are poor, and to poor women who are white as well as poor women who are Native American, African American, and Latino American. As the anthropologist Johnetta Cole (1986) explains, gender is experienced differently depending on one's race and social class, and the experience of race and class is mediated through one's gender.

Third, our exploration in *Worlds of Difference* has been guided by a life course perspective. A number of the readings introduce students to the historical conditions different categories of people experienced at particular chronological ages. People who are elderly today lived through the Great Depression of the 1930s, World War II, postwar prosperity and optimism, and the Civil Rights movement. Elderly African Americans grew up in a legally segregated world that not only limited their economic options but also provided a particular worldview and encouraged special adaptive resources. Exploration of the diversity in the social and historical contexts within which today's cohorts of elderly people experienced significant life course events is essential to understanding their experience of old age. We chose to explore these contexts by providing views of social reality through the eyes of young and middle-aged adults in the 1930s, 1940s, and 1950s, those cohorts that make up the older population today.

The book is organized by topic rather than by group or by dimension of inequality. We want to emphasize diversity in older people's encounters with negative images, in their experience of family, and in their productive activities. We want students to understand that the impact of gender, race, and class cannot be understood in additive terms; we are less concerned that students master a catalog of descriptive characteristics of each particular group. The aging experience of an affluent African American woman and a working-class white woman are very different, even though both are disadvantaged on two hierarchies and privileged on a third. To achieve this understanding, we have chosen readings that give voice to people whose perspectives have been overlooked. The readings emphasize what Johnetta Cole describes as "commonalities" as well as differences, that is, recognition that part of the social construction of gender, race, and class involves emphasizing differences and suppressing similarities (Hess, 1990). We also highlighted these issues in the discussion questions at the end of each part and in the test bank, which is available to instructors.

We met several challenges in compiling this anthology. We were unable to include a number of excellent readings that provide compelling glimpses of social reality; we share these with our readers through the list of supplementary readings at the end of each part. Our attempt to provide multiple lenses was sometimes hampered by a shortage of writings about particular categories of older people. Locating readings about older men of color that illustrated our themes was especially difficult. We hope that greater interest in an inclusive approach to the study of aging will make this task easier for editors in the future.

Worlds of Difference reflects the work of more than two people. The idea for this anthology emerged from a roundtable, Innovations in Courses on Aging in the Undergraduate Curriculum, organized by Pine Forge President Stephen Rutter during the 1991 meetings of the Gerontological Society of America. We are grateful to Steve for providing the catalyst for the book. We learned from each other and emerge from this collaborative venture with an understanding of aging that is greater than the sum of the knowledge we brought to the project.

Ingrun Lafleur merits our special thanks for introducing one of us to the meaning of an inclusive curriculum. Over the past five years, she was a mentor, a colleague, and, most important, a friend. For those who knew Ingie, her influence will be obvious throughout the anthology.

Many other people contributed to the project. We are indebted to Penny Dugan for her creative lending library of literary anthologies, to Susan McKie for her efforts in obtaining permissions, to Lesa L. Ball for her diligent work in preparing the bibliography, to Jeff Stoller for his double role as student reader and editor, to Amy Stoller and Charmaine Judon for helping us complete the manuscript on schedule. Most of all, we want to thank our husbands, Michael A. Stoller and Ralph M. Gibson, and our children, Jeffrey Mark Stoller, Kirsten Elin Stoller, Ralph M. Gibson, Jr., and John S. Gibson, for giving us the love and understanding—and time—we needed to finish *Worlds of Difference.*

E.P.S.
R.C.G.

Introduction

Different Worlds in Aging: Gender, Race, and Class

Gerontologists have long stressed the heterogeneity of the elderly population. People enter old age with an accumulation of experiences gained over six or seven decades, experiences that influence their attitudes, behaviors, and resources. Some of these experiences, such as wars, economic fluctuations, technological developments, and cultural change, are shared with other people in their age cohort. Others emerge from biographical experiences unique to the individual. The strength of a social gerontological approach to the study of late life is that it enables us to understand the ways in which what is occurring within the larger society shapes the life course of individuals. As the sociologist C. Wright Mills (1959) put it, social gerontology allows us to see the link between history and biography.

Even though older people today have lived through the same historical period, the impact of that history on their individual biographies varies with their position in society. Some characteristics of individuals and of their personal histories may appear unique, but there are also discernible patterns in the experiences of different segments of the older population. These patterns reflect social structural arrangements and cultural blueprints within society both today and during the decades in which people lived and grew old. In this book, we will examine three dimensions of experience that structure both allocation of resources and expectations about old age: gender, race or ethnicity, and social class. We frequently think of these factors as attributes of individuals. In classifying people into categories based on gender, race or ethnicity, and social class, people often emphasize biological characteristics. Clearly, there are biological differences between men and women. We often try to classify people into racial or ethnic groups on the basis of skin color or facial features. Some people have even argued that differences in intelligence determine social class placement. Social Darwinists, for example, applying the "survival of the fittest" principle to human societies, attributed the failure of the lower classes to improve their socioeconomic status to their natural inferiority.

Without denying that there are differences among individuals that are grounded in biology, our emphasis will be on gender, race or ethnicity, and social class as social constructs, or classifications based on social values. The sociologist Beth Hess (1990) describes the process through which the biological category of sex is transformed into the social construct of gender:

> Layers of meaning have been wrapped around the distinguishing feature of biological sex to produce a palimpsest of gendered reality-socially constructed systems of thought and action that organize perception, identities, and the allocation of scarce resources. Thus, rather than being a property of the individual, maleness and femaleness are products of the operation of social systems on both the variability and similarities provided by nature. . . . Gender is created by suppressing similarities, and it is maintained by a deep ideological commitment to differences between women and men. The basic process is categorization, the establishment of a gender hierarchy in which a superstructure of social, political, and economic differences have been superimposed on the biological. (pp. 83-84)

The social process of categorizing people that Hess describes is also evident in racial and ethnic labels. A child whose mother is African American and whose father is white is considered African American, whereas a child whose mother is white and whose father is Japanese American is considered Asian (Cyrus, 1993). Jews have traditionally traced group membership through the mother. A person was considered Jewish if his or her mother was Jewish, regardless of the background of the father. In the United States, a person with any African heritage has been classified as black, whereas the U.S. Census Bureau requires at least one-eighth native American lineage to qualify as Native American (Cyrus, 1993).

These labels not only influence the way people are counted in social surveys but also structure the opportunities and constraints people encounter as they move throughout their life course. They shape our self-concepts and the ways other people respond to us. There is no biological reason for classifying a child according to the racial status of the minority parent rather than the white parent or in determining what percentage of lineage is required for identification with a particular group. These distinctions reflect the social process Hess described: a process of categorization that superimposes social hierarchies on biological differences.

Our exploration of gender, race, and class as social constructs will emphasize these variables both as labels attached to individuals and as properties of hierarchical social structures within which people form identities and through which they realize their life chances (Hess, 1990). We will also investigate the ways in which chances (Hess, 1990). We will also investigate the ways in which people's positions along these multiple hierarchies generate diverse views of social reality. This involves listening to descriptions of aging and old age from multiple perspectives, of "giving voice" to people whose perspectives have been overlooked. Integrating this chorus of voices will enrich our understanding of aging by highlighting common motifs as well as the tonal and rhythmic complexity that characterize the experience of aging in the contemporary United States.

Our journey through the "worlds of difference" shaped by these social constructs will be guided by several themes. We begin by emphasizing that hierarchies based on gender, race, and class create systems of privilege as well as of disadvantage. When we think about these hierarchies, it is often easier to recognize elements of discrimination. Gerontologists have documented multiple ways in which discrimination throughout the life course translates into an accumulation of disadvantage in old age. We know, for example, that legally segregated school systems and legally sanctioned discriminatory hiring practices limited the opportunities of today's elderly African Americans to accumulate financial assets during their younger years. Research has demonstrated how a lifetime of poverty translates into poor health in later life. Other studies have shown how the rules regulating pension benefits increase the financial risks associated with widowhood for older women. The concept of "multiple jeopardy" reminds us that occupying several disadvantaged positions simultaneously compounds the risk of negative outcomes in old age. For example, both African Americans and women face higher risks of being poor in old age than do white men, but the probability of poverty is even higher for elderly African American women.

This emphasis on disadvantage, however, sometimes masks the ways in which these same hierarchies create systems of privilege. By focusing on the discrimination experienced by people at the lower end of these hierarchies, we sometimes overlook the ways in which being white, being male, and being middle or upper class provide unearned advantages. Being able to ignore issues surrounding race is one aspect of privilege, an advantage denied people of color, who are constantly reminded of their disadvantaged status. The political scientist Andrew Hacker (1992) reminds us that "what every black American knows, and whites should try to imagine, is how it feels to have an unfavorable—and unfair—identity imposed on you every waking day" (p. 21). Because white Americans spend most of their time in environments in which being white is taken for granted, they need pay little attention to race. Advantages associated with one's race, class, or gender are taken for granted by members of the dominant group. Hacker (1992) suggests a parable to elucidate the often overlooked advantages of being white. He asks his white students to imagine that tonight:

You will be visited by an official you have never met. He begins by telling you that he is extremely embarrassed. The organization he represents has made a mistake, something that hardly ever happens.

According to their records, he goes on, you were to have been born black: to another set of parents, far from where you were raised.

However, the rules being what they are, this error must be rectified, and as soon as possible. So at midnight tonight, you will become black. And this will mean not simply a darker skin, but the bodily and facial features associated with African ancestry. However, inside you will be the person you always were. Your knowledge and ideas will remain intact. But outwardly you will not be recognizable to anyone you now know.

Your visitor emphasizes that being born to the wrong parents was in no way your fault. Consequently, his organization is prepared to offer you some reasonable recompense. Would you, he asks, care to name a sum of money you might consider appropriate? He adds that his group is by no means poor. It can be quite generous when the circumstances warrant, as they seem to in your case. He finishes by saying that their records show you are scheduled to live another fifty years—as a black man or woman in America. (pp. 31-32)

How much financial recompense would you request?

Most of Hacker's students report that "it would not be out of place to ask for $50 million, or $1 million for each coming black year," a calculation he interprets as clear evidence of the value that white people place on their race.

Peggy McIntosh (1988) draws another analogy in illustrating the privilege dimension of systems of inequality. She explains: "As a white person, I realized that I had been taught about racism as something that puts others at a disadvantage, but had been taught not to see one of its corollary aspects, white privilege, which puts me at an advantage" (p. 4). She equates white privilege with an "invisible package of unearned assets," and provides a number of illustrations of the ways in which her everyday life is made easier because of her race. For example:

I can, if I wish, arrange to be in the company of people of my race most of the time. I can avoid spending time with people whom I was trained to mistrust and who have learned to mistrust my kind or me. . . . I can go shopping alone most of the time, fairly well assured that I will not be followed or harassed by store detectives. . . . Whether I use checks, credit cards, or cash, I can count on my skin color not to work against the appearance that I am financially reliable. I did not have to educate my children to be aware of systematic racism for their own daily physical protection. . . . I can do well in a challenging situation without being called a credit to my race. (McIntosh, 1988, pp. 8-82)

These advantages or assets are unearned, because access to them is determined by an ascribed rather than an achieved status. They are rendered invisible by the ideology of a meritocracy and a classless society, which teaches us that the United States is a land of equal opportunity where ambition, intelligence, and hard work are responsible for success. This is a comfortable explanation for people who are successful, because it tells them they deserve the advantages they enjoy. Affluent retired people pursuing a life of leisure in the Sunbelt can tell themselves that they earned their piece of "the American Dream," a lifestyle available to anyone with talent, intelligence, and the willingness to work hard. At the same time, this explanation holds less affluent elders responsible for their lack of success. If only they had worked harder or been more clever or intelligent, they would have reaped more rewards. In explaining poverty in old age, it is an example of an explanation that "blames the victim."

Sorting out privilege and disadvantage is sometimes complicated, because people can experience disadvantage along one dimension but privilege along others. To assume that all men are privileged over all women or that all whites are advantaged relative to all people of color is to ignore intersections among multiple hierarchies. A woman who is married to a wealthy industrialist can express dissatisfaction with the expectation that she accommodate her life to the demands of her husband's career, with her unequal voice in family decisions, and with her sole responsibility for managing home and family (Ostrander, 1984), but it is difficult to argue that she is disadvantaged relative to an African American man struggling to escape poverty as a sharecropper in the rural South or a Mexican American agricultural laborer as he follows the demand for migrant workers. As we explore the impact of gender, race, and class on the experiences of older Americans today, we will look for evidence of these intersections. We will learn that race, gender, and class represent interlocking systems of experience that affect all aspects of human life, not simply separate features of experience that can be understood in additive terms (Andersen & Collins, 1992). Gender is experienced differently depending on one's race and social class (Cole, 1986). Analogously, the constraints or privileges of race and class are mediated through one's gender. A lifetime of experiences at various points along these hierarchies contributes to diversity in old age, diversity not only in the quantity of resources people have accumulated but also in their relationships, the meanings attached to aging, and their definitions of social reality.

As we explore these worlds of difference, we will emphasize strengths as well as deficits. The "multiple jeopardy" approach to studying inequality in old age has emphasized the negative outcomes of occupying disadvantaged positions along several of these hierarchies. Social gerontologists working from this perspective have documented the accumulation of deficits across the life course that produce poverty, poor health, and inadequate living conditions in old age. Although it is important to recognize the problems faced by older people coping with the effects of disadvantaged status, it is equally important to learn how these older Americans create meaning in their lives despite barriers based on gender, race, and class. Through the readings, we will meet older people who are active creators of culture and not merely passive victims reacting to systems of oppression. We will learn to view social reality from multiple perspectives and discover that particular institutional arrangements can provide protection against oppression in some segments of society while simultaneously reinforcing oppression in others.

To illustrate this seeming contradiction, we will consider the role of religion in the lives of older African American women. In many respects, religion as an institution appears to reinforce these women's subordinate position in society. Religious doctrines defining women's proper place emphasize their role as mothers and justify their subordination to men. Although black churches are estimated to be 75% female, and women perform the majority of the work in local congregations (Gilkes, 1985), women are selected for leadership positions less often than men. The African Methodist Episcopal Church, which began ordaining women in 1948, was the first denomination in the United States to accept women into the clergy, but interviews with male clergy reveal continuing prejudice against women in the ministry (Grant, 1982). Some critics have argued that although religion can serve as a coping mechanism for adversity, dependence on prayer can serve as a substitute for direct action (S. Taylor, 1982). The dominance of European imagery and an emphasis on rewards in the afterlife also have been criticized for reinforcing racism and fostering passive acceptance of inequality in this life.

A more complex view of religion in the life of older African American women is provided by Johnetta Cole (1986). Cole, an anthropologist who is currently president of Spellman College, describes the Southern A.M.E. congregation in which she grew up and its role in the life of Sister Minnie:

> In this black church where we sang "Jesus will wash me whiter than snow" in Sunday school, the superintendent was my great-grandfather but most of the teachers were women. We looked up at stained glass windows depicting a blond, blue-eyed image of Jesus and showing Mary as a white woman. However, as the choir my mother directed sang "Amazing Grace," Sister Minnie would begin to twitch as the spirits moved her, and she began to speak in tongues and shout and dance in expressions of

"getting happy." Her religion, its imagery as Eurocentric and male as it was, also involved the retention of elements of an African religion. And importantly, it was obviously a source of tremendous relief and satisfaction to a woman who somehow had to support herself and several children on the less-than-minimum wages she received as a domestic for a Southern white lady, living in a city where even the water fountains were marked "white" and "colored."

Sister Minnie was never in the pulpit, nor did anyone who shared her gender ever hold forth as a preacher. Yet she and other women were always frying chicken and preparing the potato salad that were essentials for many church suppers. Without defending this division of labor, it is necessary to note that on those Sundays when Sister Minnie's usher board served and she brought men and women to their seats, or even more so, when, with one arm folded behind her back, she brought some of the collection plates to the minister, one saw a woman who in Mt. Olive A.M.E. church was able to play a public role of dignity and consequence denied her in much of the racist, sexist, and elitist southern United States. (pp. 309-310)

For Sister Minnie, the church was a source of recognition and self-esteem. But this is only one way in which churches have provided support in African American communities. The black church also provided both emotional and material support at a time when these were not available to African Americans through public services (R. J. Taylor & Chatters, 1986; Walls & Zarit, 1991). L. Steinitz (1981) concluded that churches served as surrogate families, offering both concrete help and psychological assurance, especially to older people without family nearby. In addition to religious activities and social support, black churches have had a major role in political mobilization (Walls & Zarit, 1991) and provided a strong foundation for the Civil Rights movement that emerged during the 1950s and 1960s.

We will see similar contradictions in our examination of family and of productive activity, including paid employment and unpaid assistance to family and friends. Listening to Sister Minnie and to the voices of other people introduced in the readings will help us begin to answer a question Ralph Ellison (1952) posed over four decades ago: "Can a people . . . live and develop for over three hundred years simply by reacting? Are American Negroes simply the creation of white men, or have they at least helped to create themselves out of what they found around them?" (pp. 316-317).

Recognition of the adaptive strategies of elders of color, however, should not blind us to the societal arrangements that demanded these strategies. For example, sharing resources across networks of extended kin and fictive kin enhance survival among poor women, but this strategy does not eliminate the economic barriers that maintain economic inequality. The increasing number of elderly people who are assuming the role of surrogate or custodial parents for their grandchildren cannot reduce the prevalence of unemployment, substance abuse, or incarceration in the middle generation. And the ability of families of color to teach children to survive prejudice and discrimination while maintaining their self-esteem does not alter the strains of everyday racism. In periods of fiscal restraint and political conservatism, gerontologists must remain alert that these celebrations of strength are not redefined as rationales for not providing much needed services.

In addition to issues of social inequality, we also will explore variations in cultural meanings and the dynamics of aging both among and within different population categories. Often this requires moving beyond research, which tends to reflect the experiences of the dominant group. Recognizing this limitation in the gerontological literature does not mean that researchers are purposely distorting information or are insensitive to concerns of older women or older people of color. Biases and oversights reflect the fact that knowledge is socially constructed. Gerontologists, like other scientists, approach their research from a specific social location that shapes what they know about the world (Andersen, 1992). The past experiences and current attitudes that researchers bring to their subject shape the questions they ask, what they observe, and how they interpret their observations.

Listening to diverse voices enriches our perspective by giving us new lenses through which to view the multiple social worlds that can exist within a particular setting. Trying on lenses can bring into focus dimensions of social reality that were overlooked from the perspective of the dominant group. Feminist research on family care of the elderly provides an example of this process. When one of the editors of this reader was in school, she was taught that many traditional functions of the family had been shifted to specialized, bureaucratic institutions. One example used to illustrate this shift was the growth of nursing homes. As she heard about the decline in family care of the elderly and the plight of older people isolated in nursing homes, she watched her own mother struggling to meet the expanding physical and emotional needs of her increasingly frail, elderly grandmother. The contradiction between the stereotype of abandonment of older people and the strains experienced by family caregivers is more evident to women than to men. Adult daughters are more likely than adult sons to provide care to older relatives. Furthermore, they tend to absorb the costs of that care themselves, struggling to meet the demands of their other roles both within and beyond the family. Jane Lewis (1986) reports that caregiving daughters struggle to "keep life as 'normal' as possible for their own family, . . . [which] entailed assuming the whole burden of care themselves and keeping it as unobtrusive as possible" (chap. 6, p. 10). We should not be surprised that male researchers were slower than women to design research projects exploring the burdens and rewards of family care of frail elders. This aspect of the aging experience was less likely to be visible to men than to women. Dorothy Smith (1987) notes that all research is done from a particular standpoint or location in the social system and is shaped by the perspective of the researcher. Throughout this reader, we will introduce examples of the ability of diverse perspectives to yield new insights. We will see, for example, how abandoning definitions of kin based on white families makes visible the richness and complexity of kin and kinlike relationships within African American communities. We will discover how expanding definitions of productivity based on the paid employment experience of white men reveals unpaid productive work performed by people throughout their lives. We will uncover the biases in retirement research that emphasize pension income and explore a variety of strategies people use in reinterpreting negative stereotypes based on age, gender, race, and class.

A final theme shaping our journey through different worlds of aging is an emphasis on the life course. A life course perspective, which we will explore in detail in the next chapter, highlights the ways in which people's location in the social system, the historical period in which they live, and their unique personal biography shape the experience of old age. This perspective allows us to explore how occupying different positions along dimensions of gender, race, and class over one's lifetime can lead to different aging experiences. It also reminds us of the importance of the historical period in which people live. People who are the same age experienced particular segments of history at the same stage of life. They experienced life transitions within similar sociohistorical contexts. The intersection of historical trends with hierarchies based on gender, race, and class produce variation both among older people from different population categories and among people of different age within particular categories. To illustrate this process, consider the historical context experienced by a particular set of elderly Americans: African Americans who will be 80 years of age in the year 2000 were born in 1920. Most completed their education in racially segregated schools, many similar to the one Maya Angelou (1969) describes in her autobiographical novel *I Know Why the Caged Bird Sings:*

> Unlike the white high school, Lafayette County Training School distinguished itself by having neither lawn, nor hedges, nor tennis court, nor climbing ivy. Its two buildings (main classrooms, the grade school and home economics) were set on a dirt hill with no fence to limit its boundaries or those of bordering farms. . . . Rusty hoops on the swaying poles represented the permanent recreational equipment. . . . Only a small percentage [of the graduates] would be continuing on to college—one of the South's A & M (agricultural and mechanical) schools, which trained negro youths to be carpenters, farmers, handymen, masons, maids, cooks, and baby nurses. (p. 163)

In 1954, the U.S. Supreme Court in *Brown v. Board of Education of Topeka* declared separate but unequal treatment unconstitutional and overturned segregation laws officially sanctioned since the *Plessy v. Ferguson* ruling in 1896. But these African American elders were 34 years old in 1954, and they had long completed their formal education. Despite the limited opportunities constraining their own youth, many foresaw possibilities of change for their children. Barbara Smith (1983) describes this vision in the introduction to her anthology *Home Girls:*

> The women in my family, and their friends, worked harder than any people I have known before or since, and despite their objective circumstances, they believed . . . that Beverly and I could have a future beyond theirs, although there was little enough indication in the 40s and 50s that Negro girls would ever have a place to stand. (p. xxi)

African Americans born in 1920 witnessed the Civil Rights movement of the 1950s and 1960s—some were among its leaders—but they witnessed these events as adults in their thirties and forties. Their childhoods were lived within a racially segregated world in which they struggled to maintain self-respect while avoiding direct challenges to the rules for "living Jim Crow":

> There were many times when I had to exercise a great deal of ingenuity to keep out of trouble. It is a southern custom that all men must take off their hats when they enter an elevator. And especially did this apply to blacks. One day I stepped into an elevator with my arms full of packages. I was forced to ride with my hat on. Two white men stared at me coldly. Then one of them very kindly lifted my hat and placed it upon my armful of packages. Now the most accepted response for a Negro to make under such circumstances is to look at the white man out of the corner of his eye and grin. To have said: "Thank you!" would have made the white man think that you thought you were receiving from him a personal service. For such an act I have seen Negroes take a blow in the mouth. Finding the first alternative distasteful, and the second dangerous, I hit upon an acceptable course of action which fell safely between these two poles. I immediately—no sooner than my hat was lifted—pretended that my packages were about to spill, and appeared deeply distressed with keeping them in my arms. In this fashion, I evaded having to acknowledge his service, and, in spite of adverse circumstances, salvaged a slender shred of personal pride. (Wright, 1937/1991, p. 50)

A life course perspective also reminds us to expect diversity among today's older population. Although all people celebrating their eightieth birthday at the turn of the century lived through the same segment of history, their experience of this history—the meanings they attach to particular events and the impact of these events on their lives—varies depending on their social location. We have introduced you to some variations in the experience of the past seven decades from the standpoint of an 80-year-old African American. Consider the contrasting life experiences of other people who were also born in 1920: a white woman born on a small farm in rural Mississippi, a Jewish man who escaped the horrors of Nazi Germany as a teenager, the now elderly daughter of a wealthy family from the Mainline in Philadelphia, or the aging son of Polish immigrants who prides himself on his own son's graduation from medical school.

At the same time, a life course perspective sensitizes us to diversity among people of different ages within the same population category. Middle-aged people today who grew up in the middle-class suburbs of the 1950s can be expected to have different attitudes toward saving and spending money than their parents, whose childhoods coincided with the Great Depression of the 1930s. Young-old people whose first experiences with government assistance programs were social security and economic recovery programs of the 1930s may be less reluctant to use public services than will old-old people who associate public assistance with the stigma of welfare. We encourage our readers to exercise their gerontological imaginations as they hypothesize about the effects of (a) increasing rates of women's labor force participation on future retirement decisions, (b) greater knowledge of and emphasis on preventing future patterns of morbidity and mortality, and (c) the widening gap between the rich and poor on future income and service needs among older people. The most difficult hurdle we encounter in developing these hypotheses is the interaction among physical changes associated with aging, the historical context in which people have lived, and the social context within which they find themselves in late life. The challenge of a life course perspective is to recognize continuity in the experience of aging within a context of population diversity and social change.

We have emphasized the importance of diversity in enriching our understanding of aging and old age. Others have advocated inclusion of women and minorities on the grounds of fairness and equal treatment. But there is a yet more urgent reason for incorporating a more inclusive approach to our study of aging. Projected increases in diversity within the elderly population over the next decades demand that people working in geriatric and gerontological positions be knowledgeable about the experiences of people of different genders, races or ethnic groups, and social classes. As the anthropologist Yolanda Moses (1992), who is currently president of City College of New York, explains, designing an inclusive curriculum is not just a matter of fairness or affirmative action. It is a central component of educating people to live and work in the twenty-first century.

The time frame available for achieving this goal is shrinking as population changes demand social policies reflecting concerns of an increasingly diverse older population. As recently as 1980, more than 90% of all Americans over 65 years of age were white. By 2025, 15% of the elderly population are projected to be minority, increasing to 20% by the year 2050. The number of minority elderly is growing more rapidly than the number of white elderly, with the most rapid growth occurring within Hispanic and Asian populations (Stanford & Yee, 1991). These population shifts will be even more dramatic in particular locations. For example, almost 40% of the elderly population in California will be ethnic minorities by 2020 (Torres-Gil & Hyde, 1990).

Increasing diversity in attitudes, behavior, and resources among older people will require reconsideration of policies and programs designed originally for a homogeneous population composed of white, English-speaking elderly people (Wray, 1991). Disadvantaged ethnic minority elderly, like their younger counterparts, are disproportionately represented among people with income below the federal poverty level. Older women, particularly minority women, are more vulnerable to poverty than are older men. Older members of minority groups have a lower life expectancy and poorer health than members of the dominant group (Torres-Gil & Hyde, 1990). Meager financial resources limit access to health care. For many older persons, including ethnic minorities and women living alone, medical expenses increase their risk of poverty, often forcing them to choose between accepting Medicaid or going without medical care (Hurd, 1989). Linda Wray (1991) summarizes the policy challenge accompanying the increasing diversity among the older population:

> Looking ahead, how do we fashion public policy that serves to ameliorate the obstacles—often constructed earlier in the life course—that handicap many ethnic and minority elderly? Further, how can public policy offer equal access to social and economic opportunities to minority and nonminority elders alike? (p. 243)

Achieving these policy goals requires sensitivity to the diversity in resources and preferences among older people. Although the concept of color-blind or gender-neutral policies sounds fair and equitable, it is important to remember the sociological maxim that "equal rules applied to unequal situations produce unequal outcomes." Even ostensibly neutral social policies can produce outcomes that are structured by older people's gender, race, and class. We can illustrate this process by returning to our example of family care of frail elderly relatives. One policy that has been considered for relieving financial strains and recognizing contributions of relatives who care for older people is providing some form of payment to family caregivers. This strategy, however, would have different effects on different caregivers. The current political and economic climate makes it likely that any payments to family caregivers would be fairly small. These relatively low payments would likely reinforce the class bias of informal caregiving, as only carers with restricted earning potential would trade paid employment for a caregiving allowance. Middle- and upper-class women would be better off financially if they entered the labor force and used part of their wages to hire supplementary services. They would become care managers by delegating responsibilities to formal care providers, mostly other women working for minimal wages (Archbold, 1983). Significantly, from our perspective stressing interlocking hierarchies based on class, race, and gender, these formal care providers are most often poor or working-class women, frequently members of racial or ethnic minority groups, who return home from performing the personal care and household tasks of more affluent women to their own "second shift" of unpaid domestic work.

The readings that follow will explore the themes introduced here. We begin in Part I with an examination of the life course perspective. A life course perspective emphasizes the ways in which people's social location, the historical period in which they live, and their personal biographies shape their experience of the aging process. We shall see how particular time periods relegate people to circumscribed roles that limit their life chances, increase the likelihood of experiencing negative life events, and weaken their adaptive resources. The readings also illustrate the ways in which the impact of various events experienced prior to old age are filtered through people's position on the interlocking hierarchies. In Part II, we explore cultural images about old age and the ways older people respond to them. We will see how these images vary along dimensions of gender, race, and class, and explore strategies used by older people for maintaining personal integrity within a context of negative stereotypes. Part III introduces the world of productivity. Economists have traditionally defined productive activities as those behaviors that add to the stock and flow of valued goods and services. Because productivity has been measured by counting exchanges of money, choices regarding productivity in old age traditionally have been framed as a dichotomy of work versus leisure. Here we will consider unpaid as well as paid activity and consider ways in which productive activity across the life course influences resources in old age. Part IV considers the diversity in family structure and kin relations among older people. We will return to the theme of family care of frail elders. But we will also look beyond ideologies describing "the American Family" to consider the diversity of families experienced by today's cohorts of older people across the life course. Finally, in Part V, we will examine gender, race, and social class differences in disease, disability, and mortality in old age. Here we explore differences in exposure to biomedical, social, and psychological risk factors and in access to medical care in shaping the health status of older people.

PART I

The Life Course Perspective

Aging in Individual, Sociocultural, and Historical Contexts

Advantages of Using the Life Course Framework in Studying Aging

Here we introduce the life course perspective as a framework for an inclusive approach to the study of aging. As we indicated in the Introduction, a life course perspective emphasizes the ways in which people's location in the social system, the historical period in which they live, and their unique personal biographies shape their experience of old age. Our approach to the life course perspective has four main premises, which we will explain and illustrate:

1. The aging process is affected by individuals' personal attributes, their particular life events, and how they adapt to these events.

2. Sociohistorical times shape opportunity structures differently for individuals with specific personal characteristics, such as being in a subordinate position on a social hierarchy. Thus people's life events, adaptive resources, and aging experiences differ.

3. Membership in a specific birth cohort (i.e., being born in a particular time period) shapes the aging experience. Within cohorts, however, the experience of aging differs depending on one's position in systems of inequality based on gender, race or ethnicity, and class.

4. Sociohistorical periods shape the aging experiences of cohorts. These historical times, however, have different impacts on the experiences of disadvantaged and privileged members of the same cohort.

What Is the Life Course Perspective?

The life course perspective merges theoretical orientations from several disciplines. Proponents of the life course framework argue that developmental changes across the life span "arise from a mixture of biological, psychological, social, historical, and evolutionary influences and their timing across the lives of individuals" (Featherman, 1983, p. 622). The life course perspective, then, broadens our approach to the aging process by introducing important elements that earlier theories of aging neglected: personal biographies, sociocultural factors, and sociocultural times.

The life course framework focuses on ways in which individuals' multiple attributes, the social roles they occupy, their unique life events, and their adaptive resources interrelate within particular sociohistorical contexts to affect their aging processes. Different sociohistorical periods provide different opportunity structures and different social roles for individuals with different personal characteristics. These opportunities and roles in turn determine the particular life events people experience and the adaptive resources with which they respond to these life events. Ways in which people adapt to life stressors shape their aging experiences.

This summary of the life course perspective contains a number of concepts that may be unfamiliar. By *opportunity structures* we mean the various restrictions prevailing social orders place on individuals with certain personal attributes, thus reducing their life chances. For example, elderly African Americans probably attended racially segregated schools that were separate but rarely equal. Even those few who managed to receive college degrees faced discriminatory hiring practices and were often not considered for jobs that were open to whites with similar or even lesser qualifications. We use the term *structure* to emphasize the fact that these limited opportunities are based on social arrangements that exist beyond individuals, not on their personal talents or efforts. By *personal attributes* we mean characteristics of individuals that determine their positions in systems of inequality. In the previous example, being an African American is a personal attribute that limits a person's chances for occupational mobility because educational experiences and access to jobs are differentially distributed on the basis of race. Some personal attributes enhance rather than limit opportunity structures. Many of us were taught in elementary school that the United States is a land of opportunity where "any little boy [sic] can grow up to be president." Although presidential candidates frequently stress their humble origins, history has shown us that this goal is more achievable by white, male children born into affluent families.

By *life events* we mean either normal events that happen over the life course, such as the birth and death of loved ones, or other more unique stressful events, such as loss of a job, declining health, declining economic status, or chronic discriminatory treatment. By *adaptive resources* we mean conditions or strategies that help the individual cope with life events and life problems. Some of these adaptive resources are strong interpersonal relationships and social supports, beneficial personal coping strategies and behaviors, personal and family values, and economic security. Both the likelihood of experiencing stressful life events and the resources available to cope with them are differentially distributed according to position along hierarchies of gender, race or ethnicity, and class. Older women, for example, are more likely than older men to experience widowhood. This difference in the probability of experiencing a life event reflects both gender differences in life expectancy and the culturally based tendency of women to marry men older than they are. Widowhood is more likely to be accompanied by declining economic status for older women than it is for older men. Some pension benefits based on husbands' earnings stop payment at death, and older wives are less likely to have adequate pension benefits based on their own past earnings. There are also differences in the availability of adaptive resources. Older widows are more likely to be surrounded by a support group of female friends, many of whom have already faced the death of their husband. Older widowers, on the other hand, have more opportunity to remarry. These differences also vary by social class and race or ethnicity. Working-class women have fewer personal resources with which to cope with widowhood and are more likely to be isolated and lonely than are middle-class widows (Atchley, 1991), and women of disadvantaged racial and ethnic minorities experience transitions such as parental death and widowhood at younger ages than white women (George, 1993).

Do Particular Historical Times Shape the Opportunity Structure of Individuals With Certain Personal Characteristics?

The following account by an educated African American woman suggests that they do. The excerpt is from Mary Church Terrell, "What It Means to Be Colored in the Capital of the United States," reprinted in Gerda Lerner, *Black Women in White America* (1973). The original article was written in 1907. The discriminatory practices it describes remained unchanged until 1949, when a suit brought by Mrs. Terrell as one of the plaintiffs resulted in outlawing racial discrimination in eating places in the nation's capital. Other segregation practices continued unchanged until the civil rights struggles of the 1950s and 1960s.

> As a colored woman I might enter Washington any night, a stranger in a strange land, and walk miles without finding a place to lay my head. As a colored woman I may walk from the Capitol to the White House, ravenously hungry and abundantly supplied with money with which to purchase a meal, without finding a single restaurant in which I would be permitted to take a morsel of food, if it was patronized by white people, unless I were willing to sit behind a screen. As a colored woman, I cannot visit the tomb of the Father of this country, which owes its very existence to the love of freedom in the human heart and which stands for equal opportunity to all, without being forced to sit in the Jim Crow section of an electric car. If I refuse thus to be humiliated, I am cast into jail and forced to pay a fine for violating the law. As a colored woman I may enter a white church in Washington without receiving that welcome which as a human being I have the right to expect in the sanctuary of God. Unless I am willing to engage in a few menial occupations, there is no way for me to earn an honest living. From one Washington theater I am excluded altogether. In the remainder, certain seats are set aside for colored people. With the exception of Catholic University, there is not a single white college in the national

capital to which colored people are admitted. (Lerner, 1973, pp. 79-80)

The above passage also illustrates how privilege in one system of inequality—class—but disadvantage in two systems—race and gender—still can close opportunities to individuals in specific historical times. Terrell was the daughter of a former slave who had become one of the wealthiest African Americans in the country. She graduated from Oberlin College. Her husband was a lawyer with a degree from Harvard University. But these social class credentials did not exempt her from discriminatory treatment on the basis of her race.

Are the Life Events, Adaptive Resources, and Aging Experiences Different for Some Individuals in Certain Sociohistorical Times?

Before the Civil Rights movement, many opportunities were closed to African Americans. These blocked opportunities produced certain negative events—the effects of racial discrimination. Special adaptive resources were called into play to deal with these stressors, and these resources affected the aging experience. Annette Jones White (1991) describes these resources as "living constantly on tiptoe and in a react mode" (p. 190). Harriet McAdoo (1986) characterizes this climate of racism as a

mundane extreme environment: . . . The "extreme" difficulties which white society imposes on Black people by denying their identity, their values, and their economic opportunities are not unusual or extraordinary but "mundane," daily pressures for Blacks. The concept of a mundane extreme environment suggests vividly how racism is a pervasive, daily reality for Black families. (p. 189)

White describes learning these adaptive strategies from her mother:

She taught me how to turn away wrath with a soft answer but without letting anybody make me think I was inferior to them. She also tried to keep me informed of the dangers I might face so that I could avoid situations that would put me in danger. She tried to keep me out of situations that could lead to humiliation and "incidents." For example, on one of the few times she took me downtown, she avoided a confrontation. It was generally known that Blacks were supposed to step off the sidewalk if they were meeting a group of Whites. To not do so invited several things—a tongue lashing, a vicious elbow to the chest or side, or, possibly, arrest. As we walked, we approached a group of Whites. My mother quickly walked to a store window and we window shopped until the Whites passed by. I knew why and she knew I knew why but we never discussed it. That was her way of avoiding an incident. (pp. 190-191)

The quote from Richard Wright in the Introduction provides another of what Wright described as "lessons in how to live as a Negro." In neither of these illustrations was the narrator a passive victim of discrimination. They developed adaptive strategies that enabled them to survive in a social context characterized by racism but at the same time enabled them to maintain their personal integrity.

Another example of adaptive resources comes from a study of coping strategies and adaptations to aging among 60 African American women leaders aged 60 to 94 at the time of the study. The researchers Hill, Colby, and Phelps (1983) analyzed oral history transcripts collected for the Black Women's Oral History Project conducted by the Schlesinger Library of Harvard University/Radcliffe College. A major finding of their study was that one specific type of response was significantly related to adaptation to aging—direct instrumental coping. The authors speculated that the use of direct instrumentality when managing life problems, including those relating to racial discrimination, required great personal strength and courage, resources that these women were able to apply in adapting to old age. The following passage from their study provides yet another illustration of an instrumental coping response to the stress of racial discrimination:

> And I have been refused . . . well the first time I ever went to Orlando, my cousin went with me to the airport and the plane was late and we went into the dining room to get a cup of coffee and they made us leave. And when I said I had just come back from a trip around the world for the State Department and I refused to move, they sent a policeman to get me. Yeah, I've had plenty of things happen to me because I was black as a handicap. But I made a speech before they got me out of there. (p. 16)

Patricia Hill Collins (1991) describes the dilemma African American women encountered in teaching their daughters to live within a system of racial discrimination, of maintaining a

> delicate balance between conformity and resistance: . . . To ensure their daughters' physical survival, they must teach their daughters to fit into systems of oppression. . . . And yet mothers know that if daughters fit too well into the limited opportunities offered Black women, they become willing participants in their own subordination. . . . The issue is to build emotional strength, but not at the cost of physical survival. (pp. 53-54)

The adaptive resources of these African American mothers is illustrated in the selection by Alice Walker, "In Search of Our Mothers' Gardens."

How Does Membership in a Specific Birth Cohort Shape the Aging Experience?

First, what is a cohort? Understanding the cohort construct is central to understanding the life course perspective. *Cohort*, as we use the term in this book (there are other types of cohorts), is an aggregate of people born during the same time period—a birth cohort. Thus members of this type of cohort have similar chronological ages. They also experience particular segments of history at similar ages. The concept of cohort thus links the life course to history. As Anne Foner (1986) explains, "Each cohort brings to old age its own unique history, and this past influences the nature of the later years of cohort members" (p. 134).

How, Within Cohorts, Does the Aging Experience Differ by Membership in Systems of Inequality—Gender, Race or Ethnicity, and Class?

Despite similarity in chronological age, cohorts are not homogeneous collections of people. Cohorts exhibit considerable diversity along dimensions of gender, race, social class, ethnicity, religion, and sexual orientation. Although all members of a cohort experience segments of history at similar chronological ages, the impact of particular events often varies along these other dimensions. One way of sharpening our understanding of the life course perspective and cohort membership is to consider the impact of the same historical events on different cohorts: the Great Depression of the 1930s; World War II in the 1940s; and the Civil Rights movement in the 1950s, 1960s, and 1970s.

The Great Depression of the 1930s. The cohort born between 1931 and 1940 was smaller in size than were cohorts born either before or after. This relatively small size meant that members of this cohort encountered less competition and more opportunities for advancement than members of larger cohorts. They entered the workforce during the postwar prosperity of the 1950s, when an expanding economy provided employment opportunities. Many members experienced upward mobility during their lives, from relative poverty during the Depression to middle-class status by the 1950s and 1960s. But their relatively small numbers can also bring unique challenges. For example, when their parents encounter poor health and disability, members of this Depression cohort will have fewer siblings with whom to share the responsibility of caring for their parents. They themselves, however, will have a larger number of children on whom to rely for support, as members of this cohort were among the parents of the large post-World War II baby boom.

The Depression had a different impact on the cohort born between 1901 and 1910. When the stock market crash of 1929 ushered in the Depression of the 1930s, members of this cohort were entering their early marriage and childbearing years. Because of difficult economic conditions, some delayed marriage and childbearing. Compared with younger and older cohorts, a larger proportion never married, and those who married had smaller families. Rather than individual histories of upward mobility, most members of this cohort experienced a decline in financial resources during the early decades of their lives. People in this cohort are the parents of the small Depression-era cohort. Survivors of the 1901-1910 cohort, who are now about 87 years of age and older, have fewer children on whom to rely for help in coping with disability.

Hard times like those experienced during the Depression years can strengthen as well as weaken adaptive resources. The selection by Elder and Liker, "Hard Times in Women's Lives: Historical Influences Across Forty Years," describes the long-term effects of coping with financial hardship during the Depression among women in this cohort. Their analysis also demonstrates the significance of adaptive resources in coping with negative life events and the ways in which these resources are differentially distributed according to social class.

The World War II years. The imprint of World War II on today's cohorts of older adults also illustrates the differential impact of the same historical event on individuals with different characteristics. For many older men today, World War II involved military service. War meant combat and risks of death or injury, and 291,557 young male members of this cohort never returned from battlefields in Europe, North Africa, or the South Pacific. Wartime also meant geographic mobility, long separation from family, exposure to different people, and the mastery of new skills. For many, World War II was the central experience of their lives. In recalling his wartime experiences, one man mentioned his senior officer's response to the jubilation he and his fellow soldiers expressed at the dismissal and separation-from-service parade at the end of the war:

> "You just don't understand how big a part of your life this has been," [he told us.] "When you hear a marching band sometime in the future, you'll pick up the beat and you'll be right back here on the parade ground marching again." And he was right. That's the way it's turned out. (Schecter, 1985)

The postwar years provided unprecedented opportunity for returning soldiers. Many purchased homes or pursued college educations with funding provided through the G.I. Bill. Economic expansion, coupled with entry into the labor force of relatively small cohorts of new workers, generated upward mobility for many members of this cohort, whose lives seemed to capture the essence of the American Dream.

Women also endured wartime separation as husbands, boyfriends, fathers, and brothers were shipped overseas, but for women the greatest impact of World War II centered on the occupational sphere. Between 1941 and 1944, the number of employed women in the United States increased by almost 5 million, from 14,600,000 to 19,367,000 (Clive, 1987). The composition of the female labor force changed after the war. Earlier in the century, women who worked for wages were disproportionately young, unmarried, and poor. By 1950, the majority of women workers were married and middle aged, with an increasing proportion from the middle and working classes. The occupational distribution of the workforce also changed. Women were employed not only in unprecedented numbers but also in unprecedented jobs—"jobs that were well paid, were industrialized, and that gave a new legitimacy and value to the work that women did" (Andersen, 1993, p. 106). Although women were laid off at double the rate of male workers after the war and were resegregated into clerical and service sectors of the workforce, their labor force participation rate continued to increase in the decades following World War II.

Expanding economic opportunities accompanying World War II did not extend to all U.S. citizens. Scarcely four months after the Japanese attack on Pearl Harbor, the U.S. government posted civilian exclusion orders, which required the evacuation of 125,000 people of Japanese ancestry living along the Pacific Coast; 70% of these people were U.S.-born U.S. citizens. The orders to these Japanese citizens were often terse:

> Dispose of your homes and property. Wind up your businesses. Register the family. One seabag of bedding, two suitcases of clothing allowed per person. People in District #1 must report at 8th and Lane Street, 8 p.m. on April 28.

The selection "Pearl Harbor Echoes in Seattle" from Monica Sone's *Nisei Daughter* provides a glimpse of the effect of the relocation orders on one Japanese American family.

Despite the demand for workers, employers were slow to hire African Americans, who remained concentrated in positions with low wages, such as janitor and domestic worker. But as wartime production continued to expand, employers were forced to forgo their prejudices. At the urging of African American labor leader A. Philip Randolph, President Roosevelt issued an executive order banning employment discrimination on the basis of race in all defense industries. For people of color, World War II brought unprecedented employment opportunities and, for many, marked the end of the Depression. The selection from Piri Thomas's novel *Down These Mean Streets* illustrates this economic impact of World War II on the life of a Puerto Rican family.

The Civil Rights movement. Before the Civil Rights movement of the 1950s, 1960s, and 1970s, legally enforced racial segregation existed throughout the United States. This was the social context in which today's cohorts of elderly African Americans lived the first half of their lives. Integrated work settings during World War II provided many Americans with their first experiences interacting as coworkers across racial lines. Demands for equal rights grew quickly; then, in the postwar era, African American soldiers confronted the disparity between fighting fascism abroad and confronting racism at home. Political pressure from African American leaders encouraged President Truman to integrate the military and establish a Civil Rights Commission (Bullard, 1989/1993). The Civil Rights movement had begun. The Civil Rights movement expanded opportunities for many African Americans, but it influenced the lives of white Americans as well.

> The 1950s and 1960s bore witness to significant events, which made lasting impressions among many white Americans who, until this time, had been either satisfied with or unconcerned about the institutional and individual discrimination facing Black Americans. . . . Older cohorts were as aware as younger cohorts of these changing norms. (Danigelis & Cutler, 1991, p. 400)

The movement left in its aftermath some changed as well as some unchanged behaviors and attitudes. But older Americans were no more resistant to these changes than were younger Americans. The sociologists Nick Danigelis and Steve Cutler (1991) found that older cohorts changed their attitudes about race at about the same rate and degree as younger cohorts. A white Chicago restaurant owner interviewed by the writer Studs Terkel (1992) illustrates these changing attitudes and behaviors:

> It is different than it was. In the earlier years, I'll admit to a lot of preconceptions based on race. . . . In recent years, with the integration of offices, people are working together. They learn to work with each other. They respect each other a lot more. . . . We are much more liberal than we were back then. I sense it in myself. (pp. 314-315)

Key Issues

This discussion and the accompanying readings illustrate several points:

1. The advantages of using a life course perspective when studying the aging process
2. How the aging process is affected by individuals' personal attributes, their particular life events, and the ways in which they adapt to these events

3. How particular historical events differently shape the opportunity structures of people with certain personal characteristics

4. How life events, adaptive resources, and aging experiences differ for some individuals in certain sociohistorical times

5. How membership in a specific cohort affects the aging experience

6. Differences within cohorts due to position along interlocking systems of inequality based on gender, race or ethnicity, and social class

7. How sociohistorical events shape the aging experiences of cohorts

8. How the same historical event differently shapes the experiences of individuals who occupy different and unequal statuses within a cohort

The Readings

The reading by Elder and Liker, excerpted from their article "Hard Times in Women's Lives: Historical Influences Across Forty Years" illustrates the advantage of using a life course perspective and the concept of cohort to study people's lives and their responses to old age. This selection also shows how a particular historical event—the Great Depression—differently shaped the opportunity structures, life problems, and adaptive resources of individuals with different characteristics, in this case women of the lower class versus women of the middle class. In showing how the Depression was imprinted on the aging processes of children born during that time, the article is an example of the intersection of cohort and history.

Elder and Liker also highlight the point that occupying a disadvantaged position in one system of inequality and a privileged position in another—being women and being middle class—resulted in Depression experiences that were different than those of people who were disadvantaged in two systems—being women and lower class. Like the example of the older African American woman described by Hill, Colby, and Phelps, whose coping with racial discrimination was tied to her adaptation to aging, in this study, "The women's effective coping with personal economic loss in the middle years represented valuable preparation for the inevitable losses of old age." One conclusion suggested by these two examples is that smooth sailing in a protected environment may not develop one's adaptive skills.

The remaining selections introduce the social context in which older people from different gender and race or ethnic groups lived their lives. Each of these readings illustrates the ways in which people in certain historical time periods are relegated to circumscribed roles that narrow their opportunity structures, increase their negative life events, and weaken their adaptive resources. A life course perspective suggests that these factors combine to structure experiences of old age that differ from the experience of the dominant group.

The excerpt from Monica Sone's *Nisei Daughter* recaptures the evacuation and internment experience of today's Japanese American elderly from the eyes of a young woman. Born in 1919, the narrator was 23 years old at the time of the internment. She will celebrate her 80th birthday in 1999. This reading about the Itoi family in Seattle, Washington, illustrates how the same historical period—World War II—had different impacts on the opportunity structure and adaptive resources (in this case, economic security) of different segments of the population. World War II provided expanded occupational opportunities for many Americans, but for Japanese Americans the war meant loss of homes and businesses.

The selection by Piri Thomas from his novel *Down These Mean Streets* illustrates the economic function of World War II for a Puerto Rican family in New York City. Thomas, who was born in 1928, was a teenager in El Barrio in Manhattan during World War II. The reading also illustrates the adaptive resources available to disadvantaged members of systems of inequality. In the period before World War II, the family coped with the stressful life events accompanying poverty by using the special resources of family closeness and escaping to memories of better times—to Mrs. Thomas's "Isla Verde." Although these adaptive resources did not eliminate problems of poverty, they enabled the family to survive under oppressive economic conditions.

World War II is also addressed in the selection from Studs Terkel's (1980) book, *American Dreams: Lost and Found,* which recounts some of the World War II experiences of Coleman Young. An African American man born around the time of World War I, Young went on to become mayor of Detroit, Michigan. The article highlights the effects of legal racial discrimination in the United States on the lives of African Americans before the Civil Rights movement. The selection illustrates two points we make in this section: (a) how the aging process is affected by individuals' personal attributes, their particular life events, and the ways in which they adapt to these events and (b) how the same historical event (World War II) differently shaped the experiences of individuals who occupied different and unequal statuses within a cohort.

The selection "In Search of Our Mothers' Gardens" by Alice Walker helps us understand the experiences of African American women of Walker's mother's and grandmother's generation who spent their early lives in an era of legalized racial segregation. Walker begins with the question, "What did it mean for a black woman to be an artist in our grandmothers' time?" Clearly, talent and genius were not nourished, yet some of these women found ways of keeping creativity alive, "year after year and century after century" in music, oral history, needlework, or, in the case of Walker's mother, gardening. Caught in an oppressive environment, these women "handed on the creative spark, . . . the respect for the possibilities—and the will to grasp them." This reading illustrates how the same historical period can have different effects on the lives of people who occupy different and unequal statuses (African American women and white women), even though they are members of the same birth cohort.

The excerpt from *Lame Deer: Seeker of Visions* by Lame Deer (John Fire) and Richard Erdoes is the story of a Lakota/Sioux Native American born in 1903. His life was influenced by the historical period in which he lived and by his status as a Native American. A history of broken treaties and misguided federal policies has produced a situation in which today's elderly Native Americans have the lowest incomes and highest risk of substandard housing of any segment of the older population. During this century, Native peoples lost vast regions of tribal land, their children were educated in boarding schools where speaking their own language was prohibited, and federal policies repeatedly redefined their relationship with the federal government. Many of these policies were guided by a "melting pot model," which assumed that different groups should lose their cultural uniqueness and "melt" or blend into the dominant culture. In this selection, Lame Deer remembers his encounters with the Bureau of Indian Affairs schools, encounters in which there was insistence on learning the dominant language and culture by throwing away the old ways of the Lakota. This reading illustrates two of the issues in this section: how particular historical events differently shape the opportunity structures of people with certain personal characteristics, and how life events, adaptive resources, and aging experiences differ for some individuals in certain sociohistorical times.

The selection from Connie Wu, *World of Our Grandmothers*, chronicles the experiences of Chinese immigrants who arrived in the late nineteenth century to work on the transcontinental railroads. The struggles to immigrate and to overcome discriminatory barriers in the new country are recounted by a fourth-generation Chinese American woman. The selection illustrates a point made in this section: There are differences within cohorts due to positions along interlocking systems of inequality based on gender and ethnicity. The main characters in this excerpt were Chinese American women who were uniquely affected by the confluence of racial discrimination and U.S. immigration laws in the new country and traditional gender-related cruelties in the old. Wu's narrative also illustrates the impact of distance from the immigration experience and reminds us that, although some Asian American families are newcomers to the United States, others have lived in the United States for generations.

The impact of the immigration experience is also illustrated in Carolina Hospital's poem "Dear Tía." *Tía* is the Spanish word for "aunt," and Hospital's poem laments lost relationships—and disappearing memories—with relatives separated by geographic distance and political barriers. When Fidel Castro took over Cuba in 1959, many Cubans fled to the United States, particularly Miami, where they were granted political refugee status. The professional and managerial skills many brought with them, as well as the fact that the great majority were Caucasian and did not experience overt racial prejudice, contributed to the ability of this first wave of Cubans to achieve economic success in their new country (Novas, 1994). But the political relationship between the United States and Cuba severed relationships with relatives still in Cuba, and Hospital's poem tells of the pain of forgetting people left behind. Cubans who fled to the United States as adults are among today's Latino elders.

Paula Dressel's article, "Gender, Race, and Class: Beyond the Feminization of Poverty in Later Life," shows how hierarchies can create systems of privilege as well as systems of disadvantage. People can be disadvantaged on some hierarchies but privileged on others, and these interlocking positions influence their access to financial resources across the life course. Dressel demonstrates how poverty in later life results from the interlocking of gender and race with social class. She shows us how an emphasis on gender alone misrepresents the phenomenon of poverty in late life. This reading also illustrates how ostensibly neutral social policies can have outcomes structured according to gender, race, or class, thus illustrating the sociological maxim (mentioned in the Introduction) that "equal rules applied to unequal situations produce unequal consequences."

1

Hard Times in Women's Lives:
Historical Influences Across Forty Years

Glen H. Elder, Jr.
Jeffrey K. Liker

A recurring theme in the human drama of rapid change centers on the fragmentation of lives and their internal discontinuities in a transformed environment. When such changes occur midway in life, initial purposes and directions lose meaning for the anticipated future. The ends of life may become obscure. Migration from rural to urban areas is one potential source of disjuncture in the life course; economic cycles provide another. Americans who grew up in Depression scarcity soon faced the problems and temptations of prosperity. Now their postwar offspring must cope with a period of retrenchment that calls for the scar-

Source: Excerpted from Elder, Glen H., Jr. and Jeffrey K. Liker, "Hard Times in Women's Lives: Historical Influences Across Forty Years," 1982, *American Journal of Sociology* 88(2), 241-269. Chicago: University of Chicago Press. Reprinted with permission of the University of Chicago Press and the authors. This study is based on a program of research on social change in the family and life course. Support from the National Institute of Mental Health (grant MH-34172, Glen H. Elder, Jr., principal investigator) is gratefully acknowledged. We are indebted to the Institute of Human Development (University of California, Berkeley) for permission to use archival data from the Berkeley Guidance Study. In the course of this research, Paul Allison, Paul Baltes, and John Nesselroade provided much-appreciated counsel on matters of design and analysis. Editorial recommendations by anonymous reviewers were most helpful. Requests for reprints should be sent to Glen H. Elder, Jr., Social Change Project, NG-22, MVR, Cornell University, Ithaca, New York 14853.

city virtues of thrift and conservation. In various ways, historical change thrusts people into new situations that can challenge the means, pathways, and ends of accustomed life.

An alternative or supplementary account of social change in life experience stresses the preparatory influence of certain historical transitions for subsequent life adaptations. This alternative account can be illustrated by the military and home-front demands of wartime America. Military service in World War II and the Korean War opened up developmental experiences and educational opportunities that improved career prospects for some veterans. Wartime employment opportunities also enabled some women to acquire skills and confidence by supporting themselves. Most occasions of social change defy a simple account of life effects by giving rise to contradictory or varied consequences, depending on the individual's exposure to changes and adaptations in the new situation.

This research explores the long-term consequences of one type of social change for the life experiences of women who lived through that change; we trace the influences of the economic collapse of the 1930s on the life course development of a small number of women who were born at the turn of the century (from about 1890 to 1910). A common theme running through the Depression years and the later years of life for these women is the prevalence of loss. This study investigates the hypothesis that their degree of well-being in old age is partly a function of how they dealt with the problems of human and material loss during the 1930s, some 40 years earlier. Adaptations to loss are contingent on both the severity of the deprivation and the resources brought to the situation. From both perspectives, women in the middle class appear to have clear advantages over women in lower-status families. Indeed, few relationships in social science have been more widely documented than the inverse association between impaired health and socioeconomic position (Kohn, 1972, 1977; Langner & Michael, 1963; Srole, 1978). Among plausible accounts of this outcome, one theme stands out: *health is a product of the interaction between stressor and resources.*

Women in this study started their families during the prosperous 1920s and experienced the bust and boom of the 1930s and 1940s as wives, mothers, and often earners. All are members of the well-known Berkeley Study (Macfarlane, 1938), a longitudinal investigation of normal development in a sample of 211 middle- and working-class children and their families. The children were systematically selected from a list of Berkeley births in 1928–29. Approximately 81 of their mothers were interviewed during the 1930s and then again in 1969–70 (mean age = 70). As might be expected from class differences in mortality and social participation, high-status and well-educated women were more likely than other women to be contacted in old age (Maas & Kuypers, 1974). These differences remain even with the deceased (about half of those lost in sample attrition) excluded from the comparison. Even so, the 1969–70 participants resemble other women of the original sample with regard to the incidence and severity of economic loss during the 1930s.

We view loss and adaptation as a conceptual bridge between hard times during early adulthood and later life some 40 years after the stock market crash. Losses after midlife generally represent a more expectable, culturally patterned sequence of experiences than the seemingly arbitrary deprivations of

the 1930s. Nonetheless, the experience of having coped with such hardships in early adulthood is a potential resource among aging women who face social, material, and physical losses. On the other hand, a prolonged sequence of Depression misfortunes might have precisely the opposite effect through diminished inner resources and greater health risk when the inevitable losses and separations of old age occur. For middle-class families, the Great Depression often created a temporary economic setback lasting several years, while working-class adults were more likely to experience the economic losses of the 1930s as more of the same economic misfortunes that already characterized their lives (Elder, 1974). We begin the study with an examination of class differences in the social and economic resources Berkeley women brought to the 1930s and then employ measurement and causal models (Jöreskog & Sörbom, 1979) to assess their psychological health in old age. Some preliminary issues are worth noting as background to the research.

A life course perspective on aging assumes that individuals assess and react to new situations in the light of their personal biographies. The ups and downs of a lifetime furnish lessons, liabilities, and resources that influence the ways in which men and women age and meet the realities of later life (Butler, 1975). The wisdom to make sound choices stemming from life experiences, positive and negative, may ensure a legacy of good health, adaptive skills, and material security in old age.

The course of individual development prompts a number of questions. What are the life course antecedents of successful aging (Neugarten, 1970)? How are life events distributed across the life span (Pearlin & Johnson, 1977)? Why do similar misfortunes during the early years appear to lead one person to become bitter (Bowlby, 1980) and another grateful? How can we account for the large number of lower-status people who manage adversity so well in their lives (Mechanic, 1972)? How do people in crisis or deprivational conditions manage without longstanding injury or impairments to self or others? Can we account for this difference between successful copers and the people who become ill or disabled?

For American women born around 1900, answers to these questions involve recognition of differential exposure to historical change, such as the economic collapse of the 1930s, as well as the differential resources families brought to the situation. Some families were exposed to severe economic hardship; others managed to avoid misfortune altogether. We shall use economic variation as a starting point in assessing the long-term effects of the Depression experience among the Berkeley women. The strategy entails systematic comparisons of the psychological health and coping resources of women who suffered economic hardships in the 1930s with those of women who managed to avoid such deprivations.

Four conditions bear upon the long-term effects of economic deprivation: (1) the degree or severity of the loss; (2) adaptive resources and options brought to this new situation (education, problem-solving skills, sense of efficacy); (3) definitions and assessments of the situation (causal attribution, cognitive appraisal, etc.); and (4) action or responses, such as job seeking or taking in boarders. The first two conditions influence definitions and responses which can produce such varying outcomes as enhanced efficacy and sense of control, on the one hand, and social withdrawal and disorganization, on the other. These outcomes, in turn, affect the likelihood of subsequent difficulties and the development of effective coping strategies, perpetuating cycles of advantage and disadvantage (Bandura, 1977; Duncan & Morgan, 1980; Peterson, 1980).

As the Berkeley women entered the 1930s, class position tells us something important about their Depression experience (severity of loss, adaptive resources, modes of response) and later life in the 1960s. According to the Oakland study (Elder, 1974, chap. 3), loss of status was especially painful to middle-class women, but they had more resources than lower-status women for dealing effectively with family hardship. Their educational, economic, and status advantages were expressed in stronger feelings of personal worth and more developed skills in problem solving. In contrast, working-class women were more vulnerable to the very real economic hardships that often seemed unmanageable. For them, family hardships reinforced feelings of inadequacy and helplessness. These issues are consistent with a "class interaction" hypothesis (see Kohn's [1972] interaction model): low socioeconomic status among women before the 1930s increased chances that hardship would impair their life prospects in old age (economic, health). Beneficial effects from Depression losses are found mainly among women who entered the 1930s as members of the middle class.

The analysis is organized in three phases. We begin with women's resources when entering the early 1930s as young mothers. Do we find differences in social support and problem-solving skill between women from high- and low-status families or between the economically deprived and the nondeprived? The most general issue here is whether social class and economic loss produced different pathways for women and their life outcomes. The second part of the analysis puts the "class interaction" hypothesis to a direct test by comparing the effects of the Depression on the mental health of elderly women from the middle and working classes. The analytic technique, LISREL (see Jöreskog & Sörbom, 1978), enables a comparative assessment of these effects in the middle and working classes while taking measurement error into account. The estimated models include pre-Depression psychological states so that analyses examine change in relative functioning as an outcome of differential exposure to Depression hardship (Bohrnstedt, 1969). Finally, we examine the long-term effects of economic loss on certain attitudes and behaviors that are related to an efficacious life-style for women in the later years.

Women's Resources From Childbearing to Old Age

In general, higher-status women had more in reserve cognitively and emotionally when they entered the 1930s, a decade that magnified many times over the life stresses that ordinarily pile up during the childbearing years. Hence, even before the Depression, working-class women were especially vulnerable to setbacks, barriers, and criticism, factors that soon became commonplace.

Economic loss did shape the lives of these women in at least two ways. First, women in the deprived middle-class group were much more likely than their nondeprived counterparts to go to work in the 1930s and to continue into the postwar years. Indeed, in the late 1930s (1936–39), 41% of the high-status women in deprived homes spent some time on a job, while only 10% of the nondeprived middle-class women did so. This difference was much less pronounced in the working class, where women in both the nondeprived and deprived groups commonly entered the labor market. In the late 1930s, 49% of the deprived and 43% of the nondeprived working-class women spent time in the paid labor force. Hence, any developmental value of working is likely to be confined to middle-class women who generally had the luxury of staying home if their families were sheltered from Depression hardship.

Second, deprived middle-class women were much more likely than the nondeprived to be widowed in 1969. Among the deprived high-status women, only one-fourth of the 1929 marriages survived to 1969. This figure, well below the 71% survival rate for middle-class marriages in families that were spared major setbacks in the 1930s, may reflect the pathogenic effects of job and income loss on men (see Brenner, 1973, p. 973; Cohn, 1978). In any case, the high rate of widowhood among women from the deprived middle class is manifested in their relative disadvantage with regard to financial status. Widows generally rank below married women in economic status.

Considering the available data on economic welfare and social networks in old age, there is little evidence of markedly different objective pathways from the Depression into the later years. Possibly, postwar affluence eliminated many of the economic disadvantages of the Depression (Elder & Rockwell, 1978). Hence, any long-term effects of the Depression are likely to operate through psychological resources and adaptive capacities. Resources brought to the 1930s lead to the expectation that economic deprivation will have a negative effect on well-being in old age among the working class and a possibly benign effect among the middle class. Limited resources and acute survival pressures in the deprived working class increased the risk of helplessness among these women. Feelings of efficacy had a better chance of evolving through the adaptational and problem-solving efforts of women in the deprived middle class. Having managed on very little during the 1930s, these women could at least view the adversity of their later years with a belief that they had been there before and survived. Are such variations in health part of the Depression's legacy for women from the middle and working class?

Early Hardship and Subsequent Well-Being in Old Age

Overall, Depression loss added to the psychological disadvantage of working-class women—to their low self-esteem, feelings of insecurity, and dissatisfaction with life—but posed no such handicap for the middle class. Two groups of middle-class women, the privileged nondeprived and the economically deprived, entered the 1930s with similar inner resources. After the economic decline of the Depression, financial pressures, husband disability, and employment on a paid job were all more common in the latter group. Despite conditions of this sort, middle-class women who lived through Depression hardships occupy a position of relative advantage on psychological well-being in their later years. They claim less in the way of material goods than women from the nondeprived middle class but show greater acceptance of what they have. Gratitude and satisfaction are more common in their lives. For them, less is truly more.

Consistent with the interaction hypothesis, hardship experience during the 1930s is linked with assertiveness and mastery feelings among elderly women from the middle class, whereas passivity and helplessness stand out as more typical outcomes of early deprivation among lower-status women. Depression hardship increased the risk of widowhood and economic pressure for working-class women and both factors, as well as the direct effect of economic loss, favored a relatively passive, dependent adaptation in old age.

Resourcefulness and confidence in old age represent the more common legacy of Depression adversity among middle-class women. Neither hard times in the thirties nor economic misfortune and loss of spouse during the later years managed to turn these women toward a dysphoric outlook or helplessness. Even serious health problems became just another problem to some. "I get in a little difficulty," a Berkeley woman observed (Maas & Kuypers, 1974, p. 136); "I've had eight surgeries trying to correct it, but now I've just given up. I do the best I can and most of the time I get along very well." It is the middle-class women from the privileged, non-deprived sector and not the economically deprived who display a more victimized outlook during the later years of their life. The effects of Depression hardship varied across class strata as expected and the class difference is statistically reliable.

Economic Change and Health in the Life Course: A Concluding Note

These contrasting outcomes of Depression experience in the lives of middle- and working-class women are partly anticipated in the empirical literature on socioeconomic factors in health. This research links the risk of impaired health to lower socioeconomic status and especially to economic setbacks in the lower strata. The direction of influence between economics and health has been questioned by analysts and the temporal span of longitudinal studies has been too short to permit estimates of the duration or persistence of economic effects. Also, research to date has viewed the economic factor largely in terms of men and their unemployment (Kasl, 1979) rather than as an influence in the lives of women. With its focus on hard times in the lives of women, this longitudinal study traces conditions of economic deprivation to psychological health in old age. Over a span of 40 years, we see diverse imprints of the Great Depression on patterns of aging.

From the evidence at hand, different processes seem to be at work in the life trajectories of middle- and working-class women. Depression hardship increased the emotional resources, vitality, and self-efficacy of women from the deprived middle class as compared with the privileged nondeprived. For working-class women in the later years, exposure to Depression hardship generally entailed a set of disadvantages, including diminished mental skills and self-confidence, lower morale, and a sense of helplessness. The consistency of this class reversal is perhaps more impressive than its size. In the working class, the modest size of the negative effect leaves open for investigation the important question of how some women from deprived circumstances managed to rise above the limitations of their world. A larger sample and more complete life records are needed to specify elements in the causal process of change and continuity and in life patterns that break with customary schedules. Social support, as a moderator of economic pressures, should be examined across the life course of marriage, parent-child relations, distant kin, and friends.

Our theoretical rationale for linking the Depression and aging experiences of the Berkeley women centers on their common ground in losses and related adaptations. We argue that women who experienced particular losses and learned to deal with them are better equipped to manage subsequent events of this type. The particular coping skills acquired in periods of hard times are not activated by tranquil stages of the life course. It is only during trying periods of decremental change, such as the later years, that coping resources are brought forth and distinguish the prepared woman from the sheltered or untested one. From this perspective, there is reason to expect the health effects of Depression hardship in the late 1930s to be weaker than those observed in old age.

Despite the daily pressures on hard-pressed families, the relative health of the Berkeley women in the late 1930s shows no reliable differences between the deprived and nondeprived in either the middle or the working class. Two types of measures were used in the analysis: (1) a simple index of behavioral impairment in performing social roles (some evidence [1936–39] or no evidence) and (2) a five-point interviewer rating on "worrisome behavior" (1936–38) identical to the worrisome ratings (1930 and 1969) used in the causal models. Of the Berkeley women, 86% were judged as showing no evidence of behavioral impairment by the end of the thirties, and the likelihood of some impairment did not vary by hard times in either social class, although it was more prevalent in the working class. A similar picture emerges from the ratings on worrisome behavior. Average scores for the nondeprived and deprived were virtually identical in the two social classes. Though much additional work is needed on Depression influences during the 1930s, and their precise timing and form, these empirical observations generally support a situational thesis on loss and life-course development: that differential experiences with problems of loss are most visibly expressed in subsequent life situations that are typified by such events, as during old age.

To a remarkable degree, the contrasting effects of Depression hardship reported in this analysis parallel the life experience of a younger group of women who were born in 1920–21 and grew up in Oakland, California,

during the 1930s. These women were young adolescents in the Depression era, and economic loss often forced them to take on adult work and domestic roles that normally would have been their parents' responsibilities. At the age of 40, when they generally had families of their own, these women were found to have long-term effects of their Depression experiences that differed by social class origin (Elder, 1974, p. 242). The assumption that "smooth sailing" in a protected childhood may not develop adaptive skills was borne out in the lives of women who had grown up in nondeprived homes in the middle class. They ranked lower on psychological health and resourcefulness at the age of 40 than middle-class women who as adolescents had encountered the emotional trauma and pressure of hard times at first hand. As in the Berkeley study, the health of the Oakland women from the deprived working class was impaired relative to that of women from the nondeprived working class. Neither a privileged life nor one of unrelenting deprivation ensures the inner resources for successful aging.

Social change and the normative order bring many contradictions to the life course. Some old people encounter losses without the prior experience that enables them to cope effectively with such events. The wisdom to make appropriate decisions may arrive too late, at a time when the most important choices have been made. In the words of a Berkeley woman: "It's only when you have lived through experiences and digested them that you come to acquire enough sense to know how to deal with them." According to both this personal perspective and scientific knowledge of behavioral adaptation, effective coping with personal loss through the middle years represents valuable preparation for the inevitable losses of old age.

References

Bandura, A. (1977). Self-efficacy: Toward a unifying theory of behavioral change. *Psychological Review, 84,* 191-215.

Bohrnstedt, G. W. (1969). Observations on the measurement of change. In E. F. Borgatta (Ed.), *Sociological methodology*. San Francisco: Jossey-Bass.

Bowlby, J. (1980). *Loss: Sadness and depression* (Vol. 3). New York: Basic Books.

Brenner, M. H. (1973). *Mental illness and the economy*. Cambridge, MA: Harvard University Press.

Butler, R. N. (1975). *Why survive? Being old in America*. New York: Harper & Row.

Cohn, R. M. (1978). The effect of employment status change on self-attitudes. *Social Psychology Quarterly, 41*, 81-93.

Duncan, G., & Morgan, J. (1980). The incidence and some consequences of major life events. In G. Duncan & J. Morgan (Eds.), *Five thousand American families* (Vol. 8, pp. 183-240). Ann Arbor: Institute for Social Research, University of Michigan.

Elder, G. H., Jr. (1974). *Children of the great depression*. Chicago: University of Chicago Press.

Elder, G. H., Jr., & Rockwell, R. C. (1978). Economic depression and postwar opportunity: A study of life patterns and health. In R. A. Simmons (Ed.), *Research in community and mental health* (pp. 249-303). Greenwich, CT: JAI.

Jöreskog, K. G., & Sörbom, D. (1978). *LISREL IV: Analysis of linear structural relationships by the method of maximum likelihood*. Chicago: International Educational Services.

Jöreskog, K. G., & Sörbom, D. (Eds.). (1979). *Advances in factor analysis and structural equation models*. Cambridge, MA: Abt.

Kasl, S. V. (1979). Changes in mental health status associated with job loss and retirement. In J. E. Barrett et al. (Eds.), *Stress and mental disorder* (pp. 179-200). New York: Raven.

Kohn, M. L. (1972). Class, family and schizophrenia: A reformulation. *Social Forces, 50*, 295-304.

Kohn, M. L. (1977). *Class and conformity*. Chicago: University of Chicago Press.

Langner, T. S., & Michael, S. T. (1963). *Life stress and mental health*. New York: Free Press.

Maas, H. S., & Kuypers, J. A. (1974). *From thirty to seventy: A forty-year longitudinal study of adult life styles and personality*. San Francisco: Jossey-Bass.

Macfarlane, J. W. (1938). Studies in child guidance: 1. Methodology of data collection and organization. *Monographs of the Society for Research in Child Development, 3*, 1-254.

Mechanic, D. (1972). Social class and schizophrenia: Some requirements for a plausible theory of social influence. *Social Forces, 50*, 305-309.

Neugarten, B. L. (1970). Dynamics of transition of middle age to old age: Adaptation and the life cycle. *Journal of Geriatric Psychiatry, 4*, 71-87.

Pearlin, L. I., & Johnson, J. S. (1977). Marital status, life-strains, and depression. *American Sociological Review, 42*, 704-715.

Peterson, C. (1980, October 5-6). *The sense of control over one's life: A review of recent literature*. Paper prepared for the Social Science Research Council Meeting, "Self and Personal Control Over the Life Span," New York.

Srole, L. (1978). *Mental health in the metropolis: The midtown Manhattan study* (rev. and enl. ed.). New York: New York University Press.

2

Pearl Harbor Echoes in Seattle

Monica Sone

On a peaceful Sunday morning, December 7, 1941, Henry, Sumi and I were at choir rehearsal singing ourselves hoarse in preparation for the annual Christmas recital of Handel's "Messiah." Suddenly Chuck Mizuno, a young University of Washington student, burst into the chapel, gasping as if he had sprinted all the way up the stairs.

"Listen, everybody!" he shouted. "Japan just bombed Pearl Harbor . . . in Hawaii! It's war!"

The terrible words hit like a blockbuster, paralyzing us. Then we smiled feebly at each other, hoping this was one of Chuck's practical jokes. Miss Hara, our music director, rapped her baton impatiently on the music stand and chided him, "Now Chuck, fun's fun, but we have work to do. Please take your place. You're already half an hour late."

But Chuck strode vehemently back to the door. "I mean it, folks, honest! I just heard the news over my car radio. Reporters are talking a blue streak. Come on down and hear it for yourselves."

With that, Chuck swept out of the room, a swirl of young men following in his wake. Henry was one of them. The rest of us stayed, rooted to our places like a row of marionettes. I felt as if a fist had smashed my pleasant little existence, breaking it into jigsaw puzzle pieces. An old wound opened up again, and

I found myself shrinking inwardly from my Japanese blood, the blood of an enemy. I knew instinctively that the fact that I was an American by birthright was not going to help me escape the consequences of this unhappy war.

One girl mumbled over and over again. "It can't be, God, it can't be!" Someone else was saying, "What a spot to be in! Do you think we'll be considered Japanese or Americans?"

A boy replied quietly, "We'll be Japs, same as always. But our parents are enemy aliens now, you know."

A shocked silence followed. Henry came for Sumi and me. "Come on, let's go home," he said.

We ran trembling to our car. Usually Henry was a careful driver, but that morning he bore down savagely on the accelerator. Boiling angry, he shot us up Twelfth Avenue, rammed through the busy Jackson Street intersection, and rocketed up the Beacon Hill bridge. We swung violently around to the left of the Marine Hospital and swooped to the top of the hill. Then Henry slammed on the brakes and we rushed helter-skelter up to the house to get to the radio. Asthma skidded away from under our trampling feet.

Mother was sitting limp in the huge armchair as if she had collapsed there, listening dazedly to the turbulent radio. Her face was frozen still, and the only words she could utter were, "*Komatta neh, komatta neh.* How dreadful, how dreadful."

Source: Excerpted from *Nisei Daughter* by Monica Sone. Copyright 1953 by Monica Sone. Copyright renewed 1981 by Monica Sone. Reprinted by permission of Little, Brown and Company.

Henry put his arms around her. She told him she first heard about the attack on Pearl Harbor when one of her friends phoned her and told her to turn on the radio.

We pressed close against the radio, listening stiffly to the staccato outbursts of an excited reporter: "The early morning sky of Honolulu was filled with the furious buzzing of Jap Zero planes for nearly three hours, raining death and destruction on the airfields below. . . . A warship anchored beyond the Harbor was sunk. . . ."

We were switched to the White House. The fierce clack of teletype machines and the babble of voices surging in and out from the background almost drowned out the speaker's terse announcements.

With every fiber of my being I resented this war. I felt as if I were on fire. "Mama, they should never have done it," I cried. "Why did they do it? Why? Why?"

Mother's face turned paper white. "What do you know about it? Right or wrong, the Japanese have been chafing with resentment for years. It was bound to happen, one time or another. You're young, Ka-chan, you know very little about the ways of nations. It's not as simple as you think, but this is hardly the time to be quarreling about it, is it?"

"No, it's too late, too late!" and I let the tears pour down my face.

Father rushed home from the hotel. He was deceptively calm as he joined us in the living room. Father was a born skeptic, and he believed nothing unless he could see, feel and smell it. He regarded all newspapers and radio news with deep suspicion. He shook his head doubtfully. "It must be propaganda. With the way things are going now between America and Japan, we should expect the most fantastic rumors, and this is one of the wildest I've heard yet." But we noticed that he was firmly glued to the radio. It seemed as if the regular Sunday programs, sounding off relentlessly hour after hour on schedule, were trying to blunt the catastrophe of the morning.

The telephone pealed nervously all day as people searched for comfort from each other. Chris called, and I told her how miserable and confused I felt about the war. Understanding as always, Chris said, "You know how I feel about you and your family, Kaz. Don't, for heaven's sake, feel the war is going to make any difference in our relationship. It's not your fault, nor mine! I wish to God it could have been prevented." Minnie called off her Sunday date with Henry. Her family was upset and they thought she should stay close to home instead of wandering downtown.

Late that night Father got a shortwave broadcast from Japan. Static sputtered, then we caught a faint voice, speaking rapidly in Japanese. Father sat unmoving as a rock, his head cocked. The man was talking about the war between Japan and America. Father bit his lips and Mother whispered to him anxiously, "It's true then, isn't it, Papa? It's true?"

Father was muttering to himself. "So they really did it!" Now having heard the news in their native tongue, the war had become a reality to Father and Mother.

"I suppose from now on, we'll hear about nothing but the humiliating defeats of Japan in the papers here," Mother said, resignedly.

Henry and I glared indignantly at Mother, then Henry shrugged his shoulders and decided to say nothing. Discussion of politics, especially Japan versus America, had become taboo in our family for it sent tempers skyrocketing. Henry and I used to criticize Japan's aggressions in China and Manchuria while Father and Mother condemned Great Britain and America's superior attitude toward Asiatics and their interference with Japan's economic growth. During these arguments, we had eyed each other like strangers, parents against children. They left us with a hollow feeling at the pit of the stomach.

Just then the shrill peel of the telephone cut off the possibility of a family argument. When I answered, a young girl's voice fluttered through breathily, "Hello, this is Taeko Tanabe. Is my mother there?"

"No, she isn't, Taeko."

"Thank you," and Taeko hung up before I could say another word. Her voice sounded strange. Mrs. Tanabe was one of Mother's poet friends. Taeko called three more times, and each time before I could ask her if anything was wrong, she quickly hung up. The next day we learned that Taeko was trying desperately to locate her mother because FBI agents had swept into their home and arrested Mr. Tanabe, a newspaper editor. The FBI had permitted Taeko to try to locate her mother before they took Mr. Tanabe away while they searched the house for contraband and subversive material, but she was not to let anyone else know what was happening.

Next morning the newspapers fairly exploded in our faces with stories about the Japanese raids on the chain of Pacific islands. We were shocked to read Attorney General Biddle's announcement that 736 Japanese had been picked up in the United States and Hawaii. Then Mrs. Tanabe called Mother about her husband's arrest, and she said at least a hundred others had been taken from our community. Messrs. Okayama, Higashi, Sughira, Mori, Okada—we knew them all.

"But why were they arrested, Papa? They weren't spies, were they?"

Father replied almost curtly, "Of course not! They were probably taken for questioning."

The pressure of war moved in on our little community. The Chinese consul announced that all the Chinese would carry identification cards and wear "China" badges to distinguish them from the Japanese. Then I really felt left standing out in the cold. The government ordered the bank funds of all Japanese nationals frozen. Father could no longer handle financial transactions through his bank accounts, but Henry, fortunately, was of legal age so that business could be negotiated in his name.

In the afternoon President Roosevelt's formal declaration of war against Japan was broadcast throughout the nation. In grave, measured words, he described the attack on Pearl Harbor as shameful, infamous. I writhed involuntarily. I could no more have escaped the stab of self-consciousness than I could have changed my Oriental features.

Monday night a complete blackout was ordered against a possible Japanese air raid on the Puget Sound area. Mother assembled black cloths to cover the windows and set up candles in every room. All radio stations were silenced from seven in the evening till morning, but we gathered around the dead radio anyway, out of sheer habit. We whiled away the evening reading instructions in the newspapers on how to put out incendiary bombs and learning about the best hiding places during bombardments. When the city pulled its switches at blackout hour and plunged us into an ominous dark silence, we went to bed shivering and wondering what tomorrow would bring. All of a sudden there was a wild screech of brakes, followed by the resounding crash of metal slamming into metal. We rushed out on the balcony. In the street below we saw dimension shapes of cars piled grotesquely on top of each other, their soft blue headlights staring helplessly up into the sky. Angry men's voices floated up to the house. The men were wearing uniforms and their metal buttons gleamed in the blue lights. Apparently two police cars had collided in the blackout.

Clutching at our bathrobes we lingered there. The damp winter night hung heavy and inert like a wet black veil, and at the bottom of Beacon Hill, we could barely make out the undulating length of Rainier Valley, lying quietly in the somber, brooding silence like a hunted python. A few pinpoints of light pricked the darkness here and there like winking bits of diamonds, betraying the uneasy vigil of a tense city.

It made me positively hivey the way the FBI agents continued their raids into Japanese homes and business places and marched the Issei men away into the old red brick immigration building, systematically and efficiently, as if they were stocking a cellarful of choice bottles of wine. At first we noted that the men arrested were those who had been prominent in community affairs, like Mr. Kato, many times president of the Seattle Japanese Chamber of Commerce, and Mr. Ohashi, the principal of our Japanese language school, or individuals whose business was directly connected with firms in Japan;

but as time went on, it became less and less apparent why the others were included in these raids.

We wondered when Father's time would come. We expected momentarily to hear strange footsteps on the porch and the sudden demanding ring of the front doorbell. Our ears became attuned like the sensitive antennas of moths, translating every soft swish of passing cars into the arrival of the FBI squad.

Once when our doorbell rang after curfew hour, I completely lost my Oriental stoicism which I had believed would serve me well under the most trying circumstances. No friend of ours paid visits at night anymore, and I was sure that Father's hour had come. As if hypnotized, I walked woodenly to the door. A mass of black figures stood before me, filling the doorway. I let out a magnificent shriek. Then pandemonium broke loose. The solid rank fell apart into a dozen separate figures which stumbled and leaped pell-mell away from the porch. Watching the mad scramble, I thought I had routed the FBI agents with my cry of distress. Father, Mother, Henry and Sumi rushed out to support my wilting body. When Henry snapped on the porch light, one lone figure crept out from behind the front hedge. It was a newsboy who, standing at a safe distance, called in a quavering voice, "I . . . I came to collect for . . . for the *Times*."

Shaking with laughter, Henry paid him and gave him an extra large tip for the terrible fright he and his bodyguards had suffered at the hands of the Japanese. As he hurried down the walk, boys of all shapes and sizes crawled out from behind trees and bushes and scurried after him.

We heard all kinds of stories about the FBI, most of them from Mr. Yorita, the grocer, who now took twice as long to make his deliveries. The war seemed to have brought out his personality. At least he talked more, and he glowed, in a sinister way. Before the war Mr. Yorita had been uncommunicative. He used to stagger silently through the back door with a huge sack of rice over his shoulders, dump it on the kitchen floor and silently flow out of the door as if he were bored and disgusted with food and the people who ate it. But now Mr. Yorita swaggered in, sent a gallon jug of soy sauce spinning into a corner, and launched into a comprehensive report of the latest rumors he had picked up on his route, all in chronological order. Mr. Yorita looked like an Oriental Dracula, with his triangular eyes and yellow-fanged teeth. He had a mournfully long sallow face and in his excitement his gold-rimmed glasses constantly slipped to the tip of his long nose. He would describe in detail how some man had been awakened in the dead of night, swiftly handcuffed, and dragged from out of his bed by a squad of brutal, tight-lipped men. Mr. Yorita bared his teeth menacingly in his most dramatic moments and we shrank from him instinctively. As he backed out of the kitchen door, he would shake his bony finger at us with a warning of dire things to come. When Mother said, "Yorita-San, you must worry about getting a call from the FBI, too," Mr. Yorita laughed modestly, pushing his glasses back up into place. "They wouldn't be interested in anyone as insignificant as myself!" he assured her.

But he was wrong. The following week a new delivery boy appeared at the back door with an airy explanation, "Yep, they got the old man, too, and don't ask me why! The way I see it, it's subversive to sell soy sauce now."

The Matsuis were visited, too. Shortly after Dick had gone to Japan, Mr. Matsui had died and Mrs. Matsui had sold her house. Now she and her daughter and youngest son lived in the back of their little dry goods store on Jackson Street. One day when Mrs. Matsui was busy with the family laundry, three men entered the shop, nearly ripping off the tiny bell hanging over the door. She hurried out, wiping sudsy, reddened hands on her apron. At best Mrs. Matsui's English was rudimentary, and when she became excited, it deteriorated into Japanese. She hovered on her toes, delighted to see new customers in her humble shop. "Yes, yes, anything you want?"

"Where's Mr. Matsui?" a steely-eyed man snapped at her.

Startled, Mrs. Matsui jerked her thumb toward the rear of the store and said, "He not home."

"What? Oh, in there, eh? Come on!" The men tore the faded print curtain aside and rushed into the back room. "Don't see him. Must be hiding."

They jerked open bedroom doors, leaped into the tiny bathroom, flung windows open and peered down into the alley. Tiny birdlike Mrs. Matsui rushed around after them. "No, no! Whatsamalla, whatsamalla!"

"Where's your husband? Where is he?" one man demanded angrily, flinging clothes out of the closet.

"Why you mix 'em all up? He not home, not home." She clawed at the back of the burly men like an angry little sparrow, trying to stop the holocaust in her little home. One man brought his face down close to hers, shouting slowly and clearly, "WHERE IS YOUR HUSBAND? YOU SAID HE WAS IN HERE A MINUTE AGO!"

"Yes, yes, not here. *Mah, wakara nai hito da neh.* Such stupid men."

Mrs. Matsui dove under a table, dragged out a huge album and pointed at a large photograph. She jabbed her gnarled finger up toward the ceiling, saying, "Heben! Heben!"

The men gathered around and looked at a picture of Mr. Matsui's funeral. Mrs. Matsui and her two children were standing by a coffin, their eyes cast down, surrounded by all their friends, all of whom were looking down. The three men's lips formed an "Oh." One of them said, "We're sorry to have disturbed you. Thank you, Mrs. Matsui, and good-by." They departed quickly and quietly.

Having passed through this baptism, Mrs. Matsui became an expert on the FBI, and she stood by us, rallying and coaching us on how to deal with them. She said to Mother, "You must destroy everything and anything Japanese which may incriminate your husband. It doesn't matter what it is, if it's printed or made in Japan, destroy it because the FBI always carries off those items for evidence."

In fact all the women whose husbands had been spirited away said the same thing. Gradually we became uncomfortable with our Japanese books, magazines, wall scrolls and knickknacks. When Father's hotel friends, Messrs. Sakaguchi, Horiuchi, Nishibue and a few others vanished, and their wives called Mother weeping and warning her again about having too many Japanese objects around the house, we finally decided to get rid of some of ours. We knew it was impossible to destroy everything. The FBI would certainly think it strange if they found us sitting in a bare house, totally purged of things Japanese. But it was as if we could no longer stand the tension of waiting, and we just had to do something against the black day. We worked all night, feverishly combing through bookshelves, closets, drawers, and furtively creeping down to the basement furnace for the burning. I gathered together my well-worn Japanese language schoolbooks which I had been saving over a period of ten years with the thought that they might come in handy when I wanted to teach Japanese to my own children. I threw them into the fire and watched them flame and shrivel into black ashes. But when I came face to face with my Japanese doll which Grandmother Nagashima had sent me from Japan, I rebelled. It was a gorgeously costumed Nfiyazukai figure, typical of the lady in waiting who lived in the royal palace during the feudal era. The doll was gowned in an elegant purple silk kimono with the long, sweeping hemline of its period and sashed with rich-embroidered gold and silver brocade. With its black, shining coiffed head bent a little to one side, its delicate pink-tipped ivory hand holding a red lacquer message box, the doll had an appealing, almost human charm. I decided to ask Chris if she would keep it for me. Chris loved and appreciated beauty in every form and shape, and I knew that in her hands, the doll would be safe and enjoyed.

Henry pulled down from his bedroom wall the toy samurai sword he had brought from Japan and tossed it into the flames. Sumi's contributions to the furnace were books of fairy tales and magazines sent to her by her young cousins in Japan. We sorted out Japanese classic and popular music from a stack of records, shattered them over our knees and fed the pieces to the furnace. Father piled up his translated Japanese volumes of philosophy and religion and carted them reluctantly to the basement. Mother had the most to eliminate, with her scrapbooks of poems cut out from newspapers and magazines, and her private collection of old Japanese classic literature.

It was past midnight when we finally climbed upstairs to bed. Wearily we closed our eyes, filled with an indescribable sense of guilt for having destroyed the things we loved. This night of ravage was to haunt us for years. As I lay struggling to fall asleep, I realized that we hadn't freed ourselves at all from fear. We still lay stiff in our beds, waiting.

3

Puerto Rican Paradise

Piri Thomas

Poppa didn't talk to me the next day. Soon he didn't talk much to anyone. He lost his night job—I forget why, and probably it was worth forgetting—and went back on home relief. It was 1941, and the Great Hunger called Depression was still down on Harlem.

But there was still the good old WPA. If a man was poor enough, he could dig a ditch for the government. Now Poppa was poor enough again.

The weather turned cold one more time, and so did our apartment. In the summer the cooped-up apartments in Harlem seem to catch all the heat and improve on it. It's the same in the winter. The cold, plastered walls embrace that cold from outside and make it a part of the apartment, till you don't know whether it's better to freeze out in the snow or by the stove, where four jets, wide open, spout futile, blue-yellow flames. It's hard on the rats, too.

Snow was falling. "My *Cristo*," Momma said, "*qué frío*. Doesn't that landlord have any *corazón*?[1] Why don't he give more heat?" I wondered how Pops was making out working a pick and shovel in that falling snow.

Momma picked up a hammer and began to beat the beat-up radiator that's copped a plea from so many beatings. Poor steam radiator, how could it give out heat when it was freezing itself? The hollow sounds Momma beat out of it brought echoes from other freezing people in the building. Everybody picked up the beat and it seemed a crazy, good idea. If everybody took turns beating on the radiators, everybody could keep warm from the exercise.

We drank hot cocoa and talked about summertime. Momma talked about Puerto Rico and how great it was, and how she'd like to go back one day, and how it was warm all the time there and no matter how poor you were over there, you could always live on green bananas, *bacalao*,[2] and rice and beans. "*Dios mío*," she said, "I don't think I'll ever see my island again."

"Sure you will, Mommie," said Miriam, my kid sister. She was eleven. "Tell us, tell us all about Porto Rico."

"It's not Porto Rico, it's Puerto Rico," said Momma.

"Tell us, Moms," said nine-year-old James, "about Puerto Rico."

"Yeah, Mommie," said six-year-old José.

Even the baby, Paulie, smiled.

Moms copped that wet-eyed look and began to dream-talk about her *isla verde*,[3] Moses' land of milk and honey.

"When I was a little girl," she said, "I remember the getting up in the morning and getting the water from the river and getting the wood for the fire and the quiet of the greenlands and the golden color of the morning sky, the grass wet from the *lluvia*[4] . . . *Ai*, *Dios*, the *coquís*[5] and the *pajaritos*[6] making all the *música* . . ."

Source: Excerpted from *Down These Mean Streets* by Piri Thomas. Copyright © 1967 by Piri Thomas. Reprinted by permission of Alfred A. Knopf, Inc.

"Mommie, were you poor?" asked Miriam.

"*Sí, muy pobre,* but very happy. I remember the hard work and the very little bit we had, but it was a good little bit. It counted very much. Sometimes when you have too much, the good gets lost within and you have to look very hard. But when you have a little, then the good does not have to be looked for so hard."

"Moms," I asked, "did everybody love each other—I mean, like if everybody was worth something, not like if some weren't important because they were poor—you know what I mean?"

"*Bueno hijo,* you have people everywhere, who, because they have more, don't remember those who have very little. But in Puerto Rico those around you share *la pobreza*[7] with you and they love you, because only poor people can understand poor people. I like *los Estados Unidos,* but it's sometimes a cold place to live—not because of the winter and the landlord not giving heat but because of the snow in the hearts of the people."

"Moms, didn't our people have any money or land?" I leaned forward, hoping to hear that my ancestors were noble princes born in Spain.

"Your grandmother and grandfather had a lot of land, but they lost that."

"How come, Moms?"

"Well, in those days there was nothing of what you call *contratos,*[8] and when you bought or sold something, it was on your word and a handshake, and that's the way your *abuelos*[9] bought their land and then lost it."

"Is that why we ain't got nuttin' now?" James asked pointedly.

"Oh, it—"

The door opened and put an end to the kitchen yak. It was Poppa coming home from work. He came into the kitchen and brought all the cold with him. Poor Poppa, he looked so lost in the clothes he had on. A jacket and coat, sweaters on top of sweaters, two pairs of long johns, two pairs of pants, two pairs of socks, and a woolen cap. And under all that he was cold. His eyes were cold; his ears were red with pain. He took off his gloves and his fingers were stiff with cold.

"*Cómo está?*"[10] said Momma. "I will make you coffee."

Poppa said nothing. His eyes were running hot frozen tears. He worked his fingers and rubbed his ears, and the pain made him make faces. "Get me some snow, Piri," he said finally.

I ran to the window, opened it, and scraped all the snow on the sill into one big snowball and brought it to him. We all watched in frozen wonder as Poppa took that snow and rubbed it on his ears and hands.

"Gee, Pops, don't it hurt?" I asked.

"*Sí,* but it's good for it. It hurts a little first, but it's good for the frozen parts."

I wondered why.

"How was it today?" Momma asked.

"Cold. My God, ice cold."

Gee, I thought, *I'm sorry for you, Pops. You gotta suffer like this.*

"It was not always like this," my father said to the cold walls. "It's all the fault of the damn depression."

"Don't say 'damn,'" Momma said.

"Lola, I say 'damn' because that's what it is—*damn.*"

And Momma kept quiet. She knew it was "damn."

My father kept talking to the walls. Some of the words came out loud, others stayed inside. I caught the inside ones—the damn WPA, the damn depression, the damn home relief, the damn poorness, the damn cold, the damn crummy apartments, the damn look on his damn kids, living so damn damned and his not being able to do a damn thing about it.

And Momma looked at Poppa and at us and thought about her Puerto Rico and maybe being there where you didn't have to wear a lot of extra clothes and feel so full of damns, and how when she was a little girl all the green was wet from the *lluvias.*

And Poppa looking at Momma and us, thinking how did he get trapped and why did he love us so much that he dug in damn snow to give us a piece of chance? And why couldn't he make it from home, maybe, and keep running?

And Miriam, James, José, Paulie, and me just looking and thinking about snowballs and Puerto Rico and summertime in the street and whether we were gonna live like this forever and not know enough to be sorry for ourselves.

The kitchen all of a sudden felt warmer to me, like being all together made it like we wanted it to be. Poppa made it into the toilet and we could hear everything he did, and when he finished, the horsey gurgling of the flushed toilet told us he'd soon be out. I looked at the clock and it was time for "Jack Armstrong, the All-American Boy."

José, James, and I got some blankets and, like Indians, huddled around the radio digging the All-American Jack and his adventures, while Poppa ate dinner quietly. Poppa was funny about eating—like when he ate, nobody better bother him. When Poppa finished, he came into the living room and stood there looking at us. We smiled at him, and he stood there looking at us.

All of a sudden he yelled, "How many wanna play 'Major Bowes' Amateur Hour'?"

"Hoo-ray! Yeah, we wanna play," said José.

"Okay, first I'll make some taffy outta molasses, and the one who wins first prize gets first choice at the biggest piece, okay?"

"Yeah, hoo-ray, *chevere*."

Gee, Pops, you're great, I thought, *you're the swellest, the bestest Pops in the whole world, even though you don't understand us too good.*

When the candy was all ready, everybody went into the living room. Poppa came in with a broom and put an empty can over the stick. It became a microphone, just like on the radio.

"Pops, can I be Major Bowes?" I asked.

"Sure, Piri," and the floor was mine.

"Ladies and gentlemen," I announced, "tonight we present 'Major Bowes' Amateur Hour,' and for our first number—"

"Wait a minute, son, let me get my ukulele," said Poppa. "We need music."

Everybody clapped their hands and Pops came back with his ukulele.

"The first con-tes-tant we got is Miss Miriam Thomas."

"Oh no, not me first, somebody else goes first," said Miriam, and she hid behind Momma.

"Let me! Let me!" said José.

Everybody clapped.

"What are you gonna sing, sir?" I asked.

"Tell the people his name," said Poppa.

"Oh yeah. Presenting Mr. José Thomas. And what are you gonna sing, sir?"

I handed José the broom with the can on top and sat back. He sang well and everybody clapped.

Everyone took a turn, and we all agreed that two-year-old Paulie's "gurgle, gurgle" was the best song, and Paulie got first choice at the candy. Everybody got candy and eats and thought how good it was to be together, and Moms thought that it was wonderful to have such a good time even if she wasn't in Puerto Rico where the grass was wet with *lluvia*. Poppa thought about how cold it was gonna be tomorrow, but then he remembered tomorrow was Sunday and he wouldn't have to work, and he said so and Momma said "*Sí*," and the talk got around to Christmas and how maybe things would get better.

The next day the Japanese bombed Pearl Harbor.

"My God," said Poppa. "We're at war."

"*Dios mío*," said Momma.

I turned to James. "Can you beat that," I said.

"Yeah," he nodded. "What's it mean?"

"What's it mean?" I said. "You gotta ask, dopey? It means a rumble is on, and a big one, too."

I wondered if the war was gonna make things worse than they were for us. But it didn't. A few weeks later Poppa got a job in an airplane factory. "How about that?" he said happily. "Things are looking up for us."

Things *were* looking up for us, but it had taken a damn war to do it. A lousy rumble had to get called so we could start to live better. I thought, *How do you figure this crap out?*

I couldn't figure it out, and after a while I stopped thinking about it. Life in the streets didn't change much. The bitter cold was followed by the sticky heat; I played stickball, marbles, and Johnny-on-the-Pony, copped girls' drawers and blew pot. War or peace—what difference did it really make?

Notes

1. heart
2. codfish
3. green island
4. rain
5. small treetoads
6. little birds
7. poverty
8. contracts
9. grandparents
10. How are you?

Coleman Young: The Mayor of Detroit

Studs Terkel

My father was many things. After World War One, he became a tailor under the GI Bill. He was already a barber and a waiter. The army was strictly Jim Crow at the time. He was a buffalo soldier in World War One, 370th Infantry.

"Following the Civil War, there were four cavalry regiments assigned to the West. The Seventh and Eighth were white. Everyone's heard of the Seventh, Custer's outfit. The Ninth and Tenth were black.

"They had quite a reputation. The Indians named them buffalo soldiers because of their curly, cropped hair. The Tenth Cavalry was with Teddy Roosevelt at San Juan Hill. History does not record that it was the Tenth that saved his ass. In World War Two, I was a member of the buffalo division.

"I got a lot of this information from my father. There is more continuity among blacks, more preservation of their history, than is commonly recognized. I remember, as a boy of six, my grandmother had a big book. It was the history of colored soldiers. I read everything I could about black history. And labor."

Like most blacks in the twenties, my father was a Republican. With the crash of '29, he became an avid supporter of FDR. He read every damn thing he could lay his hands on. My mother was a school-teacher. He was very militant. She was the stable one. She worried about me because I was like my father. He

Source: "The Mayor of Detroit" from *Coming of Age* by Studs Terkel, copyright © 1995 by The New Press. Reprinted by permission of The New Press.

was constantly in some argument. He wasn't a big man, but I've seen him beat up guys twice his size by pickin' up a bottle or a scissors or anything at hand. He hated white people until he met a guy who treated him as a peer. A Catholic. We all converted to Catholicism.

My mother insisted on neatness and that we use good English. As the oldest of five, I became her lieutenant in looking out for the rest of the kids. I became a sort of disciplinarian, a stool pigeon. (Laughs.) An enforcer for my mother. (Laughs.)

We came to Detroit from Alabama in December of '23. We lived on the Lower East Side, which was the major ghetto at the time. I was a good student and arrogant. At St. Mary's, I became Scout troop leader. We went on an excursion, but I was turned back from the island because I was black. This was the first conscious anger I felt. After that, I became more alert. That's probably part of my history in becoming a radical. I had so many rebuffs along the way.

When I finished St. Mary's, I was among the city's top ten and entitled to a scholarship. Some brother friar comes along, looks at me in puzzlement, and says: "What the hell are you, Japanese or somethin'?" I said: "No, brother, I'm colored." He took my paper and tore it up, right there in my face. I went back to public schools. That was the end of me and the Catholic church.

The year 1928 had a big impact on me, the boom year. I was ten, workin' for a tailor.

After school and all day Saturday, I'd sweep the floor, deliver suits. This is a street unlike any you'd find. It was a neighborhood street. Everybody was doin' something wrong on this street. The tailor was very good, but his back room was a crap game. Next-door was the shoeshine parlor, which had the biggest poker game on the East Side. Down the street, there was black jack and Georgia skin. Mr. Latimer, who ran the confectionery store, made moonshine.

I was gettin' three dollars a week plus tips. People were very generous then, and money was plentiful. It cost a dollar and a half to clean a suit. I'd get two bucks: Keep the change, kid. Mr. Latimer, the bootlegger, bought used bottles. I'd go to fifteen, twenty places, pick up the empty bottles, and sell 'em back to him for two cents each. Hell, I musta made nine, ten dollars a week from the bottles. If I was quiet and stayed in the corner, I could watch the crap game. At the tender age of ten, I knew the odds on all the dice. (Laughs.) These guys were doin' so well, they were admired by the blacks coming up from the South, whose only models for respectability and success were the slave masters, with their delicate hands and fancy clothes. These guys were all dressed fancy and had exotic names like Tricky Sam and Fast Black. There are many people today I don't know by their real name. (Laughs.)

So I'm listenin' to all this crap. These guys had contempt for guys who worked. They called 'em Ford mules. Most of the guys worked at Ford. They'd talk about how they'd go around with the guys' wives while they were at work. They had a motto for Ford: You feed 'em, we'll fuck 'em. I learned from them somethin' I later rejected, 'cause across the street from all this was a little barbershop run by a man named Williams, who was somethin' of a Marxist. I was the pet of the barbers until I was twelve or thirteen, because I would speak out. The guys encouraged me. By the time I was fifteen, I was pretty well accepted.

Now I'm goin' to Eastern High, where I was an all-A student. I graduated in 1935, at seventeen. I thought I wanted to be a lawyer.

It seemed as a lawyer, I could fight discrimination. It was a personal thing with me. I read a lot of Dickens. And that's when I discovered *The Souls of Black Folk* by Du Bois. I was reading everything I could by and about blacks.

A week before graduation, the principal called me in and said: "We have four scholarships, two to the University of Michigan and two to City College. You got your choice." I said University of Michigan, of course. He says: "Do you have a job? Money for your board?" I said: "No, I thought the job went with the scholarship." He said: "No." I said: "In that case, I'll go to City College." "Too late," he said, "that's been taken." I found out another black kid had been done the same way the year before. I got screwed and resented it very much. Almost subconsciously, I'm beginnin' to take on an adversary role toward society.

This is '35, '36. I got into Ford as an electrical apprentice. You went to school every night to learn about voltage and electricity. It's basically algebra, and I had taken every mathematics course that was in school. I was heavy in math. So I got a flat one hundred on all the damn stuff. There was one job open, and two of us came out at the same time. I was the only black in the apprentice program. The other guy's average was somethin' like sixty-two. His father was a foreman so he got the job.

I was still goin' to night school with the illusory hope of becomin' a skilled electrician. They didn't have any black electricians at Ford. I was assigned to the motor building, and there I heard talk about the labor union. I'd go around Williams's barbershop, where I got my hair cut, and it turned out to be a hangout for black UAW organizers. And all kinds of philosophy and arguments over who was the greater man, Booker T. Washington or Frederick Douglass or Du Bois.

I was attracted to this exchange of ideas and way of fighting back at the thing that had been fuckin' me over all my life. It wasn't a sudden thing. I didn't desert my basic hooliganism right away. I still screwed around the poolroom and did a few things. But I was in transition. I was stealin' less and fuckin' less. (Laughs.)

I knew three aspects of black life. I knew the working-class part. I knew the slicker, the gambler. There was also a middle-class part that I became alienated from. My mother and father were both light-skinned. Blacks in the early days in the South took their values from the whites. The admonition was: Always marry someone lighter than you, so you'll be whiter. That's a way of escape. I rejected this because some of my best friends were very dark. Guys I had known all my life. We were poor, not middle-class, but since I was light, I could have been accepted. There were Negro churches where, if you were darker, you weren't accepted.

Before I went to Ford and started messin' around with all those labor guys and thought I was goin' to college, I was pledged to a black fraternity. It was a society, exclusive-type club, light-skinned. They were the social dictators of the college-age group. I was invited to a dance, a signal honor. I take my friend to the dance with me, a dark guy. The black society people, the elites, we called 'em, took on the mannerisms of whites. They danced stiffly, not naturally. Everybody's dancin' naturally now. (Laughs.) My friend was the best dancer there, havin' a regular ball. The guys resented Frank and were mad at me for bringin' him. He was too dark. We wound up in a fight, and that was the end of me and black society.

If these kind of people were going to college, fuck college. I didn't want to be a gambler and shoot dice all my life. So I got involved in the labor movement and for the first time hearin' a philosophy that made sense to me: unity between black and white.

It was almost a dual life. I'd go into the poolroom and whatever con game I could, I'd make a couple of bucks. The next minute, I'm across the street in the barbershop arguing some Marxist theory. I found them both attractive. But gradually one took over. You can't do both, right?

By '37, I'm a member of the union, very subterranean. At that time, Ford had a goon squad. They called 'em service men. They couldn't be distinguished from the workers. One of the first things we did when we organized the plant, we made 'em put those in uniform so you could tell 'em.

They'd be in greasy old overalls, and they'd count how many minutes you sat in the goddamn can. The work was so rough, guys got old before their time. If you were workin' at forty-five, you were lucky, 'cause when you slowed down the production line, out you went. You'd go to the toilet, not to take a shit, but just to rest. There was no door, no privacy. I've seen guys go in the damn toilet and get five minutes' sleep. The way they did it, they'd take a newspaper and learned how to tap their feet while they were sleepin'. The service guy comes through and sees him with the paper and tappin' his feet and figures he's awake. It's funny what humans can do to survive.

One of the first UAW guys I met was a southern white. He and I got to be very good friends. Southern whites and blacks have so much in common culturally. They talk the same way, they eat the same way, they come from the same region. Once you get past racism, there's a better exchange.

The major stress was between blacks and Poles. The Poles had been the last group to migrate to Detroit, so they were at the bottom of the ladder. The blacks and the Poles were fighting for a hold on the bottom. They were constantly pitted against each other for the dirtiest job.

Even though the black community had been bulldozed out, the Poles haven't moved. Home really means home to them. Hamtramck is still a major Polish city, and all around you find neat painted wooden houses, old as hell but well-kept. It's really a city within the city.

The guys Bennett (Harry Bennett had been hired by Henry Ford to establish the service department. Its primary purpose was surveillance of workers who might be "troublemakers.") recruited were ex-thugs, wrestlers, boxers—the rougher, the better. They put a guy across from me, a big son of a bitch, musta been about two hundred eighty pounds, six foot three. He knew I was union and kept baiting me. There was a conveyer line that ran between my rollin' machine and his. I had a steel pipe that I used to clear the machine when it became jammed. This guy zeroes in on me. If he got his hands on me, there is no way in hell I could have survived. I could see, he starts across the line at me. I picked up that damn steel pipe and laid it across his head. I stretched him out on that damn conveyer, and it carried him and dumped him into a freight car. (Laughs.) It didn't hurt him that much. Five, six stitches and a few lacerations. They ran my ass outa there. (Laughs.) Officially, I was fired for fighting. The real reason was my union activity.

I went to the post office and began to organize a union. There was a six-month probationary period. Son of a bitch let me work five months and twenty-nine days, and then fired me. I was a volunteer organizer for UAW. Worked on the Sojourner Truth housing project. In and out of several jobs, had to eat. I went in the army, February 1942.

"They set up this Jim Crow Air Forces OCS School in Tuskegee. They made the standards so damn high, we actually became an elite group. We were screened and super-screened. We were unquestionably the brightest and most physically fit young blacks in the country. We were super-better because of the irrational laws of Jim Crow. You can't bring that many intelligent young people together and train 'em as fighting men and expect them to supinely roll over when you try to fuck over 'em, right? How does that go? Sowing the seeds of their own destruction. (Laughs.)

"I was washed out as a fighter pilot. I'm told it was because of FBI intervention. I had already graduated from officers' school in October of '42, at Fort Benning. They literally pulled guys off the stage, 'cause FBI, Birmingham, was accusin' them of subversion, which may have been attendin' a YMCA meeting in protest against discrimination.

"The army was dominated by southern generals, and most of the posts were old, dating back to World War One. Either all white or all black. The air force introduced a new wrinkle. They started from scratch.

"I wrote a letter to the inspector general. You become a little bit of a shithouse lawyer and learn all the army regulations for your own protection. Here we officers were barred from the officer's club. The inspector general flew down and made some changes. This was '44 and the real beginnin' of integration in the army.

"From there we went to Midland, Texas, the bombardier training school. Five of us had the whole visiting officers' quarters to ourselves. Each of us had two suites, but we still resented the fact that we were not allowed to go to the officers' club. We wrote the inspector general again. The post commander was a Texan but also a soldier. This was after V-E Day. He called every officer on the post together and said in the classic military manner: 'I may not like this and you may not like this, but these are orders. These officers will be treated as officers, they will have full access to all privileges and nobody will fuck with them, is that clear?' (Laughs.) We're now veterans of two successful struggles, but, wait, there's more to come.

"We're now, forty-five of us, at Godman Field, attached to Fort Knox. We're boxed in, Jim Crow. The white officers could go to the officers' club as guests of Fort Knox officers. Nobody invited us. I guess I'd become pretty disgusted, so they removed me from my division and put me in RTU, the Reserve Training Unit, where the troublemakers wound up. We began hearing rumors that they were going to make the Godman Officers' Club all white and the black officers would go to the noncom club. To add insult to injury, we had a few thousand bucks in the officers' club. We swore we weren't going to take this. Well, they shipped us out, one squadron at a time, to Freeman Field, near Seymour, Indiana.

"They were prepared for our arrival, expectin' trouble. MPs were there to keep us out of the club the night we arrived. We decided to go in groups of eight and nine. We were gonna scatter, play pool, get a drink, buy cigarettes. I'm in the first wave. This white captain says: 'You can't go in here.' We just brushed past him and scattered. The commandin' officer was livid and placed us under arrest, at quarters.

"It was my job to convince the other guys that they should go in and get arrested. (Laughs.) After the first nine, it was tough gettin' the next nine.

But we broke the ice, and two more groups went in and were placed under arrest. They had to close the son of a bitch down because the whole post would have been under arrest, at quarters. They wanted to put us in the position of disobeying post command.

"The commanding officer read the damn thing and ordered each of us to come up and sign it. If you did that and disobeyed, they could prosecute you. The post commander says: 'Do you recognize that under the sixtieth article of war, in time of war, disobedience to a direct order can be punished by death? Okay, give him an order. I hereby command you to sign this.' He knocked off a bunch of guys. I'm lucky. They called us alphabetically, right? (Laughs.) I got a little breathing spell. I remembered an article of war that roughly is the equivalent of the Fifth Amendment. We devised a strategy. We'd go through all the formalities, salute properly and say, 'Yes, sir.' Where he gives you a direct order, you say: 'I'm sorry, sir, but under the sixty-sixty article of war, I'm afraid this might incriminate me. I refuse to sign.' There were a hundred and one guys who stood up under that one, one by one. We were all placed under arrest.

"The word spread all over. The black enlisted men were pissed. They stopped gassin' the airplanes. It was chaos. They had five or six C-47s to fly us away, we were such a source of unrest. They had the officers' quarters enclosed in barbed wire, with white MPs patrolling it. And spotlights. Here again, the contradictions of racism screwed them. They wanted to isolate us. But they couldn't bring themselves to ignore the military code: officers are "gentlemen" and therefore entitled to valet service, right? You gotta have somebody make your bed and shine your shoes and cook for you. They could not see themselves assignin' white soldiers to perform these tasks for black officers. So they put some black guys in. (Laughs.) As luck would have it, the sergeant commanding the outfit, I used to play pool with him in Detroit. These guys were our keys to the outside world. They were gettin' our message out. We were heroes all over Fort Knox. Chappie James, the general, was among those arrested.

"They let Chappie go because he flew the C-47, our communications ship. Every day he went to Washington with orders. He also carried press releases from us, letters to Mrs. Roosevelt, to Judge Hastings, to the NAACP. We had a guy in our outfit who typed damn near as quick as I could talk. I'd dictate a press release, give it to the sergeant, who got it to Chappie, who would fly it in. (Laughs.)

"They sent in investigators and they were never able to get one out of a hundred and one guys to identify a leader. That, I think, is really something.

"It was only a month later that V-J day occurred. We chose that day to invade the white officers' club in Monroe. It's the same damn thing. We were told the next morning that we had an option of signin' up for three more years or gettin' the hell out immediately. Of course, I opted for immediate and got out.

"As a result of that incident, they published a war department memorandum, 450-50, which was the beginning of integration in the army. All officers' clubs, service clubs, and recreational facilities are open to all military personnel, regardless of race. Shortly afterward, Truman integrated the army. Oh, I remember 450-50 very clearly. It didn't come easy."

Back in Detroit, I became an international rep for the United Public Workers Union, which was eventually run out of the CIO as subversive. It included the garbage men, the hospital workers, all city workers. The same guys I negotiate with today. (Laughs.)

We had one strike, a garbage workers' strike. We were fightin' for a pay increase. The arguments were interminable. So we got about twenty garbage trucks and filled 'em up. These were open trucks, they just had tarps over 'em. It's in the summertime. You never have a garbage strike in the winter, always in the summer, when the garbage stinks. We let this garbage ripen for about four days and then just parked the goddamn trucks around City Hall and threw the fuckin' keys down the sewer. (Laughs.) Needless to say, the strike was settled pretty quickly.

In 1947, I was elected executive vice-president of the Wayne County CIO Council. I was the first black elected. A bunch of young guys, black and white, who'd come back from the army gave us some zip. They knew I wasn't an Uncle Tom, but I'd be a sleeper, acceptable to the white guys. I was under no illusions. I was at the right place at the right time. That's the way history goes.

I became active in the city. Two black families moved into what's now a slum near Tiger Stadium. They were terrorized by guys runnin' around in Ku Klux robes. We sent a group of white and black trade unionists in with shotguns to protect them. Then we had white guys of the building trade, union leaders, paint the buildings, replace the broken glass, repair the fences. When we got through, the house was worth four thousand dollars more than when they moved in. It cooled everything, just the sight of the these white union local presidents doin' this work. I was pretty well known in the black community by then.

I came from the East Side, so I knew everybody in Detroit. Detroit was a pretty small place, and then it grew suddenly. Most of the guys who became leaders came from my neighborhood. Another thing made me better known. The Red scare was on, the witch hunt. The House Un-American Activities Committee came to town. These guys would come to a city, terrorize it, put a goddamn stool pigeon on the stand. He rattles off a list of names and that person is fired, hung in effigy, blacklisted.

I was called before the committee. The first thing I found out, the chairman of the damn thing was from Georgia. I said to myself: Why should I take any shit off a son of a bitch from Georgia? How can he question my Americanism? I took the trouble to research. Ninety percent of his district was black, so less than ten percent of the people down there elected this son of a bitch. And he's gonna talk about my un-Americanism!

My lawyer advised me to take the Fifth Amendment. I thought the first should have been enough. But he convinced me to use the fifth also. I told them if they want to talk about un-American activities, I'm prepared to do so. Lynchin', the poll tax. We just got it on. (Laughs.) The damn thing was broadcast, and everybody in the city heard it. It was as big as the World Series. We had the national

Negro Council down and Local 600 of the UAW. We were the first group to go on the attack. The next stop was Chicago, where you guys kicked 'em in the ass a little bit more. They just went downhill from there. It was all over the front pages. They were sayin' I was a surly witness. But that single incident endeared me to the hearts of black people. Fightin' back, sayin' what they wanted to say all their lives to a southern white.

I went through about five years, from '55 to '60, during which I was blacklisted. I couldn't get into any shop at all. Drove cabs, found that interesting. I was cleaning and spotting for about three years. I had little money. From drivin' a taxi to luggin' beef to painting and decorating, whatever I could do. Then I decided to take a shot at politics.

I ran for the city council. I knew damn well I couldn't win, but I tested the political waters. I found I had great strength on the East Side, where I was raised. I ran as a delegate for the Constitutional Convention. It was a real heavyweight affair because it was the first time the constitution had been changed in half a century. There were some big issues at stake. That convention produced a whole new crop of political leaders. Comin' from the left, I won the nomination and surprised the Democrats and the labor movement. The Democrats disowned me and ran a sticker candidate against me. I was still looked upon as a dangerous Red. I won the damn election. At the convention, we were successful in getting a number of things done. I wrote the first version of the civil rights commission from the state of Michigan. It's the only state that has a civil rights commission as part of the state constitution.

I ran for state rep. Labor was neutral. Three of the black candidates I had beaten decisively before were put back into the race and split the vote. I was defeated by four votes. In '64, I won as state senator and have been elected to office ever since.

I felt the climate was right for a black mayor. I had come to believe we were fast approaching a military state. The pattern was developing with police chiefs being elected mayors of cities. The code words against blacks were "war on crime." I felt deeply that unless blacks were given fair representation within the department, the police would run our cities.

In '73 I was one of five principal candidates for mayor. There were two other black candidates, a liberal white, and the police chief, John Nichols. I entered late and was considered number five. If there's no majority, the two top guys run off. I ran second to Nichols.

We had a series of head-to-head debates, a classic confrontation. Unfortunately, it was the black community against the white, although it was a clean race. Nichols and I agreed not to engage in overt race baiting, and we adhered to it. I've always respected him for that.

One of the major issues was STRESS, an acronym for Stop the Robberies, Enjoy Safe Streets. The use of decoys. It can be effective, but these cowboys in Detroit turned the damn thing into a shoot-out. I've forgotten how many citizens were killed. It was in excess of twenty and at least six or seven cops. The police paper constantly referred to blacks as jungle bunnies.

One of the major issues was residency. I insisted that as mayor, I'd eliminate STRESS and create a police department that would represent Detroit, half black and half white. And mutual respect between police and people. I was gonna see to it that it would be fifty-fifty in all the civil service departments, with many more women. I surprised a lot of people in doing just that. They expected me to go ninety-five percent black and five percent white. That would've been stupid. I retained a white police chief until I had to fire him. I had a black executive deputy chief. Now that I have a black police chief, I have a white executive.

We've established something new in police work: mini-stations. Fifty in high-crime areas where old people are often victims. People of the neighborhood volunteer, man the stations, give out dog licenses and whatever other small things you do, and free the police-

man to walk the beat. We have at least two pairs of officers walkin' the beat.

In the old black bottom area, of old people, ADC mothers, and the Brewster housing project, we opened our first mini-station. When I was elected, only fifteen percent of the police were black. So it was warming to see the welcome the white cops received from gals bringin' 'em doughnuts and coffee. You have to extend a hand to the police, and they have to respect you. The white cops were surprised: old black women and kids bringin' 'em coffee. Most of 'em were scared at first. There's a new attitude in the city. The police are no longer looked upon as a foreign army of occupation.

I think the police expected retribution from me. That's the kind of world they lived in: Knock 'em on the head. They expected me to knock 'em on the head. I had no purpose in punishing police. I only insist they be professional and fair.

During my first two months as mayor, I must have attended at least three police funerals. Always in the cold of winter, it seems. Young men. A terribly sad thing. But since '74, not a single Detroit police officer has been killed in the line of duty. This must be an all-time record for the city. It can't be luck. It reflects a new respect between the people and the police.

One incident, I feel, was the turning point. It was the summer of '74. I'd barely been in office six months. A white bar owner killed a young black man. The same incident started riots before. The usual rumors: he was shot in the back. Ugly crowds gathered. I rushed out there. I stood on top of a car and exhorted the young people tryin' to ram in the door of the bar. They wanted to burn the place down and take the guy. The usual provocateurs I've known all my life. I told my police chief I wanted every black officer out on the street. He said: "How can I know who the blacks are?" I said: "You know goddamn well who they are. Get 'em out here." In about an hour, they were all out there. We had a great number of new black commanders to help control the crowd. Most importantly, we already had a relationship with the people. Ministers and block-club leaders joined me. We walked in advance of the police, pushin' people back, dispersin' 'em, urgin' 'em to go home.

What made it even more terrible: an innocent Polish immigrant, a baker on his way home, was passing through the area. His car was stopped. He was dragged out and literally stoned to death. You can imagine what was happenin'. I immediately summoned Bishop Kravchek and other Polish leaders and expressed my sympathy and asked for their cooperation. They and the black ministers came together. I visited his widow, it was a pretty hostile area, and the mother of the young black who'd been killed. I think this turned the situation around, my being there.

The next day, I said the police behaved in a most professional manner under extreme provocation, bricks and what not. Not a single shot was fired. Here were cops in their riot gear, a lot of 'em were women, little bitty women standin' there with those big truncheons. To me, this was a turning point.

The police and I still have big differences. I don't think they deserve the big pay raise they're gettin'. They're the highest-paid police in the nation. They just received an award through an arbitrator that could break the city. There's something wrong with a system whereby an arbitrator, not elected by anybody, can impose taxes on the people of the city.

Hey, Mr. Mayor, you're an old labor guy talkin', remember? (Laughs.)

Yeah, but I would rather let the damn matter go to a strike than have an artificial settlement. Again, it's my faith in the people. If the policemen have a legitimate grievance, the public will back 'em. If they do not, damn it, the public won't back 'em. That's the way I was brought up in the labor movement, right? You take it to the streets. That's where I came from—the streets. And I'm proud of it. I think if you listen, you can get a hell of an education out there.

I got support from only one industrialist: Henry Ford. He gave me three thousand dollars. He also gave Nichols three thousand dollars. I told him: "You ought to put most of your money on the winner, and I'm the winner." He laughed. (Laughs.)

I think they were also a little concerned about Nichols. He was a no nonsense, take-the-gloves-off type of cop who could cause more explosions. They were worried about their investments in the city. In askin' for their cooperation, I was workin' in their self-interest.

In the last four years, they've been convinced that I'm not a wild man. When the budget had to be cut, I cut the damn budget. It was painful. We have a number of laws on the books which gives a tax preference to businesses located in the city, encourages them to stay rather than leave. It's subject to a lot of argument. Some say this is subsidizing business. I say it's the name of the game. As long as we live in a society which pits workers in Mississippi against workers in Michigan, we have to make concessions to keep our plants. We've made more jobs for people.

We've begun to reverse the flight from the city. We've created new communities within Detroit. In some cities, with urban renewal, they've bulldozed whole communities. Movin' the blacks out and movin' middle-class whites into choice locations. As long as I'm mayor, we're not gonna have that. We'll have an integrated occupancy of the central city.

Do you have a funny feeling, a sense of irony, when you're having lunch with Henry Ford?

It is ironic. You reflect on how unlikely this was twenty, thirty years ago. Yet, I'm not doing anything differently. I've always felt people act out of self-interest, not for any utopian reasons. If you understand that, you understand coalition: a commonality of interests. You always move from point one.

We've come a long way from Harry Bennett. Of course, reaction rears its ugly head constantly. We're still plagued with racism. But I've always had great faith in the intelligence of people—if you can get to them. I'm not among those who believe you can package bull-shit and sell it to people as long as you tie a pretty ribbon around it.

I'm sixty now, and I'd like to produce a cadre of young people, black and white, who can carry on this work. It's not guaranteed. It would be a big mistake for anyone to believe that the great American Dream is apple pie and a happy endin'. It ain't necessarily so. The whole goddamn thing could go up in smoke. Reconstruction teaches you that, right? It's a continuous struggle all the time. The minute you forget that, you wind up on your ass.

I realize the profit motive is what makes things work in America. If Detroit is not to dry up, we must create a situation which allows businessmen to make a profit. That's their self-interest. Ours is jobs. The more they invest in Detroit, the more their interest becomes ours. That is the way the game is played in America today. I don't think there's gonna be a revolution tomorrow. As a young man, I thought it. I think the revolution's for someone else.

(He laughs softly; a sudden remembrance.) Had I stayed in Catholic school, I would probably have become an altar boy. I would like to have been one. St. Mary's is a beautiful, old German church. It's truly an architectural gem. I was fourteen when I was last there. You come back as mayor for the one hundred seventy-fifth anniversary of the Sisters of Holy Name. The altar's much the same. The nuns prepared a chair for me on the altar, a big chair, like a throne. (Laughs.) I'm sitting on it. That's the highlight of my life as mayor. It impressed me more, thinking back to my childhood, than sitting down with Henry Ford or President Carter. (Laughs.) My American Dream. (Laughs.)

5

In Search of Our Mothers' Gardens

Alice Walker

I described her own nature and temperament. Told how they needed a larger life for their expression. . . . I pointed out that in lieu of proper channels, her emotions had overflowed into paths that dissipated them. I talked, beautifully I thought, about an art that would be born, an art that would open the way for women the likes of her. I asked her to hope, and build up an inner life against the coming of that day. . . . I sang, with a strange quiver in my voice, a promise song.

> Jean Toomer, "Avey"
> CANE

The poet speaking to a prostitute who falls asleep while he's talking—

When the poet Jean Toomer walked through the South in the early twenties, he discovered a curious thing: black women whose spirituality was so intense, so deep, so *unconscious*, that they were themselves unaware of the richness they held. They stumbled blindly through their lives: creatures so abused and mutilated in body, so dimmed and confused by pain, that they considered themselves unworthy even of hope. In the

selfless abstractions their bodies became to the men who used them, they became more than "sexual objects," more even than mere women: they became "Saints." Instead of being perceived as whole persons, their bodies became shrines: what was thought to be their minds became temples suitable for worship. These crazy Saints stared out at the world, wildly, like lunatics—or quietly, like suicides; and the "God" that was in their gaze was as mute as a great stone.

Who were these Saints? These crazy, loony, pitiful women?

Some of them, without a doubt, were our mothers and grandmothers.

In the still heat of the post-Reconstruction South, this is how they seemed to Jean Toomer: exquisite butterflies trapped in an evil honey, toiling away their lives in an era, a century, that did not acknowledge them, except as "the *mule* of the world." They dreamed dreams that no one knew—not even themselves in any coherent fashion—and saw visions no one could understand. They wandered or sat about the countryside crooning lullabies to ghosts, and drawing the mother of Christ in charcoal on courthouse walls.

They forced their minds to desert their bodies and their striving spirits sought to rise, like frail whirlwinds from the hard red clay. And when those frail whirlwinds fell, in scattered particles, upon the ground, no one mourned. Instead, men lit candles to celebrate the emptiness that remained, as people do who enter a beautiful but vacant space to resurrect a God.

Source: "In Search of Our Mothers' Gardens" from *In Search of Our Mothers' Gardens: Womanist Prose,* copyright © 1974 by Alice Walker. Reprinted by permission of Harcourt Brace & Company. "Women" from *Revolutionary Petunias & Other Poems,* copyright © 1970 by Alice Walker. Reprinted by permission of Harcourt Brace & Company.

Our mothers and grandmothers, some of them: moving to music not yet written. And they waited.

They waited for a day when the unknown thing that was in them would be made known; but guessed, somehow in their darkness, that on the day of their revelation they would be long dead. Therefore to Toomer they walked, and even ran, in slow motion. For they were going nowhere immediate, and the future was not yet within their grasp. And men took our mothers and grandmothers, "but got no pleasure from it." So complex was their passion and their calm.

To Toomer, they lay vacant and fallow as autumn fields, with harvest time never in sight: and he saw them enter loveless marriages, without joy; and become prostitutes, without resistance; and become mothers of children, without fulfillment.

For these grandmothers and mothers of ours were not Saints, but Artists; driven to a numb and bleeding madness by the springs of creativity in them for which there was no release. They were Creators, who lived lives of spiritual waste, because they were so rich in spirituality—which is the basis of Art— that the strain of enduring their unused and unwanted talent drove them insane. Throwing away this spirituality was their pathetic attempt to lighten the soul to a weight their work-worn, sexually abused bodies could bear.

What did it mean for a black woman to be an artist in our grandmothers' time? In our great-grandmothers' day? It is a question with an answer cruel enough to stop the blood.

Did you have a genius of a great-great-grandmother who died under some ignorant and depraved white overseer's lash? Or was she required to bake biscuits for a lazy back-water tramp, when she cried out in her soul to paint watercolors of sunsets, or the rain falling on the green and peaceful pasturelands? Or was her body broken and forced to bear children (who were more often than not sold away from her)—eight, ten, fifteen, twenty children—when her one joy was the thought of modeling heroic figures of rebellion, in stone or clay?

How was the creativity of the black woman kept alive, year after year and century after century, when for most of the years black people have been in America, it was a punishable crime for a black person to read or write? And the freedom to paint, to sculpt, to expand the mind with action did not exist. Consider, if you can bear to imagine it, what might have been the result if singing, too, had been forbidden by law. Listen to the voices of Bessie Smith, Billie Holiday, Nina Simone, Roberta Flack, and Aretha Franklin, among others, and imagine those voices muzzled for life. Then you may begin to comprehend the lives of our "crazy," "Sainted" mothers and grandmothers. The agony of the lives of women who might have been Poets, Novelists, Essayists, and Short-Story Writers (over a period of centuries), who died with their real gifts stifled within them.

And, if this were the end of the story, we would have cause to cry out in my paraphrase of Okot p'Bitek's great poem:

O, my clanswomen
Let us all cry together!
Come,
Let us mourn the death of our mother,
The death of a Queen
The ash that was produced
By a great fire!
O, this homestead is utterly dead
Close the gates
With *lacari* thorns,
For our mother
The creator of the Stool is lost!
And all the young women
Have perished in the wilderness!

But this is not the end of the story, for all the young women—our mothers and grandmothers, *ourselves*—have not perished in the wilderness. And if we ask ourselves why, and search for and find the answer, we will know beyond all efforts to erase it from our minds, just exactly who, and of what, we black American women are.

One example, perhaps the most pathetic, most misunderstood one, can provide a backdrop for our mothers' work: Phillis Wheatley, a slave in the 1700s.

Virginia Woolf, in her book *A Room of One's Own*, wrote that in order for a woman to write fiction she must have two things, certainly: a room of her own (with key and lock) and enough money to support herself.

What then are we to make of Phillis Wheatley, a slave, who owned not even herself? This sickly, frail black girl who required a servant of her own at times—her health was so precarious—and who, had she been white, would have been easily considered the intellectual superior of all the women and most of the men in the society of her day.

Virginia Woolf wrote further, speaking of course not of our Phillis, that "any woman born with a great gift in the sixteenth century [insert "eighteenth century," insert "black woman," insert "born or made a slave"] would certainly have gone crazed, shot herself, or ended her days in some lonely cottage outside the village, half witch, half wizard [insert "Saint"], feared and mocked at. For it needs little skill and psychology to be sure that a highly gifted girl who had tried to use her gift for poetry would have been so thwarted and hindered by contrary instincts [add "chains, guns, the lash, the ownership of one's body by someone else, submission to an alien religion"], that she must have lost her health and sanity to a certainty."

The key words, as they relate to Phillis, are "contrary instincts." For when we read the poetry of Phillis Wheatley—as when we read the novels of Nella Larsen or the oddly false-sounding autobiography of that freest of all black women writers, Zora Hurston—evidence of "contrary instincts" is everywhere. Her loyalties were completely divided, as was, without question, her mind.

But how could this be otherwise? Captured at seven, a slave of wealthy, doting whites who instilled in her the "savagery" of the Africa they "rescued" her from . . . one wonders if she was even able to remember her homeland as she had known it, or as it really was.

Yet, because she did try to use her gift for poetry in a world that made her a slave, she was "so thwarted and hindered by . . . contrary instincts, that she . . . lost her health. . . ." In the last years of her brief life, burdened not only with the need to express her gift but also with a penniless, friendless "freedom" and several small children for whom she was forced to do strenuous work to feed, she lost her health, certainly. Suffering from malnutrition and neglect and who knows what mental agonies, Phillis Wheatley died.

So torn by "contrary instincts" was black, kidnapped, enslaved Phillis that her description of "the Goddess"—as she poetically called the Liberty she did not have—is ironically, cruelly humorous. And, in fact, has held Phillis up to ridicule for more than a century. It is usually read prior to hanging Phillis's memory as that of a fool. She wrote:

The Goddess comes, she moves divinely *fair, Olive and laurel binds her golden* hair.
Wherever shines this native of the skies,
Unnumber'd charms and recent graces rise.
[My italics]

It is obvious that Phillis, the slave, combed the "Goddess's" hair every morning; prior, perhaps, to bringing in the milk, or fixing her mistress's lunch. She took her imagery from the one thing she saw elevated above all others.

With the benefit of hindsight we ask, "How could she?"

But at last, Phillis, we understand. No more snickering when your stiff, struggling, ambivalent lines are forced on us. We know now that you were not an idiot or a traitor; only a sickly little black girl, snatched from your home and country and made a slave; a woman who still struggled to sing the song that was your gift, although in a land of barbarians who praised you for your bewildered tongue. It is not so much what you sang, as that you kept alive, in so many of our ancestors, *the notion of song.*

Black women are called, in the folklore that so aptly identifies one's status in society, "the *mule* of the world," because we have been handed the burdens that everyone else—*everyone* else—refused to carry. We have also been called "Matriarchs," "Superwomen," and "Mean and Evil Bitches." Not to mention "Castraters" and "Sapphire's Mama." When we have pleaded for understanding, our character has been distorted; when we have asked for simple caring, we have been handed empty inspirational appellations, then stuck in the farthest corner. When we have asked for love, we have been given children. In short, even our plainer gifts, our labors of fidelity and love, have been knocked down our throats. To be an artist and a black woman, even today, lowers our status in many respects, rather than raises it: and yet, artists we will be.

Therefore we must fearlessly pull out of ourselves and look at and identify with our lives the living creativity some of our great-grandmothers were not allowed to know. I stress *some* of them because it is well known that the majority of our great-grandmothers knew, even without "knowing" it, the reality of their spirituality, even if they didn't recognize it beyond what happened in the singing at church—and they never had any intention of giving it up.

How they did it—those millions of black women who were not Phillis Wheatley, or Lucy Terry or Frances Harper or Zora Hurston or Nella Larsen or Bessie Smith; or Elizabeth Catlett, or Katherine Dunham, either—brings me to the title of this essay, "In Search of Our Mothers' Gardens," which is a personal account that is yet shared, in its theme and its meaning, by all of us. I found, while thinking about the far-reaching world of the creative black woman, that often the truest answer to a question that really matters can be found very close.

In the late 1920s my mother ran away from home to marry my father. Marriage, if not running away, was expected of seventeen-year-old girls. By the time she was twenty, she had two children and was pregnant with a third. Five children later, I was born. And this is how I came to know my mother: she seemed a large, soft, loving-eyed woman who

was rarely impatient in our home. Her quick, violent temper was on view only a few times a year, when she battled with the white landlord who had the misfortune to suggest to her that her children did not need to go to school.

She made all the clothes we wore, even my brothers' overalls. She made all the towels and sheets we used. She spent the summers canning vegetables and fruits. She spent the winter evenings making quilts enough to cover all our beds.

During the "working" day, she labored beside—not behind—my father in the fields. Her day began before sunup, and did not end until late at night. There was never a moment for her to sit down, undisturbed, to unravel her own private thoughts; never a time free from interruption—by work or the noisy inquiries of her many children. And yet, it is to my mother—and all our mothers who were not famous—that I went in search of the secret of what has fed that muzzled and often mutilated, but vibrant, creative spirit that the black woman has inherited, and that pops out in wild and unlikely places to this day.

But when, you will ask, did my overworked mother have time to know or care about feeding the creative spirit?

The answer is so simple that many of us have spent years discovering it. We have constantly looked high, when we should have looked high—and low.

For example: in the Smithsonian Institution in Washington, D.C., there hangs a quilt unlike any other in the world. In fanciful, inspired, and yet simple and identifiable figures, it portrays the story of the Crucifixion. It is considered rare, beyond price. Though it follows no known pattern of quilt-making, and though it is made of bits and pieces of worthless rags, it is obviously the work of a person of powerful imagination and deep spiritual feeling. Below this quilt I saw a note that says it was made by "an anonymous Black woman in Alabama, a hundred years ago."

If we could locate this "anonymous" black woman from Alabama, she would turn out to be one of our grandmothers—an artist who left her mark in the only materials she could afford, and in the only medium her position in society allowed her to use.

As Virginia Woolf wrote further, in *A Room of One's Own:*

Yet genius of a sort must have existed among women as it must have existed among the working class. [Change this to "slaves" and "the wives and daughters of sharecroppers."] Now and again an Emily Brontë or a Robert Burns [change this to "a Zora Hurston or a Richard Wright"] blazes out and proves its presence. But certainly it never got itself onto paper. When, however, one reads of a witch being ducked, of a woman possessed by devils [or "Sainthood"], of a wise woman selling herbs [our root workers], or even a very remarkable man who had a mother, then I think we are on the track of a lost novelist, a suppressed poet, of some mute and inglorious Jane Austen. . . . Indeed, I would venture to guess that Anon, who wrote so many poems without signing them, was often a woman. . . .

And so our mothers and grandmothers have, more often than not anonymously, handed on the creative spark, the seed of the flower they themselves never hoped to see: or like a sealed letter they could not plainly read.

And so it is, certainly, with my own mother. Unlike "Ma" Rainey's songs, which retained their creator's name even while blasting forth from Bessie Smith's mouth, no song or poem will bear my mother's name. Yet so many of the stories that I write, that we all write, are my mother's stories. Only recently did I fully realize this: that through years of listening to my mother's stories of her life, I have absorbed not only the stories themselves, but something of the manner in which she spoke, something of the urgency that involves the knowledge that her stories—like her life—must be recorded. It is probably for this reason that so much of what I have written is about characters whose counterparts in real life are so much older than I am.

But the telling of these stories, which came from my mother's lips as naturally as breathing, was not the only way my mother showed herself as an artist. For stories, too, were subject to being distracted, to dying without conclusion. Dinners must be started, and cotton must be gathered before the big rains. The artist that was and is my mother showed itself to me only after many years. This is what I finally noticed:

Like Mem, a character in *The Third Life of Grange Copeland*, my mother adorned with flowers whatever shabby house we were forced to live in. And not just your typical straggly country stand of zinnias, either. She planted ambitious gardens—and still does—with over fifty different varieties of plants that bloom profusely from early March until late November. Before she left home for the fields, she watered her flowers, chopped up the grass, and laid out new beds. When she returned from the fields she might divide clumps of bulbs, dig a cold pit, uproot and replant roses, or prime branches from her taller bushes or trees—until night came and it was too dark to see.

Whatever she planted grew as if by magic, and her fame as a grower of flowers spread over three counties. Because of her creativity with her flowers, even my memories of poverty are seen through a screen of blooms—sunflowers, petunias, roses, dahlias, forsythia, spirea, delphiniums, verbena . . . and on and on.

And I remember people coming to my mother's yard to be given cuttings from her flowers; I hear again the praise showered on her because whatever rocky soil she landed on, she turned into a garden. A garden so brilliant with colors, so original in its design, so magnificent with life and creativity, that to this day people drive by our house in Georgia—perfect strangers and imperfect strangers—and ask to stand or walk among my mother's art.

I notice that it is only when my mother is working in her flowers that she is radiant, almost to the point of being invisible—except as Creator: hand and eye. She is involved in work her soul must have. Ordering the universe in the image of her personal conception of Beauty.

Her face, as she prepares the Art that is her gift, is a legacy of respect she leaves to me, for all that illuminates and cherishes life. She has handed down respect for the possibilities—and the will to grasp them.

For her, so hindered and intruded upon in so many ways, being an artist has still been a daily part of her life. This ability to hold on, even in very simple ways, is work black women have done for a very long time.

This poem is not enough, but it is something, for the woman who literally covered the holes in our walls with sunflowers:

They were women then
My mama's generation
Husky of voice—Stout of
Step
With—fists as well as
Hands
How they battered down
Doors
And ironed
Starched white
Shirts
How they led
Armies
Headragged Generals

Across mined
Fields
Booby-trapped
Kitchens
To discover books
Desks
A place for us
How they knew what we
Must know
Without knowing a page
Of it
Themselves

Guided by my heritage of a love of beauty and a respect for strength—in search of my mother's garden, I found my own.

And perhaps in Africa over two hundred years ago, there was just such a mother; perhaps she painted vivid and daring decorations in oranges and yellows and greens on the walls of her hut; perhaps she sang—in a voice like Roberta Flack's—*sweetly* over the compounds of her village; perhaps she wove the most stunning mats or told the most ingenious stories of all the village storytellers. Perhaps she was herself a poet—though only her daughter's name is signed to the poems that we know.

Perhaps Phillis Wheatley's mother was also an artist.

Perhaps in more than Phillis Wheatley's biological life is her mother's signature made clear.

6

Lame Deer: Seeker of Visions

Lame Deer (John Fire)
Richard Erdoes

I was born a full-blood Indian in a twelve-by-twelve log cabin between Pine Ridge and Rosebud. *Maka tanhan wicasa wan*—I am a man of the earth, as we say. Our people don't call themselves Sioux or Dakota. That's white man talk. We call ourselves Ikce Wicasa—the natural humans, the free, wild, common people. I am pleased to be called that.

As with most Indian children, much of my upbringing was done by my grandparents—Good Fox and his wife, Pte-Sa-Ota-Win, Plenty White Buffalo. Among our people the relationship to one's grandparents is as strong as to one's own father and mother. We lived in that little hut way out on the prairie, in the back country, and for the first few years of my life I had no contact with the outside world. Of course we had a few white man's things—coffee, iron pots, a shotgun, an old buckboard. But I never thought much of where these things came from or who had made them.

When I was about five years old my grandma took me to visit some neighbors. As always, my little black pup came along. We were walking on the dirt road when I saw a rider come up. He looked so strange to me that I hid myself behind Grandma and my pup hid behind me. I already knew enough about riding to see that he didn't know how to handle a horse. His feet were hanging

down to the ground. He had some tiny, windmill-like things coming out of his heels, making a tinkling sound. As he came closer I started to size him up. I had never seen so much hair on a man. It covered all of his face and grew way down to his chest, maybe lower, but he didn't have hair where it counted, on top of his head. The hair was of a light-brown color and it made him look like a mattress come to life. He had eyes like a dead owl, of a washed-out blue-green hue. He was chewing on something that looked like a smoking Baby Ruth candy bar. Later I found out that this was a cigar. This man sure went in for double enjoyment, because he was also chomping on a wad of chewing tobacco, and now and then he took the smoking candy bar from his mouth to spit out a long stream of brown juice. I wondered why he kept eating something which tasted so bad that he couldn't keep it down.

This strange human being also wore a funny headgear—a cross between a skillet and a stovepipe. He had a big chunk of leather piled on top of his poor horse, hanging down also on both sides. In front of his crotch the leather was shaped like a horn. I thought maybe he kept his man-thing inside to protect it. This was the first saddle I had seen. His pitiful horse also had strings of leather on its head and a piece of iron in its mouth. Every time the horse stuck out its tongue I could hear some kind of roller or gear grinding inside it. This funny human

Source: Reprinted with the permission of Simon & Schuster from *Lame Deer: Seeker of Visions* by John Fire/Lame Deer and Richard Erdoes. Copyright © 1972 by John Fire/Lame Deer and Richard Erdoes.

being wore leather pants and had two strange-looking hammers tied to his hips. I later found out these were .45 Colts.

The man started to make weird sounds. He was talking, but we couldn't understand him because it was English. He pointed at my grandmother's pretty beaded moccasins and he took some square green frog hides from his pocket and wanted to trade. I guess those were dollar bills. But Grandma refused to swap, because she had four big gold coins in her moccasins. That man must have smelled them. This was the first white man I met.

When I got home I had a new surprise waiting for me. My grandpa was butchering something that I had never seen before, an animal with hoofs like a horse and the body of a dog. Maybe somebody had mated a dog with a horse and this funny creature was the result. Looking at its pink, hairless body, I was reminded of scary old tales about humans coupling with animals and begetting terrifying monsters. Grandpa was chopping away, taking the white meat and throwing the insides out. My little puppy was sure enjoying this, his first pig. So was I, but the pig smelled terrible. My grandpa said to save the fat for axle grease.

Most of my childhood days weren't very exciting, and that was all right with me. We had a good, simple life. One day passed like another. Only in one way was I different from other Indian kids. I was never hungry, because my dad had so many horses and cattle. Grandma always got up early in the morning before everybody else, taking down the big tin container with the Government-issue coffee. First I would hear her roasting the beans in a frying pan, then I would hear her grind them. She always made a huge pot holding two gallons of water, put in two big handfuls of coffee and boiled it. She would add some sweetener—molasses or maple syrup; we didn't like sugar. We used no milk or cream in our *pejuta sapa*—our black medicine.

Before anything else Grandma poured out a big soup spoon of coffee as an offering to the spirits, and then she kept the pot going all day. If she saw people anywhere near the house she called out to them, regardless of who they were, "Come in, have some coffee!" When the black medicine gave out, she added water and a lot more coffee and boiled the whole again. That stuff got stronger and stronger, thicker and thicker. In the end you could almost stick the spoon in there and it would keep standing up-right. "Now the coffee is real good," Grandma would say.

To go with the coffee Grandma got her baking powder each morning and made soda bread and squaw bread. That squaw bread filled the stomach. It seemed to grow bigger and bigger inside. Every spring, as the weather got warmer, the men would fix up Grandma's "squaw-cooler." This was a brush shelter made of four upright tree trunks with horizontal lodge poles tied to the top. The whole was then covered with branches from pine trees. They rigged up an old wood burner for Grandma to cook on, a rough table and some logs to sit on. In the summer, much of our life was spent in the squaw-cooler, where you could always feel a breeze. These squaw-coolers are still very popular on the reservation.

Grandma liked to smoke a little pipe. She loved her *kinnickinnick*—the red willow-bark tobacco. One time she accidentally dropped some glowing embers into an old visitor's lap. This guy still wore a breech cloth. Suddenly we smelled something burning. That breech cloth had caught fire and we had to yank it off and beat the flames out. He almost got his child-maker burned up. He was so old it wouldn't have made a lot of difference, but he still could jump.

One of my uncles used to keep a moon-counting stick, our own kind of calendar and a good one. He had a special staff and every night he cut a notch in it until the moon "died"—that is, disappeared. On the other side of his staff he made a notch for every month. He started a new stick every year in the spring. That way we always knew when it was the right day for one of our ceremonies.

Every so often my grandparents would take me to a little celebration down the creek. Grandpa always rode his old red horse, which was well known in all the tribes. We always brought plenty of food for everybody, squaw bread, beef, the kind of dried meat we called *papa,* and *wasna,* or pemmican, which was meat pounded together with berries and kidney fat. We also brought a kettle of coffee, wild mint tea, soup or stuff like that. Grandfather was always the leader of the *owanka osnato*—the rehearsal ground. He prepared the place carefully. Only the real warriors were allowed to dance there—men like Red Fish or Thin Elk, who had fought in the Custer battle. With the years the dancers grew older and older and fewer and fewer. Grandfather danced too. Everybody could see the scars all over his arm where he had been wounded by the white soldiers.

Some women had scars, too. Grandpa's brother, White Crane Walking, had three wives. They were not jealous of one another. They were like sisters. They loved one another and they loved their husband. This old man was really taking it easy; the women did all the work. He just lay around the whole day long, doing nothing. Once in a while some men called him lazy, but he just laughed and told them, "Why don't you get a second wife?" He knew their wives were jealous and didn't want them to get a second one. When this old man finally passed away, the two wives who survived him buried him in the side of a hill. They took their skinning knives and made many deep gashes in their arms and legs to show their grief. They might have cut off their little fingers too, but somebody told them that this was no longer allowed, that the Government would punish them for this. So they cut off their hair instead. They keened and cried for four days and nights; they loved their husband that much.

I was the *takoja*—the pampered grandson—and like all Indian children I was spoiled. I was never scolded, never heard a harsh word. "*Ajustan*—leave it alone"—that was the worst. I was never beaten; we don't treat children that way. Indian kids are so used to being handled gently, to get away with things, that they often don't pay much attention to what the grownups tell them. I'm

a grandfather now myself and sometimes I feel like yelling at one of those brash kids, "Hey, you little son of a bitch, listen to me!" That would make him listen all right, but I can't do it.

When I didn't want to go to sleep my grandma would try to scare me with the *ciciye*—a kind of bogeyman. "*Takoja, istima ye*—Go to sleep, sonny," she would say, "or the *ciciye* will come after you." Nobody knew what the *ciciye* was like, but he must have been something terrible. When the *ciciye* wouldn't work anymore, I was threatened with the *siyoko*—another kind of monster. Nobody knew what the *siyoko* was like, either, but he was ten times more terrible than the *ciciye*. Grandma did not have much luck. Neither the *ciciye* nor the *siyoko* scared me for long. But when I was real bad, Grandma would say, "*Wasicun anigni kte*—the white man will come and take you to his home," and that scared me all right. *Wasicun* were for real.

It was said that I didn't take after my grandpa Good Fox, whom I loved, but after my other grandfather, Crazy Heart, whom I never knew. They said I picked up where he left off, because I was so daring and full of the devil. I was told that Crazy Heart had been like that. He did not care what happened to other people, or to himself, once he was on his way. He was hot-tempered, always feuding and on the warpath. At the same time he saved lots of people, gave wise counsel, urged the people to do right. He was a good speech-maker. Everybody who listened to him said that he was a very encouraging man. He always advised patience, except when it came to himself. Then his temper got in the way.

I was like that. Things I was told not to do—I did them. I liked to play rough. We played shinny ball, a kind of hockey game. We made the ball and sticks ourselves. We played the hoop game, shot with a bow and arrow. We had foot races, horse races and water races. We liked to play *mato kiciyapi,* the bear game, throwing sharp, stiff grass stems at each other. These could really hurt you and draw blood if they hit the bare skin. And we were always at the *isto kicicastakapi*, the pit-slinging game. You chewed the fruit from the rosebush or wild cherries, spit a fistful of pits into your hand and flung them into the other fellow's face. And of course I liked the Grab-Them-by-the-Hair-and-Kick-Them game, which we played with two teams.

I liked to ride horseback behind my older sister, holding onto her. As I got a little bigger she would hold onto me. By the time I was nine years old I had my own horse to ride. It was a beautiful gray pony my father had given me together with a fine saddle and a very colorful Mexican saddle blanket. That gray was my favorite companion and I was proud to ride him. But he was not mine for long. I lost him through my own fault.

Nonge Pahloka—the Piercing of Her Ears—is a big event in a little girl's life. By this ceremony her parents, and especially her grandmother, want to show how much they love and honor her. They ask a man who is respected for his bravery or wisdom to pierce the ears of their daughter. The grandmother puts on a big feed. The little girl is placed on a blanket surrounded by the many gifts her family will give away in her name. The man who does the piercing is much admired and gets the most valuable gift. Afterward they get down to the really important part—the eating.

Well, one day I watched somebody pierce a girl's ears. I saw the fuss they made over it, the presents he got and all that. I thought I should do this to my little sister. She was about four years old at the time and I was nine. I don't know anymore what made me want to do this. Maybe I wanted to feel big and important like the man whom I had watched perform the ceremony. Maybe I wanted to get a big present. Maybe I wanted to make my sister cry. I don't remember what was in my little boy's mind then. I found some wire and made a pair of "ear rings" out of it. Then I asked my sister, "Would you like me to put these on you?" She smiled. "*Ohan*— yes." I didn't have the sharp bone one uses for the ear-piercing, and I didn't know the prayer that goes with it. I just had an old awl but thought would do fine. Oh, how my sister

yelled. I had to hold her down, but I got that awl through her earlobes and managed to put the "ear rings" in. I was proud of the neat job I had done.

When my mother came home and saw those wire loops in my sister's ears she gasped. But she recovered soon enough to go and tell my father. That was one of the few occasions he talked to me. He said, "I should punish you and whip you, but I won't. That's not my way. You'll get your punishment later." Well, some time passed and I forgot all about it. One morning my father announced that we were going to a powwow. He had hitched up the wagon and it was heaped high with boxes and bundles. At that powwow my father let it be known that he was doing a big *otuhan*—a give-away. He put my sister on a rug, a pretty Navajo blanket, and laid out things to give away—quilts, food, blankets, a fine shotgun, his own new pair of cowboy boots, a sheepskin coat, enough to fit out a whole family. Dad was telling the people, "I want to honor my daughter for her ear-piercing. This should have been done openly, but my son did it at home. I guess he's too small. He didn't know any better." This was a long speech for Dad. He motioned me to come closer. I was sitting on my pretty gray horse. I thought we were both cutting a very fine figure. Well, before I knew it, Dad had given my horse away, together with its beautiful saddle and blanket. I had to ride home in the wagon and I cried all the way. The old man said, "You have your punishment now, but you will feel better later on. All her life your sister will tell about how you pierced her ears. She'll brag about you. I bet you are the only small boy who ever did this big ceremony."

That was no consolation to me. My beautiful gray was gone. I was heart-broken for three days. On the fourth morning I looked out the door and there stood a little white stallion with a new saddle and a silver-plated bit. "It's yours," my father told me. "Get on it." I was happy again.

After I was six years old it was very hard to make me behave. The only way one could get me to sit still was to tell me a story. I loved to listen to my grandparents' old tales, and they were good at relating the ancient legends of my people. They told me of the great gods Wi and Hanwi, the sun and the moon, who were married to each other. They told me about the old man god Waziya, whom the priests have made into Santa Claus. Waziya had a wife who was a big witch. These two had a daughter called Ite—the face—the most beautiful woman in the universe. Ite was married to Tate, the wind.

The trouble with this pairing was that Ite got it into her mind that the sun, Wi, was more handsome than her own husband, the wind. Wi, on his part, thought that Ite was much more beautiful than his own wife, the moon. Wi was having a love affair with Ite, and whenever the moon saw them misbehaving she hid her face in shame. "That's why on some nights we don't see the moon," Grandma told me.

The Great Spirit did not like these goings-on, and he punished Ite. She still remained the most beautiful creature in the world, but only if one looked at her from one side. The other half of her face had become so hideous and ugly that there were no words to describe it. From that time on she was known as Anunk-Ite, or Double-Face. When it comes to love the women always have the worst of it.

Many of these legends were about animals. Grandma told me about the bat who hid himself on top of the eagle's back, screaming, "I can fly higher than any other bird." That was true enough; even the eagle couldn't fly higher than somebody who was sitting on top of him. As a punishment the other birds grounded the bat and put him in a mouse hole. There he fell in love with a lady mouse. That's why bats now are half mouse and half bird.

Grandpa Good Fox told me about the young hunters who killed a buffalo with a big rattle for a tail. After eating of its meat these young men were changed into giant rattlesnakes with human heads and human voices. They lived in a cave beneath the earth and ruled the underworld.

The stories I liked best had to do with Iktome, the evil spiderman, a smart-ass who played tricks on everybody. One day this spider was walking by a lake where he saw many ducks swimming around. This sight gave him a sudden appetite for roast duck. He stuffed his rawhide bag full of grass and then he showed himself. When the ducks saw him they started to holler, "Where are you going, Iktome?"

"I am going to a big powwow."

"What have you got in your bag, Iktome?"

"It's full of songs which I am taking to the powwow, good songs to dance to."

"How about singing some songs for us?" begged the ducks.

The tricky spider made a big show of not wanting to do it. He told the ducks he had no time for them, but in the end he pretended to give in, because they were such nice birds. "I'll sing for you," he told the ducks, "but you must help me."

"We'll do what you want. Tell us the rules."

"Well, you must form three rows. In the front row, all you fat ones, get in there. In the second row go all those who are neither fat nor thin—the in-betweens. The poor scrawny ones go in the third row, way down there. And you have to act out the song, do what the words tell you. Now the words to my first song are 'Close your eyes and dance!' "

The ducks all lined up with their eyes shut, flapping their wings, the fat ones up front. Iktome took a big club from underneath his coat. "Sing along as loud as you can," he ordered, "and keep your eyes shut. Whoever peeks will get blind." He told them to sing so that their voices would drown out the "thump, thump" of his club when he hit them over the head. He knocked them down one by one and was already half done when one of those low-down, skinny ducks in the back row opened its eyes and saw what Iktome was up to.

"Hey, wake up!" it hollered. "That Iktome is killing us all!"

The ducks that were left opened their eyes and took off. Iktome didn't mind. He already had more fat ducks than he could eat.

Iktome is like some of those bull-shipping politicians who make us close our eyes and sing and dance for them while they knock us on the head. Democratic ducks, Republican ducks, it makes no difference. The fat, stupid ones are the first in the pot. It's always the skinny, no-account, low-class duck in the back that doesn't hold still. That's a good Indian who keeps his eyes open. Iktome is an evil schemer, Grandpa told me, but luckily he's so greedy that most of the time he outsmarts himself.

It's hard to make our grandchildren listen to these stories nowadays. Some don't understand our language anymore. At the same time there is the TV going full blast—and the radio and the phonograph. These are the things our children listen to. They don't care to hear an old-fashioned Indian story.

I was happy living with my grandparents in a world of our own, but it was a happiness that could not last. "Shh, *wasicun anigni kte*— be quiet or the white man will take you away." How often had I heard these words when I had been up to some mischief, but I never thought that this threat could become true, just as I never believed that the monsters *ciciye* and *siyoko* would come and get me.

But one day the monster came—a white man from the Bureau of Indian Affairs. I guess he had my name on a list. He told my family, "This kid has to go to school. If your kids don't come by themselves the Indian police will pick them up and give them a rough ride." I hid behind Grandma. My father was like a big god to me and Grandpa had been a warrior at the Custer fight, but they could not protect me now.

In those days the Indian schools were like jails and run along military lines, with roll calls four times a day. We had to stand at attention, or march in step. The B.I.A. thought that the best way to teach us was to stop us from being Indians. We were forbidden to talk our language or to sing our songs. If we disobeyed we had to stand in the corner or flat against the wall, our noses and knees touching the plaster. Some teachers hit us on the hands with a ruler. A few of these rulers were covered with brass studs. They didn't have much luck redoing me though. They could make me dress up like a white man, but they couldn't change what was inside the shirt and pants.

My first teacher was a man and he was facing a lot of fearful kids. I noticed that all the children had the same expression on their faces—no expression at all. They looked frozen, deadpan, wooden. I knew that I, too, looked that way. I didn't know a word of the white man's language and very little about his ways. I thought that everybody had money free. The teacher didn't speak a word of Lakota. He motioned me to my seat. I was scared stiff.

The teacher said, "Stand," "Sit down!" He said it again and again until we caught on. "Sit, stand, sit, stand. Go and stop. Yes and no." All without spelling, just by sound.

We also had a lady teacher. She used the same method. She'd hold up one stick and say, "One." Then she'd hold up two sticks and say, "Two," over and over again. For many weeks she showed us pictures of animals and said "dog" or "cat." It took me three years to learn to say, "I want this."

My first day in school was also the first time I had beans, and with them came some white stuff, I guessed it was pork fat. That night, when I came home, my grandparents had to open the windows. They said my air was no good. Up to then I had eaten nothing but dry meat, *wasna, papa,* dry corn mixed with berries. I didn't know cheese and eggs, butter or cream. Only seldom had I tasted sugar or candy. So I had little appetite at school. For days on end they fed us cheese sandwiches, which made Grandma sniff at me, saying, "Grandson, have you been near some goats?"

After a while I lost some of my fear and recovered my daring. I called the white man teacher all the bad names in my language, smiling at him at the same time. He beamed and patted me on the head, because he thought I was complimenting him. Once I found a big picture of a monkey in the classroom, a strange animal with stiff, white side whiskers. I thought this must be the Great White Father, I really did.

I went to the day school on the Rosebud Reservation, twelve miles south of Norris, South Dakota. The Government teachers were all third-grade teachers. They taught up to this grade and that was the highest. I stayed in that goddam third grade for six years. There wasn't any other. The Indian people of my generation will tell you that it was the same at the other schools all over the reservations. Year after year the same grade over again. If we ran away the police would bring us back. It didn't matter anyway. In all those years at the day school they never taught me to speak English or to write and read. I learned these things only many years later, in saloons, in the Army or in jail.

When I was fourteen years old I was told that I had to go to boarding school. It is hard for a non-Indian to understand how some of our kids feel about boarding schools. In their own homes Indian children are surrounded with relatives as with a warm blanket. Parents, grandparents, uncles, aunts, older brothers and cousins are always fussing over them, playing with them or listening to what they have to say. Indian kids call their aunt "Mother," not just as a polite figure of speech but because that aunt acts like a mother. Indian children are never alone. If the grown-ups go someplace, the little ones are taken along. Children have their rights just as the adults. They are rarely forced to do something they don't like, even if it is good for them. The parents will say, "He hates it so much, we don't have the heart to make him do it."

To the Indian kid the white boarding school comes as a terrific shock. He is taken from his warm womb to a strange, cold place. It is like being pushed out of a cozy kitchen into a howling blizzard. The schools are better now than they were in my time. They look good from the outside—modern and expensive. The teachers understand the kids a little better, use more psychology and less stick. But in these fine new buildings Indian children still commit suicide, because they are

lonely among all that noise and activity. I know of a ten-year-old who hanged herself. These schools are just boxes filled with homesick children. The schools leave a scar. We enter them confused and bewildered and we leave them the same way. When we enter the school we at least know that we are Indians. We come out half red and half white, not knowing what we are.

When I was a kid those schools were really bad. Ask the oldtimers. I envied my father, who never had to go through this. I felt so lonesome I cried, but I wouldn't cooperate in the remaking of myself. I played the dumb Indian. They couldn't make me into an apple—red outside and white inside. From their point of view I was a complete failure. I took the rap for all the troubles in the school. If anything happened the first question always was "Did you see John do it?" They used the strap on us, but more on me than on anybody else.

My teacher was a mean old lady. I once threw a live chicken at her like a snowball. In return she hit my palms with a ruler. I fixed an inkpot in such a way that it went up in her face. The black ink was all over her. I was the first to smile and she knew who had done it right away. They used a harness thong on my back that time and locked me up in the basement. We fullbloods spent much time down there. I picked up some good fox songs in that basement.

I was a good athlete. I busted a kitchen window once playing stickball. After that I never hit so good again. They tried to make me play a slide trombone. I tore it apart and twisted it into a pretzel. That mean old teacher had a mouth like a pike and eyes to match. We counted many coups upon each other and I still don't know who won. Once, when they were after me again for something I didn't do, I ran off. I got home and on my horse. I knew the Indian police would come after me. I made it to Nebraska, where I sold my horse and saddle and bought a ticket to Rapid City. I still had twelve dollars in my pocket. I could live two days on one dollar, but the police caught me and brought me back. I think in the end I got the better of that school. I was more of an Indian when I left than when I went in. My back had been tougher than the many straps they had worn out on it.

Some doctors say that Indians must be healthier than white people because they have less heart disease. Others say that this comes from our being hungrier, having less to eat, which makes our bodies lean and healthy. But this is wrong. The reason Indians suffer less from heart disease is that we don't live long enough to have heart trouble. That's an old folks' sickness. The way we have to live now, we are lucky if we make it to age forty. The full-bloods are dying fast. One day I talk to one, the next day he is dead. In a way the Government is still "vanishing" the Indian, doing Custer's work. The strange-looking pills and capsules they give us to live on at the Public Health Service hospitals don't do us much good. At my school the dentist came once a year in his horse and buggy with a big pair of pliers to yank our teeth, while the strongest, biggest man they could find kept our arms pinned to our sides. That was the anesthesia.

There were twelve of us, but they are all dead now, except one sister. Most of them didn't even grow up. My big brother, Tom, and his wife were killed by the flu in 1917. I lost my own little boy thirty-five years ago. I was a hundred miles away, caught in a blizzard. A doctor couldn't be found for him soon enough. I was told it was the measles. Last year I lost another baby boy, a foster child. This time they told me it was due to some intestinal trouble. So in a lifetime we haven't made much progress. We medicine men try to doctor our sick, but we suffer from many new white man's diseases, which come from the white man's food and white man's living, and we have no herbs for that.

My big sister was the oldest of us all. When she died in 1914 my folks took it so hard that our life was changed. In honor of her memory they gave away most of their possessions, even beds and mattresses, even the things without which the family would find it hard to go on. My mother died of tuberculosis in 1920, when I was seventeen years old, and that was our family's "last stand." On her last day I felt that her body was already gone; only her soul was still there. I was holding her hand and she was looking at me. Her eyes were big and sad, as if she knew that I was in for a hard time. She said, "*Onsika, onsika*—pitiful, pitiful." These were her last words. She wasn't sorry for herself; she was sorry for me. I went up on a hill by myself and cried.

When grandfather Crazy Heart died they killed his two ponies, heads toward the east and tails to the west. They had told each horse, "Grandson, your owner loved you. He has need of you where he's going now." Grandfather knew for sure where he was going, and so did the people who buried him according to our old custom, up on a scaffold where the wind and the air, the sun, the rain and the snow could take good care of him. I think that eventually they took the box with his body down from the scaffold and buried it in a cemetery, but that happened years later and by then he and his ponies had long gone to wherever they wanted to be.

But in 1920 they wouldn't even allow us to be dead in our own way. We had to be buried in the Christian fashion. It was as if they wanted to take my mother to a white boarding school way up there. For four days I felt my mother's *nagi*, her presence, her soul, near me. I felt that some of her goodness was staying with me. The priest talked about eternity. I told him we Indians did not believe in a forever and forever. We say that only the rocks and the mountains last, but even they will disappear. There's a new day coming, but no forever, I told him. "When my time comes, I want to go where my ancestors have gone." The priest said, "That may be hell." I told him that I'd rather be frying with a Sioux grandmother or uncle than sit on a cloud playing harp with a pale-faced stranger. I told him, "That Christian name, John, don't call me that when I'm gone. Call me Tahca Ushte— Lame Deer."

7

The World of Our Grandmothers

Connie Young Wu

Our grandmothers are our historical links. As a fourth-generation Chinese American on my mother's side, and a third-generation on my father's, I grew up hearing stories about ancestors coming from China and going back and returning again. Both of my grandmothers, like so many others, spent a lot of time waiting in China.

My father's parents lived with us when I was growing up, and through them I absorbed a village culture and the heritage of my pioneer Chinese family. In the kitchen my grandmother told repeated stories of coming to America after waiting for her husband to send for her. (It took sixteen years before Grandfather could attain the status of merchant and only then arrange for her passage to this country.) She also told stories from the village about bandits, festivals, and incidents showing the tyranny of tradition. For example, Grandma was forbidden by her mother-in-law to return to her own village to visit her mother: A married woman belonged solely within the boundaries of her husband's world.

Sometimes I was too young to understand or didn't listen, so my mother—who knew all the stories by heart—told me those stories again later. We heard over and over how lucky Grandpa was to have come to America when he was eleven—just one year before the

gate was shut by the exclusion law banning Chinese laborers. Grandpa told of his many jobs washing dishes, making bricks, and working on a strawberry farm. Once, while walking outside Chinatown, he was stoned by a group of whites and ran so fast he lost his cap. Grandma had this story to tell of her anger and frustration: "While I was waiting in the immigration shed, Grandpa sent in a box of *dim sum.* I was still waiting to be released. I would have jumped in the ocean if they decided to deport me." A woman in her position was quite helpless, but she still had her pride and was not easily pacified. "I threw the box of *dim sum* out the window."

Such was the kind of history I absorbed. I regret deeply that I was too young to have asked the questions about the past that I now want answered; all my grandparents are now gone. But I have another chance to recover some history from my mother's side. Family papers, photographs, old trunks that have traveled across the ocean several times filled with clothes, letters, and mementos provide a documentary on our immigration. My mother—and some of my grandmother's younger contemporaries—fill in the narrative.

A year before the Joint Special Committee of Congress to investigate Chinese immigration met in San Francisco in 1876, my great-grandmother, Chin Shee, arrived to join her husband, Lee Wong Sang, who had come to America a decade earlier to work on the transcontinental railroad. Chin Shee arrived with two brides who had never seen their husbands. Like her own, their marriages had

Source: "The World of Our Grandmothers" by C. Young Wu, from *Making Waves,* by Asian Women United of California, copyright © 1989 by Asian Women United of California. Reprinted by permission of Beacon Press, Boston.

been arranged by their families. The voyage on the clipper ship was rough and long. Seasick for weeks, rolling back and forth as she lay in the bunk, Chin Shee lost most of her hair. The two other women laughed, "Some newlywed you'll make!" But the joke was on them as they mistakenly set off with the wrong husbands, the situation realized only when one man looked at his bride's normal-sized feet and exclaimed, "But the letter described my bride as having bound feet!" Chin Shee did not have her feet bound because she came from a peasant family. But her husband did not seem to care about that nor that the back of her head was practically bald. He felt himself fortunate just to be able to bring his wife to Gum San.

Chin Shee bore six children in San Francisco, where her husband assisted in the deliveries. They all lived in the rear of their grocery store, which also exported dried shrimp and seaweed to China. Great-Grandma seldom left home; she could count the number of times she went out. She and other Chinese wives did not appear in the streets even for holidays, lest they be looked upon as prostitutes. She took care of the children, made special cakes to sell on feast days, and helped with her husband's work. A photograph of her shows a middle-aged woman with a kindly, but careworn face, wearing a very regal brocade gown and a long, beaded necklace. As a respectable, well-to-do Chinese wife in America, married to a successful Chinatown merchant, with children who were by birthright American citizens, she was a rarity in her day. (In contrast, in 1884 Mrs. Jew Lim, the wife of a laborer, sued in federal court to be allowed to join her husband, but was denied and deported.)

In 1890 there were only 3,868 Chinese women among 103,620 Chinese males in America. Men such as Lee Yoke Suey, my mother's father, went to China to marry. He was one of Chin Shee's sons born in the rear of the grocery store, and he grew up learning the import and export trade. As a Gum San merchant, he had money and status and was able to build a fine house in Toishan. Not only

did he acquire a wife but also two concubines. When his wife became very ill after giving birth to an infant who soon died, Yoke Suey was warned by his father that she was too weak to return to America with him. Reminding Yoke Suey of the harsh life in Gum San, he advised his son to get a new wife.

In the town of Foshan, not far from my grandfather's village, lived a girl who was recommended to him by his father's friend. Extremely capable, bright, and with some education, she was from a once prosperous family that had fallen on hard times. A plague had killed her two older brothers, and her heartbroken mother died soon afterwards. She was an excellent cook and took good care of her father, an herb doctor. Her name was Jeong Hing Tong, and she was pretty, with bound feet only three and a half inches long. Her father rejected the offer of the Lee family at first; he did not want his daughter to be a concubine, even to a wealthy Gum San merchant. But the elder Lee assured him this girl would be the wife, the one who would go to America with her husband.

So my maternal grandmother, bride of sixteen, went with my grandfather, then twenty-six, to live in America. Once in San Francisco, Grandmother lived a life of confinement, as did her mother-in-law before her. When she went out, even in Chinatown, she was ridiculed for her bound feet. People called out mockingly to her, "*Jhat!*" meaning bound. She tried to unbind her feet by soaking them every night and putting a heavy weight on each foot. But she was already a grown woman, and her feet were permanently stunted, the arches bent and the toes crippled. It was hard for her to stand for long periods of time, and she frequently had to sit on the floor to do her chores. My mother comments: "Tradition makes life so hard. My father traveled all over the world. There were stamps all over his passport—London, Paris—and stickers all over his suitcases, but his wife could not go into the street by herself."

Their first child was a girl, and on the morning of her month-old "red eggs and ginger party" the earth shook 8.3 on the Richter scale. Everyone in San Francisco, even Chinese women, poured out into the streets. My grandmother, babe in arms, managed to get a ride to Golden Gate Park on a horse-drawn wagon. Two other Chinese women who survived the earthquake recall the shock of suddenly being out in the street milling with thousands of people. The elderly goldsmith in a dimly lit Chinatown store had a twinkle in his eye when I asked him about the scene after the quake. "We all stared at the women because we so seldom saw them in the streets." The city was soon in flames. "We could feel the fire on our faces," recalls Lily Sung, who was seven at the time, "but my sister and I couldn't walk very fast because we had to escort this lady, our neighbor, who had bound feet." The poor woman kept stumbling and falling on the rubble and debris during their long walk to the Oakland-bound ferry.

That devastating natural disaster forced some modernity on the San Francisco Chinese community. Women had to adjust to the emergency and makeshift living conditions and had to work right alongside the men. Life in America, my grandmother found, was indeed rugged and unpredictable.

As the city began to rebuild itself, she proceeded to raise a large family, bearing four more children. The only school in San Francisco admitting Chinese was the Oriental school in Chinatown. But her husband felt, as did most men of his class, that the only way his children could get a good education was for the family to return to China. So they lived in China and my grandfather traveled back and forth to the United States for his trade business. Then suddenly, at the age of forty-three, he died of an illness on board a ship returning to China. After a long and painful mourning, Grandmother decided to return to America with her brood of now seven children. That decision eventually affected immigration history.

At the Angel Island immigration station in San Francisco Bay, Grandmother went through a physical examination so thorough that even her teeth were checked to determine whether she was the age stated on her passport. The health inspector said she had filariasis, liver fluke, a common ailment of Asian immigrants which caused their deportation by countless numbers. The authorities thereby ordered Grandmother to be deported as well.

While her distraught children had to fend for themselves in San Francisco (my mother, then fifteen, and her older sister had found work in a sewing factory), a lawyer was hired to fight for Grandmother's release from the detention barracks. A letter addressed to her on Angel Island from her attorney, C. M. Fickert, dated 24 March 1924, reads: "Everything I can legitimately do will be done on your behalf. As you say, it seems most inhuman for you to be separated from your children who need your care. I am sorry that the immigration officers will not look at the human side of your case."

Times were tough for Chinese immigrants in 1924 . Two years before, the federal government had passed the Cable Act, which provided that any woman born in the United States who married a man "ineligible for citizenship" (including the Chinese, whose naturalization rights had been eliminated by the Chinese Exclusion Act) would lose her own citizenship. So, for example, when American-born Lily Sung, whom I also interviewed, married a Chinese citizen she forfeited her birthright. When she and her four daughters tried to re-enter the United States after a stay in China, they were denied permission. The immigration inspector accused her of "smuggling little girls to sell." The Cable Act was not repealed until 1930.

The year my grandmother was detained on Angel Island, a law had just taken effect that forbade all aliens ineligible for citizenship from landing in America. This constituted a virtual ban on the immigration of all Chinese, including Chinese wives of U.S. citizens.

Waiting month after month in the bleak barracks, Grandmother heard many heart-rending stories from women awaiting deportation. They spoke of the suicides of several despondent women who hanged themselves in the shower stalls. Grandmother could see the calligraphy carved on the walls by other detained immigrants, eloquent poems expressing homesickness, sorrow, and a sense of injustice.

Meanwhile, Fickert was sending telegrams to Washington (a total of ten the bill stated) and building up a case for the circuit court. Mrs. Lee, after all, was the wife of a citizen who was a respected San Francisco merchant, and her children were American citizens. He also consulted a medical authority to see about a cure for liver fluke.

My mother took the ferry from San Francisco twice a week to visit Grandmother and take her Chinese dishes such as salted eggs and steamed pork because Grandmother could not eat the beef stew served in the mess hall. Mother and daughter could not help crying frequently during their short visits in the administration building. They were under close watch of both a guard and an interpreter.

After fifteen months the case was finally won. Grandmother was easily cured of filariasis and was allowed—with nine months probation—to join her children in San Francisco. The legal fees amounted to $782.50, a fortune in those days.

In 1927 Dr. Frederick Lam in Hawaii, moved by the plight of Chinese families deported from the islands because of the liver fluke disease, worked to convince federal health officials that the disease was noncommunicable. He used the case of Mrs. Lee Yoke Suey, my grandmother, as a precedent for allowing an immigrant to land with such an ailment and thus succeeded in breaking down a major barrier to Asian immigration.

My most vivid memory of Grandmother Lee is when she was in her seventies and studying for her citizenship. She had asked me to test her on the three branches of government and how to pronounce them correctly. I was a sophomore in high school and had entered the "What American Democracy Means To Me" speech contest of the Chinese American Citizens Alliance. When I said the words "judicial, executive, and legislative," I looked directly at my grandmother in the audience. She didn't smile, and afterwards, didn't comment much on my patriotic words. She had never told me about being on Angel Island or about her friends losing their citizenship. It wasn't in my textbooks either. I may have thought she wanted to be a citizen because her sons and sons-in-law had fought for this country, and we lived in a land of freedom and opportunity, but my guess now is that she wanted to avoid any possible confrontation—even at her age—with immigration authorities. The bad laws had been repealed, but she wasn't taking any chances.

I think a lot about my grandmother now and can understand why, despite her quiet, elegant dignity, an aura of sadness always surrounded her. She suffered from racism in the new country, as well as from traditional cruelties in the old. We, her grandchildren, remember walking very slowly with her, escorting her to a family banquet in Chinatown, hating the stares of tourists at her tiny feet. Did she, I wonder, ever feel like the victim of a terrible hoax, told as a small weeping girl that if she tried to untie the bandages tightly binding her feet she would grow up ugly, unwanted, and without the comforts and privileges of the wife of a wealthy man?

We seemed so huge and clumsy around her—a small, slim figure always dressed in black. She exclaimed once that the size of my growing feet were "like boats." But she lived to see some of her granddaughters graduate from college and pursue careers and feel that the world she once knew with its feudal customs had begun to crumble. I wonder what she would have said of my own daughter who is now attending a university on an athletic scholarship. Feet like boats travel far?

I keep looking at the artifacts of the past: the photograph of my grandmother when she was an innocent young bride and the sad face in the news photo taken on Angel Island. I visit the immigration barracks from time to time, a weather-beaten wooden building with its walls marked by calligraphy bespeaking the struggles of our history. I see the view of sky and water from the window out of which my grandmother gazed. My mother told me how, after visiting hours, she would walk to the ferry and turn back to see her mother waving to her from this window. This image has been passed on to me like an heirloom of pain and of love. When I leave the building, emerging from the darkness into the glaring sunlight of the island, I too turn back to look at my grandmother's window.

Dear Tía

Carolina Hospital

I do not write.
The years have frightened me away.
My life in a land so familiarly foreign,
a denial of your presence.
Your name is mine.
One black and white photograph of your youth,
all I hold on to.
One story of your past.

The pain comes not from nostalgia.
I do not miss your voice urging me in play,
your smile,
or your pride when others called you my mother.
I cannot close my eyes and feel your soft skin;
listen to your laughter;
smell the sweetness of your bath.
I write because I cannot remember at all.

Source: "Dear Tía" from *Cuban American Writers: Los Atrevidos*, Carolina Hospital, editor. Copyright © 1988 Ediciones Ellas/Linden Lane Press.

Gender, Race, and Class:
Beyond the Feminization of Poverty in Later Life

Paula L. Dressel

Increasing popular and scholarly attention is devoted to the feminization of poverty argument, which is focused both on women in general (Ehrenreich & Piven, 1984; Pearce, 1978) and on older women in particular (Minkler & Stone, 1985; Older Women's League, 1986). Such publications have made important contributions to the understanding of gender inequalities. For example, their discussions of the family wage system, the sexual division of paid and unpaid labor, and the existence of dual labor markets have highlighted structural and ideological bases of different economic opportunities and barriers for men and women. The writings have also provided a wealth of statistics that have documented gender inequalities and described the many social policies that undergird and reproduce different experiences by gender. Political activism by various age-based and feminist advocacy organizations has been fueled by the growing literature on the feminization of poverty across women's lives.

Although acknowledgment is due to the contributions made in the literature, a concern is that the feminization of poverty argument in isolation also has the potential for distorting and simplifying the issue of old

age poverty and for being politically divisive. In the subsequent sections, it is maintained that gerontology scholars and activists need to move beyond the feminization of poverty argument to acknowledge how complexly the factors of race and gender are interlocked with the variable of social class in the United States. Emphasis on only one of these factors, gender, seriously misrepresents the phenomenon of poverty in later life, promotes policy and programming decisions whose efficacy is limited, and has the potential to undermine broad-based political coalitions seeking economic equality.

In part, in the arguments which follow, recent criticisms of social science in general and specific criticisms of the feminization of poverty argument in particular (Burnham, 1985) are applied to the topic of the feminization of poverty in later life. Recent general criticisms (Scott, 1982; Zinn, Cannon, Higginbotham, & Dill, 1986) explicated ways in which social science research and theory reflect racism, either by omission (such as through the untested assumption that research findings or theoretical formulations apply similarly across groups) or commission (such as through the use of biased research instruments). Writings on the feminization of poverty in later life revealed both types of errors: Authors tended to ignore the inextricable link between race and social class in the U.S. and they bolstered their claims through selective utilization and interpretation of statistics.

Source: Excerpted from "Gender, Race, and Class: Beyond the Feminization of Poverty in Later Life," P. Dressel, 1988, The Gerontologist 28(2), 177-180. Copyright © 1988 The Gerontological Society of America. Reprinted with permission.

The purpose herein is not to challenge the argument that patriarchy creates significant burdens for older (as well as younger) women. Nor is it to engage in debate over whether one form of stratification is more oppressive than another or that the experiences of one oppressed group are any more tolerable than those of another. Rather, the point is to argue that racial stratification is also a primary feature of the political economy of the U.S. Once the racialized character of social class is made explicit, it is then possible to show how this feature of the political economy differentiates women with regard to later life experiences and vulnerabilities and renders racial-ethnic men disproportionately vulnerable to poverty in old age. The criticisms and reconceptualizations that follow are offered with the hope that a more complex understanding of poverty in later life will generate more effective efforts to eliminate economic inequalities.

Acknowledging Racial Oppression

The writings of selected Black political economists (Baron, 1985; Hogan, 1984; Marable, 1983) have detailed the central way in which racial oppression informs the development of the U.S. political economy. Although the forms of oppression have changed historically with transformations of the economic base, shifting from slavery to sharecropping to low-wage labor, racism is nevertheless an ever-present, if increasingly subtle characteristic of U.S. capitalism.

The economic marginality of racial-ethnic groups is built on capital's need for low-wage labor. Ideologies that systematically devalue racial-ethnic groups rationalize their low pay and occupational clustering and legitimatize their location at the bottom of the socioeconomic structure. Within a dual labor market racial-ethnic workers are found disproportionately in the peripheral sector, where jobs are characterized by low wages, minimal, if any, fringe benefits, virtually no union protection, and high vulnerability to economic fluctuations (O'Connor, 1973). The limited individual mobility that has occurred for some Black Americans since the 1960s is due largely to government employment and work in Black-owned businesses, both of which are highly vulnerable to economic downturns and to government anti-discrimination initiatives whose level of enforcement varies with political administrations (Collins, 1983).

As a result, racial-ethnic group members, male and female alike, are more susceptible to the experiences of unemployment, underemployment, and unstable low-wage employment than are their white counterparts (U.S. Commission on Civil Rights, 1982). As noted elsewhere (Dressel, 1986), the limited upward mobility that has occurred within the past 2 decades for some members of racial-ethnic groups has not significantly altered inter-group inequalities (Collins, 1983; Oliver & Glick, 1982; U.S. Commission on Civil Rights, 1982). Furthermore, any advances may be short-lived, having most recently been negatively affected by economic decline (Gramlick & Laren, 1984; U.S. Commission on Civil Rights, 1982), judicial action upholding the primacy of seniority over affirmative action (Jacobs & Slawsky, 1984), and budgetary cutbacks for civil rights enforcement by the federal administration (U.S. Commission on Civil Rights, 1981).

In sum, race is a primary stratifier of people's lives, as is gender. Recognition of this fact mandates reconceptualization of the bases of poverty in later life. Furthermore, it challenges implicit assumptions of the feminization of poverty argument.

Burnham (1985) cited several problems created by the feminization of poverty argument precisely because it fails to account for the complex interplay of gender, race, and class in the U.S. Among the problems are that it obscures class differences among women, understates racial oppression, and ignores the poverty of Black men. Furthermore, she took issue with what gerontologists have frequently conceptualized as double or triple jeopardy by arguing that oppression is not an additive phenomenon. Rather, because Black women experience the intersection of racism and sexism, their circumstances are qualitatively, not quantitatively, different from those of white women. Although Burnham speaks to the general feminization of poverty argument, her criticisms are applicable to its specialized emphasis on later life as well.

Racial-ethnic women have not been overlooked in most writing on the feminization of poverty in later life. The tendency has been, however, to take the add and stir approach (Andersen, 1983), which leads to race-blind theoretical formulations. That is, what are meant to be general statements about gender and poverty are made, and then, as an afterthought or elaboration, specialized statements about Black (or Hispanic or Native American) women are made. For example, "In 1982, over half of women aged 65 and over with incomes below the poverty level reported fair or poor health. . . . Among poor Black women the proportion approaches two-thirds" (Older Women's League, 1986).

The point here is subtle but critical. In the illustration of the add and stir approach (of which there are many instances in a variety of gerontological publications) it is implied that similar outcomes in women's lives are produced by the one and only factor of patriarchy. Acknowledged but not accounted for are the worse (and sometimes different) conditions faced by racial-ethnic women. Indeed, the differences cannot be accounted for because the model of the feminization of poverty glosses over the variable of race for heuristic and political purposes. In other words, racial-ethnic women's experiences are forced into the model rather than being utilized to refine or critique the model itself.

The important fact that racial-ethnic men are systematically rendered economically marginal is also ignored in the literature on the feminization of poverty in later life. An insistence on dichotomizing elders by gender alone dismisses fundamental political economic dynamics with respect to race as unimportant for understanding poverty in old age. In other words, the claim that poverty is "feminized" makes patriarchy the primary factor in socioeconomic stratification.

A parallel argument could be developed about the "racialization of poverty" in later life (as well as across the life span), thereby claiming white supremacy as the primary motive in socioeconomic stratification. The point, however, is that neither argument integrates the variables of gender, race, and class into a richer appreciation of poverty and economic vulnerability. What is required is movement away from debates in which implicitly, if not explicitly, one form of oppression is posited as more serious, primary, or worthy of attention than another.

Reexamining Statistics

Once race is acknowledged as a central factor in how people fare economically, statistics can be reexamined with race and gender in mind. Upon reexamination, what is frequently found is that white women fare better than Blacks and Hispanics, female or male, and that white family units fare better than other family units.

With gender as a filter for examining statistics it can be argued that elderly women are worse off than their male counterparts. For example, Minkler and Stone (1985) reported that 49% of non-married elder white women compared to 34% of non-married elder white men fell below 125% of the poverty line; similarly, 80% of non-married elder Black women compared to 64% of non-married elder Black men fell below that line. They also found that non-married white women have a median Social Security income of $4,490 compared to $5,080 for their male counterparts; similarly, non-married Black women receive a median $3,050 from Social Security compared to $3,710 for their male counterparts. If the analysis stopped here, then the conclusion that "elderly women represent . . . the single poorest segment of American society" (Minkler & Stone, 1985) might be tenable. Now let race be used as a filter for examining the same sets of statistics. What is seen is that non-married Black men are more likely (64%) to fall below 125% of the poverty line than non-married white women (49%); the median income from Social Security for non-married Black men is $3,710 compared to $4,490 for non-married white women; married white couples receive a median $7,670 from Social Security benefits compared to $5,920 for their Black counterparts. From this perspective an argument could be made for the racialization of poverty in later life.

But again, the point is not to debate which oppression is worse, gender or race. Rather, it is to argue that the history of the U.S. political economy mandates that analysts take race into account, along with gender, age, and other relevant factors (Palmore & Manton, 1973; R. Whittington, personal communication, 1986) when trying to understand economic inequality and impoverishment. Patriarchy and racism are played out similarly in some respects (such as with occupational clustering) but differently in other respects (such as with opportunities for advancement). Consequently, both must be considered for a more complete understanding of economic marginality. Furthermore, because some sources indicated that race-sex patterns of economic marginality characterizing current elders are not substantially different for younger cohorts of workers (U.S. Commission on Civil Rights, 1982), gerontologists cannot assume that each succeeding cohort of elders will have benefitted (or benefitted equally [Palmore & Manton, 1973]) from anti-discrimination legislation, whether directed toward race or gender.

In part the feminization of poverty argument depends on selectively interpreted statistics. Caution must also be employed in terms of what particular statistics are utilized to develop arguments about poverty in later life. For example, if Social Security benefits alone (including SSI) are analyzed, economic differences between Blacks and whites appear considerably smaller than when private pensions and income from assets are also factored in. Schulz (1985) cited data indicating the differential sources of income for Black and white elders, with the latter more likely to be covered by private pensions and to receive income from assets. Although it is true

that women's work is also less likely than men's to offer pensions as a fringe benefit, it is also true that white women married to white men have greater access to private pension benefits than Black women married to Black men. Once again, the picture is incomplete unless both race and gender are taken into account.

Rethinking Political Action

For several reasons the feminization of poverty argument is politically appealing to various age-based and feminist advocacy groups. Most importantly, it directs much-needed attention to the widespread implications of patriarchy for women of all ages. No doubt it has also engendered sympathy for the poor by being focused on a relatively non-threatening sub-segment, women. Indeed, elderly women may be the least threatening and politically palatable of all possible categories of economically marginal adults. Finally, the feminization of poverty argument underlies attempts to develop links across age, racial-ethnic, and social class strata of women, whose political alliances historically have been problematic (Davis, 1981; Dill, 1983; hooks, 1981, 1984). To be sure, exposing sexism, generating concern over poverty, and attempting to unite women are all worthy goals. The pursuit of these goals through emphasis on the feminization of poverty, however, has important shortcomings as well.

As suggested earlier, a singular focus on gender and a consequent disregard for the factor of race as another primary stratifier of people has negative latent functions. First, it creates the tendency for fruitless and diversionary debates about which form of oppression is worse. Second, it disregards the fact that some men also are systematically marginalized in the economy, thereby diminishing opportunities for cross-gender coalitions. Third, by failing to paint the full picture of exploitation and discrimination, it impedes a more complex analysis of both welfare state and capitalist contradictions.

Furthermore, whatever concern the feminization of poverty argument generates about the poor will be limited because of the inherent limitations of the analysis. That is, all who are poor will not be embraced by whatever policy and programmatic actions arise from attention to the feminization of poverty. As already noted, racial-ethnic men's systematic marginality is ignored. In addition, there is legitimate concern that only selected groups of impoverished women will become the focus of political interventions, namely downwardly mobile white women who comprise the "nouveau poor" (Ehrenreich & Stallard, 1982). For example, displaced homemaker legislation, in which critical needs of a specific segment of women are addressed, provides politicians with evidence of their concern over the feminization of poverty. It also enables them to sidestep long-entrenched working class and underclass poverty whose alleviation requires far more extensive social change. Even progressive social democratic groups have purposefully emphasized the female nouveau poor and underplayed race and class issues in efforts to broaden their base of political support (Burnham, 1985). In other words, the feminization of poverty argument has been appropriated to serve limited ends at the expense of other historically dispossessed groups.

Consequently, the feminization of poverty analysis may prove to be a fatal remedy (Sieber, 1981), despite the desire of its proponents to build coalitions among diverse groups of women. That is, they may accomplish just the opposite of their intentions. In the analysis, the failure to acknowledge race as a primary stratifier of peoples' life chances diminishes its utility for Black and other racial-ethnic women; its insistence on the primacy of gender implies the unrealistic expectation that racial-ethnic women separate their political interests from those of racial-ethnic men. Finally, the failure to incorporate class and race into the analysis of women's conditions provides convenient opportunities for politicians to target for intervention those women who are the least fiscally and politi-

cally costly. As a result, women may become divided because only some will benefit from the selective targeting of putatively limited resources.

A more complex understanding of old age poverty is needed by gerontology scholars and activists. Single-variable conceptualizations of political economic dynamics (whether based on gender, race, age or any other variable) may serve short-term consciousness-raising functions for select categories of people. But the detail necessary for the formulation of well-targeted social policies cannot be provided (F. Whittington, personal communication, 1986). And in the long run, the potential for broad-based political alliances among the heterogeneous people comprising the working poor, the underclass, and other economically vulnerable groups in the U.S. can be undermined. Gerontologists have realized the diversity contained within age groups; likewise they must recognize the diversity within gender groups and move beyond the feminization of poverty argument. To do so does not require abandoning concern over women's disproportionate impoverishment. But it does require abandoning appealing political rhetoric that is built on an incomplete model of the U.S. political economy.

References

Andersen, M. L. (1983). *Thinking about women: Sociological and feminist perspectives.* New York: Macmillan.

Baron, H. M. (1985). Racism transformed: The implications of the 1960s. *Review of Radical Political Economics, 17,* 10-33.

Burnham, L. (1985). Has poverty been feminized in Black America? *Black Scholar, 16,* 14-24.

Collins, S. M. (1983). The making of the Black middle class. *Social Problems, 30,* 369-382.

Davis, A. (1981). *Women, race and class.* New York: Vintage.

Dill, B. T. (1983). Race, class, and gender: Prospects for an all-inclusive sisterhood. *Feminist Studies, 9,* 131-150.

Dressel, R. (1986). Civil rights, affirmative action, and the aged of the future: Will life chances be different for Blacks, Hispanics and women? An overview of the issues. *The Gerontologist, 26,* 128-131.

Ehrenreich, B., & Piven, F. R (1984). The feminization of poverty. *Dissent, 31,* 162-170.

Ehrenreich, B., & Stallard, K. (1982). The nouveau poor. *Ms., 11,* 217-224.

Gramlick, E. M., & Laren, D. S. (1984). How widespread are income losses in a recession? In D. L. Bawden (Ed.), *The social contract revisited: Aims and outcomes of President Reagan's social welfare policy.* Washington, DC: Urban Institute Press.

Hogan, L. (1984). *Principles of Black political economy.* Boston: Routledge & Kegan Paul.

hooks, b. (1981). *Ain't I a woman: Black women and feminism.* Boston: South End Press.

hooks, b. (1984). *Feminist theory from margin to center.* Boston: South End Press.

Jacobs, J., & Slawsky, N. (1984). Seniority vs. minority. *Atlanta Journal and Constitution, 35,* 1D, 7D.

Marable, M. (1983). *How capitalism underdeveloped Black America.* Boston: South End Press.

Minkler, M., & Stone, R. (1985). The feminization of poverty and older women. *The Gerontologist, 25,* 351-357.

O'Connor, J. (1973). *The fiscal crisis of the state.* New York: St. Martin's.

Older Women's League. (1986). *Report on the status of midlife and older women.* Washington, DC: Author.

Oliver, M. L., & Glick, M. A. (1982). An analysis of the new orthodoxy on Black mobility. *Social Problems, 29,* 511-523.

Palmore, E. B., & Manton, K. (1973). Ageism compared to racism and sexism. *Journal of Gerontology, 28,* 363-369.

Pearce, D. (1978). The feminization of poverty: Women, work, and welfare. *Urban and Social Change Review, 11,* 28-36.

Schulz, J. H. (1985). *The economics of aging* (3rd ed.). Belmont, CA: Wadsworth.

Scott, P. B. (1982). Debunking Sapphire: Toward a non-racist and non-sexist social science. In G. T. Hull, P. B. Scott, & B. Smith (Eds.), *But some of us are brave.* Old Westbury, NY: Feminist Press.

Sieber, S. (1981). *Fatal remedies: The ironies of social intervention.* New York: Plenum.

U.S. Commission on Civil Rights. (1981). *Civil rights: A national, not a special interest.* Washington, DC: Author.

U.S. Commission on Civil Rights. (1982). *Unemployment and under-employment among Blacks, Hispanics, and women* (Clearinghouse Publication 74). Washington, DC: Author.

Zinn, M. B., Cannon, L. W., Higginbotham, E., & Dill, B. T. (1986). The costs of exclusionary practices in women's studies. *Signs, 11,* 290-303.

1 The readings in Part I all illustrate how particular historical times differently shape the opportunity structures of individuals who are disadvantaged by systems of inequality. In what ways were the opportunities of people in the readings limited by the historical experience in which they lived?

2 A major theme of Part I has been that certain individuals in certain historical time periods are relegated to circumscribed roles that narrow their life chances, increase their negative life events, and influence their adaptive resources. How were the life chances of the women of Elder and Liker's study, the Itoi family, the Thomas family, Lame Deer, and the mothers and grandmothers in Walker's essay circumscribed by the particular historical period? What adaptive resources were available to these people?

3 We have emphasized the fact that the same historical period can differently shape the experiences of individuals who belong to the same cohort but occupy different positions in systems of inequality. Demonstrate your understanding of this principle by comparing the impact of the Depression of the 1930s on the lower- and middle-class women in Elder and Liker's study and of World War II on the Itoi and Thomas families and on Coleman Young.

4 People's experiences in old age are influenced by the ways in which they adapt to particular life events. Both their life events and adaptive resources are influenced by the historical time period in which they live and their positions in interlocking systems of inequality. Illustrate this life course approach to old age by comparing Elder and Liker's lower-class women with the mothers and grandmothers in Walker's essay and the Chinese American women in Wu's article. In what ways were the life courses of these women similar? In what ways were they different?

5 Talk to older relatives or friends about their memories of the Great Depression, World War II, and the Civil Rights movement. In what ways do you think these events affected their lives? How was the impact of these events influenced by their age cohort? By their gender, race or ethnicity, or social class?

6 The sociologists Howard Schuman and Jacqueline Scott (1989) studied the ways a generation can be marked by the political

events and social changes of its era. They concluded that the events and changes we experience during adolescence and early adulthood have the greatest impact in creating what they call "generational memories." What events or changes do you think will have the greatest impact on your cohort? Can you predict the long-term effects of these events or changes on your life as you grow old?

7   Native Americans were not the only group within U.S. society to encounter the effects of government policies based on the "melting pot" model. This model was also applied to the wave of immigrants who came to the United States from southern and eastern Europe between 1880 and 1920. The children of these immigrants are among today's elderly Americans. Interview older relatives or family friends whose parents were part of this immigration. Do they have any memories of living between "two worlds": that of their immigrant parents and the Americanized world of their friends and school? How do they think these early experiences have affected their lives? What special strategies might be required in delivering services to these older individuals?

8   Political barriers precluded visits by Cuban Americans to their island homeland. How do you think open immigration and more frequent visits "back home" might have affected the aging experience among elderly Cuban Americans? How do the experiences of first-generation Cuban Americans compare with the experiences of other Latino immigrants to the United States? Of immigrants from various Asian countries?

SUGGESTIONS FOR FURTHER READING

1   Elder, G. H., Jr. (1985). Perspectives on the life course. In G. H. Elder, Jr. (Ed.), *Life course dynamics: Trajectories and transitions, 1968-1980* (pp. 23-27). Ithaca, NY: Cornell University Press.

An introduction to the life course perspective. In this introductory chapter, Elder develops a framework for the study of lives and aging based on life trajectories and social change.

2   Bengtson, V. L., Cutler, N., Mangen, D. J., & Marshall, V. W. (1985). Generations, cohorts, and relations between age groups. In R. H. Binstock & E. Shanas (Eds.), *Handbook of aging and the social sciences* (2nd ed., pp. 304-338). New York: Van Nostrand Reinhold.

What is a cohort? This chapter examines the empirical evidence concerning differences between and relationships across groups and individuals of contrasting age. A more sophisticated introduction to cohorts and the life course perspective.

3   Wilson, E. H., & Mullalley, S. (Ed.). (1983). *Hope and dignity: Older black women of the South.* Philadelphia: Temple University Press.

An anthology of short biographies based on interviews with older African American women. Although all of the central characters are disadvantaged on two hierarchies (gender and race), they represent a range of social class backgrounds, including a successful stockbroker on Wall Street and the wife of a college president.

4   Angelou, M. (1969). *I know why the caged bird sings.* New York: Random House.

This first of several autobiographical novels by the author illustrates the impact of race and sociohistorical time on the early life of the African American poet Maya Angelou, now in her sixties. This book chronicles her experiences growing up in Arkansas during the 1930s, and introduces readers to the racially segregated world before the Civil Rights movement and the adaptive strategies African Americans developed to survive both physically and emotionally.

5   Jen, G. (1991). *Typical American.* Boston: Houston Mifflin.

This novel traces the experiences of three young Chinese immigrants—two women and one man—who come to the United States to study in the early 1950s. This contemporary story of the immigrant experience describes the experiences of a cohort of Chinese Americans who are in their sixties today.

6   Shurkin, J. N. (1992). *Terman's kids: The groundbreaking study of how the gifted grow up.* Boston: Little, Brown.

This renowned study by Lewis Terman, begun in 1921, followed a group of gifted children throughout their lives. The survivors are now in their seventies and eighties. The stories of "Ancel," "Jess," "Shelley," and "Emily Tadashi" illustrate how hierarchies based on gender and social class produce varied lives—even among these gifted children who grew up and grew old in the same historical period.

7   CBS Fox Video. (1990). *Come see the paradise* [Film]. New York.

The Japanese internment during World War II is experienced through the eyes of a Japanese American family living in "Little Tokyo" in Los Angeles at the outbreak of the war. The film traces the family's experience through the war, including the realities of internment, and illustrates the way particular life events can both strengthen and weaken adaptive resources.

8   National Film Board of Canada. (1991). *Strangers in good company* [Film]. Burbank, CA: Buena Vista Home Video.

This film introduces us to a group of women who discover friendship and resourcefulness when their bus breaks down in the Quebec wilderness. The women confront old age and share their lives through reminiscences and old photographs. The women are not professional actresses, and the film lets each woman tell her story in her own way.

9   Dorris, M. (1987). *A yellow raft in blue water*. New York: Warner.

Beginning in the present and told backward in time, Dorris's novel tells the stories of three generations of Native American women. Hearing three versions of events in their lives illustrates dramatically the impact of historical time on three women who share similar positions on hierarchies based on gender, race or ethnicity, and social class but experience particular segments of historical time at different points in the life course.

10 Clausen, J. A. (1993). *American lives*. New York: Free Press.

Drawing on the groundbreaking Berkeley studies of human development, this book traces the lives of a sample of people born in the 1920s. Clausen demonstrates how adaptive strategies developed during an adolescence that coincided with the Great Depression continue to influence the lives of these individuals as they enter old age.

11 Silko, L. M. (1981). Lullaby. In *The storyteller*. New York: Seaver.

The limited lifetime options and powerlessness of a Native American couple weaken their adaptive resources in old age.

PART II

Social and Psychological Contexts of Aging

Cultural Images of Old Age

Old age is accompanied by physical changes. Our immune systems are less able to fight off disease, and our capacity to mobilize physical energy declines. Our hearing and vision become less acute. Changes in appearance, such as gray hair and wrinkled skin, become more prevalent. In the absence of disease, these changes seldom interfere with the ability to pursue desired activities or fulfill social obligations (Atchley, 1991). Age-related physical changes, however, occur within a cultural context that assigns meanings to physical characteristics, and often the symbolic rather than the functional consequences of age-related changes have the most negative impact on older people. Here we will explore the impact of cultural images about old age and the ways older people respond to them. Our discussion will emphasize

1. the images of old age reflected in our culture and the ways in which these images vary along hierarchies based on gender, race, and class;
2. the consequences of these images for older people and the strategies older people use to maintain positive self-concepts in the face of negative images or of positive images they cannot attain; and
3. the importance of considering variation within groups in interpreting comparisons between groups.

Contemporary U.S. culture reflects mixed images of older people. On the positive side, older people are viewed as wise, understanding, generous, happy, knowledgeable, and patriotic. On the negative side, they are depicted as forgetful, lonely, dependent, demanding, complaining, senile, selfish, and inflexible (Schmidt & Boland, 1986). Despite this mix of positive and negative stereotypes, most people do not want to get old. Only 2% of respondents in a national survey believed that the sixties are "the best years of a person's life." Older people themselves were not much more positive. Only 8% of people 65 years and older thought their sixties and seventies were their best years (National Council on the Aging, 1976).

Interest in ways to avoid the most negative aspects of aging has grown rapidly over the past several decades. Bookstores stock an expanding collection of titles advising older readers about fitness, nutrition, finances, and sexuality. Elderly Americans are advised to "keep their emotional balance," "stay active and involved," "pursue new interests," and "lead productive lives." What was once described as a "roleless role" has been transformed into a prescription for activity and personal growth, for an awareness of expanded options and possibilities. Marilyn Zuckerman's poem "After Sixty," one of the selections that follows, illustrates this redefinition of older women's lives.

Positive though these images of aging may be, they depict a lifestyle predicated on class privilege. Recommendations to join an exercise class, learn ballroom dancing, or take up lap swimming imply sufficient discretionary income to purchase lessons or gain access to appropriate facilities. Retirement financial planning assumes assets to invest, and preventive health care recommendations require insurance or other financial resources to pay for physician visits and laboratory tests. Older people with meager incomes and poor health as well as older people isolated in rural settings by lack of transportation or in inner cities by fear of crime are hard pressed to fulfill these popular recommendations for "successful aging."

The images of successful aging reflected in popular guides are more applicable to people in their sixties and seventies than to people in their eighties and nineties. Extreme old age is more often characterized by losses—loss of a future, of health and mobility, of cherished roles, of people one loves. Shortly before she died, Caroline Preston commented on the downside of these prescriptions for successful aging: "Such optimistic views of aging are as hard on us as our previous invisibility. We find ourselves yearning to be like people in these pictures and belabor ourselves for failing these role models" (quoted in Thone, 1992, p. 15). Norms for appropriate behavior in extreme old age are more nebulous. Ruth Raymond Thone (1992) suggests that emergent norms, at least for old women, can be captured in the phrase "aging gracefully," which she defines as being

> flexible, loving, a lady, positive, appreciative, accepting, tidy, active, open-minded, optimistic, proud of one's achievements, to have a zest for life, inner beauty, a sense of humor, to still learn and take risks, not to complain of one's aches and pains or other's faults, and not to worry about old age. (p. 13)

The selection from "Voices: An Epilogue" by actress Helen Hayes provides one woman's script for aging gracefully.

Not all elderly Americans define successful aging by positive adaptation and optimism. For many elders of color, aging is perceived "not as a series of adjustments, but rather as a process of survival" (Burton, Dilworth-Anderson, & Bengston, 1991). These contrasting images can be seen in the poem "Mother to Son" by Langston Hughes and the brief essay "If I Had My Life to Live Over" by Nadine Stair. Reflecting on her life, Stair concludes that she was "too sensible," that she worried about and prepared too much for difficulties that never materialized. She learned from her life experiences that many anticipated troubles were "imaginary" and that her efforts to avoid problems were often unnecessary. The elderly mother in Hughes's poem has reached no such conclusion. The struggle for survival that characterized her younger years is still the dominant theme in old age. She reflects not on daisies and merry-go-rounds but on tacks and splinters. Rather than advising the reader to travel lighter and be sillier, she admonishes her son not to fall or sit down on the steps, but to follow her example of "still climbin'."

Permutations in Images and Meanings of Old Age Images Related to Gender

Satchell Paige, who would never reveal his age but was probably the oldest man ever to play professional baseball, recognized old age as a social construct when he asked, "How old would you be if you didn't know how old you was?" For women in our society, the answer might well be "older than a man my age." Women are viewed as old at least a decade sooner than are men, and old age brings greater loss of status for women than for men. These gender differences in the social construction of age can be attributed to the emphasis on youth within our culture and to the association between youth and sexuality, especially for women (Andersen, 1993): "A man's wrinkles will not define him as sexually undesirable until he reaches his late fifties. For him, sexual value is defined much more in terms of personality, intelligence, and earning power than physical appearance. Women, however, must rest their case largely on their bodies" (Bell, 1989, p. 236). Internalization of negative images of aging is reinforced by advertisements for face creams and hair dyes and by birthday cards depicting women as "over the hill" at 40 or even 30. Given this double standard of aging, it is no wonder that many women are reluctant to reveal their age, try to "pass" as younger than they are, and are complimented when told they don't "look their age" (Bell, 1989). In her essay "Growing to Be an Old Woman," Shevy Healey shares her mixed reactions to such comments.

Although men also face negative stereotypes and loss of status as they get older, these experiences occur at a more advanced age. Compare, for example, the complexion of the female model who plans to fight aging "every step of the way" by using a popular moisturizer to that of the male model who touches up his graying hair. Negative consequences of aging for men focus more on occupational success than physical attractiveness (Andersen, 1993). That male model touching up his graying temples in the commercials is most concerned about his impression on his boss.

Negative though cultural images appear, older people do not internalize them uncritically. Older women retain an image of themselves grounded in the past, a sense of self that stays the same despite physical changes (Kaufman, 1986). The essay by Helen Hayes describes this strategy in another actress: "She was a little dumpy, she had lost a bit of her shape, but as far as she was concerned, she had not aged." A common device in comedy involving older women has the character exclaim, "Who's that?" after catching an unexpected glimpse of herself in a passing window. A 70-year-old woman interviewed by Kaufman (1986) explains the discrepancy between her chronological age and her subjective experience:

> I don't feel 70. I feel about 30. . . . I just saw some slides of myself and was quite taken aback. That couldn't be me. That's a nice looking woman, but it couldn't possibly be me. Even though I look in the mirror all the time, I don't see myself as old. (p. 8)

Dean Rodeheaver and Joanne Stohs (1991) argue that such misperceptions are adaptive strategies that help older women overcome the effects of negative images of aging. These subjective notions of age incorporate several dimensions: how old people feel (the psychological dimension), how old they think they look (the biological dimension), the age associated with the things they do (the social dimension), and the age associated with their interests (the cognitive dimension). Ronald Goldsmith and Richard Heims (1992) found that age is positively related to the likelihood that people report younger subjective rather than chronological age. For example, none of their respondents in their twenties thought they looked younger than their chronological age, but 73% of respondents in their sixties, 83% of respondents in their seventies, and all of the respondents in their eighties thought they looked younger than their chronological age. Similarly, whereas no one in their twenties said they felt younger than their chronological age, 77% of respondents in their sixties, 72% of respondents in their seventies, and 86% of respondents in their eighties felt younger than their chronological age. The age contrasts were even more striking with respect to interests and activities. Summarizing all four dimensions, no one in their twenties, but 80% of people in their sixties and seventies and 97% of people in their eighties, reported a subjective age below their chronological age. In contrast, 20% of people in their twenties reported a subjective age older than their chronological age, in comparison to 1% of people in their sixties and seventies and no one in their eighties!

Older people can also diminish the impact of negative images by reinterpreting them from the standpoint of their own experiences. Jenny Joseph's poem "Warning" illustrates this process by turning upside down the negative stereotype of the senile old woman wearing inappropriate clothes of clashing colors as she spends her money frivolously and violates rules of proper decorum. To Joseph, this behavior reflects greater freedom from social sanctions that constrain women "to set a good example." For today's older women, who were told that happiness came from fulfilling the needs of people they love, old age can be a time of autonomy, a time for "rediscovering and recreating themselves" (Thone, 1992, p. 63).

Images Related to Race/Ethnicity

Images of older people also vary by race and ethnicity. In some cases, these images reflect stereotypes based on the group in general, whereas in other cases, they apply primarily to old people.

Classic descriptions of old age in Native American cultures emphasized the respect accorded elderly people. Councils of elders were the centers of political decision making, and elders were responsible for transmitting culture across generations (Weibel-Orlando, 1989). The anthropologist Joan Weibel-Orlando (1989) studied contemporary characteristics of successful aging by interviewing Native American elders. She identified six criteria, all of which reflected an active engagement in ethnic life. Native American elders who ranked high on successful aging were involved in charitable activities with a wide range of kin, friends, and other coethnics. They evidenced a high level of involvement in community roles (e.g., head dancers at powwows, song and prayer leaders at sun dances, medicine men and women, tribal council members, family heads, and caretaking grandparents), roles for which elderly Native Americans are revered and that provide service to the ethnic community. Good health in late life was also associated with successful aging. As Weibel-Orlando (1989) explains,

> Good health in old age is not thought to be a given. Rather, it is a blessing. Long life is an indicator that a person may have been protected by powerful guardian spirits that kept him or her from harm's way when less well-endowed and protected age peers succumbed to diabetes, hypertension, alcoholism, and depression. (p. 63)

Older African Americans have confronted multiple negative images throughout their lives. African American women have been objectified as mammies, matriarchs, welfare recipients, and hot mommas (P. H. Collins, 1990), whereas African American men have been stereotyped as lazy workers, unstable husbands and fathers, and dangerous criminals. These controlling images are not the province of isolated individuals. Racist images have permeated political discourse. Public debates on African American families, for example, often use value-laden terms such as "disorganization, maladjustment, and deterioration" (Andersen, 1993). The infamous Moynihan report, published in 1965, attributed the "deterioration of the fabric of Negro society" (p. 5) to the matriarchal structure of African American families. Moynihan (1965) attributed poverty, welfare dependency, crime, and out-of-wedlock births to the fact that over 20% of African American households were headed by women. Moynihan's description of the "tangle of pathology" characterizing female-headed households assumed that family arrangements were the cause rather than the consequence of discrimination. Citing evidence that African American women had surpassed African American men in educational achievement and entrance in professional and semiprofessional occupations, the report suggested that African American women "slow down, become less achievement-oriented, and give up their independence" (Giddings, 1984, p. 328). It also urged the government not to rest "until every able-bodied Negro man was working, even if this meant that some women's jobs had to be redesigned to enable men to fulfill them" (Rainwater & Yancey, 1967, p. 29). As the historian Paula Giddings (1984) observed, "Not *White men's* jobs, mind you—women's jobs. . . . The Moynihan report was not so much racist as it was sexist" (pp. 328-329).

Stereotypical images also emerge from the popularization of research results. Studies of older minority populations often involve statistical comparisons of people of color with whites. Readers are shown, for example, that the average income of older African Americans is lower than the average income of older whites, that the percentage of elderly Hispanic Americans living below the poverty level is higher than the percentage of elderly whites, or that the probability of living in substandard housing is higher for Native Americans than for older whites. These statistical comparisons are accurate, and analyses of this type have been used successfully to justify allocating government dollars for public programs addressing the plight of low-income minority elders. Comparisons of group means, however, tell only part of the story. To fully comprehend the situation of any group of older people, we also need to consider differences within that group. From a statistical perspective, we need to consider dispersion or variation as well as central tendency (as introductory statistics students are often told, a person who doesn't swim can drown crossing a river that has an average depth of 3 feet). Statistical descriptions based on means can create an artificial picture of an "average" old person, such as the characterization of old African American women Jacqueline Jackson (1988) extracted from published reports:

> To illustrate with only slight exaggeration, the average old black woman lives in a blighted section of an inner-city or in an isolated rural area. Poor, poorly educated, and in poor health, she is economically dependent upon Social Security and other income transfer or in-kind programs (e.g., food stamps, subsidized housing, and Medicaid).
>
> This average old black woman is beset by problems, not the least of which are substandard housing in high crime areas, insufficient transportation, and inadequate access to mainstream health facilities, in part because she is stymied by and unable to cope successfully with bureaucratic institutions. If she is not gainfully employed, it is only because she is unemployed, involuntarily retired, or too ill or disabled to work. Old black women like to work because they gain dignity through working.
>
> A poor woman, she rarely uses community resources for the elderly, such as a center for senior citizens, most often because

she does not know about them nor of their eligibility requirements. . . . Extremely religious and often the matriarch of an extended family, [she] is surrounded by children, grandchildren, other relatives, or fictive kin, and by friends and neighbors who gleefully minister to her instrumental and emotional needs. "Granny" is also very happy when she is given the responsibility of rearing her grandchildren. (pp. 31-32)

Generalizing statistics based on aggregate data to predict the behavior or experiences of individuals is a type of error referred to as the "ecological fallacy." Although some older African American women are surrounded by supportive children and extended kin, others are isolated or are themselves caring for grandchildren whose parents are struggling with drug addiction or economic survival. Many older African American women are destitute, but others enjoy considerable affluence. Although their risk of poverty is considerably higher than it is among either white women or African American men, many older African American women live above the poverty line. And although some older African American women lack the educational resources to negotiate medical and social welfare organizations, others pursue careers as nurses, social workers, lawyers, or physicians. The biographical selection "Esse Quam Videri" in Part III, "Productive Activity," illustrates the ways in which a person can be advantaged on one hierarchy (social class) yet disadvantaged on others (race and gender). Mrs. Jones's life provides a sharp contrast to the image J. J. Jackson abstracted from accumulated averages.

Stereotypes need not always be negative in content to be detrimental in their consequences. The "model minority" myth applied to Asian Americans implies that unlike other people of color, Asians have "made it," that their diligence and hard work have been rewarded by economic success. This myth has several outcomes. First, like the composite of the "average African American woman," the image of the model minority ignores variation both among Asian American nationality groups in the United States and between generations within groups, thus obscuring the economic hardship and cultural isolation that many older Asian Americans experience. Studies reporting higher incomes among Asian American households often fail to adjust for the greater prevalence of multiple wage earners in Asian households and for the higher cost of living in geographic regions with high concentrations of Asian Americans (Woo, 1989). Second, they fail to report the situation of elderly households with low incomes, an omission that highlights again the importance of dispersion. The myth also overlooks the isolation experienced by recent elderly immigrants from Southeast Asia, who feel isolated not only by a different language and way of life but by the acculturation of their children and grandchildren. As we discuss in Part IV, "Family," first-generation Asian immigrants, who adhere more strongly to traditional views of old age and filial piety, are often confused and disappointed by the treatment they receive from their more Americanized children and grandchildren (Cheung, 1989). Finally, the model minority myth reinforces the ideology of a meritocracy and creates divisions among racial and ethnic groups. Claims that Asian Americans have succeeded because of values stressing hard work in school and career imply that the stratification system in the United States is open and fair and that other groups could be equally successful if only they had appropriate values.

As we saw with negative images based on gender, older people do not incorporate ethnic stereotypes uncritically. The combination of controlling images and a system of racial oppression taught minority elders the necessity of reflecting dominant images in many contacts outside their own communities. Although this behavior may have reinforced dominant group stereotypes, it did not necessarily mean that people of color had internalized negative stereotypes. Public displays of compliance with expectations of the dominant group often coexist with alternative conceptions of self. Ella Surrey, an elderly African American respondent in John Gwaltney's (1980) *Drylongso: A Self-Portrait of Black America*, described this situation: "We have always been the best actors in the world. . . . We've always had to live two lives—one for them and one for ourselves" (pp. 238, 240). The older domestic workers interviewed by the sociologist Judith Rollins (1985) had maintained positive self-concepts despite "attempts to lure them into accepting their employers' definition of them as inferior" (p. 212). Among the most powerful weapons in this resistance was their familiarity with intimate details of their employers' lives:

> Raising their voices to little girl pitch, adding hand and facial gestures suggesting confusion and immaturity, my interviewees would act out scenes from their past experiences—typically scenes in which the employer was unable to cope with some problem and had to rely on the guidance and pragmatic efficiency of the domestic. It was interesting that these domestics, described historically and by some of the employers as childlike, perceived their employers as "flighty" and childlike. How *could* they buy into the evaluations of women they so perceived? (p. 215)

Resistance to controlling images and assertions of alternative definitions of self have been important themes in writings by African Americans. Patricia Hill Collins (1990) explains that these alternative definitions have "allowed Black women to cope with and, in most cases transcend the confines of race, class and gender oppression. . . . Most African-American women simply don't define ourselves as Mammies, Matriarchs, welfare mothers, mules or sexually denigrated women" (p. 93). This process of reclaiming the power of self-definition is a major component in the struggle to maintain personal integrity in a climate of racism. Zora Neale Hurston's essay "How It Feels to Be Colored Me" illustrates the ways in which race influenced her identity.

In Part I, "The Life Course Perspective," we described the struggles of African American women to teach their daughters to confront negative images and racial discrimination while maintaining the emotional strength needed to survive. Elizabeth ("Bessie") Delany, who, with her sister Sarah ("Sadie"), chronicled her "first 100 years" in the book *Having Our Say* (1993), describes her early encounters with racism:

> This race business does get under my skin. I have suffered a lot in my life because of it. If you asked me how I endured it, I would have to say it was because I had a good upbringing. My parents did not encourage me to be bitter. If they had, I'd have been so mean it would have killed my spirit a long, long time ago.
>
> As a child, everytime I encountered prejudice—which was rubbed in your face, once segregation started under Jim Crow—I would feel it down to my core. I was not a crying child, except when it came to being treated badly because of my race, like when they wouldn't serve us at the drugstore counter. In those instances, I would go home and sit on my bed and weep and weep and weep, the tears streaming down my face.
>
> Now, Mama would come up and sit on the foot of my bed. She never said a word. She knew what I was feeling. She just did not want to encourage my rage. So my Mama would just sit and look at me while I cried, and it comforted me. I knew that she understood, and that was the most soothing salve. (p. 74)

As their collaborator Amy Heart explains, each sister developed her own strategies for coping with racism. Bessie, who was a dentist, espoused confrontation. For some of today's African Americans, struggles against racism included confrontation, coupled with efforts to change the fabric of U.S. society. Today's elders of color were among the leaders of the Civil Rights movement, which began in the 1950s. Although most civil rights leaders in history books are African American men, women also provided leadership. The writers Gloria Hull, Patricia Bell Scott, and Barbara Smith captured this omission in the title of their anthology, *All the Women Are White, All the Blacks Are Men, But Some of Us Are Brave*. For example, the organizing efforts of the Women's Political Council, an organization of middle-class African American women in Montgomery, Alabama, played a central role in organizing that city's bus boycott, which was sparked by the arrest of Rosa Parks. An activist with the National Association for the Advancement of Colored People (NAACP), Mrs. Parks was arrested when she refused to give up her seat to a white male passenger.

Confrontation is not the only strategy for coping with racism. Sadie Delany, who was a schoolteacher, manipulated the system by role-playing, a strategy of which her sister did not always approve. Bessie describes one incident:

> Once, when we were new to the neighborhood, a white policeman came knocking on the door. We were a little afraid. What did he want from us? Well, we went upstairs and opened the window and called down to him. That's what we do when we aren't sure about opening the door for someone. Sadie said to me, "Let me handle him." She leaned out the window and said:
> "Officer, can I help you?"
> And he called up: "We're raising money for the auxiliary, and I'm selling tickets to a dance."
> And she giggled and said, "Why officer, thank you very much, but I'm too old to go to a dance!" And she giggled some more and shut the window.
> Now, I just hate it when Sadie plays dumb like that! I told her, "Sadie, that fella must think you're the dumbest nigger alive." And she said, "So what? I didn't make him angry, did I? And I've still got my money, don't I?" It annoys me, but I have to admit she was right. (Delany & Delany, 1993, p. 194)

The excerpt from Pardee Lowe's autobiographical story "Father Cures a Presidential Fever" provides another illustration of childhood encounters with racism among people who are elderly today. Lowe's selection describes a young Chinese American boy's encounter with what Marie Hong (1993) describes as "the precarious position of Asian Americans during the 1910s and 1920s" (p. 175).

Images Related to Social Class

Images of older people have always been tied to social class, but our cultural images of poverty and affluence in old age have changed in recent years. Along with poor health, poverty is one of the most dreaded aspects of old age. Images of destitute old men subsisting in skid row hotels or of "shopping bag ladies" carrying their lifetime of accumulated possessions in grocery carts have replaced images of the county poor farm in popular representations of poverty in late life. People today are less likely to blame older people for low economic status than they were earlier in this century. Pre-Depression beliefs that poverty in old age resulted from laziness and failure to save for the future have been displaced by images of older people as the "deserving poor," images that provide political justifications for income transfers such as Social Security and Medicare. These changes are recent, however, and today's older people grew up with the pre-Depression stereotypes of the elderly poor, stereotypes that blamed the victim. Values emphasizing hard work, thrift, and self-reliance can still undermine self-esteem and discourage acceptance of programs viewed as "welfare" or "poverty" among some old people, particularly those in the oldest cohorts.

Older people today are less likely to be poor than were older people in the past, and the economic situation of older Americans has improved dramatically over the past two decades, particularly in comparison to younger people (Minkler, 1989). Median family incomes for older families (i.e., families headed by people 65 years and older) more than doubled between 1970 and 1980, whereas family income for young families (i.e., families headed by people younger than 25) declined by 15% (Congressional Budget Office, 1988). The percentage of older people living in poverty has also declined, from 35% in 1960 to just over 11% in 1990 (McLaughlin & Jensen, 1993).

The relative improvement in the economic status of the older population has given rise to a new class-related stereotype: the affluent older person who collects unearned and unneeded benefits at the expense of less affluent workers. Former President Reagan's political strategy of argument by anecdote gave credence to the image of wealthy widows in their penthouse apartments collecting monthly Social Security checks withheld from the earnings of young, working-class fathers struggling to support their family on wages that barely covered fixed expenses. Older people have also become scapegoats for the burgeoning budget deficit. According to this "intergenerational inequity" argument, elderly people receive too large a portion of public social expenditures, primarily through Social Security and medical care benefits. Social Security and Medicare expenditures were not only producing a tax burden on current generations of young workers, the argument goes, they were also diminishing the standard of living for subsequent generations, because paying interest on the federal debt will limit economic growth and future productivity (Kingson, 1988).

This new stereotype of the affluent elderly population has also been reflected in advertising. Twenty years ago, old people were absent from advertisements, except those selling products such as laxatives and denture adhesives. Today, advertisements geared specifically to older consumers feature tennis rackets, luxury automobiles, and Caribbean cruises as well as vitamins, health insurance, and (almost-invisible) hearing aides. The models in these ads, although visibly gray (or, more likely, silver haired), are active, physically fit adults enthusiastically pursuing or sagely planning their retirement leisure. These new marketing strategies provide a welcome contrast to the negative images of old age in past advertising, but as Meredith Minkler (1989) warns, the new stereotype they create can deflect attention from the needs of low-income elderly people. Although only 11.4% of Americans over 65 have incomes below the poverty line, the risk of poverty increases to 31% for elderly African Americans and nearly 21% for elderly Hispanic Americans (McLaughlin & Jensen, 1993). Among

African American elders living alone, the poverty rate increases to more than 60%. The selection "Survival Strategies of Older Homeless Men" by Carl Cohen, Jeanne Teresi, Douglas Holmes, and Eric Roth describes the situation of some of these elderly poor. Minkler (1989) is concerned that these disadvantaged elderly people not be hidden behind what she describes as a misleadingly homogeneous picture of the affluent older consumer: "As low income elderly persons are rendered less visible, . . . governments may find increasing justification for cutbacks in the programs and services that are most needed by those elderly people who fail to fit the new, affluent stereotype" (p. 22).

Key Issues

Here we have discussed the following issues:

1. Positive and negative images of older people and popular prescriptions for "successful aging"
2. The double standard of aging and images related to gender
3. Strategies for confronting negative images based on race or ethnicity
4. Positive and negative consequences of changing images of poverty and affluence in old age

The Readings

Several of the readings that follow illustrate attempts to embrace positive definitions of aging. Marilyn Zuckerman's poem "After Sixty" reflects an awareness of expanded options and possibilities for women as they enter old age. Rejecting the view of postmenopausal women as no longer useful or productive, Zuckerman declares old age as a time to invent a new story for her life. Rather than mourning lost roles, she redefines them as "distractions" that she will "not take with her" on the rest of life's journey. On the "other side of sixty," there is still time to invent a new story.

The selection from "Voices: An Epilogue" by actress Helen Hayes illustrates Ruth Raymond Thone's notion of what it means to "age gracefully." It also illustrates Thone's point that it is easier to age gracefully when one has had a privileged life. Hayes, who was born in 1900 and died in 1993, was often called "the First Lady of the American Theater." This essay was written when she was 72 years old. Recognizing the losses that have accompanied growing old (her husband died, her son grew up, and she retired from acting), she describes her life, her enjoyment of being alone, and her feelings about old age.

Several other selections also illustrate the meanings people attach to old age. We already introduced several of these readings:

Langston Hughes's poem "Mother to Son," Nadine Stair's essay "If I Had My Life to Live Over," and Jenny Joseph's poem "Warning." Shevy Healey's essay "Growing to Be an Old Woman" illustrates a more angry response. Healey relates her mixed reactions to comments that she "doesn't look her age" and shares her struggles to understand what it means to become an old woman in contemporary U.S. society. Her essay includes a chilling indictment of the invisibility of old women in our society. "It is difficult," she writes, "to hold on to one's own sense of self, to one's own dignity when all around you there is no affirmation of you." She ends on a positive tone, illustrating once again the importance of deconstructing negative imagery and grasping the power to define oneself.

This process of defining oneself is also illustrated in Zora Neale Hurston's selection "How It Feels to Be Colored Me." Hurston's descriptions of the "day that I became colored" and of the times when "my color comes" illustrate race as a social construct rather than as a biological trait. As a child in an all-black community, Zora noticed differences in skin color, but these differences were not a central principle in organizing her identity. "During this period," she writes, "white people differed from colored to me only in that they rode through town and never lived there." Only when she left her small Florida town to attend school in Jacksonville did she become "a little colored girl . . . in my heart as well as in the mirror."

Encountering racism, however, did not mean internalizing its imagery. In recognizing the constraints a segregated world attempts to impose on her, she transcends their psychic impact. "I am not tragically colored," she writes. Instead, she confronts her world of barriers and opportunities with "a sharpened oyster knife." Not all older African Americans grew up in racially homogeneous towns. Most, however, grew up in racially homogeneous families and in racially homogeneous neighborhoods. As Jackson, McCullough, Gurin, and Broman (1991) have demonstrated, these racially homogeneous environments serve an important insulating function in developing identities independent of racist imagery.

Pardee Lowe's autobiographical account "Father Cures a Presidential Fever" provides another account of a child's encounter with the constraints of racism and with the contradiction between values and reality that the Swedish economist Gunnar Myrdahl characterized as "the American Dilemma." Told by his elementary teacher that "every single one of you can be President of the United States someday," the young Lowe is unprepared for the blatant prejudice and discrimination that faced Chinese Americans in the early decades of the century. Unlike the African American mothers we have described, Lowe's father did not grow up in the United States, and Lowe's story illustrates a cultural conflict between the Chinese father and the Chinese American son. The 1910s and 1920s were characterized by a "melting pot" ideology, which frequently produced a wedge between foreign-born parents and their

"Americanizing" children. Mr. Lowe, who is in his nineties, received an M.B.A. from Harvard University in 1932 and was the U.S. State Department officer in charge of UNESCO Affairs in Asia, Africa, and the Middle East.

Barbara Kingsolver's story "Homeland" describes a Cherokee family's encounter with commercial caricatures of Native American culture. Our excerpt begins with a family's journey to Great Mam's childhood home in the Smoky Mountains. The narrator is Great Mam's great-granddaughter. Now an adult, she recalls the episode from her childhood. As children, she and her brothers sometimes had difficulty merging popular images of Indians with their own identities. "Are we going to be Indians when we grow up?" asks her young brother. Great Mam has no such conflicts, as she fails—or refuses—to connect the constructed image of the hybrid Indian with memories of her childhood home. "I've never been here before," she says. Kingsolver's story also illustrates the role of the Native American elder as a transmitter of ethnic heritage, the cultural conservator role described by Weibel-Orlando's selection "Grandparenting Styles: Native American Perspectives" in Section IV, "Family."

The selection "Survival Strategies of Older Homeless Men" by Carl Cohen and his colleagues describes the living situation of some of the elderly poor who can be overlooked by media images stressing newfound affluence among older people. These researchers interviewed 281 homeless men aged 50 and older, 69% of whom were white, 26% of whom were African American, and 4% of whom were Latino. The experiences of these men illustrate several key points. First, not all older Americans are characterized by improvements in economic status, which are reflected in aggregate statistics. Once again, we learn the importance of considering variation as well as central tendency. Second, these men are not passive victims. Despite poor health, limited financial resources, and a treacherous environment, these men manage to survive: "The ability of these men to somehow garner the resources to endure suggests an inner strength that contrasts with a popular image of these men as helpless, passive dregs of society." Finally, the reading reminds us of interlocking hierarchies based on gender, race, and class. All of the respondents are men and the majority of them are white, yet they are clearly disadvantaged by social class.

After Sixty

Marilyn Zuckerman

The sixth decade is coming to an end
Doors have opened and shut
The great distractions are over—
    passion . . . children . . . the long
    indenture of marriage
I fold them into a chest
I will not take with me when I go

Everyone says the world is flat and finite
    on the other side of sixty
That I will fall clear off the edge
    into darkness
That no one will hear from me again
    or want to

But I am ready for the knife slicing
    into the future
    for the quiet that explodes inside
    to join forces with the strong old woman
    to throw everything away and begin
    again

Now there is time to tell the story
    —time to invent the new one
Time to chain myself to a fence outside the
    missile base
To throw my body before a truck loaded
    with phallic images
To write Thou Shalt Not Kill
    on the hull of a Trident submarine
To pour my own blood on the walls of the
    Pentagon
To walk a thousand miles with a begging
    bowl in my hand

There are places on this planet
    where women past the menopause
    put on the tribal robes
    smoke pipes of wisdom
    —fly

Source: "After Sixty" by M. Zuckerman, from *Ourselves, Growing Older,* edited by P. Doress and D. Ziegel, 1987. NY: Simon and Schuster. Reprinted with permission of the author.

Voices: An Epilogue

Helen Hayes

Sometimes in the morning I pretend I'm still a great star of the theater and very carefully carry my breakfast to my room on a tray, using my best breakfast china and my best tray cloth. Everything is exquisite. Then I put it on the little table by my bed and crawl in, putting on a very pretty bed jacket, the tray on my lap—and I'm a star in bed having breakfast. It's fun, and it brings me back into the old rhythm and feeling. But usually I don't sleep late. I don't want to miss too much of the days that are left me—it isn't as wistful an idea as that—it's just that I love to be up and about, seeing the morning. I do bits and pieces around the house that need to be done. I do some writing, letters and things of that sort. That's another hour or two. Then in the summer and autumn, I have much to do in the garden. It is a very beautiful garden which I very much love and work in a lot.

As a matter of fact, since I've been alone and had fewer responsibilities and since I have, for sure, left my profession, I find the days are too short for me. Funny. Once in a while, I do a little television. When you've had a very active life, it is frightening to try to be inactive all at once. But being alone has its good points. I like coddling myself, thinking about me first, before anybody else. I don't know that I ever did that before. But it is pleasant, and aside from a few twinges of

conscience—which happens once in a while—I'm living with that very well.

There were many times in my life, until I was left alone, that I wished for solitude. I now find that I love solitude. I never had the blessed gift of being alone until the last of my loved ones was wrested from me. Now I can go sometimes for days and days without seeing anyone. I'm not entirely alone, because I listen to the radio and read the newspapers. I love to read. That is my greatest new luxury, having the time to read. And oh, the little things I find to do that make the days, as I say, much too short.

Solitude—walking alone, doing things alone—is the most blessed thing in the world. The mind relaxes and thoughts begin to flow and I think that I am beginning to find myself a little bit.

I never had time for myself. I was always busy making the acquaintance of other people, and entertaining them in my home or in the theater. . . . Now I have that time. I've found that though I have a lot of faults, and I am aware of them, I can live with myself. I've learned to forgive myself for some of the mistakes I've made. I've learned to tell myself that when I made mistakes, I had a good reason at the time, or thought I had, and that there couldn't have been any other way than the way it was. For instance, I've refused plays that I didn't like and they've turned out to be great successes. Instead of mourning that and blaming myself for having missed out, with another actress achieving that success, I say to myself, but it would have been

Source: "Voices: An Epilogue" by H. Hayes, from *The Woman Alone*, by P. O'Brian. Copyright © 1973 by Patricia O'Brian Koval. Reprinted by permission of Times Books, a division of Random House, Inc.

so terrible not liking that play or that role if I had done it and it had been a success and I had been forced to play it every night for months.

Unfortunately, I know mostly women now. I like men better, but I am very happy with my women friends. One of the proud things in my life is that I know two women who have been my friends over sixty years. And I spent my seventy-first birthday with one of them on the tenth of October in New Hampshire. She also is a widow. My husband died fifteen years ago, and for two years I was just about as crazy as you can be and still be at large. I didn't have any really normal minutes during those two years.

It wasn't just grief. It was total confusion. A woman who loves a man, who has had the good fortune and good sense to marry a particularly bright one whom she trusts—I think she feels very helpless when he dies. I did. I've known other women, like Mrs. Wendell Willkie, who were terribly thrown by that loss when it came to them. I was frightened and alone. I felt unable to decide. Decisions were terrible—Charlie had always been watchful and supportive and protective about me in the theater. We don't all have a gift for being alone, living with ourselves. Some of us are afraid of ourselves. I don't know why. It must be something that goes way back, deep-seated in childhood. With some people it is so bad that they cannot trust themselves to be individuals and can only live as part of a group.

My great advantage was my career—it was there to protect me like a wonderful life preserver keeping me on top of it all, keeping me from sinking. A career is a good tranquilizer for the spirit when a woman is alone. I think it is good. But I've seen other women, without the advantage of a job or a career—the tranquilizers they choose are the more obvious ones, like the bottle or the bridge table.

After Charlie died, my friends finally persuaded me to do a picture, *Anastasia*, with Ingrid Bergman and Yul Brynner. I said, No, I can't, I haven't the will to do anything at the moment. They were so persistent, and they didn't realize I needed time to mend. I needed quiet time, apart time. Grief is a very feeling thing. If I had had a chance to sit still and indulge in grief, I think it would have made my time of recovery much quicker, shorter.

Instead I went over to England to do this film, and found myself doing the oddest things. I had always been so reliable and dependable, always on the job—a real trouper, they called me. Well, one time I took off, went to Brighton with a friend. I just took a fancy to go to Brighton and I went, and left no forwarding address at the hotel where I was living. Heavens, the picture company was beside itself. I had completely put it out of my mind that I was making a movie. Curious, isn't it?

That's a time I look back on and flinch to think of, because I was most unattractive. Unreliable and erratic. I squabbled with directors—I had never squabbled before. I took umbrage at nothing at all. I gave rather pompous and silly statements to the press. I was nutty, and that's the truth. How did I come out of it? I don't know, because I didn't know when I was in it that I was in it.

Now I look back and can see how my self-image had to change. Until Charlie died, I was pretty darned arrogant. There was actually a time when I felt, why did God give me this gift of being so right so much of the time? Why should I be the one who always chooses the right play, the right line of action? I literally felt infallible. I don't any more. Unfortunately, today you have to be courageous to the point of audacity in the theater. It's one of the reasons I wanted to get away from it, get out of it, because I became too nervous and too frightened of my decisions. I told you I relied on Charlie. Really, he was making the decisions, but I wasn't recognizing it or acknowledging it to myself.

I think the problems of being an actress and finding myself alone have been no different from the problems of anyone else widowed or divorced. My private life has been far removed from my theater life. It was different for Katharine Cornell—at the time Guthrie McClintic died, a good ten or fifteen years ago, Kit walked off that stage and never walked on a stage again, never wanted to, never had the nerve to. And truly, I've been marking time since Charlie died. I haven't wanted, really, to be an actress since. Without his judgments.

I'm such a compulsive planner, now. I really bore myself with the way I fuss over plans. Every once in a while my companion will say, look it's six months off, Miss Hayes, can't we just wait? And I say, no, no, no, we have to straighten this out. It's a little crazy, I think, to make all these picky plans. I do it more than I ever did before, but of course, I depended on Charlie to do a lot of that. Not that he was much of a planner, but I would go along with him, and then we would just plunge ahead with whatever was to be done.

I'm seventy-two now, and I have to face up to some of the things that happen with age. I suppose I've tried to prove to myself and the world that I'm not getting old and deteriorated. My mind is as sharp as ever. I *can* remember things. I *can* think of the right word that I want to use. I *can* converse. The effort—to prove all this makes me apt to overdo—trying to prove myself a little more than when I was young. It's nervousness about the deterioration of time—talking too much, trying to be funny too much. You have to face the idea that others have of you. As a dried-out lemon.

Oh, well, you just have to roll with the punches, to use the vernacular. For one thing, I used to take it for granted that if you were a celebrity, a star, you just walked into a room and things would happen, simply because it was you who walked in. Now I don't feel that. I take the back seat a lot, and that's a hard transition for someone who's been in the driver's seat through life.

Little things keep happening, and I'm startled. For example, there is a film I was asked to do by a producer recently. He and the writer were in love with it, and they were so eager for me to do it. They spent a year trying to raise the money to do that film in which I would have been the star. And they couldn't raise the money. That's a new thing for me—they couldn't raise the money for me to star. That means something extraordinary has happened. What do you do when you face that?

Well, I just told myself, all right, no more trying for star roles. If I want to be in the theater or films, I will play character roles, with young stars. There is nothing wrong with that. It's the general pattern of the great all-time stars. Youth should be served by age always. This is as it should be.

But this isn't the route for everyone. I remember Booth Tarkington years ago telling me about how he tried to get Maude Adams back on the stage when she had been gone many, many years. He wrote a play about an actress who was getting on and a young man who had a great feeling about this actress— two people, young and old, who come together. In the play, she taught him not to think of her age and he taught *her* not to think of it . . . but age, with capital letters, was the subject of the play. Poor Mr. Tarkington thought that was a graceful way to bring Maude Adams back. But she had been Peter Pan—how do you bring Peter Pan back as a middle-aged woman?

Well, she went to stay at his house, and he gave her the play in the evening to read. The next morning she came down and told him, "I don't understand this play at all. I couldn't possibly be in it, because I can't understand it." Puzzled, he said, "What's unclear about it?" And she said, "I have no realization of my age, I never think in terms of age. In going through this play, it is all about age. I have never aged."

And there it is. She was a little dumpy, she had lost a bit of her shape, but as far as she was concerned she had not aged. And she wasn't about to let anybody impose it on her. I wish it were possible for most of us to feel that way. Not that we would go gamboling about like lambs, but that we could stop trying to pretend we are young.

It's awfully hard to keep on remembering that I'm old. I'm as capable of romantic dreams as I have ever been in my life, but here in this country we have a sense of embarrassment about older people trying to enjoy some of the things they enjoyed in their youth. I knew a brilliant and attractive woman with money, widowed, very bright, and she was over sixty. We had supper one night in London, and she told me why she had moved there from the United States. She said, "I would have been covered with shame to be seen going out to dinner or to dance with a young man, but no one thinks anything of my doing it here in London. I don't have to be scorned for taking on a gigolo, as they call it." They were not gigolos, they were young friends. She likes to dance with young men, to be surrounded by young people, and she particularly likes having an escort.

There is nothing wrong with that woman. Her taste is impeccable. But here in the United States it would have looked atrocious, so she moved. It's almost an Oriental attitude. When I was in Korea I used to look at those elderly couples in their kind of uniforms—a gray Korean coat, the national dress, made exactly like the gay colored ones the young people wore, but gray. And their hats—the men look like old mother witch with those high-pointed crowns. All that gray stuff. They put on those uniforms when they reach a certain age, and that's that.

So here, women my age try to do the twist. Or they did—going down to the Peppermint Lounge in New York, trying to learn the twist. Why? Everybody over forty-five has a touch of arthritis and it must hurt to do the twist. That isn't natural. And it isn't natural for women whose shapes are changing—one's shape does change as one grows older—to put on miniskirts and try to wear the things youngsters look so adorable in, with their coltish figures, and their long, straight, beautiful legs. Women my age, we should wear the things that look best on us. And stop carrying on like crazy. How silly it is—but it's the philosophy of this land, I suppose.

12

Mother to Son

Langston Hughes

Well, son, I'll tell you:
Life for me ain't been no crystal stair.
It's had tacks in it,
And splinters,
And boards torn up,
And places with no carpet on the floor—
Bare.
But all the time
I'se been a-climbin' on,
And reachin' landin's,
And turnin' corners,
And sometimes goin' in the dark
Where there ain't been no light.
So boy, don't you turn back.
Don't you set down on the steps
'Cause you finds it's kinder hard.
Don't you fall now—
For I'se still goin', honey,
I'se still climbin',
And life for me ain't been no crystal stair.

Source: "Mother to Son" from *Selected Poems of Langston Hughes* by L. Hughes. Copyright © 1926 by Alfred A. Knopf, Inc., and renewed 1954 by Langston Hughes. Reprinted by permission of the publisher.

13

If I Had My Life to Live Over

Nadine Stair

I'd dare to make more mistakes next time. I'd relax, I would limber up. I would be sillier than I have been this trip. I would take fewer things seriously. I would take more chances. I would climb more mountains and swim more rivers. I would eat more ice cream and less beans. I would perhaps have more actual troubles, but I'd have fewer imaginary ones.

You see, I'm one of those people who live sensibly and sanely hour after hour, day after day. Oh, I've had my moments, and if I had it to do over again, I'd have more of them. In fact, I'd try to have nothing else. Just moments, one after another, instead of living so many years ahead of each day. I've been one of those persons who never goes anywhere without a thermometer, a hot water bottle, a raincoat and a parachute. If I had to do it again, I would travel lighter than I have.

If I had my life to live over, I would start barefoot earlier in the spring and stay that way later in the fall. I would go to more dances. I would ride more merry-go-rounds. I would pick more daisies.

Source: "If I Had My Life to Live Over" by N. Stair. Reprinted in *If I Had My Life to Live Over, I Would Pick More Daisies,* edited by Sandra Haldeman Martz. Watsonville, CA: Papier-Mache Press, 1992.

14

Warning

Jenny Joseph

When I am an old woman I shall wear
    purple
With a red hat which doesn't go, and
    doesn't suit me.
And I shall spend my pension on brandy
    and summer gloves
And satin sandals, and say we've no money
    for butter.
I shall sit down on the pavement when I'm
    tired
And gobble up samples in shops and press
    alarm bells
And run my stick along the public railings
And make up for the sobriety of my youth.
I shall go out in my slippers in the rain
And pick the flowers in other people's
    gardens
And learn to spit.

You can wear terrible shirts and grow more
    fat
And eat three pounds of sausages at a go
Or only bread and pickle for a week
And hoard pens and pencils and beermats
    and things in boxes.

But now we must have clothes that keep us
    dry
And pay our rent and not swear in the street
And set a good example for the children.
We must have friends to dinner and read
    the papers.

But maybe I ought to practise a little now?
So people who know me are not too
    shocked and surprised
When suddenly I am old, and start to wear
    purple.

Source: "Warning" from *Selected Poems,* by J. Joseph,
published by Bloodaxe Books Ltd. Copyright © 1992 by
Jenny Joseph. Reprinted with permission of John
Johnson Limited.

15

Growing to Be an Old Woman:
Aging and Ageism

Shevy Healey

In my late fifties, and then my sixties, I heard, "I can't believe you're that old. You don't look that old." At first that felt like a compliment. Then I became a bit uneasy. It reminded me of early pre-feminist days when I was complimented by some men for being "smarter," "more independent" than those "other" women. What was I now—a token "young"?

Slowly other experiences began to accumulate, reminding me of a real change in my life status.

First, I moved. And while I found easy acceptance among older people in the community, when younger people talked to me they invariably would say something like, "You remind me of my grandmother." Grandmother?! I felt labeled and diminished somehow.

Recently, I have, in fact, become a grandmother. I found most young friends expected me—automatically—to "be" a certain way. Many of those expectations were in accord with what I felt. Some were not. I did not instantly fall in love with my grandson. I was much more drawn to my daughter and what she was experiencing. I must admit that I am now a doting grandmother, but being put in a particular slot about that was a bit disquieting, as though all of my reactions could be gauged in advance and belonged to the generic group "grandmother" rather than to me.

I attended a Women's Action for Nuclear Disarmament (WAND) meeting at which a young M.D. spoke about his research with children all over the world and their responses to the atom bomb. His talk was stimulating, and after the meeting I went up to him to comment on his research. I had the most peculiar feeling of being looked through, as though, what could I, this gray-haired woman in very casual dress, know about research design. I felt patronized, a feeling I wasn't used to.

I lost some money recently through bad judgment and suddenly had the realization that I would never be able to replace it. I do not have enough time left to be able to earn that money again.

I looked in the mirror and saw lots of wrinkles. I had a hard time fitting that outward me with the me inside. I felt like the same person, but outside I looked different. I checked into a face lift, with much trepidation. What a seduction took place in that doctor's office! He told me he would make me less strange to myself. I would look more like I felt! I became frightened by the whole process. Who was I then? This face? What I felt like inside? How come the two images were not connected? My own ageism told me that

Source: Presented to the National Women's Studies Association Conference, Seattle, Washington, June 21, 1985; edited for Calyx. Excerpted from "Growing to Be an Old Woman" by S. Healey, which was first published in *Women and Aging,* edited by Jo Alexander et al. Copyright © 1986. Published by Calyx Books. Reprinted by permission of the publisher.

how I looked outside was ugly. But I felt the same inside, not ugly at all.

Finally, death entered my life as a direct reality. My oldest friend died of cancer three years ago. My father died two years ago after what turned out to be needless surgery. Another close friend died last month after a year of struggling with cancer. My mother is dying slowly and painfully after suffering a massive stroke. The realization hit me that I can expect this kind of personal contact with death to occur with greater and greater frequency.

Not just my chronological age, but life itself was telling me that I was becoming an older/old woman!

Think of all the adjectives that are most disrespectful in our society. They are all part of the ageist stereotyping of old women: pathetic, powerless, querulous, complaining, sick, weak, conservative, rigid, helpless, unproductive, wrinkled, asexual, ugly, unattractive, and on, ad nauseam. There is, by the way, an exception to this, and that is the stereotype of the wise old woman. She, of course, never complains, is never sick, and although no one really would want to *be* with her, occasionally it might be fine to sit at her feet!

How did this happen, this totally denigrating picture of old women? To understand this phenomenon we must look at sexism, for ageism is inextricably tied to sexism and is the logical extension of its insistence that women are only valuable when they are attractive and useful to men.

Under the guise of making themselves beautiful, women have endured torture and self-mutilation, cramped their bodies physically, maimed themselves mentally, all in order to please and serve men better, as men defined the serving, because only in that service could women survive.

Footbinding, for example, reminds us how false and relatively ephemeral those external standards of beauty and sexuality are. We can feel horror at what centuries of Chinese women had to endure. Do we feel the same horror at the process which determines that gray hair, wrinkled skin, fleshier bodies are not beautiful, and therefore ought to be disguised, pounded, starved to meet an equally unrealistic (and bizarre) standard set by the patriarchy? Women spend their lives accepting the premise that to be beautiful one must be young, and only beauty saves one from being discarded. The desperation with which women work to remove signs of aging attests only to the value they place upon themselves as desirable and worthwhile, in being primarily an object pleasing to men. Women's survival, both physical and psychological, has been linked to their ability to please men, and the standards set are reinforced over and over by all the power that the patriarchy commands. The final irony is that all of us, feminists included, have incorporated into our psyches the self-loathing that comes from not meeting that arbitrary standard.

As we alter and modify our bodies in the hopes of feeling good, we frequently achieve instead an awful estrangement from our own bodies. In the attempt to meet that arbitrary external standard, we lose touch with our own internal body messages, thus alienating ourselves further from our own sources of strength and power.

What does this have to do with aging and ageism? Having spent our lives estranged from our own bodies in the effort to meet that outer patriarchal standard of beauty, it is small wonder that the prospect of growing old is frightening to women of all ages. We have all been trained to be ageist. By denying our aging we hope to escape the penalties placed upon growing old. But in so doing we disarm ourselves in the struggle to overcome the oppression of ageism.

To deal with our own feelings about aging we must scrupulously examine how we have been brainwashed to believe that three-inch feet are beautiful, or whatever equivalent myth is currently being purveyed. The old have done what all oppressed people do: they have internalized the self-hatred embodied in the ageist stereotyping. First they try to pass, at least in their own minds if not in the minds of others. They separate themselves from those "others," the old people. They are youthful. I know a woman who at 80 described how she visited the "old folks' home." She was not "one of them." That's not cute on her part. It is simply an expression of how she has incorporated that "old" is "awful," and she wants no part of that powerlessness and marginality. She has found a way to affirm herself but it's at the expense of others. For all people who try to pass the price is high. In passing you are saying that who you are at 60, 70, 80 is *not* O.K. You are O.K. only to the degree that you are like someone else, someone younger, who has more value in the eyes of others.

It is difficult to hold on to one's own sense of self, to one's own dignity when all around you there is no affirmation of you. At best there may be a patronizing acknowledgment; at worst, you simply do not exist.

The oppressed old woman is required to be cheerful. But if you're smiling all the time, you acquiesce to being invisible and docile, participating in your own "erasure." If you're not cheerful then you are accused of being bitter, mean, crabby, complaining! A real Catch-22.

Old people are shunted off to their own ghettos. Frequently they will say they like it better. But who would not when, to be with younger people is so often to be invisible, to be treated as irrelevant and peripheral, and sometimes even as disgusting.

We have systematically denigrated old women, kept them out of the mainstream of productive life, judged them primarily in terms of failing capacities and functions, and then found them pitiful. We have put old women in nursing "homes" with absolutely no intellectual stimulation, isolated from human warmth and nurturing contact, and then condemned them for their senility. We have impoverished, disrespected, and disregarded old women, and then dismissed them as inconsequential and uninteresting. We have made old women invisible so that we do not have to confront our patriarchal myths about what makes life valuable or dying painful.

Having done that, we then attribute to the process of aging *per se* all the evils we see and fear about growing old. It is not aging that is awful, nor whatever physical problems may accompany aging. What is awful is how society treats old women and their problems. To the degree that we accept and allow such treatment we buy the ageist assumptions that permit this treatment.

What then does it really mean to grow old? For me, first of all, to be old is to be *myself*. No matter how patriarchy may classify and categorize me as invisible and powerless, I exist. I am an ongoing person, a sexual being, a person who struggles, for whom there are important issues to explore, new things to learn, challenges to meet, beginnings to make, risks to take, endings to ponder. Even though some of my options are diminished, there are new paths ahead.

16

How It Feels to Be Colored Me

Zora Neale Hurston

I am colored but I offer nothing in the way of extenuating circumstances except the fact that I am the only Negro in the United States whose grandfather on the mother's side was not an Indian chief.

I remember the very day that I became colored. Up to my thirteenth year I lived in the little Negro town of Eatonville, Florida. It is exclusively a colored town. The only white people I knew passed through the town going to or coming from Orlando. The native whites rode dusty horses, the Northern tourists chugged down the sandy village road in automobiles. The town knew the Southerners and never stopped cane chewing when they passed. But the Northerners were something else again. They were peered at cautiously from behind curtains by the timid. The more venturesome would come out on the porch to watch them go past and got just as much pleasure out of the tourists as the tourists got out of the village.

The front porch might seem a daring place for the rest of the town, but it was a gallery seat for me. My favorite place was atop the gate-post. Proscenium box for a born first-nighter. Not only did I enjoy the show, but I didn't mind the actors knowing that I liked it. I usually spoke to them in passing. I'd wave at them and when they returned my salute, I would say something like this: "Howdy-do-

Source: "How It Feels to Be Colored Me" by Z. Neale Hurston. Reprinted in *Speculations: Readings in Culture, Identity and Values*, edited by Charles Schuster and William Van Pelt. Englewood Cliffs, NJ: Prentice Hall, 1992.

well-I-thank-you-where-you-goin'?" Usually automobile or the horse paused at this, and after a queer exchange of compliments, I would probably "go a piece of the way" with them, as we say in farthest Florida. If one of my family happened to come to the front in time to see me, of course negotiations would be rudely broken off. But even so, it is clear that I was the first "welcome-to-our-state" Floridian, and I hope the Miami Chamber of Commerce will please take notice.

During this period, white people differed from colored to me only in that they rode through town and never lived there. They liked to hear me "speak pieces" and sing and wanted to see me dance the parse-me-la, and gave me generously of their small silver for doing these things, which seemed strange to me for I wanted to do them so much that I needed bribing to stop. Only they didn't know it. The colored people gave no dimes. They deplored any joyful tendencies in me, but I was their Zora nevertheless. I belonged to them, to the nearby hotels, to the country—everybody's Zora.

But changes came in the family when I was thirteen, and I was sent to school in Jacksonville. I left Eatonville, the town of the oleanders, as Zora. When I disembarked from the riverboat at Jacksonville, she was no more. It seemed that I had suffered a sea change. I was not Zora of Orange County any more, I was now a little colored girl. I found it out in certain ways. In my heart as well as in the mirror, I became a fast brown—warranted not to rub nor run.

But I am not tragically colored. There is no great sorrow dammed up in my soul, nor lurking behind my eyes. I do not mind at all. I do not belong to the sobbing school of Negrohood who hold that nature somehow has given them a lowdown dirty deal and whose feelings are all hurt about it. Even in the helter-skelter skirmish that is my life, I have seen that the world is to the strong regardless of a little pigmentation more or less. No, I do not weep at the world—I am too busy sharpening my oyster knife.

Someone is always at my elbow reminding me that I am the granddaughter of slaves. It fails to register depression with me. Slavery is sixty years in the past. The operation was successful and the patient is doing well, thank you. The terrible struggle that made me an American out of a potential slave said "On the line!" The Reconstruction said "Get set!"; and the generation before said "Go!" I am off to a flying start and I must not halt in the stretch to look behind and weep. Slavery is the price I paid for civilization, and the choice was not with me. It is a bully adventure and worth all that I have paid through my ancestors for it. No one on earth ever had a greater chance for glory. The world to be won and nothing to be lost. It is thrilling to think—to know that for any act of mine, I shall get twice as much praise or twice as much blame. It is quite exciting to hold the center of the national stage, with the spectators not knowing whether to laugh or to weep.

The position of my white neighbor is much more difficult. No brown specter pulls up a chair beside me when I sit down to eat. No dark ghost thrusts its leg against mine in bed. The game of keeping what one has is never so exciting as the game of getting.

I do not always feel colored. Even now I often achieve the unconscious Zora of Eatonville before the Hegira.[1] I feel most colored when I am thrown against a sharp white background.

For instance at Barnard. "Beside the waters of the Hudson" I feel my race. Among the thousand white persons, I am a dark rock surged upon, and overswept, but through it all, I remain myself. When covered by the waters, I am; and the ebb but reveals me again.

Sometimes it is the other way around. A white person is set down in our midst, but the contrast is just as sharp for me. For instance, when I sit in the drafty basement that is The New World Cabaret with a white person, my color comes. We enter chatting about any little nothing that we have in common and are seated by the jazz waiters. In the abrupt way that jazz orchestras have, this one plunges into a number. It loses no time in circumlocutions, but gets right down to business. It constricts the thorax and splits the heart with its tempo and narcotic harmonies. This orchestra grows rambunctious, rears on its hind legs and attacks the tonal veil with primitive fury, rending it, clawing it until it breaks through to the jungle beyond. I follow those heathen—follow them exultingly. I dance wildly inside myself; I yell within, I whoop; I shake my assegai[2] above my head, I hurl it true to the mark *yeeeeoouw!* I am in the jungle and living in the jungle way. My face is painted red and yellow and my body is painted blue. My pulse is throbbing like a war drum. I want to slaughter something—give paid, give death to what, I do not know. But the piece ends. The men of the orchestra wipe their lips and rest their fingers. I creep back slowly to the veneer we call civilization with the last tone and find the white friend sitting motionless in his seat, smoking calmly.

"Good music they have here," he remarks, drumming the table with his fingertips.

Music. The great blobs of purple and red emotion have not touched him. He has only heard what I felt. He is far away and I see him but dimly across the ocean and the continent that have fallen between us. He is so pale with his whiteness then and I am so colored.

At certain times I have no race, I am *me.* When I set my hat at a certain angle and saunter down Seventh Avenue, Harlem City, feeling as snooty as the lions in front of the Forty Second Street Library, for instance. So far as my feelings are concerned, Peggy Hopkins Joyce on the Boule Mich with her gorgeous raiment, stately carriage, knees knocking together in a most aristocratic manner, has nothing on me. The cosmic Zora emerges. I belong to no race nor time. I am the eternal feminine with its string of beads.

I have no separate feeling about being an American citizen and colored. I am merely a fragment of the Great Soul that surges within the boundaries. My country, right or wrong.

Sometimes, I feel discriminated against, but it does not make me angry. It merely astonishes me. How can any deny themselves the pleasure of my company? It's beyond me.

But in the main, I feel like a brown bag of miscellany propped against a wall. Against a wall in company with other bags, white, red and yellow. Pour out the contents, and there is discovered a jumble of small things priceless and worthless. A first-water diamond, an empty spool, bits of broken glass, lengths of string, a key to a door long since crumbled away, a rusty knife-blade, old shoes saved for a road that never was and never will be, a nail bent under the weight of things too heavy for any nail, a dried flower or two still a little fragrant. In your hand is the brown bag. On the ground before you is the jumble it held— so much like the jumble in the bags, could they be emptied, that all might be dumped in a single heap and the bags refilled without altering the content of any greatly. A bit of colored glass more or less would not matter. Perhaps that is how the Great Stuffer of Bags filled them in the first place—who knows?

Notes

1. Refers to Mohammad's flight from Mecca in 622 and more generally means an escape from danger. [Eds.]
2. Hunting spear. [Eds.]

17

Father Cures a Presidential Fever

Pardee Lowe

How I came to be infected with Presidentitis even now I find somewhat difficult to explain. That it was not congenital was amply demonstrated by Father's matter-of-fact superiority over such divine foolishness. And Mother, bless her realistic Chinese soul, never affected awareness of such mundane matters until the political clubs of our neighborhood (we lived in the toughest one in East Belleville) celebrated under her very nose with torchlight parades, drunken sprees, black eyes, and cracked skulls the glorious victories of their Men of the People. Whenever this happened she would exclaim, "My, my, what queer people the Americans are!"

The first time Father discovered how long the firstborn man child of his household had been exposed to the ravages of this dread disease, he was horrified. "Unbelievable!" he stormed. But Mother, who had a strong will of her own, flew right back at him. And when she cried aloud, with Heaven as her witness that she did not know how I caught it or how she could have prevented it, Father recognized the justice of her remarks. She couldn't. Kwong Chong, our own neighborhood dry-goods store, household duties, and two new babies kept Mother so harassed that she had no time to chase us about the streets or down the back alleys. Later, to still her flow of tears, Father even grudgingly admitted his full responsibility. By moving our family to an Amer-

ican neighborhood, according to Mother, he had needlessly exposed us all to the malady.

That this was the source of the trouble, probably no one knew better than Father. When the 1906 San Francisco earthquake and fire consumed all his worldly goods and forced him to flee Chinatown with his wife, two babies in arms, and a motley feudal retinue of kinsmen, relatives, and garment-sewing employees, he merely considered it more or less a blessing in disguise. From the ashes of this catastrophe, which represented for Mother the end of her Chinatownian world, Father's thoughts and plans for the future soared like a phoenix.

At long last the visions and dreams for his offspring, present and potential, would be realized. His family would rub shoulders with Americans. They would become good American citizens albeit remaining Chinese. They would inhabit a hyphenated world. By some formula, which he never was able to explain, they would select only the finest attributes of each contributory culture. They would reflect everlasting credit on him and on the name of Lowe.

(Even then, Father's faith passed all human understanding. He expected us somehow to muddle through. We did—but in a manner totally unexpected.)

From Father's point of view, we children were to be raised at home according to the old and strict Chinese ideal. But in that ever-widening circle of American neighborhood life beyond the narrow confines of our home, Father had no control. A daily commuter to

Source: "Father Cures a Presidential Fever," from *Father and Glorious Descendant*, by P. Lowe, 1943. Boston: Little, Brown. Copyright renewed 1971 by author. Reprinted by permission of author.

his shop in San Francisco's Chinatown, an hour's ride away by steam train and ferry, he was never fully apprised of our actions until too late.

He was ignorant, for instance, of what transpired in the large wooden public school situated some three short blocks from our home. He was confident we were in good hands. If he had only known what was awaiting his son there, he might not have been so eager to have me acquire an American schooling.

When at the age of five I entered the portals of this mid-Victorian architectural fire-trap, surrounded by its iron-spiked fence and tall trees, for the first time, I recognized it as an international institution in which I was free to indulge my own most un-Chinese inclinations—and, unintentionally to be sure, to undermine Father's high hopes.

I can still vividly remember the strange excitement of the first morning roll call, which was to be repeated daily for many years to come. Clumsily, the teacher pronounced our names. As we rose, she checked our nationality.

"Louisa Fleishhacker—*Austrian.*" She underlined the word *Austrian.* "Elsie Forsythe—*English.* Penelope Lincoln—*American Negro.* Yuri Matsuyama—*Japanese.* Nancy Mullins—*Irish.* Maria Pucinelli—*Italian.* Stella Saceanu—*Rumanian.* Anna Zorich—*Serbian.*" Finishing with the girls, she turned the page. "Michael Castro—*Portuguese.* Heinz Creyer—*German.* Thorvald Ericson—*Swedish.* Philippe Etienne—*French.* Nicholas Katanov—*Russian.* Pardee Lowe—*Chinese.* Robert MacPherson—*Scotch.* And Francisco Trujillo—*Mexican.*"

There we stood. In the company of fifteen other beginners no two in the entire group of the same nationality, I was embarking upon a new and glorious adventure, the educational melting pot, which was to make every one of us, beyond peradventure, an American.

It pleased Father no end to know that I liked to go to American school. He informed Mother proudly that it denoted a scholarly spirit well becoming a Chinese. If he had only glimpsed what lay back of my mind as I saw him gaily off on the morning seven-forty commuters' train he might have derived much less satisfaction.

No sooner was Father's back turned than I would dash madly to the streetcar line. On my way I would stop and pick a bunch of posies from our neighbors' back yards, praying fervently that I would be the only pupil waiting for Miss McIntyre, our teacher. Disappointment invariably awaited me, for I was not alone. Anna, Nancy, Penelope, and Robert, sharing exactly the same sentiments, always managed to get there ahead of me.

As soon as we spotted Miss McIntyre's tall figure alighting from the car, we sprang forward. With a warm smile of affection which enfolded us all, she allowed us to grab her hands, snatch her books from her arms and literally drag her from the rear step of the car to the front steps of the school, happily protesting every step of the way: "Now, children! . . . Now *children!*"

Coming mainly from immigrant homes where parents were too preoccupied with earning a living to devote much time to their children, we transferred our youthful affections to this one person who had both the time and the disposition to mother us. We showered upon our white-haired teacher the blind, wholehearted loyalty of the young. Our studies we readily absorbed, not because we particularly liked them so much as because it was "she" who taught us. Thus, with the three R's, games, stories, a weekly bath which she personally administered in the school's bathroom—two pupils at a time—and her love, she whom we staunchly enshrined in our hearts laid the rudimentary but firm foundation of our personal brand of American culture.

Then, one day it happened. Miss McIntyre, herself the daughter of an Irish immigrant who had come to California during the Gold Rush, read to us with deep emotion the life of George Washington. The virtues displayed by the Father of Our Country, particularly when confessing his act of chopping down the cherry tree, were, she led us to believe, the very ones which would, if faithfully practiced, win us equal fame. Concluding the narrative, she looked in turn at Anna, Penelope, and Robert. She was challenging us to higher things. As her eyes caught mine, she added with conviction, "And every single one of you can be President of the United States someday!"

I shall never forget that occasion. To be President in our minds was like being God, with the difference that everybody knew what the President looked like. His pictures were in every newspaper. Even in the funny sheets, I sometimes saw him. Big as life, with his grinning mouthful of teeth, eyeglasses gleaming, and his mustache bristling in the breeze of the political opposition—he looked the spitting image of Father. The only difference I could detect was that Father preferred the bamboo duster to the "Big Stick," and "*Jun Ho Ah!*" was as near as he ever came to "Bully!"

Everything I did from this moment on served only to strengthen the grandiose dream whose chief interlocking threads included myself, Father, and the Presidency. Much to the disgust of my more active playmates and the envy of my bookworm friends, I became a walking encyclopedia of American history. I could repeat the full names and dates of every President of these United States. And I knew the vivid, gory details, authentic and apocryphal, of every important military engagement in which Americans took part—and always victoriously.

I hounded the settlement librarian for books, and more books. Like one famished, I devoured all of James Fenimore Cooper's novels. Lodge and Roosevelt's *Hero Tales from American History* fascinated me. As I read Abbot's *The Story of Our Navy* and Johnston's *Famous Scouts, Including Trappers, Pioneers and Soldiers of the Frontier,* my sense of patriotism quickened. So stirred was I by Tomlinson's narrative that in my childish imagination I followed George Washington as a young scout, or marched resolutely forward to engage the Iroquois and Red Coats. Of all the books, however, Coffin's *Boys of '76* was my favorite. And many were the evenings in which I descended from the New Hampshire hills with sixteen-year-old Elijah Favor to

fight at Lexington and Concord and finally to share the fruits of Revolutionary victory at Yorktown.

However, by the time I could recite with relish and gusto Scott's lines:—

Breathes there the man, with soul so dead,
Who never to himself hath said,
This is my own, my native land! . . .

the President's picture had changed. In the course of the years, he had become huge, the size of a bear, but he still wore a mustache. He was less like Father now. And while I found it difficult to imagine myself becoming as stout, I felt that even flabby avoirdupois, if associated with the Presidency, had its compensations. No matter what his shape, I told myself, everybody still loved and worshiped the President of the United States.

Of this deadly and insidious fever that racked my chubby frame, Father was totally ignorant. Nor would he have ever divined my secret if it had not been for our journey to the Mother Lode country.

It was our first long overnight trip away from home together. The train ride, needless to say, was nothing short of glorious. For two whole days I had all to myself a father whom I seldom saw, but to whom I was thoroughly devoted. Besides, a city boy, I had never seen mountains so tall or sights so strange and fleeting. But the most enjoyable part of all was to bounce on the redplush train seats and stop the vendor whenever he passed by with his hamper filled with peanuts, candies and soda pop.

After a full day's ride, we arrived at our destination, a small silver-mining town in the Sierra Nevada. At the station platform, Father and I were met by a roly-poly Westerner dressed in baggy clothes, riding boots, and a huge sombrero and mouthing ominously an equally formidable black cigar. After "How-de-doing" us, the stranger offered Father a cigar. A "cheroot" I think he called it. Then followed a ritual that filled me with amazement.

While Mr. Brown sized up Father skeptically, Father planted himself firmly on both feet, rolled the unlighted cigar in his hands, stroked it gently, and drew it slowly beneath his nose. With a deep sigh of satisfaction, he inhaled deeply.

"Havana Perfecto?" inquired Father, more as a statement of fact than a question.

"Splendid!" assented Mr. Brown with a vigorous nod. Smiling broadly for the first time, he slapped Father approvingly on the back and swept me up into his arms. As we drove majestically down the dusty street in his creaky cart, our now genial host vouchsafed that Father was one of the few "damned furriners" and certainly the first "Chinaman" to pass this unusual inspection.

By the way that Father puffed at his cigar and blew magnificent smoke rings, I could see that he was pleased with Mr. Brown's compliment. But never a word did he mention about his being the proprietor of Sun Loy, the largest tobacco shop in Chinatown. Since he didn't, neither did I.

Arriving at a large two-story hotel, resembling in size, shape, and color an old Southern mansion, Mr. Brown, whom we now knew to be the proprietor, roared from his sagging wagon seat: "Hi there, folks! I've picked up my Chinamen!"

Out trooped the few American residents of the hotel, glad to witness anything that would break the monotony of a long hot summer's day, followed by six white-clad Chinese domestics who greeted us with an explosion of the Fragrant Mountain dialect. *"Ah Kung Ah!"* (Respected Great-Uncle!) "We hope all is well with you!"

It gave me a great thrill to see everybody, even the Americans, so deferential to Father. There was something about him that commanded universal respect. Chinese in Western clothes, especially of the latest cut, were a decided rarity in those days. And Father in his first suit of tailor-mades from a nobby American clothier looked simply grand. Tall, well-built, and sporting a bushy mustache, he looked every inch a distinguished personage. I could well understand why his American business associates persisted in nicknaming him "The Duke."

Mr. Brown, having already been informed of the purpose of our visit, drew quietly aside. So did the Americans, no longer interested in a group of jabbering, gesticulating Orientals. This gave a few of my kinsmen an opportunity to converse with me in our dialect, which I understood, but, much to their chagrin, could not speak. Shocked that a Chinese boy should be ignorant of his own dialect, the eldest exclaimed, *"Chow Mah!"* (Positively disgraceful!) The way he said it made me more than a little ashamed of myself.

However, Father cut short my uncomfortable moment by introducing me to the object of our visit. "This—" indicating a short, slender chap who appeared exceedingly glum— "is your Fourth Paternal Uncle, Precious Fortune."

Fourth Uncle, despite his title, was only a distant kinsman and, from his point of view, had every reason for sulkiness. Just as he had conveniently forgotten about his grieving mother and childless wife in China for the pleasures of Chinatown's gambling tables, Father appeared—and Fourth Uncle didn't like it one bit. Father was the personification of outraged Chinese family conscience on the warpath. To him, in place of his own father, Fourth Uncle had to account for his glaring lapses in filial piety. He had to explain, for example, why he had not written them in three years; why he never sent them money; and, worst of all, why he persisted in leaving his aging mother grandchildless.

As the Clan's Senior Elder Uncle, Father took his Greater Family responsibilities very seriously. All through dinner, he informed Mr. Brown spiritedly that Fourth Uncle would have to leave. At first, Mr. Brown replied that he hated to part with an excellent cook, but when we came to dessert he finally agreed that in view of Fourth Uncle's wicked profligacy, it appeared the wisest course.

Having disposed of the fried chicken, apple pie, and Fourth Uncle so satisfactorily, Mr. Brown next turned to me. "Son," he inquired, "what are you studying to become? Would you like to stay with me and be my cook, taking your uncle's place?"

The last question passed me by completely; I answered the first one. "I want to be President," I said.

A sharp silence smote the mellow dining room. Now the secret was out. I was amazed at my own stupidity. Happily absorbed with my second helping of apple pie and fresh rich country milk, I had recklessly given vent to my Presidential aspirations. Now what would Father say?

Father, uncertain of the exact nature of the enchantment that had suddenly ensnared his son, looked at me queerly as though he doubted his ears. Mr. Brown laughed long and loud with a strange catch in his voice. "Sure, son, that's right," he added. "Study hard and you'll be President someday."

I wondered then why Mr. Brown's laughter sounded so odd, but I never associated this with pity until much, much later. By then, however, I had been thoroughly cured by Father.

Homeward bound Father said precious little. Not even to Fourth Uncle, still glum, whom we brought home with us to start life anew. Father's silence was disturbing and he attempted to cloak it, and his thoughts, with liberal benefactions. When we reached Belleville Junction I had no further use for the newspaper vendor and his basket of allurements—and Father no use for silence. In his own mind he had worked out a series of special therapeutic treatments to counteract my desperate malady, Presidentitis.

A few days after our return from the Sierra Nevada, Father said gently, "Glorious Descendant, how would you like to go to a private boarding school in China?"

I shuddered at the full significance of his suggestion. To be separated from America and from my family? And never to see them again for years and years? "No! no!" I wailed. "I don't want to go!" Rejecting the idea with all the vehemence at my command, I added, "I want to stay in America!"

Father dwelt patiently on all the advantages of such a schooling but to no avail.

Nothing he said moved me. What about my future, inquired Father, didn't I care? Of course, I replied, but I didn't want to be a mandarin or a Chinese merchant prince at such a terrific sacrifice. Father's questions became more penetrating; they stripped the future of everything but realities. Could I, as a Chinese, ever hope to find a good job in American society? At this, I laughed. Miss McIntyre, I told him, had plainly said that I could even be President.

In these sessions, I revealed to Father the seriousness of my infection. I opened the gates to that part of my youthful life he had never known. I told him in no uncertain terms that I loved America, particularly East Belleville, which I considered to be the grandest place in all the world. Besides, I continued, why would I wish to go to China? All the things I had heard from our kinsfolk about the old country were bad, with no redeeming features. After all, I added as my clinching argument, if this were not so, why should our kinsmen wish to come to the United States?

Our cousins and uncles, Father tried desperately to explain, really wanted to stay at home with their wives and children, but because times seemed so difficult in China they were compelled, by economic necessity, to come and work in the Golden Mountains. "Don't think you're the only one who loves his family and hates to leave it," concluded Father somewhat angrily.

The argument became endless. The more Father pleaded, the more determined I became. America, I swore, was God's own country. It abounded in free public schools, libraries, newspapers, bathtubs, toilets, vaudeville theaters, and railroad trains. On the other hand, I reminded him, China was a place where anything might happen: One might be kidnapped, caught in a revolution, die from the heat, perish from the cold, or even pick up ringworm diseases which left huge bald patches on one's scalp.

Finally Father was convinced. Since I did not personally regard his idea with favor, trying to send me to China was hopeless. This by no means exhausted Father's remedial efforts on my behalf. Plan number one having failed, Father put number two into operation. He decided that if I wouldn't go to China I was to spend an extra hour each day on my Chinese studies for Tutor Chun.

Now I knew leisure no longer. My American playmates, and endless trips to the settlement library, were given up—but not forgotten. And I discovered to my painful sorrow that I had only substituted one necessary evil for another. Every evening from five to eight I despondently memorized, recited, and copied endless columns of queer-shaped characters which bore not the slightest resemblance to English. As I went to this school on Saturday mornings and studied my lessons on Sunday, I envied Penelope, Heinz and Francisco, my poorest foreign playmates, their luxurious freedom. They did not have to learn Chinese.

Unlike my American education, my Chinese one was not crowned with success. It was not that I was entirely unwilling to learn, but simply that my brain was not ambidextrous. Whenever I stood with my back to the teacher, my lips attempted to recite correctly in poetical prose Chinese history, geography or ethics, while my inner spirit was wrestling victoriously with the details of the Battle of Bunker Hill, Custer's Last Stand, or the tussle between the *Monitor* and *Merrimac*.

When it became apparent to Tutor Chun that, in spite of my extra hour a day, I was unable to balance cultural waters on both shoulders, he mercifully desisted flailing me with the bamboo duster. No amount of chastising, he informed me bitterly, would ever unravel the cultural chop suey I was making of my studies. But, in the long run, even the gentle soul of the Chinese teacher could not tolerate my muddle-headedness. One day after a particularly heart-rending recitation on my part, he telephoned Mother in despair. "Madame," he exclaimed in mortal anguish, "never have I had a pupil the equal of your son. I strain all my efforts but, alas, I profoundly regret that I am unable to teach him anything!"

Father was appalled at this news, but since he was not the kind of man who gave up eas-

ily, his determination waxed all the stronger. Subtler methods, bribery, were tried. Perhaps, he reasoned, I might develop a taste for Chinese as well as English literature if it were only made financially worth my while. Each Sunday a shining quarter would be mine, he said, if I would present him with a daily ten-minute verbal Chinese translation of the latest newspaper reports on European war developments.

Lured by this largess, I made my translations. They were, to be sure, crude and swiftly drawn. But then, ten minutes was all too brief a period in which to circumnavigate the globe and report on its current events. I endowed the military movements of von Kluck's, Foch's and Haig's armies with the élan of Sheridan's sweep down the Shenandoah, unencumbered with the intricate mechanized paraphernalia of modern warfare. And long before Wilson, Clemenceau and Lloyd George assembled at Versailles, I had made and remade the map of Europe a dozen times.

Father's clever scheme not only worked, but it proved mutually beneficial. During the four years of the war, we kept it up. Thanks to the revolutionary *Young China*, and the *Christian Chinese Western Daily*, he was never entirely in the dark as to which armies won which campaign and who finally won the war. Naturally, Father learned a great deal about history that wasn't so, but he did not particularly mind. I was improving my Chinese.

During this period my youthful cup of patriotism was filled to overflowing. In the first place our Americanism had finally reached the ears of the White House. The christening of my twin brothers brought two important letters of congratulation from Washington, which Father proudly framed and hung conspicuously in his private office. As might be imagined, they exerted a profound influence on all our lives.

When I felt particularly in need of encouragement, I would go to the back wall of Father's office and read aloud Vice-President Marshall's letter to Father. It was a human one, glowing with warmth and inspiration. There was one sentence which stood out: "To be a good American citizen, in my judgment, is about the best thing on earth, and while I cannot endow your children with any worldly goods, I can bless them with the hope that they may grow up to be an honor to their parents and a credit to the commonwealth."

I recall this Vice-Presidential blessing so vividly because it was the crux of our family problem. It summed up our difficulties as well as our goal. For me, at least, it was difficult to be a filial Chinese son and a good American citizen at one and the same time. For many years I used to wonder why this was so, but I appreciate now it was because I was the eldest son in what was essentially a pioneering family. Father was pioneering with Americanism—and so was I. And more often than not, we blazed entirely different trails.

When America finally entered the War, even Father's sturdy common sense softened somewhat under the heat waves of patriotism that constantly beat down upon us. I was in paradise. My youthful fancies appreciated that only strife and turmoil made heroes. When I recalled that practically every great President—Washington, Jackson, Lincoln, Grant, and Roosevelt—had once been a soldier, I bitterly lamented the fact that I was not old enough. I'd show those "Huns" (by this time I had already imbibed freely at the fount of propaganda) a thing or two, I informed Father. But Father only snorted something about waiting until I could shoulder a gun, and studying Chinese.

The next summer, my thirteenth, I decided to go to work during vacation. I needed spending money badly for my first term in high school. Father applauded this show of independence until I informed him that I intended, if possible, to become an office boy in an American business firm. Then he was seized with profound misgivings. "Would they hire you?" Father inquired.

Why shouldn't they, I replied, with overweening self-confidence. "See!" I pointed to the Sunday editions of the *San Francisco Chronicle*. "I can hold any of these jobs."

Father looked at the classified advertisements I had checked. Whether he knew what

all the abbreviations meant, I wasn't certain. I didn't, but that was totally immaterial. The world was new, I was young, and for $40 a month I was willing to learn the ins. or exp. bus., work for good opps., be ready to asst. on files, and, for good measure, do gen. off. wk. for perm. adv.

Father remarked that he wasn't so certain that the millennium had arrived, but he was open to conviction. He agreed to let me proceed on one condition: If I failed to find a job I was to return to Tutor Chun and study my Chinese lessons faithfully.

Blithely one sunny July morning I went forth job hunting, well-scrubbed, wearing my Sunday suit and totally unaware of the difficulties that confronted me. In my pocket were ten clipped newspaper advertisements, each one, I thought, with a job purposely made for me.

I took out the most promising one. It was for seven enterp. boys, between the ages of 12 and 16; and they were wanted at once for a bond house which offered good opps. as well as $50 per month. The address was on California Street.

Stopping in front of an imposing marble palace of San Francisco finance, I compared the address with the clipping. It checked. How simply grand it would be to work for such a firm, I thought, as the elevator majestically pulled us up to the ninth floor. I trembled with eager anticipation as I pushed open the glass door of Richards and Mathison, for it seemed as though a new world were swimming into view.

"Wad-a-ya-wunt?" barked the sharp voice of a young lady. I looked in her direction. There she sat behind a shiny, thin brass cage, just like a bank teller—or a monkey, for above her head hung a sign. It read INFORMATION.

"Please, ma'am," I asked, "can you tell me where I can find Mr. Royal?"

"Humph!" she snorted, as she looked me up and down as if to say I didn't have a chance. "He's busy, you'll have to wait."

After what seemed hours, the girl threw open the office gate and motioned me to enter. I followed her down a long aisle of desks, every one as large as a kitchen table. At each desk sat a man or a girl shuffling large cards or scribbling on long sheets of paper. As we passed, they stopped their work and looked at me queerly. I noticed several boys of my own age putting their heads together. I knew they were talking about me. And when they snickered, I wanted to punch their noses.

Opening a door marked PRIVATE, the girl announced: "Mr. Royal, here is another boy." He raised his head.

There it was. On Mr. Royal's lean, smooth-shaven face was the same look of incredulity that I had once noticed on Mr. Brown's. But only for a moment. For he suddenly reached for a cigarette, lit it and looked at me quizzically, while I hopped on one foot and then on the other.

"Young man," he said, "I understand you would like to work for us? Well then, you'd better tell us something of yourself."

"Why, of course," I said, "of course." And impulsively I told everything: all about my graduation from grammar school, my boy-scout training, and my desire to earn my own keep during the summer.

Mr. Royal seemed visibly impressed. When a faint smile replaced his frown, I stopped fidgeting. I fully expected him to ask me to come to work in the morning. Therefore, I was appalled when he told me that he was sorry, but all the jobs were taken. It never occurred to me that our interview would end like this.

My face fell. I hadn't expected such an answer. To soften the blow, Mr. Royal added that if I filled out an application he would call me if there were any openings.

I filled out the application under the unsympathetic eyes of the information girl, and stumbled miserably out of the office, vaguely sensible of the fact that there would never be any opening.

The feeling was intensified as I made the round of the other nine firms. Everywhere I was greeted with perturbation, amusement, pity or irritation—and always with identically the same answer. "Sorry," they invariably said, "the position has just been filled." My jaunty self-confidence soon wilted. I sensed that something was radically, fundamentally wrong. It just didn't seem possible that overnight all of the positions could have been occupied, particularly not when everybody spoke of a labor shortage. Suspicion began to dawn. What had Father said? "American firms do not customarily employ Chinese." To verify his statement, I looked again in the newspaper the next morning and for the week after and, sure enough, just as I expected, the same ten ads were still in the newspaper.

For another week, I tried my luck. By now I was thoroughly shellshocked. What had begun as a glorious adventure had turned into a hideous, long-drawn nightmare.

Father during this trying period wisely said nothing. Then, one morning, he dusted off my dog-eared paperbound Chinese textbooks. When I came to breakfast I found them on my desk, mute but eloquent reminders of my promise. I looked at them disconsolately. A bargain was a bargain.

When our clock struck nine, I picked up my bundle of books. Fortunately for me, Father had already commuted to work. Only Mother saw me off. Patting me sympathetically on the shoulder, she regarded me reflectively. It was an invitation for me to unburden my heart. But not even for her would I confess my full recovery from a nearly fatal disease. That moment was reserved for my long walk to language school.

I marched out of the house insouciant. When I wasn't whistling I was muttering to myself a Jewish slang phrase I had just picked up. It was "Ishkabibble" and it meant that I didn't care. And I didn't until I reached the park where all my most vivid daydreaming periods were spent. There, I broke down and wept. For the first time I admitted to myself the cruel truth—I didn't have a "Chinaman's chance" of becoming President of the United States. In this crash of the lofty hopes which Miss McIntyre had raised, it did not occur to me to reflect that the chances of Francisco Trujillo, Yuri Matsuyama, or Penelope Lincoln were actually no better than mine. But after a good cry I felt better—anyway, I could go to an American school again in the fall.

18

Homeland

Barbara Kingsolver

To look at her, you would not have thought her an Indian. She wore blue and lavender flowered dresses with hand-tatted collars, and brown lace-up shoes with sturdy high heels, and she smoked a regular pipe. She was tall, with bowed calves and a faintly bent-forward posture, spine straight and elbows out and palms forward, giving the impression that she was at any moment prepared to stoop and lift a burden of great bulk or weight. She spoke with a soft hill accent, and spoke properly. My great-grandfather had been an educated man, more prone in his lifetime to errors of judgment than errors of grammar.

Great Mam smoked her pipe mainly in the evenings, and always on the front porch. For a time I believed this was because my mother so vigorously objected to the smell, but Great Mam told me otherwise. A pipe had to be smoked outdoors, she said, where the smoke could return to the Beloved Old Father who gave us tobacco. When I asked her what she meant, she said she meant nothing special at all. It was just the simplest thing, like a bread-and-butter note you send to an aunt after she has fed you a meal.

I often sat with Great Mam in the evenings on our porch swing, which was suspended by four thin, painted chains that squeaked. The air at night smelled of oil and dust, and

Source: Excerpted from *Homeland and Other Stories* by B. Kingsolver, copyright © 1989 by Barbara Kingsolver. Reprinted by permission of HarperCollins Publishers, Inc.

faintly of livestock, for the man at the end of our lane kept hogs. Great Mam would strike a match and suck the flame into her pipe, lighting her creased face in brief orange bursts.

"The small people are not very bright tonight," she would say, meaning the stars. She held surprising convictions, such as that in the daytime the small people walked among us. I could not begin to picture it.

"You mean down here in the world, or do you mean right here in Morning Glory?" I asked repeatedly. "Would they walk along with Jack and Nathan and me to school?"

She nodded. "They would."

"But why would they come *here*?" I asked.

"Well, why wouldn't they?" she said.

I thought about this for a while, entirely unconvinced.

"You don't ever have to be lonesome," she said. "That's one thing you never need be."

"But mightn't I step on one of them, if it got in my way and I didn't see it?"

Great Mam said, "No. They aren't that small."

She had particular names for many things, including the months. February she called "Hungry Month." She spoke of certain animals as if they were relatives our parents had neglected to tell us about. The cowering white dog that begged at our kitchen door she called "the sad little cousin." If she felt like it, on these evenings, she would tell me stories about the animals, their personalities and kindnesses and trickery, and the permanent physical markings they invariably earned by doing something they ought not to have done. "Remember that story," she often commanded at the end, and I would be stunned with guilt because my mind had wandered onto crickets and pencil erasers and Black Beauty.

"I might not remember," I told her. "It's too hard."

Great Mam allowed that I might *think* I had forgotten. "But you haven't. You'll keep it stored away," she said. "If it's important, your heart remembers."

I had known that hearts could break and sometimes even be attacked, with disastrous result, but I had not heard of hearts remembering. I was eleven years old. I did not trust any of my internal parts with the capacity of memory.

* * *

When the seasons changed, it never occurred to us to think to ourselves, "This will be Great Mam's last spring. Her last June apples. Her last fresh roasting ears from the garden." She was like an old pine, whose accumulated years cause one to ponder how long it has stood, not how soon it will fall. Of all of us, I think Papa was the only one who believed she could die. He planned the trip to Tennessee. We children simply thought it was a great lark.

This was in June, following a bad spring during which the whole southern spine of the Appalachians had broken out in a rash of wildcat strikes. Papa was back to work at last, no longer home taking up kitchen-table space, but still Mother complained of having to make soups of neckbones and cut our school shoes open to bare our too-long toes to summer's dust, for the whole darn town to see. Papa pointed out that the whole darn town had been on the picket lines, and wouldn't pass judgment on the Murray kids if they ran their bare bottoms down Main Street. And what's more, he said, it wasn't his fault if John L. Lewis had sold him down the river.

My brothers and I thrilled to imagine ourselves racing naked past the Post Office and the women shopping at Herman Ritchie's Market, but we did not laugh out loud. We didn't know exactly who Mr. John L. Lewis was, or what river Papa meant, but we knew not to expect much. The last thing we expected was a trip.

My brother Jack, because of his nature and superior age, was suspicious from the outset. While Papa explained his plan, Jack made a point of pushing lima beans around his plate in single file to illustrate his boredom. It was 1955. Patti Page and Elvis were on the radio and high school boys were fighting their mothers over ducktails. Jack had a year to go before high school, but already the future was plainly evident.

He asked where in Tennessee we would be going, if we did go. The three of us had not seen the far side of a county line.

"The Hiwassee Valley, where Great Mam was born," Papa said.

My brother Nathan grew interested when Jack laid down his fork. Nathan was only eight, but he watched grownups. If there were no men around, he watched Jack.

"Eat your beans, Jack," Mother said. "I didn't put up these limas last fall so you could torment them."

Jack stated, "I'm not eating no beans with guts in them."

Mother took a swat at Jack's arm. "Young man, you watch your mouth. That's the insides of a hog, and a hog's a perfectly respectable animal to eat." Nathan was making noises with his throat. I tried not to make any face one way or the other.

Great Mam told Mother it would have been enough just to have the limas, without the meat. "A person can live on green corn and beans, Florence Ann," she said. "There's no shame in vegetables."

We knew what would happen next, and watched with interest. "If I have to go out myself and throw a rock at a songbird," Mother said, having deepened to the color of beetroot, "nobody is going to say this family goes without meat!"

Mother was a tiny woman who wore stockings and shirt-waists even to hoe the garden. She had yellow hair pinned in a tight bun, with curly bangs in front. We waited with our chins cupped in our palms for Papa's opinion of her plan to make a soup of Robin Redbreast, but he got up from the table and rummaged in the bureau drawer for the gas-station map. Great Mam ate her beans in a careful way, as though each one had its own private importance.

"Are we going to see Injuns?" Nathan asked, but no one answered. Mother began making a great deal of noise clearing up the dishes. We could hear her out in the kitchen, scrubbing.

Papa unfolded the Texaco map on the table and found where Tennessee and North Carolina and Georgia came together in three different pastel colors. Great Mam looked down at the colored lines and squinted, holding the sides of her glasses. "Is this the Hiwassee River?" she wanted to know.

"No, now those lines are highways," he said. "Red is interstate. Blue is river.

"Well, what's this?"

He looked. "That's the state line."

"Now why would they put that on the map? You can't see it."

Papa flattened the creases of the map with his broad hands, which were crisscrossed with fine black lines of coal dust, like a map themselves, no matter how clean. "The Hiwassee Valley's got a town in it now, it says 'Cherokee.' Right here."

"Well, those lines make my eyes smart," Great Mam said. "I'm not going to look anymore."

The boys started to snicker, but Papa gave us a look that said he meant business and sent us off to bed before it went any farther.

"Great Mam's blind as a post hole," Jack said once we were in bed. "She don't know a road from a river."

"She don't know beans from taters," said Nathan.

"You boys hush up, I'm tired," I said. Jack and Nathan slept lengthwise in the bed, and I slept across the top with my own blanket.

"Here's Great Mam," Nathan said. He sucked in his cheeks and crossed his eyes and keeled over backward, bouncing us all on the bedsprings. Jack punched him in the ribs, and Nathan started to cry louder than he had to. I got up and sat by the bedroom door hugging my knees, listening to Papa and Mother. I could hear them in the kitchen.

"As if I hadn't put up with enough, John. It's not enough that Murrays have populated God's earth without the benefit of marriage," Mother said. This was her usual starting point. She was legally married to my father in a Baptist Church, a fact she could work into any conversation.

"Well, I don't see why," she said, "if we never had the money to take the kids anyplace before."

Papa's voice was quieter, and I couldn't hear his answers.

"Was this her idea, John, or yours?"

When Nathan and Jack were asleep I went to the window and slipped over the sill. My feet landed where they always did, in the cool mud of Mother's gladiolus patch alongside the house. Great Mam did not believe in flower patches. Why take a hoe and kill all the growing things in a piece of ground, and then plant others that have been uprooted from somewhere else? This was what she asked me. She thought Mother spent a fearful amount of time moving things needlessly from one place to another.

"I see you, Waterbug," said Great Mam in the darkness, though what she probably meant was that she heard me. All I could see was the glow of her pipe bowl moving above the porch swing.

"Tell me the waterbug story tonight," I said, settling onto the swing. The fireflies were blinking on and off in the black air above the front yard.

"No, I won't," she said. The orange glow moved to her lap, and faded from bright to dim. "I'll tell you another time."

The swing squeaked its sad song, and I thought about Tennessee. It had never occurred to me that the place where Great Mam had been a child was still on this earth. "Why'd you go away from home?" I asked her.

"You have to marry outside your clan," she said. "That's law. And all the people we knew were Bird Clan. All the others were gone. So when Stewart Murray came and made baby eyes at me, I had to go with him." She laughed. "I liked his horse."

I imagined the two of them on a frisking, strong horse, crossing the mountain to Kentucky. Great Mam with black hair. "Weren't you afraid to go?" I asked.

"Oh, yes I was. The canebrakes were high as a house. I was afraid we'd get lost."

* * *

We were to leave on Saturday after Papa got off work. He worked days then, after many graveyard-shift years during which we rarely saw him except asleep, snoring and waking throughout the afternoon, with Mother forever forced to shush us; it was too easy to forget someone was trying to sleep in daylight. My father was a soft-spoken man who sometimes drank but was never mean. He had thick black hair, no beard stubble at all nor hair on his chest, and a nose he called his Cherokee nose. Mother said she thanked the Lord that at least He had seen fit not to put that nose on her children. She also claimed he wore his hair long to flout her, although it wasn't truly long, in our opinion. His nickname in the mine was "Indian John."

There wasn't much to get ready for the trip. All we had to do in the morning was wait for afternoon. Mother was in the house scrubbing so it would be clean when we came back. The primary business of Mother's life was scrubbing things, and she herself looked scrubbed. Her skin was the color of a clean boiled potato. We didn't get in her way.

My brothers were playing a ferocious game of cowboys and Indians in the backyard, but I soon defected to my own amusements along the yard's weedy borders, picking morning glories, pretending to be a June bride. I grew tired of trying to weave the flowers into my coarse hair and decided to give them to Great Mam. I went around to the front and came up the three porch steps in one jump, just exactly the way Mother said a lady wouldn't do.

"Surprise," I announced. "These are for you." The flowers were already wilting in my hand.

"You shouldn't have picked those," she said.

"They were a present." I sat down, feeling stung.

"Those are not mine to have and not yours to pick," she said, looking at me, not with anger but with intensity. Her brown pupils were as dark as two pits in the earth. "A flower is alive, just as much as you are. A flower is your cousin. Didn't you know that?"

I said, No ma'am, that I didn't.

"Well, I'm telling you now, so you will know. Sometimes a person has got to take a life, like a chicken's or a hog's when you need it. If you're hungry, then they're happy to give their flesh up to you because they're your relatives. But nobody is so hungry they need to kill a flower."

I said nothing.

"They ought to be left where they stand, Waterbug. You need to leave them for the small people to see. When they die they'll fall where they are, and make a seed for next year."

"Nobody cared about these," I contended. "They weren't but just weeds."

"It doesn't matter what they were or were not. It's a bad thing to take for yourself something beautiful that belongs to everybody. Do you understand? To take it is a sin."

I didn't, and I did. I could sense something of wasted life in the sticky leaves, translucent with death, and the purple flowers turning wrinkled and limp. I'd once brought home a balloon from a Ritchie child's birthday party, and it had shriveled and shrunk with just such a slow blue agony.

"I'm sorry," I said.

"It's all right." She patted my hands. "Just throw them over the porch rail there, give them back to the ground. The small people will come and take them back."

I threw the flowers over the railing in a clump, and came back, trying to rub the purple and green juices off my hands onto my dress. In my mother's eyes, this would have been the first sin of my afternoon. I understood the difference between Great Mam's rules and the Sunday-school variety, and that you could read Mother's Bible forward and backward and never find where it said it's a sin to pick flowers because they are our cousins.

"I'll try to remember," I said.

"I want you to," said Great Mam. "I want you to tell your children."

"I'm not going to have any children," I said. "No boy's going to marry me. I'm too tall. I've got knob knees."

"Don't ever say you hate what you are." She tucked a loose sheaf of black hair behind my ear. "It's an unkindness to those that made you. That's like a red flower saying it's too red, do you see what I mean?"

"I guess," I said.

"You will have children. And you'll remember about the flowers," she said, and I felt the weight of these promises fall like a deerskin pack between my shoulder blades.

* * *

By four o'clock we were waiting so hard we heard the truck crackle up the gravel road. Papa's truck was a rust-colored Ford with complicated cracks hanging like spiderwebs in the corners of the windshield. He jumped out with his long, blue-jean strides and patted the round front fender.

"Old Paint's had her oats," he said. "She's raring to go." This was a game he played with Great Mam. Sometimes she would say, "John Murray, you couldn't ride a mule with a saddle on it," and she'd laugh, and we would for a moment see the woman who raised Papa. Her bewilderment and pleasure, to have ended up with this broad-shouldered boy.

Today she said nothing, and Papa went in for Mother. There was only room for three in the cab, so Jack and Nathan and I climbed into the back with the old quilt Mother gave us and a tarpaulin in case of rain.

"What's she waiting for, her own funeral?" Jack asked me.

I looked at Great Mam, sitting still on the porch like a funny old doll. The whole house was crooked, the stoop sagged almost to the ground, and there sat Great Mam as straight as a schoolteacher's ruler. Seeing her there, I fiercely wished to defend my feeling that I knew her better than others did.

"She doesn't want to go," I said. I knew as soon as I'd spoken that it was the absolute truth.

"That's stupid. She's the whole reason we're going. Why wouldn't she want to go see her people?"

"I don't know, Jack," I said.

Papa and Mother eventually came out of the house, Papa in a clean shirt already darkening under the arms, and Mother with her Sunday purse, the scuff marks freshly covered with white shoe polish. She came down the front steps in the bent-over way she walked when she wore high heels. Papa put his hand under Great Mam's elbow and she silently climbed into the cab.

When he came around to the other side I asked him, "Are you sure Great Mam wants to go?"

"Sure she does," he said. "She wants to see the place where she grew up. Like what Morning Glory is to you."

"When I grow up I'm not never coming back to Morning Glory," Jack said.

"Me neither." Nathan spat over the side of the truck, the way he'd seen men do.

"Don't spit, Nathan," Papa said.

"Shut up," Nathan said, after Papa had gotten in the truck and shut the door.

The houses we passed had peeled paint and slumped porches like our own, and they all wore coats of morning-glory vines, deliciously textured and fat as fur coats. We pointed out to each other the company men's houses, which had bright white paint and were known to have indoor bathrooms. The deep ditches along the road, filled with blackberry brambles and early goldenrod, ran past us like rivers. On our walks to school we put these ditches to daily use practicing Duck and Cover, which was what our teachers felt we ought to do when the Communists dropped the H-bomb.

"We'll see Indians in Tennessee," Jack said. I knew we would. Great Mam had told me how it was.

"Great Mam don't look like an Indian," Nathan said.

"Shut up, Nathan," Jack said. "How do you know what an Indian looks like? You ever seen one?"

"She does so look like an Indian," I informed my brothers. "She is one."

According to Papa we all looked like little Indians, I especially. Mother hounded me continually to stay out of the sun, but by each summer's end I was so dark-skinned my schoolmates teased me, saying I ought to be sent over to the Negro school.

"Are we going to be Indians when we grow up?" Nathan asked.

"No, stupid," said Jack. "We'll just be the same as we are now."

* * *

We soon ran out of anything productive to do. We played White Horse Zit many times over, until Nathan won and we tried to play Alphabet but there weren't enough signs. The only public evidence of literacy in that part of the country was the Beech Nut Tobacco signs on barn roofs, and every so often, nailed to a tree trunk, a clapboard on which someone had painted "PREPARE TO MEET GOD."

Papa's old truck didn't go as fast as other cars. Jack and Nathan slapped the fenders like jockeys as we were passed on the uphill slopes, but their coaxing amounted to nought. By the time we went over Jellico Mountain, it was dark.

An enormous amount of sky glittered down at us on the mountain pass, and even though it was June we were cold. Nathan had taken the quilt for himself and gone to sleep. Jack said he ought to punch him one to teach him to be nice, but truthfully, nothing in this world could have taught Nathan to share. Jack and I huddled together under the tarp, which stank of coal oil, and sat against the back of the cab where the engine rendered up through the truck's metal body a faint warmth.

"Jack?" I said.

"What."

"Do you reckon Great Mam's asleep?"

He turned around and cupped his hands to see into the cab. "Nope," he said. "She's sitting up there in between 'em stiff as a broom handle."

"I'm worried about her," I said.

"Why? If we were home she'd be sitting up just the same, only out front on the porch."

"I know."

"Glorie, you know what?" he asked me.

"What?"

A trailer truck loomed up behind us, decked with rows of red and amber lights like a Christmas tree. We could see the driver inside the cab. A faint blue light on his face made him seem ghostly and entirely alone. He passed us by, staring ahead, as though only he were real on this cold night and we were among all the many things that were not. I shivered, and felt an identical chill run across Jack's shoulders.

"What?" I asked again.

"What, what?"

"You were going to tell me something."

"Oh. I forgot what it was."

"Great Mam says the way to remember something you forgot is to turn your back on it. Say, 'The small people came dancing. They ran through the woods today.' Talk about what they did, and then whatever it was you forgot, they'll bring it back to you."

"That's dumb," Jack said. "That's Great Mam's hobbledy-gobbledy."

For a while we played See Who Can Go to Sleep First, which we knew to be a game that can't consciously be won. He never remembered what he'd meant to say.

* * *

When Papa woke us the next morning we were at a truck stop in Knoxville. He took a nap in the truck with his boots sticking out the door while the rest of us went in for breakfast. Inside the restaurant was a long glass counter containing packs of Kools and Mars Bars lined up on cotton batting, objects of great value to be protected from dust and children. The waitress who brought us our eggs had a red wig perched like a bird on her head, and red eyebrows painted on over the real ones.

When it was time to get back in the truck we dragged and pulled on Mother's tired, bread-dough arms, like little babies, asking her how much farther.

"Oh, it's not far. I expect we'll be in Cherokee by lunchtime," she said, but her mouth was set and we knew she was as tired of this trip as any of us.

It was high noon before we saw a sign that indicated we were approaching Cherokee. Jack pummeled the cab window with his fists to make sure they all saw it, but Papa and Mother were absorbed in some kind of argument. There were more signs after that, with pictures of cartoon Indian boys urging us to buy souvenirs or stay in so-and-so's motor lodge. The signs were shaped like log cabins and teepees. Then we saw a real teepee. It was made of aluminum and taller than a house. Inside, it was a souvenir store.

We drove around the streets of Cherokee and saw that the town was all the same, as single-minded in its offerings as a corn patch or an orchard, so that it made no difference where we stopped. We parked in front of Sitting Bull's Genuine Indian Made Souvenirs, and Mother crossed the street to get groceries for our lunch. I had a sense of something gone badly wrong, like a lie told in my past and then forgotten, and now about to catch up with me.

A man in a feather war bonnet danced across from us in the parking lot. His outfit was bright orange, with white fringe trembling along the seams of the pants and sleeves, and a woman in the same clothes sat cross-legged on the pavement playing a tom-tom while he danced. People with cameras gathered and side-stepped around one another to snap their shots. The woman told them that

she and her husband Chief Many Feathers were genuine Cherokees, and that this was their welcoming dance. Papa sat with his hands frozen on the steering wheel for a very long time. Then suddenly, without saying anything, he got out of the truck and took Jack and Nathan and me into Sitting Bull's. Nathan wanted a tomahawk.

The store was full of items crowded on shelves, so bright-colored it hurt my eyes to look at them all. I lagged behind the boys. There were some Indian dolls with real feathers on them, red and green, and I would like to have stroked the soft feathers but the dolls were wrapped in cellophane. Among all those bright things, I grew fearfully uncertain about what I ought to want. I went back out to the truck and found Great Mam still sitting in the cab.

"Don't you want to get out?" I asked.

The man in the parking lot was dancing again, and she was watching. "I don't know what they think they're doing. Cherokee don't wear feather bonnets like that," she said.

They looked like Indians to me. I couldn't imagine Indians without feathers. I climbed up onto the seat and closed the door and we sat for a while. I felt a great sadness and embarrassment, as though it were I who had forced her to come here, and I tried to cover it up by pretending to be foolishly cheerful.

"Where's the pole houses, where everybody lives, I wonder," I said. "Do you think maybe they're out of town a ways?"

She didn't answer. Chief Many Feathers hopped around his circle, forward on one leg and backward on the other. Then the dance was over. The woman beating the tom-tom turned it upside down and passed it around for money.

"I guess things have changed pretty much since you moved away, huh, Great Mam?" I asked.

She said, "I've never been here before."

19

Survival Strategies of Older Homeless Men

Carl I. Cohen
Jeanne Teresi
Douglas Holmes
Eric Roth

In recent years there has been a surge of interest in the homeless population (Bassuk, 1984; Holden, 1986). Although much attention has been focused on the younger, or "nouveau," homeless, the Aging Health Policy Center (1985), using primarily shelter reports from eight cities, has estimated that between 14.5% and 28% are 50 or older and that as many as 27% are 60 and older. Moreover, probably underestimated in the shelter data is the proportion of elderly homeless because the aged are often crowded out of public shelters due to fears of muggings and abusive or insensitive staff, or to concerns about being institutionalized (Coalition for the Homeless, 1984). The older homeless are also ignored by existing senior programs and services. It is rare to find a senior center which serves the homeless (New York City Human Resources Ad-

Source: This study was supported by NIMH Grant No. RO1MH37562, Center for the Studies of the Mental Disorders of the Aging. Excerpted from Cohen, Carl, Jeanne Teresi, Douglas Holmes and Eric Roth. "Survival Strategies of Older Homeless Men," 1988, *The Gerontologist 28*(1), 58–65. Copyright © 1988 The Gerontological Society of America. Reprinted with permission. Carl I. Cohen, M.D., is Associate Professor of Psychiatry, SUNY Downstate Medical Center, Department of Psychiatry. Jeanne Teresi, Ph.D., and Douglas Holmes, Ph.D., are with Community Research Applications, Bronx, NY. Eric Roth is with the Bowery Residents' Committee, New York, NY.

ministration, 1983). Reported, however, by street outreach programs is a much higher percentage of older persons, ranging as high as 50% in some surveys (Coalition for the Homeless, 1984). Furthermore, although the proportion of older homeless may be declining, their absolute number appears to be increasing (Aging Health Policy Center, 1985).

Brickner (1985) has estimated that one-fifth of the homeless people live on skid row. Yet surveys of the homeless have largely ignored the men living in skid row areas. Paradoxically, Wallace (1965) has noted that the skid rower has been traditionally considered homeless even though he no longer lives exclusively on the streets. Whereas many of these men periodically live on the street, their alcohol abuse, physical impairment, lack of traditional social ties, and poverty are considered characteristics of homelessness. Furthermore, extensive urban renewal and hotel fires in recent years have placed these men at risk of becoming undomiciled. Perhaps three-quarters to four-fifths of the men living in the flophouses are age 50 and over.

The older homeless population cannot be easily ignored. Because of their age, elderly homeless may require more specialized services than do their younger counterparts. Although the elderly homeless can be found in various quarters of American cities, skid row remains one of the principal areas of concentration. It has been nearly 25 years since the last large-scale investigations were conducted on skid rows (Bahr & Caplow, 1973; Blumberg, Shipley, & Shandler, 1973). Because of the high concentration of older habitués, a study of skid row should be of great interest to gerontological researchers and service providers. Provided in this paper is an analysis of the survival skills and needs of older men living in the flophouses and streets of the Bowery in New York City. Although each skid row may have its distinctive features, earlier research (Bogue, 1963) has pointed to a number of survival technique traits that should render this study generalizable to other skid row populations.

Methods

The site for the study was the world's most renowned skid row, the Bowery. The Bowery is a two-way street running for 16 blocks in lower Manhattan, bounded by Chinatown on the South and East Greenwich Village on the North. The actual skid row section, The Bowery, encompasses a somewhat larger area of side streets and avenues running parallel to the Bowery. Only 12 flophouses and 3 missions are left on the Bowery, along with 2 taverns and a liquor store, a few used clothing stores, and perhaps 2 or 3 classic slop joints (cheap restaurants). Replacing the more traditional support system of taverns, bookie joints, restaurants, clothing stores, and the like are a variety of social service agencies. Most of the buildings lately house commercial establishments that specialize primarily in wholesale restaurant equipment and lighting accessories.

Approximately 3500 persons live on the Bowery, of whom 2500 are in the flophouses. Each flophouse shelters between 34 to 554 men on a given night. Entering the typical lodging house the visitor encounters a rather steep, dusty, dimly-lit imitation marble staircase with wooden banisters on either side. The men are housed in 4' by 7' cubicles with a bed, a locker, a night table, and whatever personal possessions the occupant can squeeze into his space. Each cubicle is separated from the adjoining one by a thin wall that extends only part way to the ceiling, the resultant space filled with a 2 foot wide strip of chicken wire. In the ticket hotel (hotels used by the Men's Shelter) there are usually several large dormitories on various floors. The dormitories are dimly lit, smelly, dirty, crowded hovels consisting of several dozen cots, frequently covered with soiled sheets and not uncommonly infested with lice or chiggers. The cheapest flops charge about $87 per month whereas the better ones charge about twice as much.

Survival Techniques and Basic Necessities: Money, Food, Shelter

Once a man arrives on the Bowery, he must develop the requisite skills to survive in this frequently treacherous environment. As one elderly Bowery man said: "With the trials and tribulations you're not living; you're just existing. And existence is very hard." One-half of the non-street (flophouse and apartment) men studied had spent 2 or more years at their current address, which suggested considerable stability. The median time spent on the Bowery was 13 years (a range of from several days to 63 years). Approximately half the street men had been living on the streets for 3 years and three men claimed to have been on the streets for 25 or more years. One ex-Bowery man summarized the plight of the skid rower, "That whatever else might be amiss, his primary problem is a physical problem. He needs food, clothing, shelter, and probably medical attention" (Parker, 1970). To what extent a skid rower's daily existence is devoted to taking care of basic needs depends on financial status, which is extremely low for the majority. Overall, half the men earned less than $3,900 per year and one-fifth earned less than $1,000 per year. Only 3 of the 281 men indicated that they had earned $10,500 or more over the previous year. Importantly, 41% of street men reported annual incomes of less than $1,000 and half the men earned under $1,300 per year. Thus, income for these men approached levels found in Third World countries. Overall, only 16% of the Bowery men earned above the 1983 poverty level of $5,061 for a single individual. Typically, the street persons had no regular income. Their lives revolved around ensuring that they had food, a few cigarette butts, some wine, a bench to sleep on, some semblance of hygiene, and a relative degree of safety. After reciting his daily routine, one street man lamented: "I'm really tired, I'm worn out. You walk back and forth from 23rd Street Madison Square Park to 42nd Street to the Bowery. I must walk 30 miles a day."

Despite the rigors of this existence, the Bowery and its environs do provide the down-and-outer with the opportunity to survive on very little. Indeed, for two-thirds of the men the low cost of living was one of the prime motivations for having come to the Bowery. For example, one man bragged, "Sometimes I live on two bucks a month."

Income is a crucial element in the quality of life. Principal sources of income were pension (19%), social security or SSI (57%), supplemental welfare benefits (14%), money from friends or relatives (10%), and other sources such as panhandling, hustling, odd jobs, and the like (20%). Only 6% had any sort of employment; however, 82% expressed a desire to work. Of all, 56% attempted to look for work, apparently without much success. Given their age and lack of skills, it is not surprising that they had failed to find employment. It should be emphasized that the men's work histories (an average of 20 years working) and current desire to work tended to undermine the notion that the men eschewed work, a point echoed in a recent study of mission users in Baltimore (Fischer, Breakey, Shapiro, & Kramer, 1986).

Finally, although most had prior work records and medical or psychiatric disorders that might have qualified them for social security disability and the fact that 73% of the

street men had annual incomes that should have qualified them for some minimal form of social service aid (i.e., they earned under $3,900 per year), only 45% of the men were receiving such assistance. Non-street men did considerably better in that 67% of the men reported receiving some form of social service aid. The 42% of non-street men who earned $3,900 or less, however, were presumably entitled to more assistance.

Although a majority of men had obtained some form of entitlement, most were receiving inadequate amounts. Thus, it behooved the Bowery man to find alternative sources of income. Popular means for obtaining money included panhandling, running (running errands for other men or agency personnel for cash), bedmaking and porter work in the flophouses, using loansharks and pawnshops, and thievery. Probably the most common way men obtained a few dollars was through loans from other men or pooling money together, usually for liquor but sometimes for food as well. Many of the more traditional skid row sources of income have disappeared. For example, the local employment agencies, pick-up jobs from trucks or at taverns, and the blood banks have vanished. Some men still obtained employment in resort hotels in the Catskills, but the number of hotels has also dwindled.

Nearly two-fifths of the men reported that they weren't eating well; 45% of the men said that they sometimes went without meals and one-fourth of the men claimed that they had lost 10 pounds in the past 3 months because they couldn't afford food. Among street men, two-thirds reported that they sometimes went without meals. The non-street men were considerably more likely to obtain a daily hot meal than the street men (61% versus 41%). This reflected the fact that 26% of non-street men had access to hotplates or stoves and 17% had access to a refrigerator. They also had a higher income and therefore 38% went daily to restaurants or cafeterias and another 34% ate in these facilities at least once a week. By contrast, only 7% of street men went daily to restaurants or cafeterias, although an additional 37% went to these facilities at least once a week.

Another primary source for obtaining hot meals was the local social service agency meal program. Both street and non-street men made equal use of agency meal programs. Of all, 49% went to such programs daily and an additional 27% went at least weekly. Clearly, such programs were the bulwark of nutritional survival for them. Because of the violence and aggressiveness on some food lines, one of the most popular places was the Bowery Residents' Committee, which has a publicly funded senior lunch program that provides over 100 hot lunches 6 days per week. This program was especially attractive because it excluded younger men, who are feared by the older men.

Missions provided another institutional alternative for meals. The price of a meal, however, was a 90-minute Bible Meeting. Most men were able to rationalize the mission routine: "They do not make you go to Mass. Your stomach might make you go in there." Finally, the hand-out is still a time-honored method for procuring food. One 60-year-old man described how he left his hotel at 4 o'clock in the morning and went to the Fulton Fish Market where he obtained discarded fish. There were also a few "bums" left on the Bowery who, because of their suspiciousness and fears, lack of initiative, or physical disabilities, did not regularly use formal agencies. These are the ragged men who seek food from garbage cans or obtain scraps from restaurants.

As with money and food procurement, economic circumstances and individual styles determined the type of shelter used. Although to the outsider, apartments and flophouses certainly seem preferable to street living, to some men the street is a better value. For example, there are men who live on the street during the summer and then move inside during the colder months. As one man described it, "I just can't see paying so much for so little, so I stay on the street."

In rating the quality of life in the flophouses it was not surprising given the close quarters of cubicles and dormitories to find that half the men complained of high noise level and two-fifths of men complained of disturbed sleep during the night due to noise. Despite the relatively poor quality of the hotels, only 6% of the men complained of problems getting repairs done and only 5% claimed to have any problems with the hotel manager. This was nearly 10% lower than the general New York City elderly sample. On the other hand, many of the men were passive and predisposed to resignation. For instance, 64% reported mice or roaches in their dwelling, yet only 1 in 5 men considered them a problem.

Urban street dwellers had a variety of colorful descriptions for this kind of living: carrying the banner, carrying the stick, and sleeping in Bush 13. The key objective for virtually all street men was to find a place to sleep that afforded safety and freedom from harassment. Despite the public image of the street man as a lone, psychotic individual, most older street men encountered were neither isolates nor psychotic. To attain some degree of security, many slept in pairs or groups: for instance, two on one bench and two on the next bench. Another street man said he shared an abandoned car with another man: one in the front and one in the back. Protection from the elements is crucial. When it rains, men who sleep in the park must run across the street and stand all night under some scaffolding or awning. In cold weather, men find a warm doorway, one that has a radiator; or they might try to get into a cellar. Some men bundle themselves inside a big cardboard box. Though group sleeping provides some security, life on the street can be intensively anxiety-provoking: "I can stretch out but I can't relax my body, lay down and sleep. It's no joke sitting up in a hard bench sleepin'. Everytime somebody passes I'm woke. My nerves is on edge 'cause I've seen people attacked in the park."

Crime is the principal fear of the older Bowery man, whether he lives in a flophouse or on the street. Of all, 65% were afraid of crime. A startling 59% of the street men and

51% of the non-street men were victims of crime during the previous year (mugging, assault, robbery). Moreover, 37% of street men and 33% of the non-street men reported having been victims of a crime involving personal injury during the previous year. By contrast, 4% of the New York City community elderly were crime victims and 2% reported a crime-induced personal injury during the previous year.

Although jackrollers (men who rob other men, usually when the latter are intoxicated) have been associated with skid rows since their origins, the general opinion is that the quantity and degree of viciousness of muggings are substantially higher than in the past. Some jackrollers travel in pairs, trios or even quintets (one notorious group was called the Filthy Five) and prowl the streets and dayrooms of the Men's Shelter around the first and sixteenth of each month when welfare checks arrive. One elderly black man told us, "I get mugged nearly every month. This month I lost my entire check right after I cashed it."

Although violent street crime is the most pronounced problem for these men, they are also victimized by various white collar crimes. Loan sharks, many of whom work in the hotels or taverns, usually ask 14 dollars back for every 10 dollars borrowed. Even more insidious is that most loan sharks often have the men's checks turned over to them. They extract the amount owed, and then the recipient is again short for the month and must borrow again. It is like the sharecropper owing the man out of the paycheck (Parker, 1970).

Health Care

Bowery men were considerably more physically impaired than their elderly male counterparts living in the general community. On 5 of 11 health scales (respiratory symptoms, hearing disorder, hypertension, edema, somatic symptoms) the Bowery men scored significantly worse than did the community men. In all, 33% of men reported that they had been hospitalized at least once in the past year. By contrast, New York City elderly community men reported symptoms at rates of approximately one-fourth to one-third that of Bowery men and 12% had been hospitalized in the previous year. Most men over age 65 seemed to have been able to obtain Medicare insurance. Despite annual incomes that made approximately one-half the men eligible for Medicaid assistance (under $3,900 per year), only 23% had such coverage. As has been found in other studies (Fischer, Shapiro, Breakey, Anthony, & Kramer, 1986), coverage was especially inadequate for street people. Although 73% had income that made them Medicaid eligible, only 15% were covered. Part of the problem in obtaining Medicaid was due to not having an address. Some street persons have used local missions as addresses, but for those who did not, the only alternative was to spend time in public shelters. At the time of this study, clients could qualify for Medicaid benefits after spending 15 days in a shelter. Benefits are granted for 90 days and clients can be recertified as long as they remain in the shelter system. Most older street persons, however, assiduously avoided shelters. Certainly, it was rare for them to spend 15 consecutive days in a shelter and to remain within the system for 90 days.

Though most men did not have their full entitlements, 77% had been to a doctor over the past year (there were no differences between street and non-street men). In all, 38% had gone only twice, but 23% had made 10 or more visits to the doctor. Most visits were to family practitioners or internists, but one-fourth had seen an eye or ear specialist. Psychiatric care was extremely limited. Although 23% of the men evidenced psychosis or had previous psychiatric hospitalization, only 3% were taking medication for mental or emotional problems. The men primarily used hospitals (73%) or neighborhood clinics (26%) for treatment. Fewer than 1 in 13 men generally sought medical care from a local doctor. Despite access to care, 44% of the men tended to postpone seeking medical attention when they felt ill. One primary reason (23%) was that they believed doctors would not help them; 19% also cited cost as a factor. The relatively high use of medical services is in agreement with some reports of skid row men in England, where these men were viewed as "high consumers of hospital outpatient services" (Scott, Gaskell, & Morrell, 1966).

Social Supports

Social support is a crucial element in the survival formula. Many earlier researchers tended to minimize the role of social supports, suggesting that these men were lifelong isolates whose poor social skills were one of the principal factors in accounting for their presence on skid row (Pittman & Gordon, 1958; Strauss, 1946). The notion that these men are total isolates or loners is false. Although the notion of isolation is untrue, the Bowery men were relatively isolated as compared to a group of elderly community dwelling men. Bowery men experienced 8.5 overall linkages versus the 11.1 among the community dwelling men. Although the difference in the total number of linkages was not statistically significant, the difference between the two populations in the number of informal linkages (kin and nonkin) was statistically significant: Bowery men had 6.4 informal ties versus 10.8 among the community men. Street men had one-third fewer overall linkages than did the non-street men (9.6 versus 6.0 linkages) and one-third fewer informal ties. Despite the relative smallness of the Bowery men's social world, it is a highly active one. The Bowery men saw network members 3.6 times per week, which was 50% more frequently than the community men. The flophouse men were especially apt to see their contacts, perhaps because the lodging house with its communal spaces served as a focal social point. Nonetheless, street men also saw their contacts quite frequently, averaging 3 times per week.

There were a handful of men who fit the stereotype of complete loners: 4.6% had only one linkage and an additional 7.1% had only two linkages. Perhaps because the flophouses tended to foster interaction, relative isolation was more common on the street: 9.3% of the street men had only one linkage and an additional 10.5% had only two linkages.

The Bowery man's social world reflected an adaptation to the needs of his environment. Compared to elderly community men who rarely used formal agencies or rarely had any personal relationships that involved exchange of sustenance items (food, money, medical aid), more than 3 of 5 Bowery relationships involved exchange of sustenance items and two-thirds of them used formal agencies. Reciprocity was the hallmark of nearly all Bowery relationships. Failure to reciprocate can quickly terminate a relationship. Indeed, Spradley (1970) has pointed out that friends are defined not only as persons to travel with, flop with, or share a jug with, but also by the kind of reciprocity involved in doing favors for each other. Reciprocity was especially strong among street men who had a mean directionality score of 2.06 (reciprocal = 2; dependency = 3; helping = 1). The non-street men showed slightly more tendency toward dependency on others, their mean directionality score being 2.13. Community elderly men who likewise viewed themselves as quite independent had mean scores of 2.17. By contrast, older men living in single room occupancy hotels evidenced the most dependency, with their mean directionality score being 2.36 (Sokolovsky, Cohen, Teresi, & Holmes, 1986).

Several empirical measures of group behavior were employed. First looked at was the number of clusters (groups of 3 or more persons in contact with each other) that each man was engaged in. Bowery men averaged 1.4 clusters: 83% of the men were enmeshed in at least one cluster and 44% were engaged in two or more clusters. Moreover, 46% of the men were engaged in clusters of five or more men. By contrast, elderly community men were engaged in twice as many clusters (mean = 2.8), but only 34% were engaged in large clusters of five or more men. Thus, the community man's social world consisted of 2 to 3 small clusters, whereas the Bowery man's social world consisted of 1 to 2 clusters, with one cluster usually being quite large and involving a substantial portion of their social network. This finding was also reflected in the empirical measures of overall network interconnectivity: Bowery men had approximately twice the number of interconnections among their network members than did the community men.

During the interviews various structures and functions of group activities were encountered. Some were small groupings of two, three or four men who might sleep together. There also were larger groups of five or six men who panhandled together, drank together, fed, and cared for each other. Although bottle gangs are usually transient, many street groups were comprised of men who had known each other for many years. Although relationships oscillated over the years, the overall mean length of acquaintance among street men was 7.7 years. Thus, such groups provided the men with emotional and material support in addition to alcohol. In a few instances, group formation revolved around father-figures who provided assistance to street men. For example, Roscoe is a 75-year-old former street person who now has his own place and serves as the superintendent of the building. He would allow men to sleep in the building's basement in inclement weather.

The importance of informal social supports was illustrated by the fact that 68% of linkages could be counted on for help. Moreover, when queried regarding whom they would turn to if they needed help with a small amount of cash, food, shopping, or if they were sick, 54%, 25%, 49%, 35% of the men, respectively, would go initially to their informal network system (hotel nonkin, outside nonkin, kin). As opposed to community men, who in roughly half the instances indicated that they would go to kin if they needed cash, food, or medication, were ill, or needed

shopping done, fewer than 1 in 30 Bowery men would rely on kin for addressing these problems. This response was markedly disproportionate to the number of kin members identified in their networks, 2.0 and 4.5 for Bowery and community men, respectively.

Although 77% of the Bowery men claimed to have at least one intimate, they were not necessarily persons to whom they could unburden their problems: 47% of the men claimed to have no one to talk to about their problems. Two-thirds said that they usually kept problems to themselves. On the other hand, the men felt that 73% of their contacts understood their problems. Thus, an intermediate level of intimacy was found among Bowery men.

As many traditional skid row institutions have disappeared, the men have come to rely more on social agencies to fulfill various needs. For example, the closing of many of the slop joints means that the men who have meager or no incomes must depend on agency food programs. Similarly, the closing of public baths and the considerable danger that exists in the remaining one leads many of the men to utilize the toilet facilities of several local agencies. The importance of formal contacts, especially agency personnel, in the lives of these men cannot be understated. Whereas relatively few elderly community men (17%) reported any regular formal linkages (to social workers and so forth) and the formal ties accounted for only 2% of their total linkages, Bowery non-street men had 2.4 formal linkages and the street men 1.2 formal ties: This represented between 20% to 25% of their total linkages. Moreover, 83% of non-street and 67% of street men had at least one formal linkage. The non-street men had more formal linkages because of the inclusion of hotel staff (desk clerks, maintenance staff) in this category. Of their 2.4 formal ties, 1.0 were with hotel staff and 1.4 were with agency staff. When queried regarding various hypothetical needs, the Bowery men (street and nonstreet) said they would use a service agency for a place to stay (51%), clothing (58%), information (74%), food (470%), and medication (28%). In addition, 24% of non-street men would rely on hotel staff if they were ill.

Conclusions

Some insight has been provided into how one segment of the aging homeless population has managed to cope with an environment that is undergoing considerable alteration. Over the past 2 decades these men have witnessed a host of rapid changes in their traditional milieu: the urban renewal and gentrification of much of skid row; the consequent diminution of many of the traditional skid row institutions such as taverns, slop joints, barber schools, used clothing stores, and job agencies; the influx of young men, minorities, and the deinstitutionalized; and a retrenchment in social service programs in the early 1980s that made obtaining entitlements more difficult. In addition, these men are often physically and emotionally ravaged by many years of heavy drinking, poor health, a treacherous environment, abject poverty, public abuse, and feelings of powerlessness and hopelessness. The ability of these men to somehow garner the resources to endure suggests an inner strength that contrasts with a popular image of these men as helpless, passive dregs of society. As one man put it, "I won't say I 'live' on the Bowery, I'd say 'survive'." Such a perspective underscores the human qualities of these men and thwarts society's attempts to invalidate and discard them. Perforce it compels rethinking the consequences of replacing a slop joint with a nouvelle cuisine bistro, a barber school with a beauty salon, or a flophouse with a condominium.

The correlation analysis has suggested several points for intervention. Physical health is a key variable in determining ability to fulfill needs. Although most men obtained health care, it was usually from large, unfriendly hospital clinics. Care was often inconsistent, with many men failing to comply with treatment. Assisting these men to obtain their medical entitlements and encouraging

the establishment of local medical facilities would serve to enhance physical care and regularity in treatment. Because use of various skid row institutions was found to enhance need fulfillment, local service agencies must be further strengthened and they must be allowed to broaden their services as traditional skid row institutions disappear. Last, although the flophouses barely provide the minimum standards for human habitation, they afford some advantages in stability, social support, and diminished life stressors when contrasted with street living. Thus, special efforts must be made to find suitable housing for the older street dwellers who have been crowded-out of public shelters and ignored by mainstream programs for seniors.

References

Aging Health Policy Center. (1985). *The homeless mentally ill elderly.* Working paper, University of California, San Francisco.

Bahr, H. M., & Caplow, T. (1973). *Old men drunk and sober.* New York: New York University Press.

Bassuk, E. L. (1984). The homelessness problem. *Scientific American, 251,* 40-45.

Blumberg, L., Shipley, T. E., & Shandler, I. W. (1973). *Skid row and its alternatives.* Philadelphia: Temple University Press.

Bogue, D. J. (1963). *Skid row in American cities.* Chicago: University of Chicago.

Brickner, R. W. (1985). Health issues in the care of the homeless. In P. W. Brickner, L. K. Schaner, B. Conanan, A. Elvy, & M. Savarese (Eds.), *Health care of homeless people.* New York: Springer.

Coalition for the Homeless. (1984). *Crowded out: Homelessness and the elderly poor in New York City.* New York: Author.

Fischer, R. J., Breakey, W. R., Shapiro, S., & Kramer, M. (1986). Baltimore mission users: Social networks, morbidity, and employment. *Psychosocial Rehabilitation Journal, 9,* 51-63.

Fischer, P. J., Shapiro, S., Breakey, W. R., Anthony, J. C., & Kramer, M. (1986). Mental health and social characteristics of the homeless: A survey of mission users. *American Journal of Public Health, 76,* 519-524.

Holden, C. (1986). Homelessness: Experts differ on root causes. *Science, 232,* 569-570.

New York City Human Resources Administration. (1983). *Project future: Focusing understanding, targeting, and utilizing resources for homeless mentally ill, older persons, youth and employables.* New York: Author.

Parker, R. (1970). *A view from the Bowery.* Unpublished manuscript.

Pittman, D. J., & Gordon, T. W. (1958). *Revolving door: A study of the chronic police case inebriate.* Glencoe, IL: Free Press.

Scott, R., Gaskell, R. G., & Morrell, D. C. (1966). Patients who reside in common lodging-houses. *British Medical Journal, 2,* 1561-1564.

Sokolovsky, J., Cohen, C. I., Teresi, J., & Holmes, D. (1986). Gender, networks, and adaptation among an inner-city elderly population. *The Gerontologist, 26,* Special Issue, 247A.

Spradley, J. P. (1970). *You owe yourself a drunk.* Boston: Little, Brown.

Strauss, R. (1946). Alcohol and the homeless man. *Quarterly Journal of Studies of Alcohol, 7,* 360-404.

Wallace, S. (1965). *Skid row as a way of life.* Totowa, NJ: Bedminister.

1 Imagine that you are a gerontologist from a distant planet sent to Earth to learn about the experience of aging in the contemporary United States. You decide to gather your information by reading magazines and watching television. What would you conclude about old age? How might your views of aging vary by gender, race, and class? How accurate and complete a picture would you likely bring back to your home planet?

2 What are the meanings of old age reflected in birthday cards? Are there any differences in cards designed for men and cards designed for women? Try your hand at designing a line of birthday greetings that avoid ageist messages.

3 A major theme of this book centers on the interlocking hierarchies based on gender, race, and social class. We argued in the Introduction that people can be privileged on some dimensions but disadvantaged on others. In what ways can this model help us understand the experiences of old men in the Bowery compared with those of Helen Hayes, of Pardee Lowe, and of the mother in Langston Hughes's poem?

4 Children who are members of disadvantaged racial or ethnic groups face the challenge of developing positive self-concepts in the face of racist imagery. How was this challenge handled by Sadie and Bessie Delany, by Pardee Lowe, by Zora Neale Hurston, and by the Cherokee family in Barbara Kingsolver's story?

5 Old age also forces us to confront physical changes in our own bodies. In the Introduction, we argued that the social context in which we experience these changes mediates their impact on how we feel about ourselves. How did the social worlds of Helen Hayes, Shevy Healey, and the old men in the Bowery influence both the consequences of and their responses to the aging process?

SUGGESTIONS FOR FURTHER READING

1 Martz, S. H. (Ed.). (1987). *When I am an old woman I shall wear purple* and (1992). *If I had my life to live over, I would pick more daisies.* Watsonville, CA: Papier-Mache.

We selected the title pieces of these anthologies of writings about older women for this book; others of the stories, poems, and essays illustrate the ways in which women's choices, from childhood to old age, are influenced by their ethnic and cultural identity, social class and economic resources, age, and gender. The women write about the personal meanings of old age in a culture that celebrates youth.

2   Banner, L. (1983). *American beauty*. New York: Knopf.

Lois Banner chronicles the history of perceptions of feminine beauty in the United States. Changing definitions and standards of beauty are linked to other social and cultural events in different historical periods. Banner interprets beauty as both a source of power and a source of oppression for women.

3   Terkel, S. (1992). *Race: How blacks and whites think and feel about the American obsession*. New York: Doubleday.

More than 80 diverse voices speak about the experience of race in U.S. society and in their everyday lives. Terkel has captured the changing social and cultural landscape through interviews with a cross section of Americans over the past three decades.

4   Collins, P. H. (1990). *Black feminist thought: Knowledge, consciousness, and the politics of empowerment*. Boston: Unwin Hyman.

The selection "Mammies, Matriarchs, and Other Controlling Images" describes how negative images and standards of beauty of African American women operate as ideological justifications for oppression. The book, which won the C. Wright Mills Award, shares the voices of many African American women and demonstrates the new insights that emerge from seeing social reality from different standpoints.

5   Myerhoff, B. (1978). *Number our days*. New York: Simon & Schuster.

The anthropologist Barbara Myerhoff studied a group of elderly Jewish people attending a community center in Venice, California. While documenting daily problems of poverty, loneliness, and poor health, Myerhoff also demonstrates how the Jewish community provided a forum for constructing meaning in old age, for celebrating individual biography, and for sharing lessons of survival. Her work expands our understanding of the impact of World War II on today's elders by exploring the impact of the Holocaust.

6   Goings, K. W. (1993). Memorabilia that have perpetuated
    stereotypes about African Americans. In V. Cyrus (Ed.),
    Experiencing race, class and gender in the United States (pp.
    165-167). Mountain View, CA: Mayfield.

    Kenneth Goings analyzes racial and gender stereotypes in
    commonplace objects such as housewares, toys, and lawn
    ornaments produced over the past 100 years. Described by
    collectors as memorabilia, these items were part of the everyday
    environment in which today's cohorts of older Americans grew
    up. The pervasiveness of the negative images contribute to their
    most pernicious effects.

7   Gates, H. L., Jr. (1989, November 12). TV's black world
    turns—but stays unreal. *New York Times*, sec. II, pp. 1 ff.

    Professor Gates analyzes images of African Americans on
    television over the past 40 years. His insightful analyses
    highlight the subtle ways in which popular television
    programming denies the reality of oppression and reinforces
    racial stereotypes. Gates provides us with a new lens through
    which to see both contemporary programs and reruns from
    decades past.

8   *The long walk home* [Film]. (1991). Van Nuys, CA: Live Home
    Video.

    The Montgomery Bus Boycott is the setting for this film about a
    domestic worker and her employer who are caught up in the
    early years of the Civil Rights movement. The courage of the
    domestic worker in risking her job to honor the boycott forces
    her employer to confront the consequences of racism in her own
    life.

9   Campbell, B. M. (1992). *Your blues ain't like mine*. New York: G. P.
    Putnam.

    Set in the American South of the 1950s, Campbell's novel
    illustrates the climate of racism and sexism and the harsh
    realities of class inequality in which current cohorts of elderly
    Americans experienced their early and middle adult years. The
    main characters illustrate the impact of varying positions along
    hierarchies of race, class, and gender on the social contexts that
    shaped their lives.

10 Delany, S., & Delany, E. (with A. H. Hearth). (1993). *Having our say:
    The Delany sisters' first 100 years*. New York: Kodansha America.

    Sisters Sadie and Bessie Delany recall growing up in
    turn-of-the-century North Carolina. They recount their

confrontations with Jim Crow and local segregation, the World War I era migration North, and their lives as professional women during the heyday of Harlem. The daughters of the nation's first elected African American Episcopal bishop, the sisters were disadvantaged by race and gender but advantaged by social class.

PART III

Productive Activity

Paid and Unpaid

Expanding the Definition of Productivity in Old Age

What are productive activities? By economic definition, they are behaviors that add to the stock and flow of valued goods and services. Traditionally, paid work has been the exclusive measure of productivity. Recent arguments, however, have favored expanding the definition to include unpaid activities. This would be useful for two reasons. First, many unpaid activities also fit the definition of productivity, because they produce valued goods or services. Second, using paid work as the only measure does not give a complete picture of productivity in certain disadvantaged groups in the population: the elderly, women, minorities, and individuals with handicapping lifetime paid work experiences. The contributions of these groups to society are underestimated when unpaid work is not included along with paid work in calculating their productivity.

Here we develop an inclusive approach to the study of productive activity in late life that will more accurately assess the contributions to society of disadvantaged members of systems of inequality. This approach has three goals:

1. To view productivity as a continuum over the life span
2. To broaden the definition of productivity to include both paid and unpaid work
3. To expand definitions of productivity beyond experiences of the dominant group

Productivity Over the Life Course

Humans have engaged in productive activity from the beginning of time. Evidence from other cultures indicates that such activity was varied and endured across the life course. Probably the most common pattern connecting age and productive roles in preindustrial societies is for people to shift to less physically demanding tasks as they get older (Cowgill, 1986). For example, among the Inuit people in Alaska, older men who could no longer hunt or fish made and repaired tools and weapons used by younger men (Guemple, 1983). Advanced age had less impact on the productivity of older women, as they could "continue their normal domestic activities into very advanced stages of debility" (Cowgill, 1986, p. 120).

In some societies, such as that of the Bushmen of the Kalahari Desert in South Africa, everyone is encouraged to work as long as possible. Older men continue to hunt to the extent they are physically able and make decisions about moving to new hunting areas (E. M. Thomas, 1959). Older women share the knowledge they have accumulated during their lives about where to find berries and tubers. Elderly people are also responsible for distributing food. In other societies, people move through a series of increasingly important productive roles as they age. Cowgill (1986) describes this pattern of ascendancy among Sidamo men in Ethiopia:

> Each life transition represents a movement toward greater responsibility and higher status. The life cycle for the male is a progression from birth and early childhood to young manhood, marriage, promotion to elderhood, exalted old age, and death. During childhood he is schooled to perform services for and to show respect for his elders. The son runs errands, works and cares for his parents. He learns to herd the cattle that are the principal form of wealth in his society. He learns to plant and cultivate maize and ensete. Initiation marked by circumcision and a period of seclusion celebrate his ascendancy to manhood, and marriage usually takes place shortly thereafter. At marriage he can expect an allocation of land from his father, and he will begin to accumulate wealth, both by working his land and by raiding the cattle herds of neighboring tribes. Daring and bravery during these raids and the resulting warfare are honored but so is excellence in oratory and debate. Promotion to elderhood is a major transition that usually takes place in middle age. Thereafter he ceases to do manual labor and gives up raiding and warfare. He becomes part of the paternal generation, which directs the work of the younger people and exercises judicial functions, settling disputes and restraining the rivalry and competition among youths. As an elder he is deferred to in both speech and services, and he is revered for his wisdom. Furthermore, as he moves on toward old age, his status and influence increase. Eventually an old man (approximately 70) may become a woma, one who personifies the highest ideals of the culture. Such a person embodies courage, truth, justice, and wisdom and is even believed to possess the power to foretell the future. (pp. 112-113)

In contrast to these images of productivity in preindustrial societies, contemporary U.S. society has not viewed productivity as continuous. Instead, the prevalent view is that productivity ends and nonproductivity begins somewhere at the end of middle age when people leave the paid workforce. Retirement is thought to mark the end of productive work and the beginning of leisure. Historical and anthropological evidence, survey research, and personal accounts, however, all belie this simplistic view. Production of valued goods and services continues well into old age, as this example from the life of an older African American woman of the rural South suggests:

Maude Lee Bryant is a midwife. She is eighty-five years old and lives on a farm which she and her husband, Gade, own in Chatham County, North Carolina. She has already put on lunch for her sons and others who work the farm and is out helping a neighbor grind his cane [sugar cane] when we arrive.

The midwife was one of the best-known members of a North Carolina rural community, and her skills, often learned from her mother, were as essential as a man's knowing how to plant and to plow. Payment for their services was as remote as the lighted rooms of a hospital. They went quickly and willingly as if hearing in their dreams the call of a woman in her need. (Wilson & Mullalley, 1983, pp. 37, 40)

New research findings on large national samples of older Americans also provide evidence that productive activity continues across the life span. For example, Herzog, Kahn, Morgan, Jackson, and Antonucci (1989) examined both paid work and unpaid productive activities, including volunteer work in organizations, informal help to family and friends, maintenance and repair of home and possessions, and housework, among a sample of people aged 25 and over. Although older people were less likely than younger people to participate in the labor force as paid workers, individuals 65 and over participated in unpaid productive activities at levels comparable to those of middle-aged and younger people.

The Impact of Ignoring Unpaid Work on Estimates of Productivity

Two social trends, societal aging and the changing characteristics of the labor force, are creating new cultural realities for studying productive activities in late life. As we move into the twenty-first century, there will be more people who will live to age 100, more minority workers in the labor force, and more people who will need to combine paid work in the labor force with the unpaid work of caring for increasing numbers of very old family members. How much sense does it make for productive activity to stop at age 65 when an individual has 35 more years to live? Will there be enough paid work for everyone who wishes to work? Is it fair to discount social care provided mainly by women in national assessments of productivity? What are the consequences of defining work and retirement according to the labor market experiences of white middle-class men? These are some of the questions that beg a reevaluation of definitions of productivity and a reconsideration of the ways different activities contribute to society.

Treating paid work as the whole of productive activity underestimates the productivity of women, minorities, and people in low-level occupations. Estimates of productivity that only count paid work will conclude that these individuals are less productive than white men employed in highly paid occupations. However, when unpaid work is also considered, these individuals are no less productive than their more privileged counterparts. People who are disadvantaged along hierarchies based on gender, race, and social class also have different patterns of paid work over their life course than their more privileged counterparts. By ignoring the restrictions on their opportunities in the labor market, culturally defined responsibility for housework and care of family members, and the adaptive strategies they develop to manage these restrictions, we overlook the ways in which they blend paid and unpaid productive work to survive and to provide for their families.

Patterns of Productivity Based on Gender

Researchers studying work and family have documented differences in the paid work patterns of men and women. First, women are less likely than men to maintain continuous labor force participation throughout their adult lives. Stone (1989) describes the checkered work histories that disadvantage women in paid work over a lifetime:

> Many women who work for pay exhibit interrupted work patterns including mid-life career entry, intermittent employment throughout the work cycle, and frequent job changes. Erratic work history is most often the consequence of childbearing and childrearing, which cause many women to delay or interrupt their work careers. Thus, women have an in and out pattern of the worklife. (p. 207)

Women are also more likely than men to participate in a broad range of unpaid activities that produce valued goods and services yet are not included in national assessments of their productivity:

> The division of labor with regard to caregiving does not stop with childrearing but continues throughout the life cycle. Just as women are beginning to anticipate the empty nest, many are faced with the responsibility of caring for disabled husbands, parents, and other adult family members. A large proportion also must deal with the competing demands of employment and eldercare. (Stone, 1989, p. 207)

In addition to caring for the needs of family members, women are responsible for the majority of housework. The economist F. Thomas Juster studied the division of household labor in 1965, when today's cohorts of elderly people were middle-aged adults, and found that, among married couples, wives performed about 80% of the unpaid housework. The productive value of these goods and services becomes obvious when we consider replacing the unpaid work that women perform in their roles as wives, mothers, and housewives with goods produced in the market or with services performed by paid workers.

Nona Malbin-Glazer (1976) estimated the value of women's unpaid family work at $13,000 per year. Translating that figure into 1995 dollars results in an estimate of $32,202. Lack of recognition of this unpaid domestic labor has long-term consequences for women's access to pension and other resources in old age, as Quadagno and Meyer illustrate in their article "Gender and Public Policy" (1990).

Herzog and her colleagues (1989) shed some additional light on women's overall productivity. Using measures of both paid work and unpaid work, including housework and caring for family members, they found that although women spend less time than men in paid work, they spend more time than men in unpaid work. These two types of activities balanced out, leading Herzog and her colleagues to conclude that the total productivity of men and women does not differ.

Patterns of Productivity Based on Social Class

As with gender inequality, people who are disadvantaged by their social class also exhibit patterns of overall productivity that differ from those of their more privileged counterparts. People from poor or working-class backgrounds have a lifetime of lower wages, less job security, fewer pension and other fringe benefits, and greater risk of occupational injury than more middle- and upper-class workers (Crystal & Shea, 1990). As a result, they are less able to afford to retire completely from paid work when they are older. Toni Calasanti and A. Bonanno (1992) describe the situation of a retired working-class woman named Betty. Despite a lifetime of paid work, she was unable to accumulate enough resources to support herself in retirement. To supplement her limited income, she continues to produce valued goods and services, which she exchanges for the support she needs. Betty survives by providing domestic labor, with irregular pay, for her live-in brother-in-law. Both recognize that he could not otherwise afford the services she provides and that his financial contributions are vital to her survival:

> I worry about him. If I lost him, I'd lose a major part out of my life because not only does he help me financially for taking care of him, which he said he'd have to pay 3 or 4 times as much if he had to be put in a nursing home. You see, you look at both sides of the question. He helps me out and I help him. Now he doesn't actually pay me money but like if something comes up, why like if I have to have something done to my car, he'll help me pay for it. Or something goes wrong with the house, why he'll have to pay for it, see. We go grocery shopping and he mostly pays for the groceries . . . so that's money in a way. (p. 144)

Patterns of Productivity Based on Race

Minority workers also have checkered work lives that lead to underestimates of their total productivity. For example, between ages 45 and 64, African Americans and Hispanic Americans constitute larger proportions of the unemployed labor force than do white Americans. Simple comparisons of the percentage of whites and nonwhites who are employed obscure the greater tendency for minorities to be part-year, part-time, and seasonal workers or to be discouraged workers (i.e., people who want to work but have given up looking for jobs) who are not even counted in labor force statistics.

The current generation of older African American women had particularly disadvantaged work lives. Comparing the work experiences of older white men and women and older African American men and women over a six-year period, Gibson (1983) found that older African American women were the most likely of the four groups to have spotty work patterns. They had been with their employers the shortest time and had the fewest years, weeks, and hours of work. Living in areas of high unemployment also decreased work time for the African American women.

As with the work patterns of women, looking only at paid work fails to tell the whole story. Older minorities are engaged in many types of unpaid, yet productive activities. James Jackson, Toni Antonucci, and Rose Gibson (1993) applied a typology of three types of economic exchange networks to illuminate the range of productive activities performed by older members of minority groups. In the regular economic network, exchanges of labor are made for pay and are regulated by government accounting and tax systems. Workers pay income taxes and Social Security contributions on the money that they earn. The government is aware of these activities, and they are counted in national estimates of productivity. In the irregular economic network, pay is also involved, but economic exchanges are informal and not subject to government regulations or taxation. Payment for services is often described as "under the table," and this exchange network is often referred to as the "underground" or "shadow" economy. The government is not likely to be aware of these activities, which include such things as cutting hair in your basement for pay or performing domestic labor or yard work when payment is in cash and the income is not reported to the government either through income tax or Social Security contributions. In the social economic network, people do not receive direct cash payments for the work they do. Goods and services are reciprocally exchanged independent of money payment—favor for favor. For example, a person who owns a car may run errands or shop for an older neighbor who, in turn, will watch the younger woman's children after school.

Production of valued goods and services in the irregular and social economic networks by African Americans and other disadvantaged Americans are well documented. Carol Stack (1974) describes exchanges within these networks among residents of The

Flats, the poorest section of an African American community in a midwestern city:

> Black families living in The Flats need a steady source of cooperative support to survive. They share with one another because of the urgency of their needs. Alliances between individuals are created around the clock as kin and friends exchange and give and obligate one another. They trade food stamps, rent money, a TV, hats, dice, a car, a nickel here, a cigarette there, food, milk, grits and children. (p. 32)

Stack concludes that it is this kin-based exchange network that protects residents of The Flats from going hungry.

Community organizations, particularly churches, provide another setting for informal exchanges of goods and services. Within African American communities, churches are a resource through which people can provide services to others and on which they can draw in times of need. Sister Minnie, the elderly member of the A.M.E. Church we met in the Introduction, relied on the church for support. As Cole (1986) explains, "When the social services she and her family needed were not provided by the city, state, or federal government, it was to her sisters and brothers in the church that she turned for help" (p. 310). Unlike social services provided by various levels of government, however, services contributed by church members are not counted in estimates of economic productivity. Neither are the child care activities of the "othermothers" we describe in Part IV on family. This kind of bartering with family, friends, church members, and neighbors in the irregular or social economic networks is facilitated by patterns of family interdependence, by the importance of religion and the church, and by values that emphasize group rather than individual achievement (Cantor, 1979; Stack, 1974).

Gibson, Jackson, and Antonucci estimated productivity levels for older African Americans, including unpaid or uncounted activities in the irregular and social economic networks. Although comparisons of time spent in paid labor often suggest that African Americans are less productive than white Americans, this more inclusive approach of counting activities in all three economic networks indicated that older African Americans are as productive as their white counterparts.

In summary, we suggest that the productivity of people who are disadvantaged in systems of inequality—women, minorities, and those of low socioeconomic status—is underestimated when paid work is the only criterion. For an inclusive approach to the study of productivity, on both individual and societal grounds, definitions of productivity need broadening to include unpaid behaviors that also produce valued goods or services. The Alzheimer patient's unpaid caretaker at home is no less productive than his or her paid caretaker in a nursing home setting. The volunteer typist in a church or hospital is no less productive than the typist sitting next to him or her who receives a salary. The person who cleans and cooks for pay in the homes of others is no more productive than the person who does the same work for his or her own household (Herzog et al., 1989). In all of these cases, the product is identical and the work equally productive.

Differences in the Availability of Productive Activity Roles

As the previous discussion suggests, people's positions within systems of inequality influence the way they allocate their time between paid and unpaid activities. Position along interlocking hierarchies based on gender, race, and social class also influences people's access to particular types of each category of productive activity. For example, although women typically perform more unpaid domestic labor than men, women's social class position determines how they execute this work. Whereas poor and working-class women generally do their own housework, more affluent women are able to delegate some of these responsibilities to paid workers. By hiring domestic help, they are "relieved of the drudgery of doing housework themselves. They become, instead, the managers of the drudgery of domestic work done by other women" (Cole, 1986, p. 8).

Social class determines access to volunteer roles. Susan Ostrander's book *Women of the Upper Class* (1984) describes the activities of upper-class volunteers. The upper-class women interviewed by Ostrander served on boards of directors of community organizations, setting policy and planning fund-raising campaigns. These leadership positions contrast with the more "hands-on" activities of middle- and working-class people, for whom volunteer work more often involves activities such as tutoring children in after-school programs, delivering flowers or mail to hospital patients, soliciting door-to-door contributions for a local charity, or staffing the entry desk at the museum. "Community Volunteer," one of the chapters in Ostrander's book, focuses on the experiences of Mrs. Sharpe, the wife of a wealthy stockbroker, now in her sixties. Mrs. Sharpe's productive activities are unpaid and therefore not counted in conventional national accounting systems that focus on wages and salaries. Because of her upper-class status, she has access to volunteer roles that enable her to exercise power and to garner respect. In fact, several of Ostrander's subjects explained that volunteer work is more rewarding psychologically than would be the paid work roles available to women. For Mrs. Sharpe, receiving a salary for her productive activity was less important than the benefits she received from her unpaid volunteer work: a context for recognition and accomplishment and an opportunity to contribute to society, while upholding and legitimating the dominance of the upper class.

People's positions on interlocking systems of inequality also influence access to different types of paid productive activity. Not all people have equal access to the most desirable occupations. Prevailing social structures limit the opportunities of people with certain sociodemographic characteristics to pursue particular jobs. Several of the selections that follow portray working conditions faced by some members of today's cohorts of older Americans during the historical period when they were entering the workforce. Tillie Olsen's poem "I Want You Women Up North to Know" describes the working conditions of Hispanic garment workers in the Southwest; Victoria Byerly's selection tells the story of southern mill worker Aliene Walser; and Studs Terkel's interview with Mike LeFevre describes work in the steel mills of Chicago.

As social structures change across historical times, however, so does the availability of certain occupations, and today's elderly members of minority groups have experienced changes in their occupational opportunities over their life course. Nevertheless, many entered the labor force at a time when their opportunities were severely constricted. We can illustrate this process by considering two types of paid productive activity traditionally available to African Americans: domestic worker and Pullman porter.

Before World War II, workers of color were locked into a narrow band of jobs at the bottom of the occupational hierarchy. Nearly all African American women workers were domestics. This was an occupation with long hours, low wages, and poor working conditions. The quotation from "Slave Markets Typify Exploitation of Domestics" written by Louise Mitchell in 1940 describes the exploitation of domestic workers in New York City:

Every morning, rain or shine, groups of women with brown paper bags or cheap suitcases stand on street corners in the Bronx and Brooklyn waiting for a chance to get some work. Sometimes they are 15, sometimes 30, some are old, many are young and most of them are Negro women waiting for employers to come to the street corner auction blocks to bargain for their labor.

They come as early as 7 in the morning, wait as late as 4 in the afternoon with the hope that they will make enough to buy supper when they go home. Some have spent their last nickel to get to the corner and are in desperate need. When the hour grows late, they sit on boxes if any are around. In the afternoon their labor is worth only half as much as in the morning. If they are lucky, they get about 30 cents an hour scrubbing, cleaning, laundering, washing windows, waxing floors and woodwork all day long; in the afternoon, when most have already been employed, they are only worth the degrading sum of 20 cents an hour.

Once hired on the 'slave market,' the women often find after a day's backbreaking toil, that they worked longer than was arranged, got less than was promised, were forced to accept clothing instead of cash and were exploited beyond human endurance. Only the urgent need for money makes them submit to this routine daily . . . they have no social security, no workmen's compensation, no old age security. (pp. 275-281)

As late as 1935, African American women did housework and laundry for $3 a week and African American washerwomen did a week's wash for 75 cents. The selection by Elsa Barkley Brown ("Mothers of Mind") in Part IV, "Family," and the selection by Gwendolyn Brooks "At the Burns-Coopers' " in this part illustrate the concentration of African American women in domestic work. Brown (1991) describes her mother's search for employment after graduating from college with a degree in mathematics in 1938: "It took some time but finally she did find a job, with an employer who was suitably impressed with all this young African American girl had accomplished; yes, it would be so refreshing to have an intelligent maid for a change" (p. 80). This restriction of African American women to domestic work, with its substandard wages and employment conditions, reflected the vulnerability of women workers combined with the effects of racial and class discrimination (Lerner, 1973).

In June 1941, however, the president of the United States issued Executive Order 8802 banning discrimination in defense industries and in government because of race, creed, color, or national origin. This governmental intervention plus increased labor shortages brought more minority workers into the labor force and began to improve their status. One of the more significant shifts in the occupational structure was the movement of African American women from domestic work into the steel foundries, munitions and aircraft plants, the army, canneries, and hospitals (Baxandall, Gordon, & Reverby, 1976). In earlier years, the majority of African American women were private household workers, but by 1960 the proportion had dropped to 34%. By 1977, only 8% were employed in domestic work.

Employment of African American men as Pullman porters is another example of how people with specific sociodemographic characteristics are channeled into certain productive activities in particular historical times. The Pullman porter was to railroad travel what the skycap and flight attendant are to airplane travel. Many black Pullman porters of the 1920s and 1930s were college and university graduates. Among them were physicians, attorneys, pharmacists, and Ph.D.s. Because they completed college and sought employment in an era of legalized racial discrimination, they were relegated to jobs near the bottom of the occupational hierarchy. The black Pullman porter is yet another example of how prevailing social structures impose limits on the types of paid productive activities available for certain individuals. The concentration of many educated African American men in this occupation also illustrates how being advantaged along two hierarchies (gender and class) but disadvantaged along another (race) still limited available employment opportunities.

The Impact of Productive Activity Across the Life Course on Economic Well-Being in Old Age

The financial resources available to people in old age reflect patterns of productive activity over the life course. For example, the "in-and-out" labor force experiences of many women decrease their opportunities to become vested in pension plans and limit their ability to establish earnings profiles that translate into higher pensions and Social Security benefits when they retire. Stone (1989) sums up the ways in which paid and unpaid productive activities of women shape their life course and financial well-being in old age:

> In order to understand why women are more likely than men to be poor in old age, it is important to recognize that the economic status of elderly persons depends on their lifelong marital and family obligations and their employment history. Paternalistic customs and laws that encouraged female dependency, the division of labor between genders with women as primary caregivers, and labor market discrimination are important determinants of gender differences in poverty among the elderly. (p. 205)

People with continuous labor force attachment generally have more resources than people who have intermittent employment patterns. But the sector of the economy in which one has been employed also influences a person's opportunity to accumulate resources. People seeking jobs face a dual labor market. Workers employed in the primary labor market enjoy higher wages, greater opportunities for advancement, greater job stability, better working conditions, and better pension and health insurance benefits. The secondary labor market, where women workers and workers of color have been disproportionately concentrated, offers poorer working conditions, lower wages, limited fringe benefits, and unstable employment. Even if they work continuously during their adult lives, workers employed in the secondary labor market enter old age with fewer resources (Dowd, 1980). Because their wages were low, their Social Security benefits will be low and they are less likely to have accumulated assets such as stocks or bonds. They are also less likely to have private pensions or private health insurance. Workers whose paid productive activity has been concentrated in the irregular economic network may not even be eligible for Social Security and Medicare because much of their income was never reported to the government.

In contrast, white men from affluent backgrounds are disproportionately concentrated in professional and managerial positions in which their continuous labor force attachment is rewarded with salary increases, promotion opportunities, job security, challenging and interesting work, pension benefits, and opportunities to shelter income in individualized retirement accounts (Crystal, Shea, & Krishnaswami, 1992). Stephen Crystal and Dennis Shea (1990) have argued that the effects of early advantages accumulate across the life course, producing large differences in economic resources in old age:

> Over the life course, the structure of retirement income programs interacts with the workings of the labor market and with patterns of consumer behavior, such as savings and investment, in producing the distribution of economic outcomes. . . .
>
> Respondents with more education had access to higher status jobs; were able to continue work longer; and were more likely to be self-employed, all tending to increase adjusted income. . . .
>
> Tax-advantaged private pension systems provide benefits predominantly to those who held the "better" jobs in the economy and had stable employment patterns; IRA, Keogh, and other industrial savings systems benefiting from tax deferral similarly benefit higher-income individuals disproportionately . . .
>
> These findings suggest that stratification established early in the life course continues at least as sharply in the later years. (Crystal et al., 1992, p. S220)

Differences in the Meaning of Retirement and Productive Activity in Old Age

Common wisdom suggests that older people retire from paid employment and shift from productive activity to leisure pursuits. The more inclusive definition of productivity we develop here indicates that retirement from paid work often means reallocation of time to various types of paid and unpaid productive activity. Choices regarding paid and unpaid activities and the meanings people attach to these choices vary according to their positions along hierarchies based on gender, race, and class.

Affluent elderly people enjoy the greatest discretion in choosing among productive and leisure activities in late life. Although they may retire from occupations they found personally rewarding, they can often continue to exert leadership roles through volunteer positions in the community. They have the financial resources to pursue leisure activities. Given the association between socioeconomic status and health (see Part V), they encounter fewer restrictions in mobility than their less affluent counterparts.

Not all older people can afford to retire completely. For some working-class elderly people, retirement income falls short of meeting their basic needs or maintaining their former lifestyles. Some of these individuals need to supplement their economic resources with part-time work. Toni Calasanti and Alessandro Bonanno (1992) introduce us to two workers facing this situation:

> After retiring from a low pay job, Lorraine continued to work part-time another eight years in low-wage positions-cleaning in a nursing home and tending a laundromat counter. Mindful of her reliance on this income, her feeling is that retirement is "wonderful, if I can work." (p. 144)

> Poor health forced Marie to retire from a monopoly firm in her fifties. Although she worked since very young, she was always a marginal worker. She held seasonal jobs, usually in a tobacco factory, waited tables, and worked for various firms as a sewing machine operator. Finally, monopoly firm work stabilized her employment, but at low pay. After 20 years, her job yields less than $100 a month in pension. Her total monthly income of about $400 must cover a house payment and all other expenses, including prescription medications. To supplement, she makes things at home to sell. She sews such things as ducks and pillows, and makes quilts until her fingers hurt from being pricked. Then she switches to crocheting things such as Easter egg covers. One of her prouder accomplishments is a yarn poodle she can now finish "in just 5 days." She sells these days of labor for $25. These activities are crucial to her survival; as she puts it, "if it's the end of the month and I can sell a duck for $5, it helps me pay my medicine." (p. 143)

Even with these financial pressures, retirement is still viewed positively by many working-class and low-income elders. Compared with more advantaged workers, disadvantaged workers are more likely to have experienced chronic unemployment, work disability, or part-time, part-year, seasonal, and joyless work. For these older people, the paid worker role may be less satisfying than for more privileged workers who were rewarded not only with high incomes but with prestige, deference, and challenging opportunities. Retirement can also have a special meaning for older people with a lifetime of sporadic work: For the first time in their lives, a check—Social Security or Supplemental Security Income payments—comes every month!

Not all older people consider themselves retired. For both older African Americans and older Mexican Americans, checkered work lives often continue into old age. Economic need requires many to continue their lifelong pattern of sporadic work in low-paying jobs. The continuation of the "in-and-out" employment pattern seems to blur the line between work and nonwork to the extent that these minority elders do not always think of themselves as retired, despite the fact they are not consistently working. The availability of disability pay provides both an alternative identity and an alternative source of income for older people who are also work disabled. Defining themselves as disabled often has greater economic benefits than calling themselves retired, because disability benefits are often higher than retirement benefits based on a lifetime of low-wage work (Gibson, 1987; Zsembek & Singer, 1990). An article by Rose Gibson, "Reconceptualizing Retirement for Black Americans" (1987), describes the situation of some of these disabled older workers. She demonstrates the ways in which productive activity roles earlier in life shape both economic well-being in old age and the meanings of work and retirement roles. The African Americans she studied had worked in "low status jobs characterized by sporadic work patterns and low earnings." These lifetime work patterns produced a precarious financial situation such that "work in old age, in the same low status jobs, becomes a necessity for many." Her article also illustrates the ways in which concepts based on the experiences of the dominant group can mask diversity in the experience of retirement. Many studies consider individuals retired if they are not working full-time, if they define themselves as retired, and if they receive retirement income (e.g., Social Security or other pension benefits). Defining retirement according to work patterns of white middle-class men causes researchers to overlook the experiences of poor African American workers who maximize their economic resources in late life by labeling themselves disabled rather than retired. By this definition, poor disabled elderly people who choose disability benefits over less lucrative Social Security or pension benefits would not be considered retired. Neither would a retired person who at the time a study was conducted had taken a temporary position to supplement inadequate retirement income. Neither would a widow who had spent most of her life caring for her children, her elderly parents, and her terminally ill husband. As Gibson warns, developing more inclusive definitions of retirement is a prerequisite to designing research and policy to "enhance the lives of all elderly individuals in American society."

The experiences of these workers provide another example of the link between productive activity throughout the life course and economic resources in late life. Rather than the "cumulative advantage" experienced by the high-status managers and professionals described by Crystal and Shea, the experiences of these minority workers illustrate a process of "cumulative disadvantage."

Key Issues

The availability and meaning of both paid and unpaid productive activities, the ways in which these activities influence the life course, and the linkages between early- and late-life productive activities are different for people who occupy different positions in systems of inequality. Our discussion and the following readings emphasize several points:

1. Productive activity continues over the life course.

2. Using traditional definitions of productivity inaccurately assesses the productivity of people who are disadvantaged in systems of inequality.

3. Differences due to membership in various systems of inequality arise in

    a. the availability of productive activity roles,

    b. the way productive activity roles affect the life course,

    c. the meanings attached to productive activity roles, and

    d. role transitions and the links between early- and late-life roles.

The Readings

Several of the readings that follow provide insight into the paid work experiences of today's cohorts of elderly Americans. The quotation from Louise Mitchell's essay, "Slave Markets in New York City," and the selection by Gwendolyn Brooks are vivid portrayals of the consequences of limited job opportunities for African American women prior to and just after World War II. The labor market for African American women during this period was almost exclusively limited to domestic work. The women in "Slave Markets in New York City" bargained for wages of 20 to 30 cents an hour (or, converted into 1995 figures, $2.14 to $3.21 per hour, considerably below minimum wage). The quotation and the article illustrate the constraints experienced by individuals who are disadvantaged on three systems of inequality: gender, race, and class.

The selection "I Didn't Have No Family Before I Was Married" from Victoria Byerly's collection *Hard Times Cotton Mill Girls* recounts the experiences of a white female mill worker, Aliene Walser, during the 1940s. Her history of paid work dramatically illustrates the way social class disadvantage constrains opportunity structures even among workers who are advantaged by their race. Orphaned at 6 years old, Walser quit school and began working as a domestic at age 14. The same year, she married and found employment in a textile mill. Within the mill, both jobs and the meager economic benefits available were structured according to gender: "There were men all around me doing jobs that were easier than what I was doing and they were making more money. . . . When Christmas-time came around, the men got a big bonus and we women might get a little one." In addition to her work in the mill, she also shouldered the unpaid domestic work typically assigned to women. Caught in a web of limited opportunities, she still hopes for a better future for her own children.

Tillie Olsen's poem "I Want You Women Up North to Know" is based on a letter written by Felipe Ibarro published in 1934 in *New*

Masses, a radical newspaper. The poem describes the paid productive activity of poor Hispanic women shortly after the Great Depression, offering another example of the relegation of poor women of color, who are disadvantaged on three hierarchies, to a narrow band of productive activities at the bottom of the occupational hierarchy. It dramatically illustrates the ways in which productive activities can severely circumscribe people's life chances. Finally, it makes visible the ways in which lives of privilege are built upon systems of oppression. Olsen pleads with the affluent women who purchase "dainty children's dresses" with "exquisite work, madame, exquisite pleats" to remember the suffering of the women who work "for three dollars a week from dawn to midnight." Olsen's argument parallels Cole's analysis of domestic work: Affluent women can be relieved of the drudgery of housework by becoming managers of the work performed by less privileged women.

Several of the other readings also illustrate the consequences of occupying privileged positions along some hierarchies and disadvantaged positions on others. The interview that Studs Terkel conducted with Chicago steelworker Mike LeFevre illustrates the work experiences of a white working-class man. Despite being advantaged by race and gender, LeFevre feels "dehumanized" by his work. He describes himself as "a dying breed. A laborer. Strictly muscle work." His position within the hierarchy based on social class constrains his options. He sees few opportunities for improving his own situation, but he, like the mill worker Aliene Walser, is determined to provide a better future for his child.

The reading "From Homemaker to Housing Advocate: An Interview with Mrs. Chang Jok Lee" focuses on the productive activities of a Chinese American woman, now in her early seventies. Mrs. Lee does volunteer work, thus her productive activities are unpaid and therefore not counted in conventional national accounting systems that focus on wages and salaries. The article underscores the point that Mrs. Lee's productivity started early in life and lasted well into older age—taking different forms as she aged. The essay also is an example of how being a member of a minority group (Mrs. Lee's family was Chinese in Japan during the Sino-Japanese war) shapes the type and duration of productive activity roles over the life course. Like Mrs. Sharpe in Ostrander's book (described earlier), Mrs. Lee finds volunteer work has psychological, if not monetary, payoffs: "Being active keeps me alive. I don't play mah-jongg or go to Reno, so I take care of my granddaughter, and I go to meetings." Unlike Mrs. Sharpe, however, Mrs. Lee is not of the upper class.

"Esse Quam Videri" is an essay about the life of an African American woman of the middle class, a college president's wife. Susie Jones is an example of how privilege in one hierarchy—class—and disadvantage in two others—gender and race—interlock to shape opportunities for productive activity. The impact of these interlocking hierarchies is evident in comparing the experiences of Mrs. Jones, Mrs. Chang Jok Lee, the women looking for work in the Brooklyn slave market, and the African American woman in Gwendolyn Brooks's story. How very different were the productive activities of the women in the slave market and those of Susie Jones, although both were disadvantaged on race and gender. Mrs. Jones and Mrs. Sharpe were both affluent women, but the social construct of race structured their lives in different ways.

The excerpt from the article "Women's Work and Caregiving Roles: A Life Course Approach," by Phyllis Moen, Julie Robison, and Vivian Fields, illustrates that role involvement varies by location in the social structure. They suggest that two productive activity roles, caregiving and employment, combine differently for men and women, and differently for women of lower and higher class. They document 30 years of transitions between caregiving and work roles to show that productive activity continues over women's adult life course. The essay also indicates that (a) using only paid work definitions of productivity inaccurately assesses the total productivity of women, and (b) differences in role transitions and the way productive activity roles affect the life course are due in part to gender and class.

The excerpt from Barbara Zsembik and Audrey Singer's article, "The Problem of Defining Retirement Among Minorities: The Mexican Americans," demonstrates the ways in which meanings attached to the productive activity roles of work and retirement differ by minority and occupational status. The Mexican Americans they studied had different views of whether they were retired based on the particular definition of retirement that was used. When asked directly, "Are you retired?" only 35% of the sample indicated they were. One-quarter implied they were retired when asked what activities they were currently engaged in; half implied they were retired when asked whether they were receiving Social Security or other retirement pensions; and fully 68% implied they were retired when asked whether they were currently working. Definitions of retirement are different for minority group members who have had spotty work lives, and concepts based on the experiences of the dominant group can mask diversity in the experiences of work and retirement.

Harvest Moon Eyes's short story, "The Day the Crows Stopped Talking" (from Clifford Trafzer's anthology *Earth Song, Sky Spirit: Short Stories of the Contemporary Native American Experience*, 1992), illustrates two key issues in this section. First, the availability of productive activity roles depends on positions in systems of inequality. Second, the meanings attached to productive activity roles differ not only by positions in systems of inequality but by birth cohort as well. This reading, about life on a Cherokee reservation, shows how older and younger generations of the same minority group are in conflict about the meaning of productive activity—traditional views of productive activity versus the new phenomenon on reservations, gambling casinos. The story illustrates how changes in economic activities can undermine the traditional authority of the Council of Elders and how positions of privilege can be used to restrict access to productive activity among people disadvantaged on systems of inequality. This is a story of generation versus generation and the powerful versus the powerless.

In the selection "On the Edge of the Barrio," from Ernesto Galarza's autobiography *Barrio Boy,* two key issues presented in this section are illustrated. First, solely using traditional definitions of productivity—paid work in the regular labor force—inaccurately assesses the productivity of the disadvantaged in systems of inequality. Second, certain productive activity roles are closed to these disadvantaged individuals. Ernesto Galarza was a Mexican American migrant worker who experienced a string of other menial jobs before going on to become a labor organizer, sociologist, and teacher. The article demonstrates how control is exerted over the productive activities of those at lower levels of the inequality hierarchy by those at the top.

"At the Burns-Coopers' " from Gwendolyn Brooks's novel *Maud Martha* (1953) was published more than 30 years ago and reflects the state of African American women's work roles in those times. Before World War II, and a few years thereafter, the majority of African American women were domestic workers—one of the few work roles open to them. The selection illustrates two key issues of this section: Differences due to membership in various systems of inequality are found in the availability of productive activity roles and the meanings attached to those roles. In this selection, an African American woman reveals her thoughts about the often demeaning and humiliating experience of domestic work.

20

I Didn't Have No Family Before I Was Married

Aliene Walser, as told to Victoria Byerly

I didn't have no family before I was married. My mother died when I was five, my father died when I was six, and I was switched here and yonder and everywhere. My mother's sister was mainly responsible for raising me. There were thirteen children in her family— three girls and ten boys. She kept me from the time I was five years old until I was ten. Then she said she couldn't keep me no more. Well, they brought me over here to the Baptist orphanage and tried to put me in that orphanage home. But they said my mother and father had died of tuberculosis, so they wouldn't take me. We had to have x-rays every six months, me and my two brothers. Honey, I can't tell you what a bad experience that was, living with my aunt. I would wake up crying for my mother and daddy at night and she'd turn the cover back and whip me. She'd whip me and shut me in the closet. Now I'm scared of getting into somewhere I can't get out of. That's the way I was treated. Then my aunt said she didn't want me no more, that they couldn't keep me no longer. So I went to stay with my grandmother and I stayed there about a year before she said that she couldn't keep me.

My brother was five years older than me and he didn't have nowhere to go. He used to sleep on porches. He'd come to my aunt's house where I was staying and sit down to eat

dinner and she'd run him away from the table. I never will forget that. He would get up crying and leave. Finally, when my brother got married, I came to live with them in Thomasville. His wife and him separated when I was fourteen years old, so I quit school and went to housekeeping for this family who had four children. Two dollars a week for cooking and scrubbing. That's when I met my husband Anderson. When me and him was dating, before we was married, we had to take the children with us, so we've been with children before we were married and ever since.

Then one day I decided to go back home. So they got me back down there below Denton, and I stayed one night with my uncle—I knew I couldn't live there and then I hired my uncle to bring me back, and me and Anderson went to Virginia to get married. Got one of my friends to go with me. He was seventeen and I was fourteen, but Anderson told them in Virginia that he was twenty and that I was eighteen. I had on my first pair of high-heel shoes. I never will forget trying to walk up them courthouse steps. And honey, I could stand under your arm, I didn't weigh but seventy-four pounds. Well, the magistrate looked at us and he said, "You younguns go home." So we come back home. See, I didn't have no one to sign for me. So his mother and one of his aunts and us went to the courthouse in Lexington and got our license. They signed for us and we came back to Thomasville. Preacher James out here on Fisher Ferry Street married us. That night, I'd say we got

Source: Excerpted from "I Didn't Have No Family Before I Was Married" by A. Walser, as told to Victoria Byerly in *Hard Times Cotton Mill Girls: Personal Histories of Womanhood and Poverty in the South* (pp. 74-86), 1986. Ithaca, NY: ILR Press. Reprinted by permission of the author.

married about one-thirty in the afternoon, at four o'clock he went in to work at the mill. The girl who lived across the street came over there and she liked to pick and joke, and oh, she had me scared to death that she was going to crawl under my bed and going to do this and going to do that. She embarrassed me to death.

Then we lived with his parents in a mill house over there on Concord Street right behind the mill. It had six rooms. We had two rooms, a kitchen and a bedroom. His parents lived in the other rooms. That was all right, Anderson's mother was like a mother to me. We lived there until my first baby was born. When I was pregnant for the first time, I was sitting there sewing with my mother-in-law one night and I said, "I wouldn't mind having this baby if I didn't have to have my stomach cut open." She looked at me and said, "Honey, you mean that you don't know no better than that and fixin' to have a baby?" I said, "What do you mean?" And when she told me I said, "Ain't no way I'm going to go through that." That like to have scared me to death. See, I didn't understand anything about my body. If I had, I wouldn't have had so many children.

The first time I ever started my period I was going to the spring to get a bucket of water. I was living with my brother and his wife then. All at once I looked and blood was going down my leg and it scared me to death. I didn't know what to do. I ran in the house and told my brother's wife and she told me what to do. She said for me to go in there and get something to put on. I was ashamed to tell my grandfather. And that was all that was ever said to me about it. That's all I ever knowed. She told me that it would happen again. I said, "What for?" She never did explain nothing like that to me. Didn't nobody.

I had my first two babies at home. His mother was there and she fixed my bed and told me to get in it. She helped me put on my gown and she would always have pads just about this wide, about four feet across, and she would put a lot of cotton padding in it to use under me. That way they could be thrown away afterwards. Then she called the doctor.

And I laid there in pain until he got there. They didn't give you anything for the pain, you know. I remember that doctor sitting there and me hurting so bad. He was sitting there beside my bed and he went off to sleep! So I kicked him. Then after my first baby was born I told him I never was having another one, this was my last. And then, when my second one came along, he looked at me and said, "I thought you weren't going to have another one."

I was fifteen when I had my first baby and thirty-two when I had my eighth. I raised seven of them. No, I didn't know how not to have babies. If I had known, I don't think I would have had eight. No, I never heard tell of birth control pills. Lordy mercy, honey, them things come out since I quit having kids. I wish I had had them back then. Maybe I wouldn't have been so tired.

I went to work in the cotton mill in 1940. I remember I was scared to death. I knowed I was doing everything wrong. I was scared the boss man would say something to me. I was actually scared to death! I didn't do anything wrong but I thought I was doing everything wrong. I was running a winder and it was called a spool winder. It had wooden tubes on it that were long and the thread went around it. When you first start them off that metal makes an awful racket. Well, I didn't know that. First time I had ever run them. Well, when I started that thing up and it started making this horrible noise, I run out of the alley and started crying like a baby. The boss man come up and said, "What's the matter?" And I said, "I've torn that thing up." Finally some women that worked around me got me calmed down and told me that it always does that. I got used to that noise finally, but I never did like to run that machine.

I stayed at the mill until World War II. Then my husband went into the service and my brother moved in with me because the children were small and I was pregnant again. I had my baby on the ninth and my husband left to go into the service that day. After he took his training, they sent him overseas. He didn't even get to come home to see the youngest until she was two years old. I waited until my baby was about four months old and then my brother's wife took care of the children so I went to work at the Erlanger Mill in Lexington. My sister-in-law taught me to wind over there. Then my husband came home and we moved down close to Charlotte. I went to work in a mill down there in the winding room. We stayed down there six years and then we came back to Thomasville. I went back to work in the Amazon Cotton Mill as a winder and I worked I don't know how many years winding. Then I was switched from that to running twisters. I don't know if you know what twisters are, but it twists yarn together, nylon and wool. I worked on that job for about four years. Then they put me to keeping the time sheets and stamping yarn and keeping what pounds the people would get off. You know, they got paid by the pound. I'd been there so long, I knew it all by heart.

There were better jobs, yeah. Some of them were happy doing the same old job day in and day out but I wasn't. I wanted more money. There were men all around me doing jobs that were easier than what I was doing and they were making more money. That bothered me. My husband was a boss man out there for a good long while, but I don't care if he was, when Christmas-time came around, the men got a big bonus and we women might get a little one. I just didn't think that was fair. We had to work as hard as the men. Harder! They were sitting on their rears writing down numbers. They said it was brain work. And I said, "What brain?" Yeah, I know I was working hard. Some of them were afraid to say anything though. See, they were scared they would lose their jobs, I reckon. And they probably would have. Mill people take a lot. But you'll find one or two that's not like that. They put me working with this man one time and he'd come in of a morning and maybe he'd be a little grouchy. I'd say, "Now listen here, I feel bad too, so get your butt off your shoulders." That's what I'd tell him and he'd start laughing at me.

Before I was married, I remember hearing that mill people wasn't nothing but slum peo-ple, that there wasn't nothing to them. I've heard it said that mill people are a lower class of people. A lot of them that worked at the furniture factory thought that they was better than mill workers. I got about seven or eight uncles that worked there and I know. They thought they was better than mill people and still do. I didn't know whether that was true or not until I went to work in the mill and learned the truth. There's a lot of good people working in there. I've got friends that work in the mill and they have been good to me. Those that think we're a lower class of people ought to go in the mill and find out for themselves, if they got sense enough to do the work. People were moving in and out all the time on mill hill. Different types that drank, fuss and fight, and goings on. But now there was some real good people on the mill hill. You could have real good neighbors. They would do anything in the world for you, they could.

We wanted to own our own home, but we had seven children to put through high school. I cooked three meals a day, forty biscuits for each meal. I got to where I knew how to make that bread so that it would be forty biscuits every time. And they would eat it up. We ate a lot of beans and potatoes and had meat about three times a week. On Sundays always. I tried to raise my girls differently than how I had been raised. I tried to tell them when they first started wanting to date that I didn't want them to start dating early, which they didn't. They said, "But Mama, you did." And I'd say, "Yes, but I don't want you to do what I done." I said, "I got married when I was just a child. You need to get a little more out of life than just getting married, having children, and working in that mill." I explained to my girls about going with boys and things like that, and having babies and things like that. We just talked about it like there wasn't nothing to it. There was some of my boys that I even talked to. My youngest one I did, about going with girls. I said, "You might think that if something happened to a girl you was going with, it wouldn't be on you," but I said it would. "You've got to be careful with girls. Anything like that you need to have marriage first before you think about it, because," I said, "anything could happen and you might have to get married. And them kind of marriages sometimes just don't work out." Yeah, I tried to bring them up in the church which I think I have, most of them. My youngest son used to have a temper like nobody's business, but now he goes to Liberty Baptist. He got saved and now he's changed.

I didn't want my girls to have to work in the mill. I know people out there who have been hurt real bad on the job. I was working on the first shift and this woman was working on the second. She had long beautiful blonde hair and she bent over some way and her hair got caught in the machine. When it did, it just pulled her scalp off. They said blood was just pouring down her. Her boss man like to have passed out. They took her on to the hospital and sent somebody to go over there and get her scalp out of that thing and see if they could, you know, but nothing they could do. She stayed in the hospital for a long time. That happened about seven or eight years ago. Last thing I knew she was still going to the doctor's because she started having severe headaches. The insurance company fought it because they didn't want to pay off. So they took her to court. She didn't like for anyone to see her without her wig but they made her pull it off in court and they said she was crying. It was so pitiful.

I was working on second or third shift until the last job I had was on the first shift. My husband worked on one shift and I worked on the other. At the mill we had an understanding, he'd leave in time to get home so that I could get there in time to start work. Well, when I worked on the second shift, I'd sleep, say, about five hours a night. I have worked on third when I wouldn't get but three hours sleep. I worked on third one time and I wouldn't get no sleep at all because I would come in from work of a morning and I'd have to cook my breakfast and get the kids off to school. My husband was working on second. Then I'd do my wash or whatever I had to do and lay down maybe about ten thirty or eleven o'clock. I got my nerves so bad that time that my boss man told me I was going to have to go on another shift. I had gotten down to seventy-some pounds.

Then I worked on that shift until I was seven months pregnant with my last child. My boss man came and told me I was going to have to quit because they didn't want nobody in there after they were six months pregnant. They were scared something would happen and it would be on their hands. So I got a leave of absence for six months, but I didn't go back for six years. I just couldn't go back.

21

I Want You Women Up North to Know

Tillie Olsen

I want you women up north to know
how those dainty children's dresses you buy
    at macy's, wannamakers, gimbels,
marshall fields,
are dyed in blood, are stitched in wasting
    flesh,
down in San Antonio, "where sunshine
    spends the winter."
I want you women up north to see
the obsequious smile, the salesladies trill
    "exquisite work, madame, exquisite
    pleats"
vanish into a bloated face, ordering more
    dresses,
    gouging the wages down,
dissolve into maria, ambrosa, catalina,
    stitching these dresses from dawn to
    night,
    In blood, in wasting flesh.

Catalina Rodriguez, 24,
    body shrivelled to a child's at twelve,
catalina rodriguez, last stages of
    consumption,
    works for three dollars a week from
    dawn to midnight.
A fog of pain thickens over her skull, the
    parching heat
    breaks over her body,

and the bright red blood embroiders the
    floor of her room.
    White rain stitching the night, the
bourgeois poet would say.
    white gulls of hands, darting, veering,
    white lightning, threading the clouds,
this is the exquisite dance of her hands over
    the cloth,
and her cough, gay, quick, staccato,
    like skeleton's bones clattering,
is appropriate accompaniment for the
    esthetic dance
    of her fingers,
and the tremolo, tremolo when the hands
    tremble with pain.
Three dollars a week,
two fifty-five,
seventy cents a week,
no wonder two thousand eight hundred
    ladies of joy
are spending the winter with the sun after
    he goes down—
for five cents (who said this was a rich
    man's world?) you can
    get all the lovin you want
"clap and syph aint much worse than sore
    fingers, blind eyes, and
    t.b."

Maria Vasquez, spinster,
    for fifteen cents a dozen stitches
    garments for children she
    has never had.

Catalina Torres, mother of four,
    to keep the starved body starving,

Source: "I Want You Women Up North to Know" by
T. Olsen, originally published in *The Partisan* (March
1934) under Tillie Lerner. Copyright Tillie Olsen. All
rights reserved. Reprinted with permission of the
author.

embroiders from dawn
to night.
Mother of four, what does she think of,
as the needle pocked fingers shift over
the silk—
of the stubble-coarse rags that stretch on
her own brood,
and jut with the bony ridge that marks
hunger's landscape
of fat little prairie-roll bodies that will
bulge in the
silk she needles?
(Be not envious, Catalina Torres, look!
on your own children's clothing,
embroidery,
more intricate than any a thousand
hands could fashion,
there where the cloth is ravelled, or
darned,
designs, multitudinous, complex and
handmade by Poverty
herself.)
Ambrosa Espinoza trusts in god,
"Todos es de dios, everything is from
god,"
through the dwindling night, the
waxing day, she bolsters
herself up with it—
but the pennies to keep god incarnate, from
ambrosa,
and the pennies to keep the priest in wine,
from ambrosa,
ambrosa clothes god and priest with
hand-made children's dresses.

Her brother lies on an iron cot, all day and
watches,
on a mattress of rags he lies.
For twenty-five years he worked for the
railroad, then they laid
him off.
(racked days, searching for work;
rebuffs; suspicious eyes of
policemen.
goodbye ambrosa, mebbe in dallas I find
work; desperate
swing for a freight,
surprised hands, clutching air, and the
wheel goes over a
leg,

the railroad cuts it off, as it cut off
twenty-five years of his
life.)
She says that he prays and dreams of
another world, as he lies
there, a heaven (which he does not
know was brought to
earth in 1917 in Russia, by workers like
him).

Women up north, I want you to know
when you finger the exquisite hand-made
dresses
what it means, this working from dawn to
midnight,
on what strange feet the feverish dawn
must come
to maria, catalina, ambrosa,
how the malignant fingers twitching over
the pallid faces jerk
them to work,
and the sun and the fever mount with the
day—
long plodding hours, the eyes bum like
coals, heat jellies
the flying fingers,
down comes the night like blindness.
long hours more with the dim eye of the
lamp, the breaking
back,
weariness crawls in the flesh like
worms, gigantic like earth's
in winter.
And for Catalina Rodriguez comes the
night sweat and the blood
embroidering the darkness.
for Catalina Torres the pinched faces of
four huddled
children,
the naked bodies of four bony children,
the chant of their chorale of hunger.
And for twenty eight hundred ladies of joy
the grotesque act gone
over—the wink—the grimace—the
"feeling like it baby?"
And for Maria Vasquez, spinster,
emptiness, emptiness,
flaming with dresses for children she
can never fondle.

And for Ambrosa Espinoza—the skeleton
    body of her brother on
his mattress of rags, boring twin holes in
    the dark with his eyes
to the image of christ, remembering a leg,
    and twenty five years

cut off from his life by the railroad.

Women up north, I want you to know,
I tell you this can't last forever.

I swear it won't.

22

Mike LeFevre

Studs Terkel

It is a two-flat dwelling, somewhere in Cicero, on the outskirts of Chicago. He is thirty-seven. He works in a steel mill. On occasion, his wife Carol works as a waitress in a neighborhood restaurant; otherwise, she is at home, caring for their two small children, a girl and a boy.

At the time of my first visit, a sculpted statuette of Mother and Child was on the floor, head severed from body. He laughed softly as he indicated his three-year-old daughter: "She Doctor Spock'd it."[1]

I'm a dying breed. A laborer. Strictly muscle work . . . pick it up, put it down, pick it up, put it down. We handle between forty and fifty thousand pounds of steel a day. (Laughs.) I know this is hard to believe—from four hundred pounds to three- and four-pound pieces. It's dying.

You can't take pride any more. You remember when a guy could point to a house he built, how many logs he stacked. He built it and he was proud of it. I don't really think I could be proud if a contractor built a home for me. I would be tempted to get in there and kick the carpenter in the ass (laughs), and take the saw away from him. 'Cause I would have to be part of it, you know.

It's hard to take pride in a bridge you're never gonna cross, in a door you're never gonna open. You're mass-producing things and you never see the end result of it.

(Muses.) I worked for a trucker one time. And I got this tiny satisfaction when I loaded a truck. At least I could see the truck depart loaded. In a steel mill, forget it. You don't see where nothing goes.

I got chewed out by my foreman once. He said, "Mike, you're a good worker but you have a bad attitude." My attitude is that I don't get excited about my job. I do my work but I don't say whoopee-doo. The day I get excited about my job is the day I go to a head shrinker. How are you gonna get excited about pullin' steel? How are you gonna get excited when you're tired and want to sit down?

It's not just the work. Somebody built the pyramids. Somebody's going to build something. Pyramids, Empire State Building—these things just don't happen. There's hard work behind it. I would like to see a building, say, the Empire State, I would like to see on one side of it a foot-wide strip from top to bottom with the name of every bricklayer, the name of every electrician, with all the names. So when a guy walked by, he could take his son and say, "See, that's me over there on the forty-fifth floor. I put the steel beam in." Picasso can point to a painting. What can I point to? A writer can point to a book. Everybody should have something to point to.

It's the not-recognition by other people. To say a woman is *just* a housewife is degrading, right? Okay. *Just* a housewife. It's also degrading to say *just* a laborer. The difference is that a man goes out and maybe gets smashed.

Source: "Mike LeFevre" excerpted from *Working* by S. Terkel. Copyright © 1972, 1974 by Studs Terkel. Reprinted by permission of Pantheon Books, a division of Random House, Inc.

When I was single, I could quit, just split. I wandered all over the country. You worked just enough to get a poke, money in your pocket. Now I'm married and I got two kids . . . (trails off). I worked on a truck dock one time and I was single. The foreman came over and he grabbed my shoulder, kind of gave me a shove. I punched him and knocked him off the dock. I said, "Leave me alone. I'm doing my work, just stay away from me, just don't give me the with-the-hands business."

Hell, if you whip a damn mule he might kick you. Stay out of my way, that's all. Working is bad enough, don't bug me. I would rather work my ass off for eight hours a day with nobody watching me than five minutes with a guy watching me. Who you gonna sock? You can't sock General Motors, you can't sock anybody in Washington, you can't sock a system.

A mule, an old mule, that's the way I feel. Oh yeah. See. (Shows black and blue marks on arms and legs, burns.) You know what I heard from more than one guy at work? "If my kid wants to work in a factory, I am going to kick the hell out of him." I want my kid to be an effete snob. Yeah, mm-hmm. (Laughs.) I want him to be able to quote Walt Whitman,[2] to be proud of it.

If you can't improve yourself, you improve your posterity. Otherwise life isn't worth nothing. You might as well go back to the cave and stay there. I'm sure the first caveman who went over the hill to see what was on the other side—I don't think he went there wholly out of curiosity. He went there because he wanted to get his son out of the cave. Just the same way I want to send my kid to college.

I work so damn hard and want to come home and sit down and lay around. *But I gotta get it out.* I want to be able to turn around to somebody and say, "Hey, fuck you." You know? (Laughs.) The guy sitting next to me on the bus too. 'Cause all day I wanted to tell my foreman to go fuck himself, but I can't.

So I find a guy in a tavern. To tell him that. And he tells me too. I've been in brawls. He's punching me and I'm punching him, because

we actually want to punch somebody else. The most that'll happen is the bartender will bar us from the tavern. But at work, you lose your job.

This one foreman I've got, he's a kid. He's a college graduate. He thinks he's better than everybody else. He was chewing me out and I was saying, "Yeah, yeah, yeah." He said, "What do you mean, yeah, yeah, yeah. Yes, *sir.*" I told him, "Who the hell are you, Hitler? What is this *'Yes, sir'* bullshit? I came here to work, I didn't come here to crawl. There's a fuckin' difference." One word led to another and I lost.

I got broke down to a lower grade and lost twenty-five cents an hour, which is a hell of a lot. It amounts to about ten dollars a week. He came over—after breaking me down. The guy comes over and smiles at me. I blew up. He didn't know it, but he was about two seconds and two feet away from a hospital. I said, "Stay the fuck away from me." He was just about to say something and was pointing his finger. I just reached my hand up and just grabbed his finger and I just put it back in his pocket. He walked away. I grabbed his finger because I'm married. If I'd a been single, I'd a grabbed his head. That's the difference.

You're doing this manual labor and you know that technology can do it. (Laughs.) Let's face it, a machine can do the work of a man; otherwise they wouldn't have space probes. Why can we send a rocket ship that's unmanned and yet send a man in a steel mill to do a mule's work?

Automation? Depends how it's applied. It frightens me if it puts me out on the street. It doesn't frighten me if it shortens my work week. You read that little thing: What are you going to do when this computer replaces you? Blow up computers. (Laughs.) Really. Blow up computers. I'll be goddamned if a computer is gonna eat before I do! I want milk for my kids and beer for me. Machines can either liberate man or enslave 'im, because they're pretty neutral. It's a man who has the bias to put the thing one place or another.

If I had a twenty-hour workweek, I'd get to know my kids better, my wife better. Some kid invited me to go on a college campus. On a Saturday. It was summertime. Hell, if I had a choice of taking my wife and kids to a picnic or going to a college campus, it's gonna be the picnic. But if I worked a twenty-hour week, I could go do both. Don't you think with that extra twenty hours people could really expand? Who's to say? There are some people in factories just by force of circumstance. I'm just like the colored people. Potential Einsteins don't have to be white. They could be in cotton fields, they could be in factories.

The twenty-hour week is a possibility today. The intellectuals, they always say there are potential Lord Byrons, Walt Whitmans, Roosevelts, Picassos working in construction or steel mills or factories. But I don't think they believe it. I think what they're afraid of is the potential Hitlers and Stalins that are there too. The people in power fear the leisure man. Not just the United States. Russia's the same way.

What do you think would happen in this country if, for one year, they experimented and gave everybody a twenty-hour week? How do they know that the guy who digs Wallace[3] today doesn't try to resurrect Hitler tomorrow? Or the guy who is mildly disturbed at pollution doesn't decide to go to General Motors and shit on the guy's desk? You can become a fanatic if you had the time. The whole thing is time. That is, I think, one reason rich kids tend to be fanatic about politics: They have time. Time, that's the important thing.

It isn't that the average working guy is dumb. He's tired, that's all. I picked up a book on chess one time. That thing laid in the drawer for two or three weeks, you're too tired. During the weekends you want to take your kids out. You don't want to sit there and the kid comes up: "Daddy, can I go to the park?" You got your nose in a book? Forget it.

I know a guy fifty-seven years old. Know what he tells me? "Mike, I'm old and tired all the time." The first thing happens at work: When the arms start moving, the brain stops. I punch in about ten minutes to seven in the morning. I say hello to a couple of guys I like,

I kid around with them. One guy says good morning to you and you say good morning. To another guy you say fuck you. The guy you say fuck you to is your friend.

I put on my hard hat, change into my safety shoes, put on my safety glasses, go to the bonderizer. It's the thing I work on. They rake the metal, they wash it, they dip it in a paint solution, and we take it off. Put it on, take it off, put it on, take it off, put it on, take it off . . .

I say hello to everybody but my boss. At seven it starts. My arms get tired about the first half-hour. After that, they don't get tired any more until maybe the last half-hour at the end of the day. I work from seven to three thirty. My arms are tired at seven thirty and they're tired at three o'clock. I hope to God I never get broke in, because I always want my arms to be tired at seven thirty and three o'clock. (Laughs.) 'Cause that's when I know that there's a beginning and there's an end. That I'm not brainwashed. In between, I don't even try to think.

If I were to put you in front of a dock and I pulled up a skid in front of you with fifty hundred-pound sacks of potatoes and there are fifty more skids just like it, and this is what you're gonna do all day, what would you think about—potatoes? Unless a guy's a nut, he never thinks about work or talks about it. Maybe about baseball or about getting drunk the other night or he got laid or he didn't get laid. I'd say one out of a hundred will actually get excited about work.

Why is it that the communists always say they're for the workingman, and as soon as they set up a country, you got guys singing to tractors? They're singing about how they love the factory. That's where I couldn't buy communism. It's the intellectuals' utopia, not mine. I cannot picture myself singing to a tractor, I just can't. (Laughs.) Or singing to steel. (Singsongs.) Oh, whoop-dee-doo, I'm at the bonderizer, oh how I love this heavy steel. No thanks. Never happen.

Oh yeah, I daydream. I fantasize about a sexy blonde in Miami who's got my union dues. (Laughs.) I think of the head of the union the way I think of the head of my company. Living it up. I think of February in Miami. Warm weather, a place to lay in. When I hear a college kid say, "I'm oppressed," I don't believe him. You know what I'd like to do for one year? Live like a college kid. Just for one year. I'd love to. Wow! (Whispers.) Wow! Sports car! Marijuana! (Laughs.) Wild, sexy broads. I'd love that, hell yes, I would.

Somebody has to do this work. If my kid ever goes to college, I just want him to have a little respect, to realize that his dad is one of those somebodies. This is why even on— (muses) yeah, I guess, sure—on the black thing . . . (Sighs heavily.) I can't really hate the colored fella that's working with me all day. The black intellectual I got no respect for. The white intellectual I got no use for. I got no use for the black militant who's gonna scream three hundred years of slavery to me while I'm busting my ass. You know what I mean? (Laughs.) I have one answer for that guy: Go see Rockefeller. See Harriman.[4] Don't bother me. We're in the same cotton field. So just don't bug me. (Laughs.)

After work I usually stop off at a tavern. Cold beer. Cold beer right away. When I was single, I used to go into hillbilly bars, get in a lot of brawls. Just to explode. I got a thing on my arm here (indicates scar). I got slapped with a bicycle chain. Oh, wow! (Softly.) Mmm. I'm getting older. (Laughs.) I don't explode as much. You might say I'm broken in. (Quickly.) No, I'll never be broken in. (Sighs.) When you get a little older, you exchange the words. When you're younger, you exchange the blows.

When I get home, I argue with my wife a little bit. Turn on TV, get mad at the news. (Laughs.) I don't even watch the news that much. I watch Jackie Gleason. I look for any

alternative to the ten o'clock news. I don't want to go to bed angry. Don't hit a man with anything heavy at five o'clock. He just can't be bothered. This is his time to relax. The heaviest thing he wants is what his wife has to tell him.

When I come home, know what I do for the first twenty minutes? Fake it. I put on a smile. I got a kid three years old. Sometimes she says, "Daddy, where've you been?" I say, "Work." I could have told her I'd been in Disneyland. What's work to a three-year-old kid? If I feel bad, I can't take it out on the kids. Kids are born innocent of everything but birth. You can't take it out on your wife either. This is why you go to a tavern. You want to release it there rather than do it at home. What does an actor do when he's got a bad movie? I got a bad movie every day.

I don't even need the alarm clock to get up in the morning. I can go out drinking all night, fall asleep at four, and bam! I'm up at six—no matter what I do. (Laughs.) It's a pseudo-death, more or less.

Notes

1. *Doctor Spock:* Dr. Benjamin Spock, prominent U.S. child-care expert (b. 1903).

2. *Walt Whitman:* influential U.S. poet (1819–1892); best known for *Leaves of Grass* (1855).

3. *Wallace:* George C. Wallace (b. 1919), governor of Alabama in three separate terms spanning three decades. Wallace was a key opponent of school desegregation in 1963, but recanted and won significant black support in the 1982 election.

4. *Harriman:* Edward Harriman, railroad tycoon (1848–1909) and father of New York governor W. Averell Harriman. Like Rockefeller, a rich, powerful man.

23

From Homemaker to Housing Advocate:
An Interview With Mrs. Chang Jok Lee

Nancy Diao

I first met Mrs. Lee in 1976 at a rally in front of the International Hotel and then again in 1985 in the midst of a financial crisis in the San Francisco Housing Authority. The agency was more than $9 million in debt, and its executive director Carl Williams had been asked to resign by Mayor Diane Feinstein. During this time, the Ping Yuen Residents Improvement Association (PYRIA) remained the best organized and most effective tenant association in the city. Much of its strength was due to the consistent participation of Mrs. Lee. She had been the backbone of a monumental effort to protect the rights of low-income tenants in San Francisco's Chinatown. This is an unusual role for an immigrant woman whose Chinese tradition frowns upon women activists.

What struck me was Mrs. Lee's dedication to working for social change, an unusual choice for a woman her age. Instead of playing mah-jongg with her contemporaries, she prefers to attend community meetings, testify at city hearings, and help fellow tenants settle disputes. Mrs. Lee is in her late fifties, but looks much younger. With glasses and short black hair, permed and fashionably kept,

she is always well groomed and impeccably dressed. For a Chinese woman, she is rather big-framed, but looks sturdy and confident. She speaks her mind freely, from telling stories about her favorite granddaughter to tales about growth pains with the tenant association or gossip in the Chinese community. Though she speaks a combination of Chinese dialects, with a mixture of some English words, she looks you straight in the eye when she talks. You can't help but notice her sincerity and passion.

Growing Up in Japan

In a 1985 interview, Mrs. Lee told of how poverty and discrimination have plagued her since her childhood in Japan. Born in 1927, in Kobe, she was the third of eight children, and the second girl. Her family suffered the hard life of Chinese immigrants in Japan, and she remembers growing up poor, segregated from the Japanese.

My family was very poor when I was born. We didn't even have money to buy soy sauce. When I was two years old, my father got a job as a chef in the Egyptian Embassy, so our entire family lived in the servants' quarters of the embassy. My mother helped out with the housecleaning and ironing.

We didn't have much contact with the Japanese except when we went shopping.

Source: "From Homemaker to Housing Advocate: An Interview with Mrs. Chang Jok Lee," by N. Diao, from *Making Waves*, by Asian Women United of California, copyright © 1989 by Asian Women United of California. Reprinted by permission of Beacon Press, Boston.

In Kobe, the Chinese operated pastry, coffee, tailoring, and other shops and had two Chinese schools. I went to the Mandarin school until the sixth grade, but we didn't have enough money for me to continue; my sister went only to night school.

The heavy responsibilities she assumed as a girl helped to groom her for her later leadership role in the Chinatown tenants' group. When her family returned to the Zhongshan district in southeastern China during the Sino-Japanese War, and while her father and older brother remained in Japan, Mrs. Lee had to bear the bulk of caring for the family though she was only eleven years old. This responsibility continued even after the family reunited in Japan one year later. More aggressive and verbal than her older, frail sister, Mrs. Lee represented the family at air raid exercises and in food ration lines. After the sixth grade, she worked in a Taiwanese-owned shoe factory and then in a candy factory to help with the family income.

Along with other Chinese in Japan, she and her family were subjected to many forms of discrimination because Japan and China were on opposite sides of a war.

Some pharmacies would use slogans like "Can even kill the Nanking Bloodsuckers" as advertisements for the effectiveness of pesticides. In many Japanese shops we would have to wait until the Japanese customers were served first. We were also discriminated against in employment and were only able to get lower class jobs regardless of our education, skills, and abilities. This situation forced many of us to start our own small businesses such as cafe/restaurants, tailor shops, and painting stores.

When the United States began bombing Kobe in 1944, life became even harsher for Mrs. Lee's family.

Whole families died in air raid shelters, smothered by smoke. When the planes came, everyone in my family went into caves or shelters; only my older brother and I stayed behind to watch our house. One time our house was firebombed, and I tried to put out the fire by stomping, but in vain. My brother went looking for me all over the place, but the fire and smoke had spread so fast that he couldn't see anything. Fortunately I had escaped, and he did thereafter. We lost our house, and our family split up. I was sent to live with a family friend who came from the Fukien province.

Romance Leads to America

While living with the Fukienese family and working for them to earn her keep, Mrs. Lee met her future husband, George, through her first boyfriend. George was a Chinese American GI who was stationed in Yokohama after the surrender of the Japanese government at the end of World War II. When asked how she met George, Mrs. Lee giggled. Her face lit up and she blushed. Then her eyes softened with a watery glow. Compared to her first boyfriend, who treated her like a "good little workhorse," George was considerate and romantic, though they didn't talk much in those days.

George always treated me with kindness and respect, very different from my first boyfriend. He always saved me a seat on the bus and gave me little gifts, whereas my boyfriend never showed any appreciation. [For instance], when my boyfriend's family's house was bombed, and he lost all of his belongings, I stayed up all night to knit him a sweater. He never even said "thank you."

Mrs. Lee and George married in 1946, and their first son was born one year later. When the son was just six months old, George returned to the United States while Mrs. Lee remained in Japan with her parents till her husband came back to get her. They arrived in San Francisco in 1950, and in two years moved into one of the Ping Yuen public housing apartments in Chinatown. She remembers her life being full, but also one of poverty.

We were so poor that most of the time we didn't even have a penny in the house, but I wasn't scared or worried. We raised eight children, four boys and four girls, and from them I learned some English.

When the children were small, Mrs. Lee spent all of her time raising them; but as they grew older, she found more time to think about her own needs and interests. She began to become more active in the community, beginning first with just singing and socializing, and then onto more serious work.

When the children were all grown up, I started learning Mandarin and singing songs at the Asian Community Center. Since I went to a Mandarin school in Japan, I wanted to keep it up. While I was learning Mandarin, I had the opportunity to read a lot of newspapers and books, and went to May Day celebrations with George. Ever since George got disabled from a car accident in 1972, he has had a lot of free time to get involved in community issues.

Confrontation With Housing Issues

The Asian Community Center was a commercial tenant of the International Hotel block, which soon became the focal point of the early conflict of interests between low-income tenants and land developers. Mrs. Lee's association with the center eventually led to her involvement with community housing issues.

In 1977, when my youngest daughters, Sylvia, Patricia, and Teresa, were twenty-one, nineteen, and ten, I became involved in the International Hotel struggle. I would take my youngest daughter, Teresa, to meetings and classes with me. Because I knew some of the tenants who lived in the International Hotel, I got upset when I saw

leaflets about the possibility of them being evicted; I did not want to see them homeless. The young people at the Asian Community Center encouraged me to go to meetings on the third floor of the I-Hotel. It took me a while to get used to meetings and rallies, but eventually I even spoke with bullhorns at demonstrations.

On August 3, 1977, the night of the eviction, George, Teresa, Patricia, and I were there. It was a warm night; there were four hundred policemen on horses, in addition to the tactical squad. The I-Hotel was surrounded by thousands of people—Asian, white, black, young and old, including many from Reverend Jim Jones's church who came in busloads. It seemed that we all stood on the sidewalk for hours. Suddenly the horses charged. I screamed, and everywhere there was yelling, screaming, and crying. We wanted the horses to stop charging, but the tactical squad used their billy clubs to hold us back on the sidewalk. As the horses rushed and trampled, the human chain around the hotel broke. People fell down. Tears poured out of my eyes as I heard Hongisto (then chief of police) breaking down the door to the I-Hotel. We stayed in front of the I-Hotel until three in the morning—watching every tenant being either dragged out or carried out of the hotel; then we went to Portsmouth Square.

Even as Mrs. Lee's support of the I-Hotel continued, she transferred more energy toward improving living conditions in Ping Yuen. In 1977 all the pipes in Ping Yuen were rotting, but in spite of repeated calls to the San Francisco Housing Authority, nothing was being done to fix the problem. Eventually George and some members of the tenant association initiated a massive petition drive to get the plumbing repaired. At the end of 1977, the housing authority finally repaired all of the pipes and painted the exterior walls of half of the buildings. And George was elected president of the association.

A year later, when the housing authority proved unresponsive in meeting the tenants' demands for better security, Mrs. Lee participated in the Ping Yuen tenants' first rent strike. The action was instigated by the brutal rape and murder of tenant Judy Wong. It was an intense period for Mrs. Lee.

I remember passing out leaflets door to door, talking to the tenants, attending lots of meetings, and collecting rent for fifteen days of each month at the association office on Pacific Avenue. The strike lasted for four months, with numerous press conferences and tedious negotiations with the housing authority, at the end of which we got our security guards.

The second strike followed at the end of 1979, when housing authority groundskeepers and office workers struck for higher pay. The city-wide Public Housing Tenants Association (PHTA) wanted to strike in support, but only the Ping Yuen tenants actually did. When the city employees went back to work, the Public Housing Tenants Association withdrew their support. But the Ping Yuen group continued the strike for maintenance issues, such as fixing apartment interiors and elevators, repairing floors, and painting. It was a long and drawn-out fight, but the tenants' persistence brought them victory.

We started with eighty households, but some tenants discontinued their strike support for fear of eviction. We held many meetings and visited people door to door. We also had membership drives and sponsored activities to keep the striking tenants together. Since I was the treasurer, I collected the rent, put it in escrow, and kept the books. After two years, we finally got our demands met.

At the end of the strike, most of the tenants chose to donate 50 percent of the escrow interest, about ten thousand dollars, to PYRIA for a color television in the community room and a banquet at Asia Garden. At the banquet the tenants surprised Mrs. Lee

and George with two round-trip tickets to Japan to show their appreciation for the couple's efforts in the strike.

During her husband's term as president of the improvement association, from 1979 to 1981, Mrs. Lee worked on two major projects that brought additional benefits to the Ping Yuen tenants. In 1979, at the request of the tenant population, Mrs. Lee went door to door at least two hours a day to sign up enough tenants to pressure Cablevision to install cable television services. Second, Mrs. Lee took over the coordination of the vegetable garden and established new rules: each member had an opportunity to have a garden and the size of all the lots was made equal. She thereby abolished all favoritism in the distribution of garden plots.

Reactions to Activism

Though Mrs. Lee can now act fearlessly, this was not so when she first became active in the community.

At first I was scared, or rather, kind of embarrassed. I didn't speak English and was not used to speaking in front of people. But after a while, I got used to it. As long as I am fighting for a just cause, then I am not scared.

Since Mrs. Lee's own family has remained in Japan, and George is also alone in the United States, neither has had to face pressure and criticism from relatives, who traditionally might have frowned on women's activism. She and her husband have, however, had some run-ins with the more conservative element of the community.

I didn't really get much reaction from getting involved in I-Hotel, but when I became active in the business of the association, I started getting a lot of harassment. The wall near our apartment was often spray painted with the word "commies!" with a black arrow pointing to our apartment. Everytime we challenged the previous PYRIA administration's way of doing things, we were called "commies." There were also flyers and posters attacking us.

Neither have her relationships with other tenants always been smooth. Some have criticized her for "doing too much." Take, for example, the laundromat project.

One of the officers of the association says that I am stupid to sweep the floors of the laundryroom. But when the laundryroom is dirty, I just can't stand it. It took so much out of us to get this project done; I feel like it's my own. So, when people don't clean up after themselves and youths abuse the furniture and write on walls, it really hurts me. But what hurts me more is when other officers nag at me for "doing too much." If they do some and if everybody does something, then I wouldn't have to do so much. Sometimes I squeeze in the sweeping when the baby is taking a nap.

After a recent officers' meeting, Mrs. Lee went home crying. The stress brought her a few sleepless nights and some additional white hair. At times like these, she wonders about whether her efforts are worth all the headaches and talks about quitting, but she stays. She remains undaunted about making Ping Yuen a better place to live and confident about the tenants' overall good feelings towards her.

Deep down, I know a lot of tenants really like me. They respect me and support George. The maintenance worker, Mr. Wong, complains about the youths not listening to him, but I don't have any problems with them. I just tell them to get out [of the laundryrooms] and they do. Most of the tenants listen to me, and whenever there is something bothering them, they always either ask me questions or ask me to help them.

Sometimes even her children scold her for "wasting her time." Yet other times they have helped out by protecting her at demonstrations or doing errands.

Some of my children get down on me for doing so much volunteer work. They say that I am crazy for spending so much time on the association when I don't get paid. They don't really understand me. I am happier when I am active, though there is nothing material to gain. It keeps me young. I don't have much white hair or wrinkles [*she points to her head*], do I?

Sylvia doesn't get down on me for doing so much. She just doesn't want me and George to be taken advantage of; she helps me out a lot. She is the one who taught me how to do books, how to do a membership drive, and keep a membership list. Her husband took off work a couple of times to take care of their daughter whom I watch [five days a week], so that I could be freed up to go to the public hearings on the Orangeland Project at the City Planning Commission.

Teresa . . . knows that I am happier when I am active. She doesn't complain when I am not home to cook dinner, and sometimes she even translates for me.

Conclusion:
Balancing Life's Demands

When asked if it has been hard to balance all the demands in her life—being a wife, mother of eight, grandmother of eleven now (eight when she was interviewed), and a housing activist—she laughed:

From these activities, I learned that there is nothing to fear. I feel alive when I come out to do things. But I do take a lot of abuse from people—gripes, complaints, blames, and a lot of headaches. Even George and I have differences sometimes, and he is very stubborn. But basically we are alike, so things don't get too bad at home. At least he doesn't bug me about housework or cooking; sometimes we just go out to eat. . . .

In the past a lot of the community leaders courted George and me. They always invited us to events and asked us to help. Now no one comes. I guess they realize that they can't just use us anymore. I try to keep up with the issues. Sometimes I get upset about association business, and I can't sleep at night. But most of the time, being active keeps me alive. I don't play mahjongg or go to Reno, so I take care of my granddaughter, and I go to meetings.

On 10 July 1985, Mrs. Chang Jok Lee was honored for her dedication and hard work with the Ping Yuen Residents Improvement Association at the eighth anniversary celebration of the Chinatown Neighborhood Improvement Resources Center, which has spearheaded much of the effort to retain housing in San Francisco's Chinatown. In front of 550 people, she said in Chinese, "I don't really deserve this, but I know that if we all work together, anything can be done." Then, the fifty-eight-year-old grandmother smiled and curtsied.

24

Esse Quam Videri: Susie Williams Jones

Emily Herring Wilson
Susan Mullalley

Susie Jones invites visitors to come in, opening the door of her comfortable white clapboard home, which served as the President's residence on the Bennett College campus in Greensboro. Mrs. Jones extends her hand, and, if there is a certain formality in the gesture, it is relieved by her smile.

The house is muted in shadows across drapery and chairs, across the ridges of many books, falling on the keys of the piano. Over the mantel there is a large abstract painting; beneath, logs are laid for use in the fireplace. Carved ivory statues rest on shelves and tables. Everywhere there are books of poetry, art, and history. There is music, but not from the piano; it comes from Mrs. Jones's high, flute-like voice. She comes to her guests with freshly made orange juice on a china plate, with a linen napkin. She turns the conversation to ask about our families. The hour passes until the room seems to be filled, with sunlight.

Here is the home to which Bennett girls came for breakfast with her husband, David

Source: Excerpted from "Esse Quam Videri" by S. Williams from *Hope and Dignity, Older Black Women of the South* edited by E. Herring Wilson, 1983, Philadelphia: Temple University Press. Copyright © 1983 by Temple University. Reprinted by permission. Acknowledgement is made to the Black Women Oral History Project, sponsored by the Arthur and Elizabeth Schlesinger Library on the History of Women in America of Radcliffe College, for permission to quote from an interview conducted with Mrs. Jones by Dr. Merze Tate.

D. Jones, who served the school from 1926 until his death in 1956. Here there were teas, parties, and dinners presided over by a woman who is widely regarded as one of the most gracious hostesses in Greensboro. Here there were the activities of their four children, encouraged to participate in the life of Bennett College. Here there was good sense, good manners, and good will.

Susie Jones, now in her ninetieth year, is one of the best-known and best loved women in North Carolina. Her years of service with her husband during his presidency of Bennett College and with the YWCA, the Methodist Church, and the United Council of Church Women have given her unique opportunities to advance humanitarian concerns and the progress of what she, in an old-fashioned way, refers to as "our group." By this she means, of course, all black Americans. Born into a family where education was more extensive than that of many Southerners and where attitudes were broadly democratic, she grew up with an informed understanding of human rights. From this kind of environment, she developed a deep resourcefulness which sustains her now.

Her lifetime of involvement in schools and organizations, her travels, and her contacts with people of national importance have not separated her from other lives unlike her own. Whether her concern is for the black children who were thrust into integrated schools or the first black contestants in the

Miss America pageant, or the numbers of blacks in jails, she is especially sensitive to the lives of members of her own race, particularly those who have had a less protected environment than her own. Although she is comfortable in the college home on the Bennett campus, Susie Jones will never be satisfied until her own comforts are shared by a larger number of black Americans. Thus, she lives both with the serenity which a long life of family success has brought her and with the quiet insistence that other black families come to experience a better day.

To begin her story, we go back from Greensboro, the center for the first civil rights sit-ins which changed the nation, to Kentucky, where her family was perhaps already preparing for a new America.

"I was born in Danville, Kentucky, April 30, 1892. This was my grandmother's home. It was our custom every year, as soon as school was dismissed, to go to Danville and spend the summer. We always went on the train from Cincinnati, Ohio, because my mother insisted that we were interstate travelers, and this meant we did not have to use the segregated coaches. I did not understand this at that time, but I can remember that she would often have arguments with the conductor as to where we would sit. We all looked forward to going to visit Grandmother, because my mother was a very practical woman, and she had many interests in the community as well as the responsibilities of her home. We lived a very simple life; we had a very simple upbringing. But Grandmother did not feel that way about it. She felt that all of our underskirts should have lace sewed on them and that it was important for children to have a party every summer. She brought lots of glamour into our lives. I think I have heard my sisters say, and I know I have said often to myself, 'I do hope I can grow old gracefully as Grandmother did.' l have my grandmother's cups and saucers. They are old Haviland, and during our summers in Danville, one of the things Grandmother did always was to entertain her club of friends. And for this club, my uncle, my mother's brother

who was a very sought-after caterer, would send her either pastries or strawberries from Cincinnati. He would send them by porters on the train, and we would go down and pick them up. He and his wife added a great deal to our lives. They thought it was important for us to have kid gloves and simple jewelry that every girl appreciates. He had great love for his family and was mindful of them. My grandmother was also a very good seamstress, and she did beautiful handiwork. Every year during the winter months, she would make her mother a cap to wear, a cap made of lace and fine material. One of our jobs when we came in the summer was to 'go out to the hill,' as we called it, where my great-grandmother lived, to carry her this cap.

"My grandmother had great influence on my life and on the lives of my sisters and brother. She was the slave of a Presbyterian minister, and it was his custom to read to his wife every evening. He always insisted on my grandmother sitting there, listening to him, and so she learned to read and was a great reader all her life. When my two oldest children were about three and four, I took them to see her, and she recited for us, sitting in her rocking chair on the front porch, all of Byron's *Prisoner of Chillon*. She had a great love for English and Irish literature. I think you can understand why she felt it was important for her daughter to go to college. My mother started her college work at Allegheny, where she had an uncle living, and then transferred to Berea, and there she met my father. She had been the favorite in her own home and family. Her college education was rare for a woman at that time. She made a brilliant record, and she would stand no interference with her plans. It was she who decided that my sister, Frances, must go to Mt. Holyoke College. They had not enrolled a colored student at Holyoke for years, and when she applied for admission for Frances, they wrote her that Frances would probably be happier in an environment where she was more at home, and she answered, 'Frances's happiness is none of your business; that's my business. I want to know if you will admit her.' And they did.

When my youngest son went to Andover, his teacher said to him, 'You are the best prepared Latin student that I have had in years. Where did you study your Latin?' His reply was, 'My grandmother.' He had studied with his grandmother while in high school. She was on the advisory committee for the national YWCA before Negroes were on the board. At seventy, she resigned all the clubs she belonged to and became a member of the recently organized League of Women Voters. At her death we found that she had adopted a child under CARE.

"My mother and father graduated from Berea College, receiving their bachelor's degrees. My first experience in race [discrimination] was when the Negro students, because of the Day Law that was passed by the legislature in Kentucky, were put out of Berea.[1] Lincoln Institute was established for them. Some of the Negro graduates of Berea protested this. My father was leader of the group that protested, so my first racial experience was hearing very heated discussions on this matter. The president at that time was Dr. Foust. He came to our house several times to meet with this group to try to work out a satisfactory arrangement, but this never was realized. Although in these later years, under Dr. Hutchins, Berea opened again her doors to Negro students, my mother never forgave them, and so she never made a contribution to the college. My father did give, but she did not. Because, you would probably remember, Berea was founded for Negroes and mountain whites, and she felt that they had in such a large way betrayed their heritage.

"My father was a great teacher. As I was growing up, he was a teacher in Louisville, Kentucky. Later, he became principal of the high school in Covington, Kentucky. This was a very significant event in our lives, because he immediately enrolled in the University of Cincinnati for advanced work. He was the only Negro principal of a high school in St. Louis for years. We saw him take demotions and new assignments. He had made Sumner High School one of the first high schools in the country, and he was moved to a down-

town high school that had a very bad image, the Vashon High School. It was located in the inner city, and the majority of the students came from deprived homes. One of the first things he did, which to me was fascinating, he sat on a stool in the hall, and as the children came into the building, he would say, 'Good morning' to each of them. He believed clearly in certain principles. One of the marked ones of these was thrift, and he thought our group would never make the kind of progress they should make until they were adequate economically. And so one of his first activities in the St. Louis community was to organize the New Age Building and Loan Association. Another thing he deplored was the housing of Negroes in St. Louis. Those of you who know St. Louis know that there were many very large houses there, and St. Louis was something like Brooklyn in that these houses were grouped around. As people moved to the west, and Negroes went into these large houses, the only way they could sustain themselves was to sublet. And so there was a feeling in St. Louis that property would go down when Negroes moved into the area. And my father was greatly concerned about this. We had all at this time graduated from college, and out of his earnings, he had saved enough money to build an apartment building for Negroes. This building was built by one of the leading construction firms of St. Louis, and the building was very adequate, very impressive looking outside. And so there happened one of these strange phenomena of how people that you're trying to help turn on you, and my father faced a severe school fight. Interestingly enough, a friend, who came by one day as he sat on his porch, said to him, since there was his own home, the apartment next door, and a housing unit next, 'Mr. Williams, this is your trouble. You are looking too prosperous.' But he did live to see all the leaders in the school fight come to him for some favor. I can well remember one time being there when a teacher came to him with his monthly check, and I said to my father, 'What does this mean?' He said, naming the teacher, 'He does not seem to be able to handle his finances, and the Board of Education is continuing his employment if he will come to me every month with his check, and we will sit down and make a budget, and he will keep out of the hand of vendors and people accusing him of not paying his bills.'"

A grandmother who recited poetry, a mother who read Latin, a father who was a community leader—these were the earliest influences in the life of Susie Williams Jones. Her future looked bright, indeed. She entered kindergarten when she was three years old and continued through elementary and high schools in Kentucky. After graduation, she took an additional year at Woodward High School in Cincinnati, the alma mater of William Howard Taft, to qualify for entrance to the University of Cincinnati. "At Woodward High School," she remembers, "there was quite a tradition not only for a certain type of education, but for relationships of students and faculty. I remember our Latin teacher, a Mr. Peabody from Boston Latin School, had been teacher there for years. The days at Woodward, you can understand, had certain adjustments that had to be made because I was entering the senior class. Most of the students had been with each other through all of their high school experiences. But I was reasonably happy. I did not feel that I had any particular problems. I think our parents had been successful in bringing us up with an acceptance of people as people, and this was the important thing. We had certain normal situations with people of the white race, but I never was particularly impressed with what color they were, or whether they were Negroes or whites. In the yearbook, the comment under my picture read: Susie believes in our class motto, *Esse quam videri*, To be rather than to seem. Our parents were very anxious, as far as their means allowed, to give us experiences of enrichment that were wider in scope than life in this small Kentucky town. One of our Christmas presents was always a season ticket to lectures given in Cincinnati on Sunday afternoons during the fall and winter. We heard prominent leaders in the country. Through this kind of an experi-

ence and attending political meetings in Cincinnati involving national politics, we had a feeling of world outreach.

"The matter of race did not really hit me until I went to college. Although there were just a very few Negroes who attended the University of Cincinnati at that time, it was largely a municipal college. It had no dormitories, and so the students came from the Cincinnati area, and if not immediately from Cincinnati, from some of the smaller Kentucky towns. One of the most outstanding irritations that I suffered was that an English teacher, who was from the North, left a vacant seat on both sides of me. I went to the head of the department and complained about this. After our initial conversation he sent for me to come back. Dr. Miller did not want me to transfer; he wanted me to stay in the class. This was a very difficult experience for me, but not difficult enough to deter me in any way. When it was necessary to use the same material, or if I wanted to see somebody else's notebook, or they wanted to see mine, we would just move in the seats of our own accord, and so it did not deter me, but it really was my most unpleasant experience in college. When I graduated, I had persuaded my father, who was not easy to persuade, to let me go to the University of Chicago for a summer session, so that I could graduate early. He granted this request. There, too, I found discrimination of a different kind, people not willing to even answer simple questions. I later found out that there were a great many Southerners who came for the summer session, and I am sure unfriendliness was more or less common because there were a great many Negroes attending the summer sessions. So my racial experiences came along at the time of life that I was mature. I must have taken them in stride as most Negroes do, and worked with them when I could. I always had enough pleasant experiences to outbalance those that were difficult. I never felt persecuted, and I really never felt that I couldn't do anything I wanted to do because of race. Those of us who grew up in a more or less protected environment, where we did not have to use public transportation, where we did not have to—now, I can remember my mother on this, you just never bought anything at a store where the clerks were in any way rude to you. You go to another store because there were plenty of stores where they were kind and gracious to you. And my grandmother's home, although it was right in the heart of the bluegrass, she had a horse and buggy and so you know you weren't up against a lot of things that some people had to contend with. I think that—I don't quite know how to say this—but I think that as I grew older and began to understand more of the system and what was happening in the world, I began to feel that I must do whatever I could to work on this matter. I was able to work in the Methodist Church and in the United Council of Church Women, where there are both white and Negro women working together for solutions. This was a most exciting experience. I also was here for the first sit-ins and marched and participated in all of the activities that were a part of this movement in Greensboro, North Carolina.

"Just as race was not emphasized in my family, neither was the matter of sex. My father had both men and women as faculty members, and so I never felt there was any question about my identity as a woman. I never grew up feeling that there should be preferences. Just as I acquired a deeper knowledge of the race issue as I grew older, so I became conscious of the problem of women. In my married life, I was always interested in the YWCA, and I inherited this from my mother. But the women's movements, except the League of Women Voters, were not as clearly defined in focus or in activities as they are today. And so I have a mixed feeling about the women's movement, not that I am specifically against it, but I feel that there are some strategies that are questionable. I feel strongly that the struggle for racial equality and the struggle for women's rights have been two parallel struggles in American life. I feel that it is important, since women are moving out into the mainstream of life, and our home responsibilities have

become less, I do think it is important that they be supported by non-discrimination of all kinds. In many ways I am very grateful for the movement, but at the same time as I have seen some of it from the sideline, which is quite different from being responsible for things, I have felt that there were certain things in our struggle for rights that we did not want to lose out on. Just as Mr. Hooks, present director of the NAACP, was saying in his 'Face the Nation' interview, that he was dedicated, he wanted liberty for everybody, but he was committed to seeking it out for people who had been deprived. I think that what we do in these movements is so dependent upon the kinds of people that we are, and I don't think that I have been over-aggressive in the area of race because that's just not my nature. I can remember a man came in my house one day; I can't remember just why he was there, but he had his hat on, and I asked him to take off his hat, please, and so I dropped my voice and he took it off. Then I can remember when we lived in Atlanta, I volunteered to take nursery school children to the clinic at Grady Hospital. Registration cards had to be made out for each child, and the woman who was head of this part of the work asked me one day, what was my name, and I said, 'My name is Mrs. Jones.' She replied, 'We do not call Negroes by titles.' I suggested that she not use my name because I would be uncomfortable if she attempted to use my first name. Her reply was, 'I will call you what you wish. I can't let you be more polite than I.' "

After marriage to David Jones in 1915, when she was twenty-three, Mrs. Jones settled down to a life in which the family and home were of primary importance. When Mr. Jones, a graduate of Wesleyan College and the University of Chicago, was interviewed by Edward R. Murrow for *This I Believe*, he said, "From the outset my wife and I have had the feeling that no matter what else we did in life, we had to devote our best thinking and our best living to our children." After Mr. Jones became president of Bennett College in 1926, Susie Jones and their four young children became part of the campus family. The children were included in receptions and dinners in the home which were given for distinguished visitors. And "there were chores to be done, the grass was to be weeded, and the trips to the post office and banks were made daily. This was a priceless heritage. The children learned to work, and they knew when work was well done. There was a far greater blessing that came to them and came to me as their mother. We were starting a new enterprise and there were people who were willing to help; and so in and out of the home there were visitors who greatly enriched all of our lives. I can remember one Sunday evening, the youngest boy was with us as we were taking Mrs. Mary McLeod Bethune to the station. And he said in the car going down, 'Daddy, you know this is the first time I ever heard a speech where I understood all the speaker said.' And Mrs. Bethune laughed in her characteristic way and said, 'Well, Dave, I really put the cookies on the lower shelf today, didn't I?'

"I would like to say a deep word of gratitude for the opportunities that were ours on the college campus. Mr. Jones's illness in the 1950s stopped all of my outside activities. At his death, the trustees were kind enough to elect me vice-president of the college. I felt that I should not accept this. I wanted to be sure not to presume on the college in any way, and whatever I did, I wanted people to understand that it would be something that was important for the on-going of the college. And so I asked that instead of being elected vice-president, I should be elected registrar, work which I had done voluntarily in the early days of the college and an office where I had started the college records. And so I worked in this office until I was seventy-two years of age."

The four children of Susie and David Jones attended public schools in Greensboro, the boys finishing their secondary training in northern preparatory schools. Later, they studied at some of the most distinguished colleges and universities in America—Wesleyan, Harvard, Boston University. Their daughter, now on the staff of Harvard University Medical School, is still proud of the training she received at Bennett College.

"I hope as I have talked," Mrs. Jones concludes, "I have not made it seem that life was without struggle, because my life has been filled with ups and down. [One of the tragedies of her life was the death of her oldest son in 1976.] My father was wont to say that the good life does not necessarily mean that you do not have trouble, but it does mean that you get the breaks. My husband used to say to the Bennett girls, 'The next most certain thing to death is that effort counts.' "

For Susie Jones the "good life" has meant a legacy of education, manners, and opportunity received from her parents, which she, in turn, has passed on to her children and grandchildren.

Note

1. The Kentucky Day Law 71904 prohibited co-racial education in the state.

25

Women's Work and Caregiving Roles: A Life Course Approach

Phyllis Moen
Julie Robison
Vivian Fields

This study drew on a life course approach and a sample of 293 women from four birth cohorts in upstate New York to examine the relationship over time between women's paid work and their informal caregiving of aging or infirm relatives. We find that such caregiving is an increasingly likely role for women, both as they age and across birth cohorts. One in four (24%) women became caregivers at some time between ages 35–44, and over one in three (36%) of these same women became caregivers between ages 55–64. Only 45 percent of the oldest cohort (born 1905–1917) were ever caregivers, compared to 64 percent of the most recent cohort (born 1927–1934), an increase of almost 20 percent. Clearly changes in the labor force participation of more recent cohorts of women do not appear to alter their caregiving responsibilities. In fact, women in this sample were equally likely to become caregivers, regardless of whether or not they were employed.

Adulthood and aging can be depicted as a series of role changes, and while role loss may be concomitant with aging, role gain may also occur (Moen, Dempster-McClain, and Williams, 1992; Riley and Riley, 1989).

Women have always been the family caregivers (Coward and Dwyer, 1990; Lee, 1992; Stoller, 1983; Stone, Cafferata, and Sangl, 1987), but an aging population and the ongoing revolution in women's roles is placing this previously taken-for-granted responsibility in the spotlight.

One concern is the extent to which women's paid employment may be disrupted by caregiving responsibilities for ailing or dependent adult kin (Breslau, Salkever, and Staruch, 1982; Brody et al., 1987; Steuve and O'Donnell, 1989). As women move into the labor force in unprecedented numbers (Moen, 1992), traditional role obligations, such as caregiving for infirm relatives, become increasingly problematic. Do prolonged caregiving spells preclude women's on-going involvement in a paid job in the same way that caring for preschoolers has? Do adult caregiving demands hinder women's entry or reentry into the labor force?

While caregiving may well curtail employment, so too may employment serve as a possible deterrent to women becoming caregivers.

Propositions. We hypothesize that role entrances and exits, whether to or from caregiv-

Source: Excerpted from "Women's Work and Caregiving Roles: A Life Course Approach," P. Moen et al., 1994, *Journal of Gerontology: Social Sciences* 49(4), S176-S186. Copyright © 1994 The Gerontological Society of America. Reprinted with permission.

ing or employment, are in fact contingent on women's current role occupancy. Specifically, we anticipate that: (a) women currently in the labor force are less likely than full-time home-makers to take on caregiving, and are un-likely to leave their jobs in the face of new or ongoing caregiving responsibilities; and (b) women who are already caregivers are un-likely to take on the additional role of paid worker.

A life course approach suggests that the relationships between employment and care-giving will vary depending on women's age. For example, as women grow older we expect caregiving to become more, and paid work less, salient. But this may also be affected by social class, with college-educated women more invested in the worker role, and corre-spondingly, less apt to take on caregiving than those with only a high school education (Stone and Short, 1990).

A life course approach also presumes that the linkages between work and caregiving may well have changed historically, with women born into different historical circum-stances having vastly different experiences with these two roles. We hypothesize that more recent birth cohorts of women will be more likely than women born earlier in the century to be involved in both roles. With increases in longevity, we in the United States are facing a situation where there will be more people requiring informal family care (Berg and Cassells, 1990; Coward, Horne, and Dwyer, 1992). At the same time, due to demo-graphic shifts in family size, families have fewer siblings to share caregiving obliga-tions. This trend was temporarily reversed for the cohorts born during the post World War II baby boom; however, the secular trend since the turn of the century has been one of reduced fertility. The women in the sample analyzed here were born before the baby boom. Therefore, despite their increasing com-mitment to employment, the more recent co-horts of women in our analyses are more likely to have both aging relatives requiring care and fewer siblings among whom to dis-tribute caregiving tasks (e.g., Seccombe, 1992; Stoller, 1983; Treas, 1977).

Sample

We draw on life history data from the Women's Role Survey, a study of 313 wives and mothers from a mid-sized community in upstate New York.

(For a more detailed description of the sample, see Moen, Dempster-McClain, and Williams, 1989, 1992.)

Measures and Procedures

To assess the patterning of paid work and caregiving roles over the prime adult years (ages 18–55), we analyzed our data for the sample as a whole, by birth cohort, by age categories, and by educational level. The four cohorts in our sample consist of women who were born between 1905–1917 ($n = 87$), 1918–1922 ($n = 88$), 1923–1926 ($n = 52$), and 1927–1934 ($n = 66$). We divided the sample into four birth cohorts in order to test for differences due to changes in the historical and social climate in which the respondents lived. The cohorts were constructed according to when these women became adults and in relation to the timing of historical events in their lives. The older of these women (born 1905 to 1917) came to adulthood during the years of the Great Depression when women's employ-ment was often economically critical for fami-lies and when caregiving was a taken-for-granted aspect of women's lives. They turned 65 in the 1970s, the decade of the women's movement. The second cohort (born 1918 to 1922) reached adulthood during the second World War, when employment of women was portrayed as a patriotic duty. They reached retirement age in the 1980s. The third cohort (born 1923 to 1926) became adults during the early postwar period, a time of transition from a wartime to peacetime economy, and are just now moving into their mid-sixties.

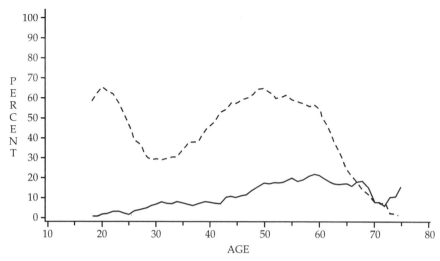

Figure 1. Percent of women working and caregiving, by age (*n* = 293). Solid line, caregiving; dashed line, working.

The youngest cohort (born 1927 to 1934) began their adulthood in the 1950s, when women's lives were expected to be family and home oriented. They will reach their 60s during the decade of the 1990s. Each of these cohorts has experienced major historical, demographic, and social changes affecting gender role expectations and, possibly, their expectations about caregiving.

To examine the possible effects of social change on women's role choices, we looked for differences among these cohorts in involvement in work and caregiving. We also describe the incidence of caregiving and paid work up until age 75 (for those respondents who were 75 or older at the time of the second interview).

We created spells (episodes) of work and caregiving, where each spell represents a particular combination of paid work and caregiving roles. For each spell there is a specific start and end date, with a change in either working or caregiving status marking the beginning of a new spell. We calculated: (1) the percent of women engaged in caregiving and or paid work for various age groups and by birth cohort; (2) the duration of time spent in various work/caregiving role combinations; (3) the probability of making a transition from one work/caregiving role combination to any

other; and (4) the relationship between educational level, paid work, and caregiving. The transitions are contingent upon: (a) the particular originating role combination and (b) the existence of a move (i.e., censored spells are eliminated). In addition, we examined various age categories to note age-related changes in roles across the course of women's lives. Because employment in particular is a function of age, when looking at both roles together we analyze the probability of paid work and caregiving from ages 18 to 55. All tests of significance were conducted with F-tests, unless otherwise noted.

Results

Figure 1 depicts the distribution of involvement in paid work and caregiving over the course of women's lives. While employment in this sample of women born before 1935 follows the traditional "M" shape (with women leaving the labor force while their children are young), the incidence of caregiving increases slowly but steadily over their life course.

The caregiving curve is quite flat compared to the employment curve. The percent-

TABLE 1 Transition Rates and Mean Durations Prior to Transition, in Years

	Number of Spells	Transition Rates	Mean Duration (in years)	Standard Deviation of Duration
1. From Working and Caregiving to:				
a. Caregiving only	20	.15	2.6	3.1
b. Working only	110	.83	1.6	2.5
c. Neither	2	.02	0.25	0.00
2. From Caregiving Only to:				
d. Caregiving and working	30	.23	1.7	2.4
e. Working only	1	.01	2.0	
f. Neither	101	.77	1.9	2.8
3. From Working Only to:				
g. Caregiving and working	119	.15	5.6	5.9
h. Caregiving only	9	.01	7.2	5.5
i. Neither	658	.85	3.5	4.1
4. From Neither Working nor Caregiving to:				
j. Working and caregiving	4	.00	8.9	8.4
k. Caregiving only	121	.15	8.3	8.9
l. Working only	707	.84	4.5	6.0
Total number of spells	1882			

age of women caregiving at any one point in time from age 46 through age 69 varies by at most 10 percent, from a low of 11 percent at age 46 to a high of 21 percent at age 59. This pattern suggests that caregiving may be less sensitive to other life course transitions, such as childbearing, than is employment. Neither does caregiving appear to be as normatively prescribed by age constraints as is employment. In other words, women apparently do not "retire" from the caregiving role at particular ages.

We analyzed data for each woman from the time she was 18 to her 55th birthday and calculated the rates of transition to four possible work and caregiving role combinations: working and caregiving, caregiving only, working only, and neither working nor caregiving (see Transition Rates column in Table 1). These transitions are conditional upon starting in a given state. For any given starting state there are three possible changes. What is important to note is that women were as likely to move from working only to caregiving and working (row g), as they were to move from neither working nor caregiving to caregiving only (row k).

For example, one woman had been working full time as a real estate agent at the time of her husband's diagnosis of Alzheimer's disease in May 1985 when she was 68. She started working part time late in 1986 and was continuing in both roles at the time of her interview. Another woman worked as a secretary for an aircraft manufacturing company from 1963 to 1981, during ages 46 to 64. She also cared for her elderly aunt who lived with her from 1967 until the aunt's death in 1977. Thus, contrary to our hypothesis, being employed does not seem to preclude becoming a caregiver. In fact, women were both workers and caregivers at the same time during as many spells (132—see row 1) as they were caregivers alone (132—see row 2). The number of years from age 18 to age 55 spent working and caregiving versus caregiving alone are almost identical (see column 3, rows 1 and 2).

Women who were both working and caregiving (row 1) were more likely to stop caregiving (row b) than to stop working (row a). Examples of women undergoing such transitions include a grade school teacher who cared for her father-in-law in her home for seven years beginning in 1954, when she was

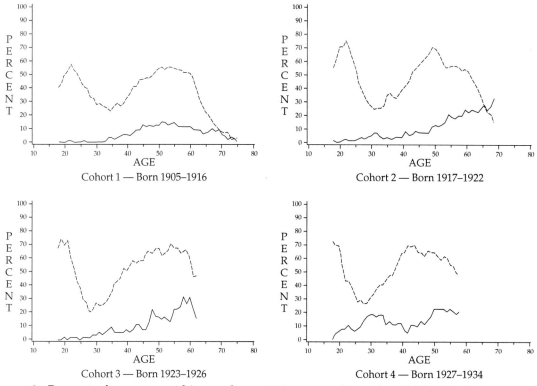

Figure 2. Percent of women working and caregiving, at each age (*n* = 293). Solid line, caregiving; dashed line, working.

43, until he moved into a nursing home; and a woman who ran a riveting machine from 1953 to 1957 (and was continuously employed in various occupations until 1980, when she was 56), who started caring for her mother in 1955 but stopped after two months and did not care for her again up to the mother's death in 1972. A significant proportion of women who were caregiving only (row 2) moved into employment (.23, see row d), although most stopped caregiving without taking on employment (.77, see row f). One woman, age 31, who had stopped working to have children, was caring for her infant daughter with cerebral palsy in 1955, but went back to work as a full-time private nurse when her daughter was 3 years old. Another woman, who had not worked outside the home since her marriage, cared for her husband who had cancer from 1975, when she

was 56, until his death in 1978, after which she remained out of the labor force.

Cohort differences in women's paid work and caregiving.—When we divide the sample into four birth cohorts we find that the earliest cohort (born 1905–1917) was the least involved in caregiving, regardless of age or stage of the life course (see Figure 2). At no age does the percentage of women in cohort 1 who were caregiving exceed 15 percent. By contrast, the caregiving curve for women in cohort 2 (born 1918–1922) rises rather steadily with age to a high of 32 percent at age 68. Women in cohort 3 (born 1923–1926) show a similar level of caregiving to those in cohort 2. Among women in cohort 3, however, caregiving activity peaks at 33 percent, 10 years earlier than for those in cohort 2. The caregiving curve for the most recent cohort (born

1927–1934) is more erratic than those of the earlier cohorts. It is flatter than those for cohorts 2 and 3. Except for a dip in activity during their early 40s, caregiving levels stay between 10 and 23 percent from age 28 to age 55 (the age of this cohort when interviewed). Since this cohort is right censored at age 55, it is quite likely that the percentage of caregiving might rise even higher as this cohort ages.

As can be seen in Table 2, women in the two most recent cohorts (born 1923–1934) tend to be more active in both work and caregiving roles than women in the two earlier cohorts (born 1905–1922). Sixty-four percent of women in cohort 4 (1927–1934) had some experience with caregiving during ages 18–55, while only 45 percent of the earliest cohort (born 1905–1917) did. We find a statistically significant ($p = .01$) difference in the likelihood of taking on the caregiving role between the two oldest and the two youngest cohorts, with the more recent cohorts more likely to have been caregivers than those born earlier, despite the fact that the most recent cohort is younger. Even more of these younger women may yet become caregivers as they move into later adulthood.

We also examined the patterns of transitions between the various combinations of working and caregiving roles across cohorts (as described for the whole sample in Table 1). We found that women in the most recent cohort (born 1927 to 1934 were significantly ($p = .0001$) more likely to make a transition from neither working nor caregiving to caregiving only than were women in the other three cohorts (data not shown).

Differences in women's paid work and caregiving as they age. In order to examine variations in work and caregiving patterns over time, we divided each woman's life into 10-year segments, starting with ages 35–44 and ending with ages 65–74. The age categories themselves were arbitrary, but provide convenient markers of moving through the adult years. We find relatively little involvement in caregiving prior to age 35, but the 35 to 44 decade

sees a fourth of women experiencing caregiving. Over the next 20 years the proportion of these women becoming caregivers increases to 35 percent. Most women were also paid workers during this same period, from ages 45–64. This finding points to the importance of caregiving in women's lives in late midlife, and the potential for role strain and overload as significant numbers of women in their forties and fifties combine employment with caregiving.

As shown in Table 3, the drop-off in involvement in caregiving as women reach age 65 is less sharp than that for employment, since a smaller proportion of women are engaged in caregiving in the first place, and since caregiving remains a significant role in the later years. Note that fully one fourth of women aged 65–74 were caregiving at some time during these years, more than were in the paid labor force. However, the proportion of years spent caregiving during these older years (65–74) is about half the time these women spent caregiving during their previous decade (ages 55–65).

Women combine caregiving and working or are caregivers exclusively for only a small percentage of time during their prime adult years from age 18 to 55. However, over the life course we see relatively more time spent caregiving exclusively and less time spent working exclusively (see Table 3).

When we test for significant differences in transition rates of change to a given work/caregiving status between age categories, we find that women ages 45 to 54 are significantly ($p = .0002$) more likely to add caregiving responsibilities to work than they are at other ages. In other words, they are significantly more likely to move from working only to working and caregiving (row g, Table 1) in their late 40s and early 50s. When women reach their late 50s and early 60s (ages 55–64), they are significantly ($p = .004$) more likely to make the transition from both working and caregiving to caregiving only than they were as younger women (row a, Table 1). This could well reflect the decision to retire in the face of caregiving responsibili-

TABLE 2 Women's Paid Work and Caregiving Experiences (Ages 18 to 55) by Cohort

	Cohort 1 (n = 87) b. 1905–1917	Cohort 2 (n = 88) b. 1918–1922	Cohort 3 (n = 52) b. 1923–1926	Cohort 4 (n = 66) b. 1927–1934	Total Sample
Paid work experience					
Ever worked in paid job	94.25[a]	95.45[a]	98.08[a]	100.00[a]	96.59
Never worked in paid job	5.75	4.55	1.92	0	3.41
Median duration (of those employed)	16.89	17.52	19.58	18.35	17.75
Percentage of 18–55 years employed	45.65	47.35	52.94	49.65	42.28
Median age first job (if by age 55)	19.28	18.61	18.08	18.00	18.29
Caregiving experience					
Ever gave care	44.83[a]	45.45[a]	53.85[a]	63.64[a]	50.9
Never gave care	55.17	54.55	46.45	36.36	49.1
Median duration (of those who gave care)	1.64	1.71	2.35	2.99	2.00
Percentage of 18–55 years caregiving	4.43	4.62	6.34	8.08	5.42
Median age first gave care (if by age 55)	43.60	43.61	43.86	37.60[b]	42.01
Joint paid work and caregiving experiences: Duration in years					
Working and caregiving					
Mean (SD)	1.2 (3.3)	.67 (1.8)	1.1 (2.5)	1.5 (3.2)[b]	1.1 (2.8)
Median	0.0	0.0	0.0	0.0	0.0
Caregiving exclusively					
Mean (SD)	1.1 (3.1)	.73 (1.9)	.8 (2)	1.5 (3.7) p = .01[b]	1.1 (2.8)
Median	0.0	0.0	0.0	0.0	0.0
Working exclusively					
Mean (SD)	14.1 (9.8)	15.6 (9.2)	15.7 (10)	16.3 (8.5)	15.3 (9.8)
Median	15.6	16.5	14.6	16.7	15.6
Neither caregiving nor working					
Mean (SD)	20.6 (9.8)	20.0 (9.3)	19.4 (10)	17.2 (9.1) p = .03[b]	19.5 (9.6)
Median	19.9	19.2	17.2	17.7	18.6

a. According to t-tests, women in earlier cohorts (1 and 2) are significantly less likely to have given care ($p = .02$) or worked ($p = .05$) than women in later cohorts (3 and 4).
b. According to t-tests, woment in the latest cohort differ significantly ($p = .05$) from women in all other cohorts combined, with respect to these variables.

TABLE 3 Women's Paid Work and Caregiving Over Their Life Course

	Ages 35–44 $n = 293^a$	Ages 45–54 $n = 289$	Ages 55–64 $n = 159$	Ages 65–74 $n = 32$	F-value	Ages 35–74 ^{b} $n = 293$
Paid work experience						
Percentage who ever worked during given ages	66.21	73.70	65.41	21.86	41.5**	84.30
Proportion of given years employed (of those who were employed)	72.10	95.80	74.84	40.84	63.92**	56.62
Caregiving experience						
Percentage who ever gave care during given ages	23.55	34.95	35.85	25.00	5.15**	62.80
Percentage of given years spent caregiving (for those who did caregiving)	10.65	24.12	39.13	19.60	6.69**	11.21
Joint paid work and caregiving experiences: Duration in years						
Working and caregiving						
Mean (SD)	.27 (1.1)	.63 (1.8)	.47 (1.5)	.0 (0)	7.27**	1.4 (3.2)
Caregiving only						
Mean (SD)	.30 (1.3)	.53 (1.7)	.95 (2.3)	.98 (2.5)	3.30*	1.8 (4.0)
Working only						
Mean (SD)	3.9 (4.0)	5.2 (4.1)	4.2 (3.8)	.73 (1.9)	55.9**	12.7 (9.3)
Neither caregiving nor working						
Mean (SD)	5.5 (4.2)	3.7 (4.0)	4.4 (3.9)	8.3 (2.9)	89.92**	14.8 (10.5)

a. Age categories include only those women who had reached the oldest age by the time of the interview, since younger women's work and caregiving experiences are not necessarily complete for the given age category.

b. This may be an undercount since at the time of the interview some women were not yet age 74. Younger women may work or caregive in the future. The figure for proportion of given years spent working or caregiving calculates the proportion of possible years spent in the given activity.

*p < .05; **p < .01.

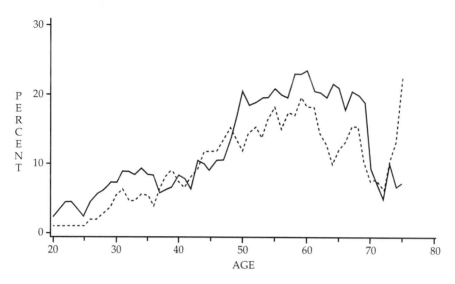

Figure 3. Percent of women caregiving over the course of their lives, by education. Solid line, high school education or less; dashed line, more than high school education.

ties, or it may simply mark the societal trend toward earlier retirement (U.S. Bureau of the Census, 1989). Another possible explanation for this finding is that older women do not earn enough to pay for formal caregivers to replace them, and find it easier to stop working than to find substitutes for their own caregiving.

Differences in women's paid work and caregiving by education level. Thus far we have considered similarities and differences in women's employment and caregiving by age and by birth cohort, but women's role involvements may also vary by their location in the social structure.

Do the pathways to caregiving in fact differ for women with different educational backgrounds?

When we examine working and caregiving in light of educational level (high school or less vs. as least some college), we find, not surprisingly, that women with college training are more likely to be working at paid jobs later in life (from age 44 to their late 60s) than are less educated women (see Figure 3). However, the opposite pattern appears with re-

spect to caregiving. That is, between ages 57 and 71, less educated women are more likely to be caregivers than are those with more education (see Figure 3). College-educated women are likely to spend more postretirement years (65–74) neither caregiving nor working than are those with only a high school education. (Note in Figure 3 that the proportion of college-educated women in the role of caregiver increases at age 71, but the very small sample size at this age level makes it unclear whether this is a true trend.)

Summary of the Findings

- Caregiving is an increasingly common role for women in the United States.

- Caregiving is usually a short-term, intermittent role, and one frequently combined with employment.

- While caregiving may be a major interruption in one's anticipated life experiences, we found that it does not necessarily interrupt women's labor force participation.

- Our findings suggest that women are as likely to be combining working and caregiving as they are to be caregivers exclusively, and in one in five cases home-makers who are caregivers take on employment in addition to caregiving. When women who are employed take on caregiving tasks, they are unlikely to leave the labor force as a result, despite any possible strains they may experience.

- Neither does employment appear to preclude women's subsequent caregiving responsibilities. Again contrary to our hypothesis, women are equally likely to become caregivers, whether or not they are employed. In the case of women who are both workers and caregivers, they are more likely to stop caregiving than to leave their jobs.

- Caregiving appears to be increasingly a role that is more, not less, characteristic of women's lives, as seen by the rising incidence of caregiving across succeeding birth cohorts. We found that more recent cohorts of American women are more likely than those born earlier in the century to take on the caregiving role, despite their increased involvement in the paid labor force and the societal revolution in gender expectations.

- Thus, it does not appear that as women become more involved in the paid labor force the prevalence of their caregiving declines. Women seem to be adding to their role repertoire rather than experiencing shifts in roles.

- The apparent disparity by cohort, evidenced by the fact that caregiving is increasing across cohorts, suggests that changes in family structure and in longevity are indeed increasing the demand for informal family care (Coward, Horne, and Dwyer, 1992; Dwyer and Coward, 1992).

- Position in the social structure, as operationalized by level of education, also affects the likelihood of working and caregiving. During the later years of adulthood, more educated women are more apt to be in the work force than are women with less education, but the pattern is reversed for caregiving. Women with only a high school education (or less) may lack the resources to purchase care for ailing relatives; they may also be less in a position to have alternative claims—such as a professional career—on their time.

Policy Implication

It is also of crucial importance that policy makers take into consideration the fact that caregiving is frequently concomitant with employment (e.g., Neal et al., 1993; Seccombe, 1992), since the odds are that combining these two roles will become more common for future cohorts. We have seen, from the findings of this study, that working women are as likely to become caregivers as are those out of the labor force. Both flexibility at work and community-based programs to aid family caregivers may help women (and men) to better manage their work and caregiving obligations. Caregiving responsibilities throughout the life course may also affect women's socioeconomic status in later life (Arendell and Estes, 1991). The development of care-providing institutional alternatives as well as job flexibility will shape family caregiving in future decades, even as advances in longevity increase its likelihood.

Acknowledgments

This research was supported by grant no. RO1 AG05450 from the National Institute on Aging, Phyllis Moen and Robin M. Williams, Jr., principal investigators, Donna Dempster-McClain, project director; by Hatch grant 3217420, Phyllis Moen, principal investigator; and by grant 1P50 AG11711-01 from the National Institute on Aging, Karl Pillemer and Phyllis Moen, principal investigators. The authors appreciate the considerable efforts of Donna Dempster-McClain in producing the data archive.

Address correspondence to Dr. Phyllis Moen, Life Course Institute, MVR Hall, Cornell University, Ithaca, NY 14853.

References

Arendell, Terry and Carroll L. Estes. 1991. "Older Women in the Post-Reagan Era." *International Journal of Health Services* 21:59-73.

Berg, Robert R. and Joseph S. Cassells (Eds.). 1990. *The Second Fifty Years: Promoting Health and Preventing Disability*. Washington, DC: National Academy Press.

Breslau, Naomi, David Salkever, and Kathleen S. Staruch. 1982. "Women's Labor Force Participation and Responsibilities for Disabled Dependents: A Study of Families with Disabled Children." *Journal of Health and Social Behavior* 23:169-183.

Brody, Elaine M. 1990. *Women in the Middle: Their Parent-Care Years*. New York: Springer.

Brody, Elaine M., Morton H. Kleban, Pauline T. Johnson, Christine Hoffman, and Claire B. Schoonover. 1987. "Work Status and Parent Care: A Comparison of Four Groups of Women." *The Gerontologist* 27:201-208.

Coward, Raymond T. and Jeffrey W. Dwyer. 1990. "The Association of Gender, Sibling Network Composition, and Patterns of Parent Care by Adult Children." *Research on Aging* 12:158-181.

Coward, Raymond T., Claydell Horne, and Jeffrey W. Dwyer. 1992. "Demographic Perspectives on Gender and Family Caregiving." In Jeffrey W. Dwyer and Raymond T. Coward (Eds.), *Gender, Families, and Elder Care*. Newbury Park, CA: Sage.

Dwyer, Jeffrey W. and Raymond T. Coward (Eds.). 1992. *Gender, Families, and Elder Care*. Newbury Park, CA: Sage.

Lee, Gary R. 1992. "Gender Differences in Family Caregiving: A Fact in Search of a Theory." In Jeffrey W. Dwyer and Raymond T. Coward (Eds.), *Gender, Families, and Elder Care*. Newbury Park, CA: Sage.

Moen, Phyllis. 1992. *Women's Two Roles: A Contemporary Dilemma*. New York: Auburn House.

Moen, Phyllis, Donna Dempster-McClain, and Robin M. Williams, Jr. 1989. "Social Integration and Longevity: An Event History Analysis of Women's Roles and Resilience." *American Sociological Review* 54:635-647.

Moen, Phyllis, Donna Dempster-McClain, and Robin M. Williams, Jr. 1992. "Successful Aging: A Life Course Perspective on Women's Multiple Roles and Health." *American Journal of Sociology* 97:1612-1638.

Neal, Margaret B., Nancy J. Chapman, Berit Ingersoll-Dayton, and Arthur C. Emlen. 1993. *Balancing Work and Caregiving for Children, Adults, and Elders*. Newbury Park, CA: Sage.

Riley, Matilda W. and John W. Riley, Jr. 1989. "The Lives of Old People and Changing Social Roles." *The Annals of the American Academy of Political and Social Science* 503:14-28.

Seccombe, Karen. 1992. "Employment, the Family, and Employer-Based Policies." In Jeffrey W. Dwyer and Raymond T. Coward (Eds.), *Gender, Families, and Elder Care*. Newbury Park, CA: Sage.

Steuve, Ann and Lydia O'Donnell. 1989. "Interactions Between Women and Their Elderly Parents: Constraints of Daughters' Employment." *Research on Aging* 11:331-353.

Stoller, Eleanor Palo. 1983. "Parental Caregiving by Adult Children." *Journal of Marriage and the Family* 45:851-858.

Stone, Robyn I., Gail Lee Cafferata, and Judith Sangl. 1987. "Caregivers of the Frail Elderly: A National Profile." *The Gerontologist* 27:616-626.

Stone, Robyn I. and Pamela F. Short. 1990. "The Competing Demands of Employment and Informal Caregiving to Disabled Elders." *Medical Care* 28:513-526.

Treas, Judith. 1977. "Family Support Systems for the Aged: Some Social and Demographic Considerations." *The Gerontologist* 17:486-491.

U.S. Bureau of the Census. 1989. "Projections of the Population of the United States, by Age, Sex, and Race: 1988 to 2080." *Current Population Reports series 25, no. 1018*. Washington, DC: U.S. Government Printing Office.

26

The Problem of Defining Retirement Among Minorities: The Mexican Americans

Barbara A. Zsembik
Audrey Singer

Using the 1979 Chicano Survey and four different operational definitions of retirement, we explored the effects of age, gender, health, birthplace, and lifetime work experience on the retirement of Mexican Americans. We found that correlates of retirement vary by the definition used. Frequent health limitations were associated with retirement defined by self-reported retirement or self-reported current work status, but not defined by respondents' self-described activities or receipt of retirement income. Operational definitions often used in discussion of timing and determinants of retirement, thus, poorly fit the lifetime work patterns and retirement process of Mexican Americans.

Of interest here is the retirement process among Mexican Americans, which has received minimal attention by social scientists (Lacayo, 1980; Markides, 1978; Markides & Martin, 1983). Although retirement is one of the most researched topics in gerontology, little is known about retirement among Hispanic groups. The conceptualization and operationalization of retirement is the first step in research on the determinants and consequences of the retirement transition, although the most useful definition of retirement remains debatable despite extensive literature (Parnes & Nestel, 1981). The major purpose of this research is to investigate correlates of retirement among Mexican Americans as they vary by definitions of retirement.

The conceptualization and operationalization of retirement among Mexican Americans requires closer examination as more traditional criteria poorly fit their lifetime work patterns and thus their retirement process. Gibson's (1987) review of two decades of major retirement studies suggests that more traditional retirement criteria are: "age 65, a clear line between work and nonwork, income primarily from retirement sources, and viewing themselves as retired" (p. 691). Gibson further argues that blacks frequently do not meet these criteria and therefore many are likely to be excluded from retirement research and from the planning and policy formulation generated by that research (Gibson, 1987). Mexican Americans have had similar experiences: lifetime work patterns that yield no clear line between work and nonwork, lack of access to private pensions, low levels of public pensions, and lengthening periods of nonwork at early ages. The lifetime work disadvantages not only cloud the more objective criteria of retirement but also may com-

Source: Excerpted from "The Problem of Defining Retirement Among Minorities: The Mexican Americans," B. Zsembik and A. Singer, 1990, *The Gerontologist* 30(6), 749-757. Copyright © 1990 The Gerontological Society of America. Reprinted with permission. An earlier version of this paper was presented at the meeting of the American Sociological Association, August 1989, San Francisco.

plicate Mexican Americans' self-definition of retirement.

Defining Retirement

Conceptualizing Retirement

Atchley's (1976) work on the sociology of retirement characterizes retirement as a process, a social role, an event, or as a phase of life. As a social role, retirement reflects a social position with attendant rights, duties, and associations. Presumably, one of the most important of these rights and duties is to remain socially and financially independent of family and community as long as possible. Neither is there sufficient evidence nor intuition to assume that the value of dependence and the meaning of retirement are constant among race and ethnic groups.

Retirement as an event reflects a ceremonial rite of passage; however, these events may more often be associated with lengthy job tenures, larger business organizations, and white-collar occupations. It is doubtful that their erratic work histories and disadvantaged placement in the labor structure expose Mexican Americans to such ceremonies.

Retirement as a phase of life refers to a well-defined period of time when "occupational responsibilities are at a minimum and in which the individual is entitled to an income by virtue of his past occupational efforts" (Atchley, 1976, p. 9). This follows a well-defined period of time in which the person was regularly and sufficiently involved in such an occupation. The discontinuous work histories of Mexican Americans cloud the distinction between occupational efforts and relaxing those efforts. Alternating spells of employment and unemployment, and the lengthening of unemployment spells associated with age, make it difficult to apply this definition to Mexican American men and women.

Similarly, Mexican American men and women may work, voluntarily or involuntarily, in part-time and seasonal jobs for much of their working life. This suggests that when retirement is described as the process of ceasing full-time year-round employment, defining the point at which Mexican Americans become retired is almost arbitrary. Given the lifetime work patterns of Mexican Americans, it is unclear how best to define retirement, identify when it occurs, and determine what retirement means.

Operationalizing Retirement

The operational definition of retirement may be subjectively or objectively defined. The subjective definition of retirement is the consideration or claim of oneself as retired. Objective indicators of retirement are more complex. Most generally objective indicators reflect some amount or change in the amount in regular hours of employment and weeks employed and the receipt of income from public or private pensions or of self-initiated retirement plans (Atchley, 1979; Palmore, 1971, 1984). At times these indicators are refined by combining these two aspects. For example, Palmore (1984) uses the following two definitions: objective dichotomous, which labels a person as retired if he or she works less than 35 hours per week and receives a retirement pension; and objective continuous, which describes a person as fully retired when not employed, partially retired when employed part-time, and minimally retired when employed full-time.

Subjective and objective indicators of retirement are not necessarily consistent with one another. A person may describe him- or herself as retired but also be gainfully employed. Likewise, a person may not declare him- or herself to be retired yet not be gainfully employed. In their study of older African American men, Jackson and Gibson (1985) call the group of nonworking men who do not claim to be retired "the unretired-retired." The choice of operational definitions of retirement not only reflects how retirement is conceptualized but also determines who is included in the study sample. Accordingly, certain groups of older adults may be inappropriately or arbitrarily omitted from retirement research and therefore not considered in policy formulation.

This research delves into the complexity of defining retirement among older Mexican Americans to begin to understand the correlates of retirement. We explore the specific retirement experience of Mexican Americans to expand our understanding of their aging experience. The effects of age, sex, acculturation, and lifetime work experience on four definitions of retirement—two more subjectively determined and two more objectively determined—are examined. Given that in the general population correlates vary according to the definition and measurement (Palmore, 1984), correlates also vary according to definition in this Mexican American sample.

Data and Methods

Data are from the Mexican Origin People in the United States: The 1979 Chicano Survey. We focus here on persons aged 50 and older to capture the full distribution of retirement, as Mexican Americans retire soon after 60 (Lacayo, 1980).

Four Definitions of Retirement

We focus here on four definitions of retirement to explore how correlates of retirement vary by which definition is used. The first two definitions essentially are self-reports of retirement. Mexican Americans who answered yes to the question "Are you retired?" are coded as 1 and those who answered no are coded as 0. Of the 162 persons in this analysis, 35.2% answered that he or she was retired (see Table 1). The second definition is based on the respondents' description of what they are "currently doing" these days. Mexican Americans who said they were retired were coded as 1, whereas respondents who named any other activity were coded as 0. Other activity states commonly named include working, housewife, and disabled. Almost one-quarter of this sample described their current activity as retirement.

TABLE 1 Percentage Distribution of Variables in the Analysis of Mexican American Retirement

Variable	%	n (N = 162)
Retirement definition		
Question[a]	35.2	57
Activity[b]	24.7	40
Income source	50.0	81
Work status	67.9	110
Age		
50–54	32.1	52
55–59	19.8	32
60–64	13.0	21
65+	35.2	57
Health limitations		
Many times	14.8	24
Occasionally	55.5	90
Never	29.6	48
Occupation		
Professional/technical	16.0	26
Skilled blue collar	43.8	71
Unskilled and laborers	40.2	65
Birthplace		
U.S. born	60.5	98
Mexican born	39.5	64
Sex		
Women	60.5	98
Men	39.5	64

a. Self-report to the question "Are you retired?"
b. Self-report as to what respondent is "currently doing."

The final two retirement definitions are more objective measures. First, individuals who reported receiving Social Security, pension, or annuity income were coded as 1, and Mexican Americans who did not report such receipts were coded as 0. Of the men and women in this analysis, 50.0% reported receipt of income from Social Security, pensions, or annuities. A relatively large percentage of elderly Mexican Americans receive neither private nor public pension income (Lacayo, 1980; Westat, Inc., 1989). Most retirement income is derived from Social Security, but the small proportion of persons who also receive private pension income has a noticeably higher level of annual income (Lacayo, 1980; Westat, Inc., 1989). Second, Mexican Americans who reported current employment (coded as 0) were compared with persons who reported no current employment (coded as 1). In contrast to the relatively small proportions of retired persons in the first two definitions, 67.9% of this sample is not currently working.

Claiming to be retired is moderately correlated with describing current activity as retired ($r = .687$) and with the receipt of retirement income ($r = .556$). Receipt of retirement income is somewhat correlated with describing current activity as retired ($r = .408$). The lower correlation of retirement income with the other definitions of retirement may be explained by the specific age thresholds of income receipt; retirement income is dependent on reaching a certain age, usually 62 or 65, whereas the more subjective definitions of retirement are not age dependent. The correlations of employment status with the other three definitions of retirement are moderate; however, employment status is most strongly correlated with retirement income ($r = .476$) and is least correlated with current activity ($r = .394$).

The two subjective definitions are linked conceptually. Indeed, the more interesting question is, why aren't the correlations higher than they are? Being retired (definition 1) and describing current activity as other than retired may occur for a number of reasons. First, older Mexican Americans with a life-time of labor market disadvantage may not easily distinguish between the cessation of working and retirement. Second, retirement status is chosen among a set of options to describe employment status; not working could also be described as disability, unemployment, discouraged worker, or homemaker status. Third, leaving a job is not equivalent to the end of productive life for many older persons. The stigma of being "nonproductive" may be averted by claiming another status. Finally, retirement is a process that reflects either leaving a particular job or leaving the labor force entirely. An older person may have retired from a long-term job or career or occupation but currently be employed. Therefore, defining retirement ac-

cording to the first definition overlooks the fact that older people are productive, and employed and employable. Moreover, retirement is both self-defined as well as structurally defined.

Age groups were defined to capture gross differences in the timing of retirement: 50–54; 55–59; 60–64; and 65 and older. Most importantly, the proportions of Mexican Americans who are not currently working are remarkably high, regardless of age group.

Health limitations are intertwined with the transition into retirement. Persons who have experienced ill health are more likely to say they are retired than persons whose work has never been adversely affected by ill health.

Acculturation implies that the values, norms, attitudes, and behaviors of the Mexican-origin population will be changed through contact with those of the non-Mexican origin majority. Acculturation is reflected in whether the respondent was born in the United States (coded as 0) or born in Mexico (coded as 1). The presumption is that Mexican-born persons have been less likely to encounter or acquire the attitudes, beliefs, customs, and skills that underlie successful work lives. More successful work lives are characterized by continuous employment in well-paying jobs, and they yield more successful economic and social adaptation to retirement. Persons continuously employed in jobs in the more productive sectors of the economy are more likely to be covered by corporate pensions and are more likely to be able to afford annuities and assets that support financial stability and well-being in the later years. Moreover, Mexican-born persons historically have been concentrated in jobs only recently covered by Social Security benefits: farm labor and domestic service workers. Consequently, less acculturated Mexican Americans may not be eligible for Social Security benefits, be covered by private pension plans, or be able to afford private financing schemes for the retirement years.

Another indicator of retirement differentials that is included in this analysis is the type of occupation in which a person is currently or was most recently employed. This indicates various dimensions of life-time work patterns. Higher levels of education underlie a more successful occupational attainment and consequently a more successful aging. Mexican Americans generally have low levels of education, which constrains them to periodic employment in low-paying, benefit-deficient, dead-end jobs; nearly 50% of these Mexican Americans have not gone to high school. Occupation indicates differences in the transition to retirement. Professional workers tend to delay retirement to later ages than other workers, whereas laborers and service workers tend to retire at earlier ages. Skilled blue-collar workers tend to be concentrated in industries that provide pension plan coverage as well as mandate at which age retirement is permitted or expected.

Elderly Hispanics are more likely to have worked in unskilled labor, service, and farm occupations (Lacayo, 1980; Westat, Inc., 1989), especially if they are Mexican-born, Spanish-speaking persons with low levels of education. Occupational histories are differentiated into professional or technical occupations, skilled blue-collar jobs, and unskilled blue-collar or farm labor occupations. We expect that skilled and unskilled blue-collar or farm employees are more likely to say that they are retired, regardless of the definition. On the other hand, we expect that professional workers are less likely to say they are retired but more likely to report the receipt of income from Social Security, pensions and annuities, and to be employed.

To examine the correlates of each of the four definitions of retirement, a series of logistic regression models were estimated. These models refer to whether a person is retired (see Table 2).

Summary of the Findings

- Correlates of retirement among Mexican Americans do vary according to the definition used. Age is significantly associated with retirement in all of the models.

- The odds of being retired increases with age.
- The association between health limitations and retirement varies in its significance among definitions.
- The likelihood of claiming retirement is more than five times greater (odds ratio = 5.22) if a respondent reported frequent health limitations as compared with persons who reported that ill health never affects their work capacity.
- Apparently degrees of health limitations affect work status but not other categorizations of retirement. However, persons who did report work limitations due to poor health may have described their current activity as disabled and not as retired. This may be especially true for younger Mexican Americans who are forced to retire early because of poor health. As Gibson (1987) suggests in her analysis of African Americans, younger Mexican Americans may be more comfortable with the sick role than with the role of the aged that accompanies retirement.
- The indicator of lifetime work patterns, occupational type, shows minor variation among definitions of retirement. Professional and technical workers are marginally more likely to be working than unskilled workers and laborers. Professional and technical workers are about two-thirds as likely as unskilled workers to be in the labor force, in contrast to the direction of the relationship expected. Unskilled workers may be less able to afford to leave the labor force than professional and technical workers. Also, unskilled workers are unlikely to encounter the work disincentives built into private pension plans. Professional and technical workers are as likely as unskilled workers and laborers to be retired when it is defined as self-reported retirement, activity status, or income source.
- Skilled blue-collar workers are about three times more likely to describe their current activity as retirement than are unskilled workers and laborers, as expected. This may reflect the unionization of blue-collar

TABLE 2 Logit Estimates of Four Definitions of Retirement Among Mexican Americans

	Definition of retirement							
	Question ("Are you retired?")		Activity ("currently doing")		Income source		Work status	
Variable	Estimate (S.E.)	Odds ratio	Estimate (S.E.)	Odds ratio	Estimate (S.E.)	Odds ratio	Estimate (S.E.)	Odds ratio
Age								
50–54	−4.441*** (.787)	.01	−3.410*** (.827)	.03	−5.418*** (.822)	.004	−3.617*** (.762)	.03
55–59	−2.830*** (.665)	.06	−1.849** (.751)	.16	−4.052*** (.863)	.02	−2.708*** (.802)	.07
60–64	−2.096*** (.617)	.12	−2.185*** (.717)	.11	−3.978*** (.831)	.02	−2.525*** (.769)	.08
65+[a]	—		—		—		—	
Health limitations								
Many times	1.653** (.768)	5.22	−.953 (.888)	.39	.050 (.764)	1.05	1.850** (.739)	6.36
Occasionally	−.021 (.505)	.98	.200 (.546)	1.22	.620 (.544)	1.86	1.424*** (.514)	4.15
Never[a]	—		—		—		—	
Occupation								
Professional/technical	.330 (.669)	1.39	.513 (.732)	1.67	−.979 (.729)	.38	−1.111* (.628)	.33
Skilled blue collar	.623 (.493)	1.86	1.022* (.541)	2.78	.048 (.503)	1.05	−.157 (.481)	.85
Unskilled and laborers[a]	—		—		—		—	
Birthplace								
Mexican born	−.473 (.488)	.62	.711 (.494)	2.04	.110 (.520)	1.12	.766 (.495)	2.15
U.S. born[a]	—		—		—		—	
Sex								
Women	.563 (.480)	1.76	1.593*** (.528)	4.92	−1.274** (.604)	.28	−2.303*** (.554)	.10
Men[a]	—		—		—		—	
Intercept	.647		−1.521		3.571		3.056	
−2 log likelihood	133.96		115.90		125.48		138.38	
Model chi-square	76.18		65.19		99.10		64.97	
Degrees of freedom	9		9		9		9	
Pseudo R^2	.277		.260		.361		.231	

NOTE: $N = 162$.
a. Included as a reference group.
*$p \leq .10$; **$p \leq .05$; ***$p \leq .001$.

occupations and its attendant policy mandates on retirement age and pension receipt. Skilled blue-collar workers are as likely to be retired as unskilled workers and laborers in the remaining three definitions. The

few significant relationships between occupational type and retirement were only marginally significant.

■ Acculturation does not seem to unambiguously differentiate Mexican Americans who are retired from those who are not retired. U.S.-born Mexican Americans are as likely as Mexican-born persons to describe their current activity as retirement.

Conclusions

It appears that even among this small sample of older Mexican Americans the concept and definition of retirement are complex. As hypothesized, correlates of retirement vary with the operationalization considered. The correlates of retirement vary by the definition used to characterize the retirement process. Therefore, any discussion of the timing of retirement or the correlates of retirement used for policy development needs to work within the context of the definition and the operationalization.

The first three definitions of retirement suggest that retirement is a change in social position. Ekerdt and DeViney (in press) argue that when revisions of identity status and social ties are the research foci, the appropriate definition of retirement may be that which highlights changes in social position. Another research orientation suggests that retirement is seen as a change in labor market position. When new economic roles, relationships, and patterns of consumption are the foci of research, the appropriate definition of retirement may center on changes in labor market position. The fourth definition reflects a change in labor market position.

We believe that the work history of Mexican Americans is different from the conceptualization of the work/nonwork lives of the non-Hispanic white population that has garnered the most attention in retirement research.

Retirement must be recast and reconceptualized to account for the distinctive patterns of lifetime work that separate minority populations from the majority. Gibson (1987) has already called for this reconceptualization of retirement for blacks, introducing the concept of the unretired-retired. We would like to extend this to the Mexican American population, as well, albeit in slightly different terms. We see it more in terms of an array of patterns of work and nonwork that have variations in their sequencing, and variations in the correlates of these types of patterns.

It is important for policymakers and policy implementors to increase their awareness of how retirement is defined. Variations in definitions of retirement yield variations in program participation, eligibility, and coverage. It would be a mistake to expect a single definition of retirement to meet multiple policy needs. Policies for the elderly center on a number of interrelated issues: health care and other social services, income maintenance, and labor supply. Hence, no one definition of retirement will identify varying levels of need for a panoply of programs. Some persons would benefit from partial retirement policies and others from job training programs. Greater communication between disability and public pension programs would better provide effective and cost-efficient income maintenance to persons retiring early due to physical limitations and who then age into public pension eligibility.

Evidence from both abroad and the U.S. suggests that as the later years of human life are extended, life remains as complex as in the early and middle years. The necessary reconceptualization of working life in the later years, and thus retirement, must account for such heterogeneity. Indeed, we call not just for a reconceptualization of retirement and working life, but also for a reconceptualization of the later years of the life cycle. This reconceptualization should directly confront issues of race, ethnicity, gender, and social class to highlight the often overlooked diversity among older persons in the United States.

References

Atchley, R. C. (1976). *The sociology of retirement.* New York: Schenkman.
Atchley, R. C. (1979). Issues in retirement research. *The Gerontologist, 19,* 44-54.
Gibson, R. C. (1987). Reconceptualizing retirement for black Americans. *The Gerontologist, 27,* 691-698.

Jackson, J. S., & Gibson, R. C. (1985). Work and retirement among the black elderly. In Z. S. Blau (Ed.), *Current perspectives on aging and the life cycle, A research annual. Work, retirement and social policy.* Greenwich, CT: JAI Press.

Lacayo, C. G. (1980). *A national study to assess the service needs of the Hispanic elderly* (Final report). Los Angeles: Asociacion Nacional Pro Personas Mayores.

Markides, K. S. (1978). Reasons for retirement and adaptation to retirement by elderly Mexican Americans. In E. P. Stanford (Ed.), *Retirement: Concepts and realities of minority elders.* San Diego: San Diego State University.

Markides, K. S., & Martin, H. W., with Gomez, E. (1983). *Older Mexican Americans: A study in an urban barrio,* (Monograph of the Center for Mexican American Studies). Austin: University of Texas Press.

Palmore, E. B. (1971). Why do people retire? *Aging and Human Development, 2,* 269-283.

Palmore, E. B. (1984). The retired. In E. B. Palmore (Ed.), *Handbook on the aged in the United States.* Westport, CT: Greenwood.

Parnes, H. S., & Nestel, G. (1981). The retirement experience. In H. S. Parnes (Ed.), *Work and retirement.* Cambridge, MA: MIT Press.

Westat, Inc. (1989). *A survey of elderly Hispanics,* (Final report). Baltimore: The Commonwealth Fund Commission on Elderly People Living Alone.

27

The Day the Crows Stopped Talking

Harvest Moon Eyes

I remember the day they found Sky dead. I was thirty-eight and I had already lived a lifetime. It was Smitty and Gray Buck that found her over by the tribal hall. Shrouded in a protective fence of oak trees, her neck had been broken and she lay crumpled. Like the oak trees, she'd never been able to bend with the wind.

Many big, black crows live in those oak trees. They talk throughout the day. Sometimes they gossip about us with visiting crows from other reservations. It is wise never to talk under the oak trees. One never knows to whom they tell our secrets. The crows cannot be trusted.

When they're not gossiping, they warn us of approaching visitors. As annoying as they can be with their constant chatter, we know that when the crows stop talking, something is very, very wrong here. The day they found Sky dead, the crows stopped talking.

* * *

Sky slowly made her way across the pasture toward the oak trees that were clustered around the tribal hall. Her long black hair was clasped tightly in a bun at the nape of her

neck. Haunted by memories of too many nights in too many different beds, dark circles had become a permanent fixture under her intense blue eyes. But last night's dream had been different.

"For once it's nice to dream about someone other than myself," Sky mused as she made her way carefully around the cow dung scattered throughout the pasture. Earlier in the day, Sky had met with her friend Maggie under the oak trees to tell her about the dream. It was Maggie who had told her to go see Aunt Lil, the reservation's resident dream interpreter. Her conversation with Aunt Lil had left her tired and confused; and now she was making her way to the hill that overlooked the reservation. For years, everyone on the reservation had watched Sky make her way to the top of that hill every time she had a problem.

Sky didn't belong to this reservation. Actually, Sky didn't belong anywhere. She was an unenrolled mixed-blood, an outsider, who years ago roamed onto the reservation in a cloud of drugs and alcohol. She ended up staying. No one seemed to mind. She was harmless and she was pretty; so she always seemed to have a bed for the night and a free meal. Everyone on the reservation knew Sky; and though she was liked, she always knew she was an outsider. Some things were just never talked about in front of her, but she didn't mind. Sky was used to it. Her entire life she had felt like an outsider—not really white, but not really Indian; and like a stray bullet looking for a place to land, she had

Source: "The Day the Crows Stopped Talking" by Harvest Moon Eyes, from *Earth Song, Sky Spirit: Short Stories of the Contemporary Native American Experience,* edited by C. Trafzer, 1992. Copyright © 1992 by Harvest Moon Eyes. Harvest Moon Eyes lives and writes in Taos, NM. She has recently finished her first novel, from which this story is an excerpt. Reprinted by permission.

often become wedged into places and things where she did not belong.

Standing on the hill at the lookout point above Aunt Lil's place, Sky could see the wind weaving its way throughout the reservation. Miniature dust balls of grit and loose ends of reservation life merged with the wind. Choking on the fragments, the wind split the dust across the valley. Settling down among the cacti, Sky's eyes rested on Aunt Lil and Maggie far below. While Lil and Maggie chattered on Lil's porch, dusk stealthily slid its way across them creating two shadows cackling in the dark.

Sky's thoughts darted back and forth like flickering shadows; dancing separately and together, they whirled around and pressed themselves against each other.

Tired from the day, Sky pulled her knees tight to her chest, wrapped her arms around her legs, and rested her chin between her knees. While she braced herself against the oncoming night, her conversation with Lil and Maggie was temporarily abandoned.

"I wonder what dusk and day do in the dark," mused Sky. Her left hand removed a strand of hair the wind had wedged between her pressed lips. She reached her hands back to the nape of her neck and checked the clasp that held her bun.

The wind reached down and slowly, steadily began to pull and tug at the roots of Sky's hairline. The wind pulled in one direction while her clasp braced itself against the onslaught.

Sky's hands moved to the nape of her neck again. Gnarled hands, hands too old for the rest of her body, held onto her bun in an attempt to keep her thoughts from escaping. But the wind would have its own way.

Sky watched her thoughts escape and she was afraid. She was afraid that her thoughts might break loose from the wind's grasp and settle in someone's mind below. Her thoughts would no longer be her own. Sky knew that the wind could sprinkle her thoughts like dust particles throughout the reservation. People would begin to talk. Secrets would come out. Sky knew she would be the one to blame.

A woman is a powerful thing, thought Sky as she tucked some loose strands of hair back into the clasp. Her eyes wandered down the length of her blue jeans, across the tips of her worn boots, and onto the particles of sand that reached out toward the horizon and the reservation far below. In the daytime, the reservation seemed so peaceful and serene. Children played among the abandoned junk cars and cows grazed lazily in the pastures. But with the night, despair whored its way throughout the reservation—seldom resting until dawn. Sun brings temporary relief and rest from the nightmares of reality. But then comes the night again, and the circle remains unbroken.

After reaching for a handful of sand, Sky watched it trickle through her fingers. The sand faded from view and in its place she saw her dream from the night before. Rising up from the faded sand, the apparition appeared cloudlike, haunting, until it came into clarity.

Sky saw silver hair braided with alternating pieces of silver and feathers. Then she saw long, dark hair moving like fingers scaling a piano. Lightly the dark hair entwined itself with the silver hair. Tears fell through the clouds to the valley below.

Maggie's spirit stood by Lil on the porch. She no longer wore peach lipstick. Her eyes no longer beckoned to the men on the reservation. She watched as Lil moved through emotional quicksand across the shadowed porch.

Lil moved toward the picture hanging crooked on the wall. The picture that captured Lil and Maggie before they both became old was placed softly across the quilt. The binoculars, Lil's eyes for so many years, hung loosely from around Lil's neck. Maggie spoke to Lil, but Lil could not hear her. Maggie was not there for Lil.

As Lil bent to lift the rocking chair into her arms, her eyes rested on the small airplanes lined up on the airfield below. The runway stretched itself tightly over the land that was once occupied by tribal buildings like tights across a whore's thighs.

The houses that once dotted the hillside had been moved. Loose dirt, dirt darker than the dirt that surrounded the empty lots, was all that remained to mark what was once reservation life.

Lil's house was still there. Her house was the last house to be moved, the last life to be uprooted. Only one slice of the past stood untouched. The lookout point with its cacti garden remained. Beyond the hill, where once there were empty valleys, estates sprawled, border to border, electric fence to electric fence, touching each other yet separate from each other. Sky wondered if something was being locked in or if something was being locked out. Maybe both.

The oak trees were gone along with the crows. Unable to compete with the airplanes, the crows moved to somewhere unknown. The crows' chatter was replaced by the high-pitched whine of dirt bikes racing along the hillside. Cows that once wandered lazily across the dirt roads were replaced by fast cars whizzing to and from the small airfield.

Sky trembled from the chill left by the dream. Stretching her bare arms forward, she pushed the dream away; and hearing a noise behind her, she turned and stood up. Struggling against the darkness that grasped her, she crumpled against its force.

It was the next morning that Smitty and Gray Buck found Sky among the oak trees next to the tribal hall.

The reservation was the only real family that Sky had, so most of the people showed up for the burning the following evening. There wasn't much to burn: a pair of blue jeans, an old flannel shirt, and a worn Bible were all that marked the passing of her life. The wake that followed was quiet: There were only a few tears, but a lot of eating; and by morning, Sky was quietly buried on top of the hill that she loved so much.

No one ever notified Les McCann, the sheriff out of Smateren Creek, about the murder. It was just one of those many tacit agreements found in reservation life. Death had long ago become an everyday matter on the reservation; and after all, why involve an outsider about someone's death if the person wasn't going to be missed? Besides, Sky's

death was of little importance compared to the larger issue that was being debated down at the tribal hall.

Tom Crow sat with his back to the open windows that faced the oak trees. Wiping sweat from his forehead, he tried again to adjust the electric fan so that the cross breeze would cool him down without blowing his papers all over the tribal council chambers. It had proven to be hotter than usual during the meeting he'd had with Aunt Lil and her Council of Elders, the Gray Panthers of the reservation.

Through years of negotiations as tribal chairman, Tom Crow had learned to affect an easygoing manner. Wearing Western clothes, chomping on a toothpick, he'd lean back in his black swivel chair, his arms and legs open for any discussion. But these theatrics had, as usual, no effect on Aunt Lil and the Council of Elders.

"They've become a collective thorn in my ass," Tom grumbled as he spit out what was left of his chewed-up toothpick. After reaching for the phone, he dialed George Brent's number. Wiping a trickle of sweat from the back of his neck, he cradled the receiver while he tried to adjust the fan again.

"Hello, George? Tom Crow here. Listen, we've got a little problem out here. We need to talk before the vote tonight. Got a few minutes?

"Yeah, George, I know I told you everything looked good for the land purchase, but some of the elders have doubts. They're capable of influencing a vote either way," said Tom as he tapped the end of his pencil on his empty coffee cup.

"Well, what they're concerned about is selling part of our land. It seems they've changed their minds; and now all they want the tribe to do is lease the land to your people on a hundred-year lease," Tom continued. "Yeah, I know I told you we were all for selling part of our land, but ever since a white girl died out here, the elders have been acting strange.

"It seems this girl told a couple of the elders about some dream she'd had, and now the elders think they're going to lose the reservation," Tom said nervously.

"You don't understand, George—wait, hold on a second," said Tom as he froze in midsentence.

"Sorry, I thought I heard something—anyway, as I was saying, there's still a lot of superstition out here. People put a lot of weight into Lil Pachuca's dream interpretations. No, I'm not saying I believe or I don't believe her, it's just that I've never known her to be wrong, that's all," Tom said as he adjusted the fan again.

"Listen, all I'm trying to say is that I can't openly go against the elders. It would show disrespect and I could just kiss my career good-bye as tribal chairman. But I've got an idea—hold on again, George." After putting down the phone, Tom quietly crossed over to the open windows. Looking out, he saw some cows grazing near the oak trees.

"Sorry about the interruptions, George, but I thought I heard someone outside my window.

"Okay, George, I'll see you out here in about an hour and we'll go over things before the vote tonight.

"Worried—no, I think we can work something out. Yeah, see ya later," said Tom. Hanging up the phone, he turned toward the open windows and watched a shadow pass out of sight among the oak trees.

Sitting in a rocking chair on her porch with an old red-and-white patchwork quilt thrown across her lap, Aunt Lil waved as Indian Joe flew by in his jeep. Long silver hair waved back at her.

Joe is still a good-lookin' man after all these years. It's too bad that his emotions are as reckless as his driving, thought Lil as she reached for the binoculars that were hidden beneath her rocking chair.

Scanning the reservation with her binoculars, she focused in on the Mercedes Benz parked outside the tribal hall. Other than George Brent's car, things seemed pretty much as usual: The tribal hall looked stark against the backdrop of grazing cattle and junk cars. But it wasn't always this empty. Anyone

could rent the tribal hall for fifty dollars a night. Lil had heard whispered that the tribal council, like a high-class call girl, went for even higher stakes than the hall. But no one had ever proven any of the talk was true.

Lil lowered the binoculars and thought about the meeting that had occurred earlier in the day between the elders and Tom Crow.

When Lil, acting as spokesperson for the Council of Elders, told Tom about Sky's dream, he had seemed genuinely interested in hearing her interpretation. This had surprised Lil and some of the other elders. Ever since Tom had graduated from college, he had seemed more white than Indian: He seldom showed up at any of the pow-wows; and he rarely consulted with the elders about tribal affairs. Although he seemed interested in what Lil had to say, when she told him the dream meant that they were going to lose their land to outsiders, Tom had patiently reminded her that Sky was white, and not one of their people. How could she have a dream about their future? This, she was at a loss to explain. But until she could adequately explain away Sky's dream, she and the other elders had vowed to Tom Crow that they would vote against the selling of the land to George Brent for the building of his casino.

But, as it turned out, Lil and the other elders lost the fight that ensued later at the tribal meeting. They were outvoted by the younger ones; and so George Brent was allowed to purchase land for his casino. In return for the vote of support, George agreed to hire only Indians to work the casino. The reservation's guaranteed 40 percent profit margin would be divided into equal shares among the heads of each family on the reservation. Everyone was happy. Everyone except the elders.

Lil never knew for sure why the elders lost the fight, but she did know that within two months of the casino's completion, some people on the reservation were driving new cars and wearing new clothes. At first she, and some of the elders, thought that Tom Crow had sold the reservation out, but his lifestyle never changed, and so once again he was voted in for another term as tribal chairman.

It's hard to believe it's been two years now since Sky was killed and the casino was built. I'm forty now, and lately I've been feeling more like fifty.

No one ever found out who killed Sky or why. It was too bad about Sky, but that silly dream of hers caused a lot of unnecessary trouble and nearly disrupted plans for a casino.

The reservation still hasn't seen its 40 percent profit, but my money's safe in a Keogh plan and my oldest boy is at Stanford. I really didn't want to kill Sky, but she never could keep her mouth shut about anything. I had to do it. I'd feel better about it, though, if the crows would start talking again.

Swiveling in his chair, Tom Crow turned his back to the open windows and the oak trees beyond.

28

On the Edge of the Barrio

Ernesto Galarza

I had been reading stories in the *Sacramento Bee* of the Spanish influenza. At first it was far off, like the war, in places such as New York and Texas. Then the stories told of people dying in California towns we knew, and finally the *Bee* began reporting the spread of the flu in our city.

One Sunday morning we saw Uncle Gustavo coming down the street with a suitcase in his hand, walking slowly. I ran out to meet him. By the front gate he dropped the suitcase, leaned on the fence, and fainted. He had been working as a sandhog on the American River, and had come home weak from fever.

Gustavo was put to bed in one of the front rooms. Uncle José set out to look for a doctor, who came the next day, weary and nearly sick himself. He ordered Gustavo to the hospital. Three days later I answered the telephone call from the hospital telling us he was dead. Only José went to Gustavo's funeral. The rest of us, except my stepfather, were sick in bed with the fever.

In the dining room, near the windows where the sunlight would warm her, my mother lay on a cot, a kerosene stove at her feet. The day Gustavo died she was delirious. José bicycled all over the city, looking for oranges, which the doctor said were the best medicine we could give her. I sweated out the fever, nursed by José, who brought me glasses of steaming lemonade and told me my mother was getting better. The children were quarantined in another room, lightly touched by the fever, more restless than sick.

Late one afternoon José came into my room, wrapped me in blankets, pulled a cap over my ears, and carried me to my mother's bedside. My stepfather was holding a hand mirror to her lips. It didn't fog. She had stopped breathing. In the next room my sister was singing to the other children, "A birdie with a yellow bill/hopped upon my window-sill,/cocked a shiny eye, and said,/'Shame on you, you sleepyhead.' "

The day we buried my mother, Mrs. Dodson took the oldest sister home with her. The younger children were sent to a neighbor. That night José went to the barrio, got drunk, borrowed a pistol, and was arrested for shooting up Second Street.

A month later I made a bundle of the family keepsakes my stepfather allowed me to have, including the butterfly sarape, my books, and some family pictures. With the bundle tied to the bars of my bicycle, I pedaled to the basement room José had rented for the two of us on O Street near the corner of Fifth, on the edge of the barrio.

José was now working the riverboats and, in the slack season, following the round of odd jobs about the city. In our basement room, with a kitchen closet, bathroom, and laundry tub on the back porch and a woodshed for storage, I kept house. We bought two

Source: "On the Edge of the Barrio" by Ernesto Galarza, from *Barrio Boy,* E. Galarza, 1971. Copyright © 1971 by the University of Notre Dame Press. Reprinted by permission.

cots, one for me and the other for José when he was home.

Our landlords lived upstairs, a middle-aged brother and sister who worked and rented rooms. They were friends of doña Tránsito, the grandmother of a Mexican family that lived in a weather-beaten cottage on the corner. Doña Tránsito was in her sixties, round as a barrel, and she wore her gray hair in braids and smoked hand-rolled cigarettes on her rickety front porch. Living only three houses from doña Tránsito, saying my saludos to her every time I passed the corner, I lived inside a circle of security when José was away.

José had chosen our new home because it was close to the Hearkness Junior High School, to which I transferred from Bret Harte. As the jefe de familia[1] he explained that I could help earn our living but that I was to study for a high school diploma. That being settled, my routine was clearly divided into school time and work time, the second depending on when I was free from the first.

Few Mexicans of my age from the barrio were enrolled at the junior high school when I went there. At least, there were no other Mexican boys or girls in Mr. Everett's class in civics, or Miss Crowley's English composition, or Mrs. Stevenson's Spanish course. Mrs. Stevenson assigned me to read to the class and to recite poems by Amado Nervo, because the poet was from Tepic and I was, too. Miss Crowley accepted my compositions about Jalcocotán and the buried treasure of Acaponeta while the others in the class were writing about Sir Patrick Spence and the Beautiful Lady Without Mercy, whom they had never met. For Mr. Everett's class, the last of the day, I clipped pieces from the *Sacramento Bee* about important events in Sacramento. From him I learned to use the ring binder in which I kept clippings to prepare oral reports. Occasionally he kept me after school to talk. He sat on his desk, one leg dangling over a corner, behind him the frame of a large window and the arching elms of the school yard, telling me he thought I could easily make the debating team at the high

school next year, that Stanford University might be the place to go after graduation, and making other by-the-way comments that began to shape themselves into my future.

Afternoons, Saturdays, and summers allowed me many hours of work time I did not need for study. José explained how things now stood. There were two funerals to pay for. He would pay the rent and buy the food. My clothes, books, and school expenses would be up to me.

On my vacations and when he was not on the riverboats, he found me a job as water boy on a track gang. We chopped wood together near Woodland and stacked empty lug boxes in a cannery yard. Cleaning vacant houses and chopping weeds were jobs we could do as a team when better ones were not to be had. As the apprentice, I learned from him how to brace myself for a heavy lift, to lock my knee under a loaded hand-truck, to dance rather than lift a ladder, and to find the weakest grain in a log. Like him I spit into my palms to get the feel of the ax handle and grunted as the blade bit into the wood. Imitating him, I circled a tree several times, sizing it up, tanteando, as he said, before pruning or felling it.

Part of one summer my uncle worked on the river while I hired out as a farmhand on a small ranch south of Sacramento. My senior on the place was Roy, a husky Oklahoman who was a part-time taxi driver and a full-time drinker of hard whiskey. He was heavy-chested, heavy-lipped, and jowly, a grumbler rather than a talker and a man of great ingenuity with tools and automobile engines. Under him I learned to drive the Fordson tractor on the place, man the gasoline pump, feed the calves, check an irrigation ditch, make lug boxes for grapes, and many other tasks on a small farm.

Roy and I sat under the willow tree in front of the ranch house after work, I on the grass, he on a creaky wicker chair, a hulking, sour man glad for the company of a boy. He counseled me on how to avoid the indulgences he was so fond of, beginning his sentences with a phrase he repeated over and over, "as the feller says." "Don't aim to tell you your business," he explained, "but as the feller says, get yourself a good woman, don't be no farmhand for a livin', be a lawyer or a doctor, and don't get to drinkin' nohow. And there's another thing, Ernie. If nobody won't listen to you, go on and talk to yourself and hear what a smart man has to say."

And Roy knew how to handle boys, which he showed in an episode that could have cost me my life or my self-confidence. He had taught me to drive the tractor, walking alongside during the lessons as I maneuvered it, shifting gears, stopping and starting, turning and backing, raising a cloud of dust wherever we went. Between drives Roy told me about the different working parts of the machine, giving me instructions on oiling and greasing and filling the radiator. "She needs to be took care of, Ernie," he admonished me, "like a horse. And another thing, she's like to buck. She can turn clear over on you if you let 'er. If she starts to lift from the front even a mite, you turn her off. You hear?"

"Yes, sir," I said, meaning to keep his confidence in me as a good tractor man.

It was a few days after my first solo drive that it happened. I was rounding a telephone pole on the slightly sloping bank of the irrigation ditch. I swung around too fast for one of the rear tracks to keep its footing. It spun and the front began to lift. Forgetting Roy's emphatic instructions, I gunned the engine, trying to right us to the level ground above the ditch. The tractor's nose kept climbing in front of me. We slipped against the pole, the tractor bucking, as Roy said it would.

Roy's warning broke through to me in my panic, and I reached up to turn off the ignition. My bronco's engine sputtered out and it settled on the ground with a thump.

I sat for a moment in my sweat. Roy was coming down the ditch in a hurry. He walked up to me and with a quick look saw that neither I nor the tractor was damaged.

"Git off," he said.

I did, feeling that I was about to be demoted, stripped of my rank, bawled out, and fired.

Roy mounted the machine, started it, and worked it off the slope to flat ground. Leaving the engine running, he said: "Git on."

I did.

"Now finish the disking," he said. Above the clatter of the machine he said: "Like I said, she can buck. If she does, cut 'er. You hear?" And he waved me off to my work.

Except for food and a place to live, with which José provided me, I was on my own. Between farm jobs I worked in town, adding to my experience as well as to my income. As a clerk in a drugstore on Second and J, in the heart of the lower part of town, I waited on Chicanos who spoke no English and who came in search of remedies with no prescription other than a recital of their pains. I dispensed capsules, pills, liniments, and emulsions as instructed by the pharmacist, who glanced at our customers from the back of the shop and diagnosed their ills as I translated them. When I went on my shift, I placed a card in the window that said "Se habla español." So far as my Chicano patients were concerned, it might as well have said "Dr. Ernesto Galarza."

From drugs I moved to office supplies and stationery sundries, working as delivery boy for Wahl's, several blocks uptown from skid row. Between deliveries I had no time to idle. I helped the stock clerk, took inventory, polished desks, and hopped when a clerk bawled an order down the basement steps. Mr. Wahl, our boss, a stocky man with a slight paunch, strutted a little as he constantly checked on the smallest details of his establishment, including myself. He was always pleasant and courteous, a man in whose footsteps I might possibly walk into the business world of Sacramento.

But like my uncles, I was looking for a better chanza, which I thought I found with Western Union, as a messenger, where I could earn tips as well as wages. Since I knew the lower part of town thoroughly, whenever the telegrams were addressed to that quarter the dispatcher gave them to me. Deliveries to the suites on the second floor of saloons paid especially well, with tips of a quarter from the ladies who worked there. My most generous customer was tall and beautiful Miss Irene, who always asked how I was doing in school. It was she who gave me an English dictionary, the first I ever possessed, a black bound volume with remarkable little scallops on the pages that made it easy to find words. Half smiling, half commanding, Miss Irene said to me more than once: "Don't you stop school without letting me know." I meant to take her advice as earnestly as I took her twenty-five-cent tip.

It was in the lower town also that I nearly became a performing artist. My instructor on the violin had stopped giving me lessons after we moved to Oak Park. When we were back on O Street he sent word through José that I could work as second fiddler on Saturday nights in the dance hall where he played with a mariachi. Besides, I could resume my lessons with him. A dollar a night for two hours as a substitute was the best wages I had ever made. Coached by my teacher, I second-fiddled for sporting Chicanos who swung their ladies on the dance floor and sang to our music. Unfortunately I mentioned my new calling to Miss Crowley when I proposed it to her as a subject for a composition. She kept me after school and persuaded me to give it up, on the ground that I could earn more decorating Christmas cards during the vacation than at the dance hall. She gave me the first order for fifty cards and got subscriptions for me from the other teachers. I spent my Christmas vacation as an illustrator, with enough money saved to quit playing in the saloon.

It was during the summer vacation that school did not interfere with making a living—the time of the year when I went with other barrio people to the ranches to look for work. Still too young to shape up with the day-haul gangs, I loitered on skid row, picking up conversation and reading the chalk signs about work that was being offered. For a few days of picking fruit or pulling hops I bicycled to Folsom, Lodi, Woodland, Freeport, Walnut Grove, Marysville, Slough House, Florin, and places that had no name. Looking for work, I pedaled through a countryside blocked off, mile after mile, into orchards, vineyards, and vegetable farms. Along the ditch banks, where the grass, the morning glory, and the wild oats made a soft mattress, I unrolled my bindle and slept.

In the labor camps I shared the summertime of the lives of the barrio people. They gathered from barrios of faraway places like Imperial Valley, Los Angeles, Phoenix, and San Antonio. Each family traveling on its own, they came in trucks piled with household goods or packed in their secondhand fotingos[2] and chevees. The trucks and cars were ancient models, fresh out of a used-car lot, with license tags of many states. It was into these jalopies that much of the care and a good part of the family's earnings went. In camp they were constantly being fixed, so close to scrap that when we needed a part for repairs, we first went to the nearest junkyard.

It was a world different in so many ways from the lower part of Sacramento and the residences surrounded by trim lawns and cool canopies of elms to which I had delivered packages for Wahl's. Our main street was usually an irrigation ditch, the water supply for cooking, drinking, laundering, and bathing. In the better camps there was a faucet or a hydrant, from which water was carried in buckets, pails, and washtubs. If the camp belonged to a contractor and it was used from year to year, there were permanent buildings—a shack for his office, the privies, weatherworn and sagging, and a few cabins made of secondhand lumber, patched and unpainted.

If the farmer provided housing himself, it was in tents pitched on the bare baked earth or on the rough ground of newly plowed land on the edge of a field. Those who arrived late for the work season camped under trees or raised lean-tos along a creek, roofing their trucks with canvas to make bedrooms. Such camps were always well away from the house of the ranchero, screened from the main road by an orchard or a grove of eucalyptus. I helped to pitch and take down such camps, on some spot that seemed lonely when we arrived, desolate when we left.

If they could help it, the workers with families avoided the more permanent camps, where the seasonal hired hands from skid row were more likely to be found. I lived a few days in such a camp and found out why families avoided them. On Saturday nights when the crews had a week's wages in their pockets, strangers appeared, men and women, carrying suitcases with liquor and other contraband. The police were called by the contractor only when the carousing threatened to break into fighting. Otherwise, the weekly bouts were a part of the regular business of the camp.

Like all the others, I often went to work without knowing how much I was going to be paid. I was never hired by a rancher, but by a contractor or a straw boss who picked up crews in town and handled the payroll. The important questions that were in my mind— the wages per hour or per lug box, whether the beds would have mattresses and blankets, the price of meals, how often we would be paid—were never discussed, much less answered, beforehand. Once we were in camp, owing the employer for the ride to the job, having no means to get back to town except by walking and no money for the next meal, arguments over working conditions were settled in favor of the boss. I learned firsthand the chiseling techniques of the contractors and their pushers—how they knocked off two or three lugs of grapes from the daily record for each member of the crew, or the way they had of turning the face of the scales away from you when you weighed your work in.

There was never any doubt about the contractor and his power over us. He could fire a man and his family on the spot and make them wait days for their wages. A man could be forced to quit by assigning him regularly to the thinnest pickings in the field. The worst thing one could do was to ask for fresh water on the job, regardless of the heat of the day; instead of iced water, given freely, the crews were expected to buy sodas at twice the price in town, sold by the contractor himself. He usually had a pistol—to protect the pay-

roll, so it was said. Through the ranchers for whom he worked, we were certain that he had connections with the Autoridades, for they never showed up in camp to settle wage disputes or listen to our complaints or to go for a doctor when one was needed. Lord of a ragtag labor camp of Mexicans, the contractor, a Mexican himself, knew that few men would let their anger blow, even when he stung them with curses.

As a single worker, I usually ate with some household, paying for my board. I did more work than a child but less than a man—neither the head nor the tail of a family. Unless the camp was a large one, I became acquainted with most of the families. Those who could not write asked me to chalk their payroll numbers on the boxes they picked. I counted matches for a man who transferred them from the right pocket of his pants to the left as he tallied the lugs he filled throughout the day. It was his only check on the record the contractor kept of his work. As we worked the rows or the tree blocks during the day, or talked in the evenings where the men gathered in small groups to smoke and rest, I heard about barrios I had never seen but that must have been much like ours in Sacramento.

The only way to complain or protest was to leave, but now and then a camp would stand instead of run, and for a few hours or a few days work would slow down or stop. I saw it happen in a pear orchard in Yolo when pay rates were cut without notice to the crew. The contractor said the market for pears had dropped and the rancher could not afford to pay more. The fruit stayed on the trees while we, a committee drafted by the camp, argued with the contractor first and then with the rancher. The talks gave them time to round up other pickers. A carload of police in plain clothes drove into the camp. We were lined up for our pay, taking whatever the contractor said was on his books. That afternoon we were ordered off the ranch.

In a camp near Folsom, during hop picking, it was not wages but death that pulled the people together. Several children in the camp were sick with diarrhea; one had been taken to the hospital in town and the word came back that he had died. It was the women who guessed that the cause of the epidemic was the water. For cooking and drinking and washing it came from a ditch that went by the ranch stables upstream.

I was appointed by a camp committee to go to Sacramento to find some Autoridad who would send an inspector. Pedaling my bicycle, mulling over where to go and what to say, I remembered some clippings from the *Sacramento Bee* that Mr. Everett had discussed in class, and I decided the man to look for was Mr. Simon Lubin, who was in some way a state Autoridad.

He received me in his office at Weinstock and Lubin's. He sat, square-shouldered and natty, behind a desk with a glass top. He was half-bald, with a strong nose and a dimple in the center of his chin. To his right was a box with small levers into which Mr. Lubin talked and out of which came voices.

He heard me out, asked me questions, and made notes on a pad. He promised that an inspector would come to the camp. I thanked him and thought the business of my visit was over; but Mr. Lubin did not break the handshake until he had said to tell the people in the camp to organize. "Only by organizing," he told me, "will they ever have decent places to live."

I reported the interview with Mr. Lubin to the camp. That part about the inspector they understood and it was voted not to go back to work until he came. The part about organizing was received in silence, and I made my first organizing speech.

The inspector came and a water tank pulled by mules was parked by the irrigation ditch. At the same time the contractor began to fire some of the pickers. I was one of them. I finished that summer nailing boxes on a grape ranch near Florin.

When my job ended, I pedaled back to Sacramento, detouring over country lanes I knew well. Here and there I walked the bicycle over dirt roads rutted by wagons. The pastures were sunburned and the grain fields had been cut to stubble. Riding by a thicket of reeds where an irrigation ditch swamped, I stopped and looked at the red-winged blackbirds riding gracefully on the tips of the canes. Now and then they streaked out of the green clump, spraying the pale sky with crimson dots in all directions.

Crossing the Y Street levee by Southside Park, I rode through the barrio to doña Tránsito's, leaving my bike hooked on the picket fence by the handlebar.

I knocked on the screen door that always hung tired, like the sagging porch coming unnailed. No one was at home.

It was two hours before time to cook supper. From the stoop I looked up and down the cross streets. The barrio seemed empty.

I unhooked the bicycle, mounted it, and headed for the main high school, twenty blocks away, where I would be going in a week. Pumping slowly, I wondered about the debating team and the other things Mr. Everett had mentioned.

Notes

1. *jefe de familia:* head of the household (literally, "head of the family")
2. *fotingos:* old cars (often travel-worn Fords)

29

At the Burns-Coopers'

Gwendolyn Brooks

It was a little red and white and black woman who appeared in the doorway of the beautiful house in Winnetka.

About, thought Maud Martha, thirty-four. "I'm Mrs. Burns-Cooper," said the woman, "and after this, well, it's all right this time, because it's your first time, but after this time always use the back entrance."

There is a pear in my icebox, and one end of rye bread. Except for three Irish potatoes and a cup of flour and the empty Christmas boxes, there is absolutely nothing on my shelf. My husband is laid off. There is newspaper on my kitchen table instead of oilcloth. I can't find a filing job in a hurry. I'll smile at Mrs. Burns-Cooper and hate her just some.

"First, you have the beds to make," said Mrs. Burns-Cooper. "You either change the sheets or air the old ones for ten minutes. I'll tell you about the changing when the time comes. It isn't any special day. You are to pull my sheets, and pat and pat and pull till all's tight and smooth. Then shake the pillows into the slips, carefully. Then punch them in the middle.

"Next, there is the washing of the midnight snack dishes. Next, there is the scrubbing. Now, I know that your other ladies have probably wanted their floors scrubbed after dinner. I'm different. I like to enjoy a bright clean floor all the day. You can just freshen it up a little before you leave in the evening, if

it needs a few more touches. Another thing, I disapprove of mops. You can do a better job on your knees.

"Next is dusting. Next is vacuuming—that's for Tuesdays and Fridays. On Wednesdays, ironing and silver cleaning.

"Now about cooking. You're very fortunate in that here you have only the evening meal to prepare. Neither of us has breakfast, and I always step out for lunch. Isn't that lucky?"

"It's quite a kitchen, isn't it?" Maud Martha observed. "I mean, big."

Mrs. Burns-Cooper's brows raced up in amazement.

"Really? I hadn't thought so. I'll bet"—she twinkled indulgently—"you're comparing it to your *own* little kitchen." And why do that, her light eyes laughed. Why talk of beautiful mountains and grains of alley sand in the same breath?

"Once," mused Mrs. Burns-Cooper, "I had a girl who botched up the kitchen. Made a botch out of it. But all I had to do was just sort of cock my head and say, 'Now, now, Albertine!' Her name was Albertine. Then she'd giggle and scrub and scrub and she was *so* sorry about trying to take advantage."

It was while Maud Martha was peeling potatoes for dinner that Mrs. Burns-Cooper laid herself out to prove that she was not a snob. Then it was that Mrs. Burns-Cooper came out to the kitchen and, sitting, talked and talked at Maud Martha. In my college days. At the time of my debut. The imported lace on my lingerie. My brother's rich wife's Stradivarius. When I was in Madrid. The charm

"At the Burns-Coopers'" by Gwendolyn Brooks, from *Maud Martha*, Chicago: Third World Press, 1993. Reprinted by permission of the author.

of the Nile. Cost fifty dollars. Cost one hundred dollars. Cost one thousand dollars. Shall I mention, considered Maud Martha, my own social triumphs, my own education, my travels to Gary and Milwaukee and Columbus, Ohio? Shall I mention my collection of fancy pink satin bras? She decided against it. She went on listening, in silence, to the confidences until the arrival of the lady's mother-in-law (large-eyed, strong, with hair of a mighty white, and with an eloquent, angry bosom). Then the junior Burns-Cooper was very much the mistress, was still, cool, authoritative.

There was no introduction, but the elder Burns-Cooper boomed, "Those potato parings are entirely too thick!"

The two of them, richly dressed, and each with that health in the face that bespeaks, or seems to bespeak, much milk drinking from earliest childhood, looked at Maud Martha. There was no remonstrance; no firing! They just looked. But for the first time, she understood what Paul endured daily. For so—she could gather from a Paul-word here, a Paul-curse there—his Boss! when, squared, upright, terribly upright, superior to the President, commander of the world, he wished to underline Paul's lacks, to indicate soft shock, controlled incredulity. As his boss looked at Paul, so these people looked at her. As though she were a child, a ridiculous one, and one that ought to be given a little shaking, except that shaking was—not quite the thing, would not quite do. One held up one's finger (if one did anything), cocked one's head, was arch. As in the old song, one hinted, "Tut tut! now now! come come!" Metal rose, all built, in one's eye.

I'll never come back, Maud Martha assured herself, when she hung up her apron at eight in the evening. She knew Mrs. Burns-Cooper would be puzzled. The wages were very good. Indeed, what could be said in explanation? Perhaps that the hours were long. I couldn't explain *my* explanation, she thought.

One walked out from that almost perfect wall, spitting at the firing squad. What difference did it make whether the firing squad understood or did not understand the manner of one's retaliation or why one had to retaliate?

Why, one was a human being. One wore clean nightgowns. One loved one's baby. One drank cocoa by the fire—or the gas range—come the evening, in the wintertime.

1 Aliene Walser, Mike LeFevre, and Mrs. Sharpe were all white and therefore privileged in one system of inequality: race. But there were differences among these three people in the availability of productive activity roles and of the economic rewards associated with these roles. What were these differences? What factors account for the differences?

2 The women in the New York City slave market, the workers in Olsen's poem, Mrs. Lee, Sky, and Mrs. Susie Jones were all women of color. Thus they were disadvantaged in two systems of inequality: race and gender. Yet there were differences in the effects of their productive activities on their lives. What were these differences? What accounts for the differences?

3 Gender structures opportunities for paid productive activity and responsibilities for unpaid productive activity. The readings introduced you to a number of women: Aliene Walser, Mrs. Jones, Mrs. Lee, the women in the New York City slave market, the African American woman at the Burns-Coopers', and the garment workers in Olsen's poem. What similarities and what differences do you see in the meanings they attached to their productive activities and in their disillusionments and satisfactions with their work? Can you explain the patterns you observe?

4 Mrs. Jones and Mrs. Sharpe were both privileged on class and disadvantaged on gender, yet there were some differences in their attitudes toward the availability and meaning of productive activity roles. What were they? Why do you think these differences existed? To what degree do their lives illustrate an "accumulation of advantage"?

5 What types of productive activity (both paid and unpaid) do you anticipate pursuing over the next 50 years? How do you think your position on hierarchies based on gender, race, and class will influence the availability of various productive roles? Place yourself about 50 years hence. How will your lifetime of productive activity influence the resources you have available in old age?

6 Tillie Olsen's poem about Hispanic garment workers is written in the form of a letter to the "women up North" who buy the clothes in local department stores. Draft a letter in response to

Olsen's poem as it might have been written by Mrs. Sharpe or by other women sharing her position of privilege.

7 Moen, Robison, and Fields's discussion of ways in which women's employment and caregiving combine over the life course illustrates how gender and class structure productive activities. How might pension policies be changed to reflect the range of productive activities of women across the life course? Can you think of other seemingly neutral policies with outcomes structured by systems of inequality?

8 Mike LeFevre and Ernesto Galarza were both men and therefore privileged in one system of inequality: gender. But there were differences between these men in the availability of productive activity roles and of the economic rewards associated with these roles. What were these differences? What factors account for the differences?

SUGGESTIONS FOR FURTHER READING

1 Cowgill, D. O. (1986). Economic systems and economic roles of the aged: Ascendancy and continuity. In *Aging around the world* (pp. 108-119). Belmont, CA: Wadsworth.

In many societies around the world, productive activity continues over the life course. Using a comparative approach, Cowgill reviews several patterns in the relationship between age and productive activity and explores variation in economic systems and the distribution of resources.

2 Allen, K. R., & Chin-Sang, V. (1990). A lifetime of work: The context and meaning of leisure for aging black women. *The Gerontologist, 30,* 734-740.

For women, productive activity is most often a tapestry of paid and unpaid work throughout the life course. In researching this article, Allen and Chin-Sang interviewed 30 aging African American women about the meanings of leisure within the context of their work histories. "Leisure" for these women most often involved a continuation of their lifetime pattern of hard work and service to others.

3 Stone, R. I. (1989, Spring/Summer). The feminization of poverty among the elderly. *Women's Studies Quarterly, 17,* 20-34.

This article explores a number of issues surrounding increasing risks of poverty for older women. Stone discusses women's economic dependence on men, labor market discrimination, unpaid family labor, and the impact of illness in old age.

4 Calasanti, T. M., & Bonanno, A. (1992). Working overtime: Economic restructuring and retirement of a class. *Sociological Quarterly, 33*(1), 135-152.

In this analysis of retirement adjustment, Calasanti and Bonanno move beyond individual-level characteristics and consider the impact of employment in the primary versus the secondary labor markets. Their analysis is particularly relevant to understanding intersections among systems of inequality, as women and people of color are disproportionately employed in secondary labor market jobs.

5 Terkel, S. (1974). *Working: People talk about what they do all day and how they feel about what they do.* New York: Pantheon.

Studs Terkel interviews a range of working people in the 1950s and 1960s about their work. Listening to the voices of these workers brings to life statistics documenting occupational distribution of the workforce. The interviews demonstrate how the meaning of work is distributed across interlocking systems of privilege and disadvantage.

6 Himes, C. B. (1975). *Black on black: Baby sister and selected writings.* London: Joseph.

What types of productivity roles were available to people disadvantaged by race and class during the Depression of the 1930s? How did this particular historical period shape the opportunity structure, life events, and adaptive resources of African American men as they aged? We recommend, in particular, the selections "Headwaiter" and "Pork Chop Paradise."

7 Clive, A. (1987). The home front and the household: Women, work and family in Detroit. In N. A. Hewitt (Ed.), *Women, families and communities: Readings in American history* (Vol. 2, pp. 188-203). Glenview, IL: Scott, Foresman/Little, Brown.

Dramatic alterations in work and home life for women occurred during World War II. The popular image of Rosie the Riveter symbolized the belief that women could move into industry and become "one of the boys." Clive traces these alterations as they were played out in Detroit, Michigan. He explores changes in the sexual and racial composition of the workforce, attitudes of employers and coworkers toward women, and the impact of federal policies on women's work and family experiences both during and after the war.

8 Lerner, G. (1973). It takes a while to realize that it is discrimination. In *Black women in white America* (pp. 275-281). New York: Vintage.

The historian Gerda Lerner traces the quest of an African American woman for equitable paid work roles. Covering the Great Depression of the 1930s and World War II of the 1940s, this selection illustrates how sociohistorical time and disadvantaged status in three systems of inequality converged to limit role availability.

9 Singer, I. B. (1988). The hotel. In *The death of Methuselah and other stories*. New York: Farrar, Straus & Giroux.

This story demonstrates how productive activity roles in early life influenced the retirement role chosen by an affluent Jewish man. The meanings Israel Danziger attached to productive activities throughout his life continued to influence his adjustment to retirement.

10 Quadagno, J., & Meyer, M. H. (1990). Gender and public policy. *Generations, 14*(3), 64-66.

This discussion of pension policy illustrates ways in which ostensibly neutral social policies can produce outcomes that are structured by older people's gender, class, and race or ethnicity. The article begs the question of how pension policies might be changed to reflect the range of productive activities of women across the life course.

11 Ostrander, S. (1984). Community volunteer. In *Women of the upper class* (pp. 111-139). Philadelphia: Temple University Press.

Productive activity takes on different meanings for women of the upper class.

12 Gibson, R. C. (1987). Reconceptualizing retirement for black Americans. *The Gerontologist, 27*(6), 691-698.

Productive activity roles in early life shape economic well-being and meanings of work and retirement roles in late life.

PART IV

Family

Variations on "the American Family"

The Diversity of American Families

Our understanding of family, perhaps more than any other institution, is clouded by myth. Masking diversity among contemporary U.S. families is an ideology that describes the American family as "one man who goes off to earn the bacon, one woman who waits at home to fry it, and roughly 2.5 children poised to eat it" (Cole, 1986, p. 11). This image of family-dominated U.S. culture during the decades following World War II, a period during which the majority of older people today experienced at least part of their child-rearing years. As described by Betty Friedan (1964) in *The Feminine Mystique,* this ideology told women that caring for their home and family was the path to fulfillment and gratification (Andersen, 1993). The sociologist Talcott Parsons (1955) described the American family as an isolated, nuclear unit in which the husband, wife, and their dependent children live geographically and economically independent from other relatives. Families were viewed as safe havens from the competitiveness of the workplace, and both popular images and social scientific treatises emphasized the split between the public sphere of employment and the private sphere of home.

In this part, we will explore the consequences of this idealized image of the American family on our efforts to understand the diversity of family experiences among older people today. Our exploration of older families will ask the following questions:

1. How does the myth of the American family mask the diversity of families in which today's cohorts of elderly people grew up and grew old?

2. How do interlocking hierarchies based on gender, race, and class structure the family experiences of today's older Americans?

3. How do definitions of family based on the experiences of the dominant groups in society bias research on other older families?

How the Myth of the American Family Masks the Diversity of Families in Which Today's Cohorts of Elderly People Grew Up and Grew Old

There are a number of problems with the ideological view of the nuclear family as a key to understanding the family experiences of older people today. First, not all older people married and not all married people had children. Of people 65 and older today, 5% never married, 6% divorced or separated, and 20% do not have adult children. Since the 1950s, the percentage of never-married older people has declined, and the percentage of divorced elderly people has begun to increase (Myers, 1990, p. 39). Marriage and divorce rates also vary by gender and ethnicity. Older Native American and Asian American women are slightly less likely to have remained single throughout their lives than are other older people. Rates of divorce and separation for elderly African Americans, Hispanic Americans, Native Americans, and Asian Americans are higher than rates for elderly whites.

Second, the idealized view of the family glorified the role of the full-time housewife, wife, and mother. Married women who did not enter the paid labor force and worked full-time at home often found that their lives did not correspond to the image fostered by popular culture. Many full-time mothers were troubled by the isolation of their daily lives, the repetitiveness of household tasks, and the invisibility of their accomplishments (Oakley, 1974). Betty Friedan (1964) labeled the vague, unspoken anxiety experienced by the full-time housewives in her study as "the problem that has no name." According to popular ideology, these women should have been among the most happy and fulfilled. Their families came closest to the idealized American family. Yet Friedan's (1964) subjects shared doubts and dissatisfactions. Moreover, they felt responsible for this unease, because the ideology of the feminine mystique shifted the blame to women themselves if they were unsatisfied with their lives. Women were taught that they

> could desire no greater destiny than to glory in their femininity. . . . If a woman had a problem in the 1950s and 1960s, she knew that something must be wrong with her marriage and with herself. . . . What kind of woman was she if she did not feel this mysterious fulfillment waxing the kitchen floor? (p. 19)

Not all women who opted for full-time work at home over paid work in the labor market were dissatisfied with their situation. Caring for a home and family offered opportunities for creativity and satisfaction. Because work at home provides freedom from supervision and some flexibility in organizing tasks, many women preferred it to the more alienating conditions they would have encountered in the paid positions available to them (Andersen, 1993). Nevertheless, as the 1960s came to a close, the vague discontent described by Friedan began to crystallize into a feminist analysis that defined motherhood as a serious obstacle to women's fulfillment. This strain of feminist thought reflects the race and class position of its creators. In gathering data for *The Feminine Mystique,* Friedan interviewed her former classmates at Smith College, and her results reflect the experiences of these white, middle-class, college-educated women. bell hooks (1984) describes the bias of an analysis developed from the standpoint of this particular group:

> [They] argued that motherhood was a serious obstacle to women's liberation, a trap confining women to the home,

keeping them tied to cleaning, cooking, and child care. . . . Had black women voiced their views on motherhood, [motherhood] would not have been named a serious obstacle to our freedom as women. Racism, availability of jobs, lack of skills or education, and a number of other issues would have been at the top of the list—but not motherhood. Black women would not have said motherhood prevented us from entering the world of paid work, because we have always worked. (p. 133)

As hooks's critique suggests, not all of today's older women were able to choose whether or not they would stay out of the paid labor force when their children were young, despite the popular and scholarly rhetoric advocating full-time motherhood. Women rearing children alone because of single motherhood, divorce, or widowhood had little choice but to combine the nurturing roles assigned to mothers with the breadwinning responsibilities supposedly reserved for fathers. Further, poor and working-class two-parent families often needed two incomes to survive. Women of color were more likely than white women to find themselves in this situation, as racial oppression denied many sufficient economic resources to maintain nuclear family households (P. H. Collins, 1990). Elderly African American women, for example, typically combined child rearing with paid work at a time when employment opportunities for women and for people of color were even more restricted than they are today.

The rigid gender-based division of labor that characterized popular constructions of the American family of the 1950s did not apply across all combinations of race and class. For example, the strict gender role segregation within the domestic sphere applied more to white families than to African American families. African American couples have traditionally been more flexible in allocating family obligations, with parents sharing household tasks and child rearing as well as responsibility for earning a living (McAdoo, 1986). Upper-class women, most of whom were white, retained personal responsibility for managing children and household but rarely did the actual work themselves (Ostrander, 1984). Rather, they supervised the work of paid domestic workers, who were usually poor or working-class women and often women of color (Cole, 1986).

Upper-class women also had more resources with which to exercise their family responsibilities than less affluent women. Susan Ostrander's (1984) wealthy subjects wanted their children "to develop to their fullest potential, . . . to be 'the best' " (p. 75). They expressed concerns about their children's personal happiness and their future success. Most important, they had resources to facilitate these goals for their children. For example, if their children encountered academic difficulties or adjustment problems, the parents often sent them to private schools. Mrs. Miles, a woman now in her seventies whose husband had been chairman of the board of a major bank, describes her decision to enroll her teenage daughter in a private boarding school: "She was a very shy child . . . so I thought . . . going away to school would be good for her, would give her some confidence and put her on her feet" (p. 85). As Ostrander explains, "Upper class children . . . are not allowed to fail academically or personally. This gives them strong advantages" (p. 84). Parents from other social classes share many of the same dreams and concerns for their children expressed by the women Ostrander interviewed, but they do not share the same resources for helping their children realize these dreams.

Another aspect of the mythic American family that clouds our understanding of the family experiences of today's elderly people is the assumption that the nuclear family is isolated from other relatives. Contrary to this image of independent nuclear households, women have traditionally maintained family relationships across households through visiting, writing letters, organizing holiday gatherings, and remembering birthdays and anniversaries—activities that have been described as "kinship work" (Rosenthal, 1985). The work of "kinkeeping" can produce complex networks of female kin who entrust confidences, pool resources, and share social activities. Furthermore, as social gerontologists have demonstrated, women are the primary caregivers for the frail elderly people in their families.

Strong female-centered networks have also linked families and households among African Americans. Mothering responsibilities have traditionally been shared among women in African American communities. Boundaries distinguishing biological mothers from other women who care for children are less rigid within these communities, and women often feel a sense of obligation for *our children*, a term that includes all of the children in their community. Patricia Hill Collins (1991) explains that "African-American communities recognized that vesting one person with full responsibility for mothering a child may not be wise or possible. As a result, 'othermothers,' women who assist bloodmothers by sharing mothering responsibilities, traditionally have been a central part of the institution of Black motherhood" (p. 47). When children are orphaned, when parents are ill or at work, or when biological mothers are too young to care for their children alone, other women in the community take on child care responsibilities, sometimes temporarily, but other times permanently.

These women-centered networks of bloodmothers and othermothers within African American communities have often been described as a reaction to the legacy of slavery and to generations of poverty and oppression. More recently, scholars have challenged this interpretation. The impact of racial oppression on African American families must be acknowledged, but it is also important to recognize the ways in which today's elderly African Americans evolved new definitions of family from their everyday experiences and cultural legacies. Networks of community-based child care, for example, provided supervision for children while biological parents worked to provide economic support. Alternative definitions of motherhood, emphasizing both emotional support and physical provision of care, were adapted from West African culture, which had been retained as a culture of resistance since slavery (Sudarkasa, 1981). Building on this cultural heritage, African American women devised strategies for ensuring their children's physical survival within a racist society (P. H. Collins, 1991). The selection "Mothers of Mind" by Elsa Barkley Brown provides a personal view of this approach to mothering.

Other examples also challenge the myth of self-reliance of isolated, nuclear households. Coontz (1992) points out that working-class and ethnic subcommunities "evolved mutual aid in finding jobs, surviving tough times, and pooling money for recreation" (p. 71). Immigrant groups developed an infrastructure of churches, temperance societies, workers' associations, fraternal orders, and cooperatives that provided instrumental and emotional aid beyond the confines of the nuclear household. Godparenting created extrafamilial bonds among Catholic populations, bonds that often cut across social class boundaries, and, as Coontz (1992) points out, "the notion of 'going for sisters' has long and still thriving roots in black communities" (p. 72). Extended networks of kin also characterize Latino families, in which child care responsibilities are often shared with older siblings, aunts, uncles, and grandparents. Ceremonial events frequently involve close friends linked to the family through *compadrazgo,* a network of kinlike ties among very close friends who exchange tangible assistance and social support (Heyck, 1994).

The idealized image of the American family also assumes a heterosexual couple. Despite more recent attention to gay and lesbian rights, it is important to remember that today's cohorts of elderly gay men and lesbians grew up in a social environment in which they encountered strong pressures to hide their sexual orientation. Many kept their relationships secret to avoid discriminatory treatment by their families, their employers, and their communities (D'Augelli & Hart, 1987). Although marriage between gay and lesbian partners is not legally sanctioned, many couples establish long-term relationships. The short story "The Linden Tree" introduces us to one such couple. Although the two men in this story are relatively isolated, gay and lesbian elders often establish networks of friends who, like family members, exchange emotional and instrumental support (Kimmel, 1992). Lipman (1986) reported that elderly gay men and lesbians tend to have more friends than heterosexuals of similar age. Most of these friends are of the same gender, and many are also gay or lesbian.

Generalizing the image of the American family to all couples masks the complexity of family experiences and resources with which older Americans face the challenges of aging. Uncritically accepting dominant stereotypes of older families is like wearing blinders. Our understanding is limited because we don't think to ask questions about dimensions of social reality that we overlook. We forget to ask how people who never married develop other relationships to meet their needs for companionship in old age. We forget to ask how gay and lesbian couples activate a support network to care for them when they are ill. We forget to ask how more fluid definitions of family and more flexible divisions of labor both within and beyond nuclear family households influence strategies used by older African Americans in coping with disability in old age. These oversights are not intentional. They reflect limited views of social reality from particular standpoints.

Plurality of Family Experience Among Older People: How Interlocking Hierarchies of Gender, Race, and Class Structure the Experience of Family Among Older People Today

Families of older people today are continuations of families established by young adults in the 1930s, 1940s, and 1950s. The composition of these families has changed over the intervening decades, as new members were added through birth, marriage, adoption, or other alliances; others were lost through death; and the remainder aged and moved through life transitions. Economic and political fluctuations produced changes in opportunities and access to resources available to support family members, and changes in attitudes regarding old age influenced older people's self-esteem and their relationships with kin. Although these demographic, socioeconomic, and political forces impinge on all families, differences in their consequences are grounded in hierarchies based on gender, race or ethnicity, and social class.

Because of sex differences in life expectancy, the tendency of women to marry men older than themselves, and higher remarriage rates among older men, the majority of older men are married and the majority of older women are widowed. Minority elders, particularly those also disadvantaged by social class, have a shorter life expectancy than elderly people privileged by race and class, but the sex differential in life expectancy persists across all racial and ethnic groups. Higher rates of divorce and separation suggest that elderly African American, Hispanic American, Native American, and Asian American women will be less likely to live with a spouse than will elderly white women (Markides, 1989).

Historical trends in fertility and differences in mortality also have influenced the number of adult children in families of today's older people. Although birthrates have evidenced a long-term decline since the early 1800s, several fluctuations in this trend influence today's elderly families. The oldest-old (i.e., people over 85 years of age) experienced their marriage and childbearing years during the Great Depression of the 1930s, a period when limited economic opportunities reduced marriage and fertility rates. In contrast, older people in their late sixties and seventies experienced their marriage and childbearing years during the prosperous decades following World War II when, as we have seen, dominant ideology emphasized marriage and motherhood as primary goals for U.S. women. This cohort of elders were the parents of the post-World War II baby boom. As a result of these demographic shifts, the current cohort of old-old people have, on the average, fewer adult children than do young-old people. This difference will shift, of course, as the parents of the baby boom reach their late eighties and will shift again as people experiencing their childbearing years during the "birth dearth" of the 1970s enter old age.

Families as well as individuals are shaped by historical context. In her book *The Way We Never Were: American Families and the Nostalgia Trap,* Stephanie Coontz (1992) interprets the "traditional" middle-class family of the 1950s as a product of a particular historical period. She argues that this family type was a qualitatively new phenomenon, reflecting a "unique and temporary conjuncture of economic, social and political factors" (p. 29): high rates of savings during the war; America's postwar industrial advantage; expansion of middle-class management occupations, a honeymoon period between management and organized labor, and a rapid growth in real wages; and expanded government subsidy of education, job training, housing loans, and highway and sewer construction. As she explains, the family arrangements that became the new standard in the 1950s were not a return to traditional patterns established in previous decades. Indeed, early marriages, high birthrates, and declines in the proportion of never-married persons stand in sharp contrast to the rest of the twentieth century, in which American families have been characterized by falling birthrates, rising divorce rates, and older ages at first marriage (Skolnick, 1991).

Decisions regarding fertility are also influenced by economic and cultural factors, so it is not surprising that family size varies by social class and by race or ethnicity. In general, more affluent families have had fewer children than poorer families, a tendency that persists across all racial groups. One exception to this negative relationship between social class and number of children occurs at the pinnacle of the class hierarchy, with upper-upper class families slightly larger than average (Ostrander, 1984). Fertility rates also vary by race or ethnicity. Hispanics have the highest fertility rate of any racial or ethnic group. Fertility rates for African Americans have been consistently higher than fertility rates for whites, with the difference most pronounced during the 1950s. Differences in mortality, however, reduce the numerical advantage of older African Americans and Hispanic Americans in number of adult children implied by these fertility differentials. Children of African American and Hispanic American parents are less likely than children of white parents to survive infancy and childhood, and young men from these groups face higher risks of death from violence. Children of today's young-old elders compose the cohort that participated in the Vietnam War. In addition to the gender difference in deaths in combat, studies of wartime mortality documented higher death rates among minority soldiers than among white soldiers, a difference that reflected race and class biases in both the military draft and assignments within the military (Waitzkin, 1974).

Family Care of Frail Elders: Why Women Are Most Often the Providers of Family Care for Frail Older People

Despite the myth that older people are dumped into nursing homes by uninterested relatives too involved in their own careers and activities to care for their frail elderly relatives, gerontologists have demonstrated that family members, particularly spouses and adult children, provide the majority of long-term care to older people in the United States today. Caring for frail elderly relatives represents a major gender difference in the experience of old age, as provision of this unpaid care is disproportionately women's work. According to the Long-Term Care Survey conducted by the U.S. Health Care Financing Administration, 71.5% of the 2.2 million caregivers of frail and disabled elderly are women (Stone, Cafferata, & Sangl, 1987). Among elderly couples, the caregiver is most likely the wife, as she is typically younger than her husband. Widowed women most often rely on adult daughters for assistance.

The research on family caregiving illustrates the intersection of hierarchies based on gender and on class. The majority of people who provide unpaid care to frail elderly people are women, but social class differences mediate the experience of family caregiving. Relatively affluent women have resources to hire supplementary assistance or purchase market alternatives for caregiving tasks or domestic work. These women become care managers, delegating responsibilities to formal providers, most of whom are women who work for minimal wages. They are relieved of some of the drudgery of housework and caregiving by "becoming managers of the drudgery of domestic work done by other women" (Cole, 1986, p. 8). These other women are most often working-class women, frequently members of racial or ethnic minority groups, who return home from performing the personal care and household tasks of more affluent women to their own second shift of unpaid domestic work.

Responsibilities of caring for a frail older relative can discourage labor force participation among women caregivers. With minimal support from either public services or male relatives, these women often experience the obligation to care for a spouse or elderly parent as a necessity rather than a choice (Aronson, 1992; Brubaker & Brubaker, 1992). But not all women faced with caregiving responsibilities are able to reduce demands on their time by withdrawing from paid labor. Poor and working-class women lack the financial resources to retire early, leave the labor force temporarily, or work part-time. Even lifelong, continuous employment in the secondary labor market fails to provide adequate pension benefits or an opportunity to accumulate savings. For unmarried women who cannot pool resources with a second wage earner, the situation is particularly bleak. Traditional notions of the "maiden aunt" as a provider of care for her frail elderly parents must be tempered by the reality that even lifelong continuous employment can fail to provide adequate pension benefits or opportunities to accumulate savings (O'Rand & Henretta, 1982a).

As with many transitions in the life course of older families, the transition from adult son or daughter to caregiver is an unscheduled one. Sometimes the shift occurs suddenly, as when an older parent suffers a stroke. More often, however, the transition begins almost imperceptibly, with caring for an older parent at first entailing more a sense of responsibility than tangible assistance. A number of the adult daughters interviewed by Jane Lewis and Barbara Meredith (1988) felt they had "just drifted into caring" and were unable to identify the point at which they had assumed a caregiving role. The narrator in Ann Tracy's short story "Between the Funerals" catches this subtle shift in dependency long before her mother needs concrete assistance.

How Definitions Based on Experiences of the Dominant Group Can Bias Research on Older Families: Methodological Issues in Studying Older Families

Exploring the implications of heterogeneity in families in late life reminds us that knowledge is socially constructed. As we have tried to demonstrate in this part, definitions of family based on the experience of white, middle-class elders can mask the richness and complexity of family structure and relationships of older people who occupy or have occupied other positions along the intersections of gender, race or ethnicity, and social class.

Research on informal caregiving has highlighted the contribution of spouses and adult children, particularly daughters, as providers of assistance to frail elderly. But these studies most often have focused on the experiences of white middle- or working-class elders. Studies of caregivers often rely on respondents recruited through newspaper advertising or from client rosters of social service agencies. This means that our knowledge of caregiving is based disproportionately on people who have sought some type of outside support. As Sarah Matthews (1988) argues, these strategies for recruiting subjects systematically bias research by emphasizing the experiences of older people with inadequate resources. People who are sharing responsibility for caring for a frail older relative with an extensive network of kin and friends or who have enough money to hire people to provide some of the care are less likely to participate in support groups or in a study of caregiver burden.

Research on family care of older people can also be biased by researchers' assumptions about definitions of family. Many studies emphasize the relationship between older care recipients and their "primary caregiver," a strategy that can overlook the contributions of other people within helping networks. Data from the national Long-Term Care Survey indicate that 28.9% of the people providing assistance to frail elders are classified as "secondary caregivers," that is, people who provide assistance but do not have the primary responsibility of coordinating care for the disabled person. These secondary caregivers are more likely to be men than women and more likely to be relatives other than spouses or adult children (Stone et al., 1987). We shouldn't be surprised, then, that researchers who ask older people to "tell me about the person who helps you the most" are most likely to obtain information about husbands, wives, and adult daughters.

In some older families, this picture of family care may be fairly accurate. But this question will provide only a partial picture of assistance to older people embedded in extensive networks of kin and "fictive kin." For example, we have already seen that definitions of kin have traditionally been more fluid and flexible within African American communities, where "institutions of community-based childcare, informal adoption, [and] greater reliance on othermothers . . . emerge as adaptations to the exigencies of combining exploitive work with nurturing children" (Collins, 1991, p. 49). The result is not a collection of isolated nuclear families but "a nurturing female community of grandmothers, aunts, and friends [encircling] their 'daughters' " (Guy-Sheftall, 1991, p. 62). These expanded definitions of family can enhance the resources available to older African Americans for coping with illness and disability. For example, Colleen Johnson and Barbara Barer (1990) studied older African Americans living in the inner city in San Francisco. They concluded that their respondents were

> quite competent in drawing on numerous mechanisms for creating extensions in the kinship system that result in dense and often emotionally supportive networks. Blacks, much more than whites, are close to relatives on the periphery of the kinship system. They are also able to create fictive kin by redefining their relationships with friends. In doing so, they add members to their networks who function like kin. (p. 732)

Definitions of family based on the experience of white, middle-class elders can mask the richness and complexity of this fluidity in the boundaries between family and community. If we don't understand how people come to define someone as kin, we will ask the wrong questions. Too often, we try to fit answers to these questions into a conceptual framework built on our own understanding of the world. The result can be inaccurate research conclusions. Elsa Barkley Brown (1991) illustrates this process when she shares her reactions to a study concluding that African American culture emphasized kinship rather than friendships among southern women:

> All of . . . my mother's closest confidantes, her support network, were her sisters and cousins and aunts. Thus, I initially thought that perhaps the article . . . captured some element of African American women's networks. . . . It was not until I sat down to write this article that I recognized the fallacy in my own thinking, even about my mother's life. Of course my mother's female network consisted almost exclusively of family members—because all those women who had become part of her support network had also become part of her family. . . . So much so that when I had attempted to really think about the female networks in my mother's life I had been unable to separate "friends" from "family" but, knowing them all to be family, had assumed my mother had no need for "friends." (p. 88)

Intergenerational Relationships and Ethnic Culture: Variation in Family Values

When politicians call for a "return to family values," they most often summon up an image of the mythical American family of the 1950s. As we have seen, American families have always exhibited more diversity than that stereotype suggests. Values concerning family relationships also vary by race or ethnicity. Hispanic American families, for example, have been described as highly integrated, intergenerational kin networks sustained by rules of mutual obligations (Hines, Garcia-Preto, McGoldrick, & Weltman, 1992). Traditional Hispanic values emphasize respect for elders (Stanford, Peddecord, & Lockery, 1990). Women assumed caregiving roles in the family, including care of older relatives, and devoted their lives to the welfare of others (Hines et al., 1992), values illustrated in Gerald Halsam's short story "The Horned Toad."

Traditional Asian American family values also emphasize respect for and care of elderly parents. Filial piety, a central value in Chinese, Korean, Japanese, and other Asian societies influenced by Confucian culture, obliges a married son and his wife to serve the husband's parents, providing physical care and social psychological comfort, consulting parents about important family and personal issues, and honoring parents through achievements and observance of ceremonial occasions (Kim, Kim, & Hurh, 1991). Traditional conceptions of filial piety, institutionalized within a patrilineal extended family system, defined the tie to one's parents as more important than the tie to one's spouse and emphasized obligations to the husband's rather than the wife's parents. Different expectations about intergenerational assistance also occur among European American families. "Whereas Italians or Greeks are likely to grow up with the expectation that eventually they will take care of their parents, white Anglo-Saxon Protestants parents' worst nightmare might be that eventually they will have to depend on their children for support" (Hines et al., 1992, p. 323).

Neither extended networks of kin and fictive kin nor traditional values stressing respect for and support of elderly parents are sufficient to guarantee that older relatives will receive the treatment they expect from younger family members. Families disadvantaged by social class often lack the economic resources to support older relatives. Meeting obligations of caring for older relatives is difficult when all adult members of the family must be employed. Unlike affluent families, poor and working-class families lack the financial resources to hire supplemental help or purchase market equivalents for their own unpaid labor. While celebrating the strength of extended kin networks sustained by values of mutual obligation, planners and policymakers must also evaluate resources available for implementing these expectations. Otherwise, images of minority elders embedded in multigenerational families can serve as rationales for failing to provide needed formal services.

How Family Relationships and Family Values Can Vary Among Generations Within Families

Variation in definitions of kin and family obligations also occur within ethnic groups and among generations within families. Sometimes these differences reflect differences in life stage. Elaine Brody and her colleagues (Brody, Johnson, Fulcomer, & Lang, 1983) interviewed three generations of women within the same families and found that those in the oldest generation were least likely to feel that children should help elderly parents and most likely to prefer hiring formal help rather than asking family members for assistance. As Gary Lee (1988) concluded, although cultural norms emphasize responsibility for family members, very few people want to be on the receiving end in family relations, especially if they cannot reciprocate for the help they receive.

Other generational differences can reflect cohort effects. For example, an elderly mother who followed the dictates of the feminine mystique and stayed out of the labor force to care for her children may disapprove of a daughter's decision to return to full-time employment while an infant grandchild stays in a day care facility. She also may interpret her daughter's decision as an implicit criticism of the way she handled work and family roles when her daughter was very young. Generational differences within ethnic families can also reflect differences in length of time in the United States. Challenges to traditional values accompanying acculturation of immigrant groups can produce generational differences in expectations about how elders should be treated. The immigrant generation tends to keep to traditional values more closely than either their children or their grandchildren. If these immigrants came to the United States as young or middle-aged adults and left their parents behind, they were probably socialized into norms regarding care of elderly parents but never experienced the difficulties that accompany implementation of those norms. As a result, they can be more demanding and less appreciative of care provided by their own adult children.

Norms based in one culture can be difficult to implement in another culture. Differences between the dominant culture and elements of ethnic cultures can also produce conflicts between generations. Children and grandchildren who embrace norms and values of the dominant culture can disappoint elderly parents and grandparents by failing to fulfill expectations delineated by traditional ethnic culture. The dominant position of the eldest generation can be undermined by their unfamiliarity with ways of life in the United States, with their children and grandchildren sometimes embarrassed by the "foreign" ways of older relatives. These types of intercultural and intergenerational conflicts are illustrated by Barbara Yee's selection, "Elders in Southeast Asian Refugee Families."

Ethnic culture is not always a source of conflict within multigenerational families. The renewed interest in ethnic cultures over the past several decades provides mechanisms through which cultural differences within families can strengthen intergenerational relationships. Renewed interest in "ethnic roots" among younger generations translates older people's knowledge of ethnic history and culture into an exchange resource. Older people's self-esteem is enhanced because they are perceived as sources of valuable information (Cool, 1980). They become the experts or the teachers. "Culture camps"—through which elderly Native Americans teach music, language, crafts, and local history to children and teenagers—not only maintain traditional knowledge but also enhance the self-esteem of the elders. Family or local history projects that record memories of elders are two other strategies for translating older people's memories into a valued resource. Joan Weibel-Orlando's selection "Grandparenting Styles: Native American Perspectives" illustrates this role of elderly family members as teachers of traditional culture.

Key Issues

This discussion and the readings in this part illustrate the following issues:

1. How earlier marriage and child-rearing experiences of today's cohorts of elderly Americans differed from the idealized image of the American family

2. How these differences in family experiences for young and middle-aged adults were patterned along hierarchies based on gender, race, and class

3. How interlocking hierarchies of gender, race, and class structure the experience of family among older people today

4. Why women are most often the providers of family care for frail older people

5. How research based on the caregiving experiences of white middle-class families can undermine our understanding of caregiving in other families

6. How family relationships and family values can vary among generations within families

The Readings

Family relationships are one example of adaptive resources on which people can call in coping with particular life events. African American families have provided a source of support against stressors of racism and economic disadvantage. African American women have developed strategies for ensuring their children's physical survival without compromising their sense of self-worth. A personal account of this redefinition of mothering is provided in the selection "Mothers of Mind" by Elsa Barkley Brown. Like other writings by African American women, this selection stresses the contributions of mothers and grandmothers in teaching the "delicate balance between conformity and resistance. . . . Black daughters must learn how to survive in interlocking structures of race, class, and gender oppression while rejecting and transcending these very same structures" (P. H. Collins, 1991, p. 54). In her essay, Brown describes this same balance as her mother's "need to socialize me to live my life one way and, at the same time, to provide me with all the tools I would need to live it quite differently."

Ella Leffland describes the two characters in her story "The Linden Tree" as "just a couple who had grown old together." In many respects, the two elderly men are similar to many couples who are facing aging and death after a lifetime together. They had learned to accept each other's idiosyncrasies and granted each other space to express their uniqueness. They had developed a division of domestic labor that spilled over into their rooming house business. They also monitored and worried over each other's health, confronting not only the pain of a beloved partner but their own impending loss. In the case of George and Guilio, however, their shared memories included discrimination grounded in racism and homophobia. Their experiences contrast with the networks of kin and friends described in some research on elderly gay men and lesbians, but perhaps this reflects patterns of isolation begun in adolescence—Guilio as a young, single immigrant from Italy and George as the son of a poor African American couple isolated in a Finnish farming community in the upper Midwest.

Although the importance of women as providers of care for frail elderly has been well documented empirically, gerontologists have devoted less attention to explaining the caregiving patterns they have described. As Jane Lewis and Barbara Meredith (1988) reported, many adult daughters are unable to pinpoint the moment at which they became caregivers for a frail older mother. The shift begins with a sense of responsibility. The selection from the short story "Between the Funerals" by Ann Tracy provides insight into the subtle ways in which this transition in the mother-daughter relationship can occur. The mother in this story lives independently and the dependence her daughter senses is more psychological than physical. The narrator is not facing demanding caregiving tasks, but she is confronting aging—both her mother's and her own. She tells us "there's a moment when I can't catch my breath and I want to scream and protest that I'm not ready for this changing of the guard."

Gerald Halsam's story "The Horned Toad" illustrates family caregiving in a Mexican American family. Described by the author as "fiction based on actual events," with Halsam as the young narrator, the story illustrates the centrality of *la familia* in Chicano culture. None of the boy's relatives questions having responsibility for the elderly grandmother. Moving from house to house within the family reflects concerns with her happiness, efforts to "find a place she'd accept." The story also illustrates the importance of place, a lesson the old woman teaches her great-grandson when she exhorted him to return the horned toad "to his own place." As she faced the end of her own life, she too focused on the open country in which she had spent most of her life. Finally, Halsam's story illustrates the importance of language as both a bridge and a barrier within Chicano culture. The young narrator has little facility in the Spanish language because his Anglo father had decided that learning "that foreign tongue" would hurt the boy's chances in school. Unlike bilingual children of immigrant parents, who serve as bridges between their parents and the Anglophone community, Halsam's family had been in the United States since his great-great-grandparents emigrated from Mexico in the 1850s. In this case, the Spanish language proved a barrier, at least initially, between the boy and his *abuelita*. Halsam's story reminds us that Hispanics in the United States differ not only by country of origin, they also differ by history of immigration both between and within cultural groups.

Immigration and acculturation can also strain family relationships. Elderly grandparents and great-grandparents adhere more closely than younger generations to traditional culture, and they can be disappointed with behaviors and attitudes of younger family members who adopt patterns of the dominant culture. These types of intercultural and intergenerational conflicts are illustrated in Barbara Yee's selection, "Elders in Southeast Asian Refugee

Families." Among these families, elderly relatives' traditional roles as family advisers and decision makers are undermined by their unfamiliarity with the culture and language of their new country.

Unfamiliarity with traditional culture among younger generations need not always lead to isolation and lack of respect for elderly relatives. Knowledge of ethnic culture and history can also be a resource that enhances the self-esteem of older people. The final selection, by Joan Weibel-Orlando, "Grandparenting Styles: Native American Perspectives," presents a typology of grandparenting roles that includes "cultural conservator," a role that can apply to grandparenting within both minority and European American cultures. The Sioux and Muskogean (Creek, Chickasaw, and Choctaw) grandparents that she interviewed sought to teach their urbanized grandchildren about traditional culture. As one respondent explained, her own children were "just too far gone" to respond to efforts to maintain their Native American heritage. Her grandchildren were "her only hope for effecting both personal and cultural continuity."

30

Mothers of Mind

Elsa Barkley Brown

My mother was born in 1916, the youngest of eight children—six of them girls—to Kentucky farmers. She was fortunate to be the youngest. Two of the three eldest sisters passed quickly through the rural elementary school, married, and moved to the city to work as domestics. More importantly for the other four daughters, their homes became one by one their sisters' homes as they came to the city to attend the colored high school. The next eldest, having finished high school and normal school, became a teacher and opened her home to her younger sisters. As was the tradition among African American families, the two brothers remained on the farm, but it was important to provide the daughters with as much education as possible so that they might escape the plight of domestic work and particularly the sexual violence and abuse. The fourth and fifth sisters then went beyond high school and normal school and were certified as teachers, the pride of the family and its collective struggles.

My mother's turn came. She too went to the city, lived in her sisters' homes, graduated from the colored high school in 1934. A new development in Louisville, Kentucky, was the opening of Louisville Municipal College for Negroes. It was now possible for African

Americans to attend college in the city. It was a difficult decision for a Black family, even one as large as this in the midst of the Depression, but it was in keeping with their traditions, their belief in education, their faith in each other that they decided that this daughter/sister would go to college. As a matter of fact, as my mother describes it, it was not a decision at all—they just assumed that she would go. They all had gone as far as was possible and for her there was a new level of possibility. Four years later, when she graduated as a mathematics major, her achievement represented the culmination of generations of struggle.

The question was, what was this African American female mathematician, pride not only of her family but of her communities—both rural and urban—going to do? Teach? Her temperament ruled that out. But there were surely other possibilities. And so she went, diploma, pride, and courage in hand, in search of her future. It took some time but finally she did find a job, with an employer who was suitably impressed with all that this young African American girl had accomplished; yes, it would be so refreshing to have an intelligent maid for a change. And so my mother, unwilling to accept the only profession open to African American women—teaching—hung her sheepskin in other women's kitchens as she cooked and washed and cleaned and tended their children.

She soon married, and as they planned their future the one thing of which she and her husband were certain was that she had

Source: Excerpted from "Mothers of Mind," by E. Brown, from *Double Stitch: Black Women Write about Mothers and Daughters*, edited by P. Bell-Scott, B. Guy-Sheftall, J. Jones Royster, J. Sims-Wood, M. DeCosta- Willis, and L. Fultz, 1991. Boston: Beacon Press. Reprinted by permission of the author.

not struggled all those years never to have a life of her own; and so she chose, as many other African American women did, despite economic hardship, to leave the world of Black women's work inside the household outside her home and raise a family which would have her time and attention. For her, as for many other women, the decision to be a wife and mother first in a world which defined African American women in so many other ways, the decision to make her family the most important priority was an act of resistance to a system which would define her place for her in terms of its own economic and racist needs.

Thus, the maintenance of her children and family became the priority of her life. She taught her three daughters that they should get good educations, including college degrees. There were more opportunities then and a degree would allow them to be something other than a domestic. But first and foremost they must maintain their family. Unless it was an economic necessity, they should never work if they had children.

Two of her daughters listened and learned and obeyed, at least for a number of years. They went to college, married, and raised their families. But one—you can probably guess which one; as my mother says, "I don't know where I got that child from"—was more restless. And so she went to college, married, had two daughters, and worked while her husband went to graduate school. One day she wrote her mother a letter telling of her own ambitions—and her frustrations. While she did not mind working while her husband went to school, what she did mind was all the talk in the family/community about his education and future and none about hers.

Mother read this letter and worried and pondered. A month later she replied in a letter which once again told her daughter that raising a family was and should be all that she concentrated on. Future schooling and careers should not be in her immediate plans. A Black woman's responsibility was to maintain her family. Enclosed in that same envelope with that letter was a check in the amount of tuition for graduate school—an enormous sum for the mothers/sisters/aunts who had pooled all and sold some to raise it—an act of faith in another generation of African American women.

When this daughter reached the stage of Ph.D. candidacy exams, this mother came and stayed a month to care for the two granddaughters. Every night at dinner she gave her daughter a lecture on the evils of pursuing a career and neglecting her children and begged her to give this up and be a proper Black mother. And every morning she got the children up quietly and tiptoed 'round the house all day so her daughter's studying would not be interrupted. When time came to take the oral exams, the sisters/aunts/mothers sent an appropriate suit for their child to wear. And the mother loudly proclaimed the evils of such careerism and neglect of family priorities as she cooked a very special dinner to celebrate.

There is much more to my mother's story but this represents the basic outline of those things with which I wish to deal.

My mother also taught me to understand theoretical concepts and to develop new frameworks. Several years ago Bonnie Thornton Dill wrote about "The Dialectics of Black Womanhood" and has since refined those ideas to give us a good basis for understanding the relationship between African American women and the society in which we live. What Dill argues is that Black women in the United States have lived in a society which defined womanhood in one way while they have been required to live lives that were in reality totally different from that definition. For example, "true women" did not work outside the home at a time when the majority of African American women were employed. And in that process, as Dill argues, African American women were forced to define themselves and to develop new definitions of womanhood—those definitions coming out of the dialectics of their lives. African American women have lived lives filled with contradictions and have formed a meaning for themselves and their people out of those contradictions.

My mother best explained that contradiction to me: when she was in college—majoring in mathematics—she worked as a live-in servant. In the mornings she rose early enough to clean house, cook breakfast, and prep the baby before she went off to classes; at noon she hurried back to the house to fix lunch and walk the dog; afternoons to class and then home to cook dinner and perform any other unfinished chores before she began a night of study. It was not just a full schedule in terms of hours taken up; but it was also a life that was built around coming to terms with contradictions. She lived a life which defied in very basic ways both the notions of the proper role of women and the proper place of Blacks. She lived a life which simultaneously conformed to notions of the proper place of Black women and defied those notions. To be a domestic worker is in many ways to be all that the larger society assumes about African American people and particularly African American females: it is to do the work that the majority women believe beneath them and fit only for those of lower status and intellect. It requires certain attitudes and actions, deferences and subserviences even in the most defiant. It requires in many ways submission to a set of notions. To be a Black female college student in the early 1930s—and to major in mathematics—was to defy notions in the larger society about both women and African American people. To do both of these simultaneously is to live a life inherently contradictory. In the process, one has to define one's self through the interrelationships of *both* of those lives. It is the dialectical process at its core which was my mother's life.

My mother's seeming contradictions don't end there. Her letter and the accompanying check for my graduate education demonstrated her understanding of the need to socialize me to live my life one way and, at the same time, to provide me with all the tools I would need to live it quite differently. When I finally comprehended that, I understood much about the unique and essential dynamics of Black mother-daughter relationships. Moreover, it helped me understand

much that seems conflicting when I study the Richmond, Virginia, Black community. Historians frequently have assumed that the seeming contradictions between the rhetoric and the actions, or differing sets of actions, of the African-American community or of some of its leaders is evidence of duplicity; "wearing the mask"; of massive confusion and disorientation; or of accommodation. Some of these interpretations may in some instances be true. But what I came to understand on a concrete level through my mother was the possible necessity of the simultaneous promotion of two contradictory sets of values. *Both* were essential to the survival—of me as a person in the society in which we lived, and of the African American community as a whole. That understanding has greatly enhanced my comprehension of political developments in Richmond and elsewhere.

Perhaps most obviously, but not always so, my mother has enhanced my understanding of familial relationships. Historians and other social scientists have difficulty grappling with the basic conceptions of African American families. There is either the tendency to try to fit them into Eurocentric notions of family, or, as Niara Sudarkasa has noted, even when it is recognized that they are not Eurocentric, Eurocentric terminology and definitions are employed to characterize them and so their difference is described in distorting ways. I understood that most clearly when a friend of mine, with whom I often share notes on teaching and writing, called me one night to say that she had been trying to talk about families in her women's studies class and that she had tried to do it in a way which did not assume Eurocentric family norms. So, having explained the differing notions of family, she asked her students to talk about their families. Teaching in a southern California university, she has a number of racial/ethnic groups in her classroom, and her students began, having heard her lecture and understanding that they could speak of more than their parents and siblings, to describe their nuclear and extended family networks. All of them spoke until she got to the one African American woman in the class, who was an older woman returning to school. The woman looked at my friend and said quite clearly, "I don't understand—I just got family." My friend Lillian came to understand what she was saying, that even in attempting to recognize that there might be a different conception of family, she had imposed a way of defining it on her students— so they could talk about whoever was their family but they still had to divide it up according to Eurocentric distinctions among who is nuclear and who is extended, who is blood kin and who is fictive kin. And this Black woman refused to try to dissect her family along Eurocentric lines, for all she had was family.

A notion of family which transcends Eurocentric notions about relationships and roles is what my mothers have clearly passed to me. Perhaps the most cogent expression of that was on my wedding day. One of my mothers/aunts sat me down to talk about many things. All that I explicitly remember is her depiction of our relationship, for she said to me, "Your mother is my sister, my daughter, my mother, my cousin, and to you I have been and always will be your aunt, your mother, your grandmother, your sister; your children will have an aunt, a grandmother, a great-grandmother, a mother, a sister, a cousin." I understood it then in sentimental ways. I comprehended it years later when I couldn't, using the paradigms I had, accurately describe the family relationships in the community which I was studying. Often as I have tried particularly to discuss relationships among African American mothers and daughters in my research and in my classroom, I have been drawn back to my mother/aunt's statements. And I have understood the fallacy of trying to impose ideas that those doing African American family studies have often tried to impose—they have required their subjects to define their relationships with the other women/people in their family by Eurocentric notions and have marveled at the difficulty.

31

The Linden Tree

Ella Leffland

In the early years there had been passion, but now they were just a couple who had grown old together. The last twenty years they had owned a rooming house, where they lived contentedly on the ground floor with their cat, Baby.

Giulio was a great putterer. You could always see him sweeping the front steps or polishing the doorknobs, stopping to gossip with the neighbors. He was a slight, pruny man of sixty-eight, perfectly bald, dressed in heavy trousers, a bright sport shirt with a necktie, and an old man's sweater-jacket, liver-colored and hanging straight to the knees. He had a thick Italian accent and gesticulated wildly when he was excited.

George was quite different. Everything about him was slow and solid, touched by grandeur. Though he was a Negro from the Midwest, he spoke with an accent that sounded British, yet not exactly. He was seventy-four, but looked much younger, with a hard body and a hard face with only a few deep fissures in it. Giulio was a neat dresser, but George was attired. His perfectly creased trousers, his crisp white shirt, smoothly knotted tie, and gray sleeveless sweater seemed out of place in the stuffy little flat.

A home is usually the wife's creation, and so it was in their case. The doilies, the vases with their wax flowers, the prints of saints

Source: "The Linden Tree" by Ella Leffland, from *Last Courtesies and Other Stories*, Ella Leffland, 1980. Copyright © 1972 Ella Leffland. Reprinted by permission of HarperCollins Publishers, Inc.

hanging among gaudy floral calendars—all these were Giulio's. George's contribution was less concrete but more important. He made their life possible, dealing with the rents and taxes, attending to the heavy chores, ousting tenants who drank or brawled. If Giulio were to run the building he would soon come to grief, for he had no real sense of work, and as for the rents, it was all he could do to add two digits together. In addition, he was fussy and fault-finding, so that he often took a dislike to perfectly good tenants, yet countenanced glib bullies.

They were a nicely balanced couple, and for years had been happy. When they were young they had had their troubles—living quarters had been hard to find not only because of George's color, but because of their relationship. In those days Giulio had had fetching ways, too obvious to be ignored. But gradually he passed into a fussy dotage, and now people thought of the pair merely as two lonely old men who lived together. George's color no longer represented problems now that he had proved what was not necessarily demanded of those who asked for proof: that he was a responsible man, an asset to the neighborhood. His building was the best kept on the block, his rents reasonable, his tenants, for the most part, permanent. He would not rent to the fly-by-night element that was slowly invading the district.

The tenants consisted of a pair of raddled, gadabout sisters, a World War I veteran with one leg, and a few clerks and students. Giulio regaled George with facts about these people he gleaned by snooping through their rooms in their absence, and George put him down for this, even threatened him, but it did no good. And in any case, the tenants did not seem to care; there was something so simple about Giulio that his spying was like that of a mouse or a bird. They called him Aunty Nellie (his last name being Antonelli), and the younger ones sometimes invited him into their rooms so that his teeth might be enjoyed. These were ill-fitting, too large for his mouth, and clicked through his speech. When he grew excited, they slipped out of place, at which he would pause in a natural, business-like way to jam them back in before going on.

Giulio was forever dragging the carpet sweeper up and down the halls, looking for an ear to gossip in. George, on the other hand, talked very little. Only tenants who had lived there a long time got to know him at all, when, once in a great while, he would invite them in for a glass of sherry when they came to pay the rent.

In his flat, the tenants found George to be a different man, less aloof and forbidding. Sitting there with Giulio and Baby, the cat, he had something patient, indulgent, altogether loving in his face. Giulio looked with pride at him, glancing now and then at the guest, as though to say: Isn't he wonderful? Sometimes he would go so far as to confess, "I no good at the paper work, but George, George, he *smart*." Or, "We live together fifty years, never a yell, always happy." And George would give him a look to show him that he was saying too much, and then Giulio would sulk and refuse to rejoin the conversation. But the next day he would be the same as ever, whirling creakily around the steps with his broom, or around his garden with a green visor clamped to his head.

He had a shrine in the garden, with statues of the saints standing in sun-blanched profusion. He was an ardent Catholic, and there was no one with a greater collection of religious objects—rosaries and crosses and vestments, which he kept in his bureau drawer and brought out to enjoy their varied glass, wooden, and satin richness. But religious as he was, he would not divest his beloved garden of one fresh bloom for his saints. It was a skimpy garden, heavily bolstered with potted geraniums, and he was so proud of each green shoot that struggled through the hard ground, and attended its subsequent flowering with such worried care, that it was only when a flower had finally begun to wither on the stem that he would pluck it as an offering to his statues.

George understood this attitude and was properly grateful when once a year on his birthday he received a sacrifice of fresh daisies and marigolds. He was amused by Giulio's niggardliness toward the saints. He himself did not care about them. He, too, was a Catholic, but had become one only so that he and Giulio might be buried together. Two fully paid-for plots, side by side, awaited them under a linden tree in Our Lady of Mercy Cemetery just outside town. Whoever was the first to go, George because he was older, Giulio because he was frailer, the other would join him in due time. Giulio had vague visions of an afterlife. The older man did not.

He had had a good life, everything considered, and he would be content to die and be done with when the time came, and have his bones rest by his friend's forever. Sometimes he thought of the linden tree and gave a satisfied nod.

But lately George had noticed something strange about Giulio. His large red ears seemed to have grown less red.

"Giulio," he said one day, "your ears don't seem to be as red as they used to be."

Giulio touched his ear. When he was young he had been sensitive about their largeness. "Nothing wrong with my ears," he said defensively.

"I'm not criticizing you, Giulio. I think it's just strange." And now he realized that some definite change had been taking place in his friend, but he could not put his finger on it. It was as though he were a little smaller. The jacket seemed to hang lower than it had.

Ah, well, he thought, we're both getting old.

A few days later, as Giulio was raking the leaves in the garden, he complained to George of shortness of breath, and there was the faintest touch of blue in his lips.

"Why don't you go to the doctor for a checkup?" George asked as casually as he could.

Giulio shook his head and continued his raking.

That night, as Giulio was turning on the television set, he suddenly stepped back and dropped into a chair with his hand spread across his chest. "Help!" he shouted into the air. "Help!" and when his friend ran to his side, he gasped, "I gotta pain. Here! Here!" And his hand clutched at his heart so hard that the knuckles were white.

The next day George took him to the doctor, and sat by his side through all the tests. Giulio was terrified, but when it was all over and they came out of the doctor's office he seemed restored.

"See," he said, "I'm okay. The doctor he say no worry."

George's face did not reflect Giulio's good spirits. "I know he says not to worry, but . . ."

"He say no worry," Giulio repeated cheerfully.

But from then on Giulio was visited frequently by the paralyzing pains. He would stop what he was doing and crouch over, his eyes darting frenziedly in their sockets. If George was there he would hurry to his friend's side, but at these moments Giulio seemed totally alone even though his hand grasped George's arm. When it was over he would be stripped of his little ways; he would wander slowly around the room or stand for long moments looking at nothing. Patiently George would wait, and eventually the old Giulio returned. Uneasily, fretfully, he would say, "I no understand. Looka me, I never hurt a fly in all my life, and this pain, he come and scare me. It's not right."

"Well," George would venture soothingly, "if you'd just eat fewer starches and stop worrying, these pains would go away. You've got plenty of years ahead of you . . ."

"Plenty years?" Giulio would break in sharply. "I *know*, I *know* I got plenty years ahead. This pain, he no *important*, he just *scare* me."

In an effort to distract him, George broke a lifelong precedent and invited Myrna and Alice Heppleworth, the two aging sisters who lived on the third floor, down to the flat for the evening. He himself did not like women, but Giulio did, in a way that George could not understand. Giulio loved to gossip with them, and afterward delighted in describing their clothes and manners, which he usually found distressing. He was more interested in the Heppleworth sisters than in anyone else in the building, and always pursed his lips when he saw them going out with their rheumy escorts, and could never forget that he once found a bottle of gin in a dresser drawer ostensibly given over to scarves and stockings.

The Heppleworth sisters came, drank all their wine, and turned the television set up as high as it would go. George grew rigid; Giulio went to bed. The sisters were not asked again.

It seemed to George that Giulio failed daily. His ears were as pale as his face, and this seemed particularly significant to George. He found himself suddenly looking at his friend to check his ears, and each time they looked whiter. He never discussed this with Giulio, because Giulio refused to speak about his fears, as though not daring to give them authority by acknowledging them.

And then one morning Giulio gave up this pretense. As he was getting out of bed he had an attack, and when he recovered this time he let out a piercing wail and began to weep, banging his head from side to side. The rest of the day he spent immobile, wrapped from head to foot in a patchwork quilt.

Toward evening George made him get up and walk in the garden with him. George pointed to the flowers, praising them, and gently turned his friend's face to the shrine. The white plaster faces looked peaceful. Even he, George, felt it, and he realized that for weeks he had been in need of some comfort, something outside himself.

"Look," he said, and that was all, fearing to sound presumptuous, because the statues belonged to Giulio and the Church—he himself understood nothing of them.

Giulio looked without interest, and then, forgetting them, he took George's arm and his eyes swam with tears. "What can I do?" he asked. "What will happen?"

As they walked slowly back to the house he drew his lips back from his big false teeth and whispered, "I'm gonna die."

"No, no, don't think that way," George soothed, but he felt helpless, and resentful that his friend must go through this terror. And now that Giulio had said the words, his terror would grow, just as the pain of a bad tooth grows when you finally acknowledge the decay and are plunged into a constant probing of it with your tongue.

When they came back inside Giulio went straight to bed. George stood in the kitchen and looked at his face in the little mirror that hung on the wall. He feared Giulio would die this very minute in the bedroom as he was removing his carpet slippers, and he wanted with every muscle to run to him. But it would not do to become as hysterical as Giulio, and he stood still. Presently the sound of the bedsprings released a sigh from his throat. The flat was silent. He looked again at his face in the mirror. It was as though he were one person and the reflection another, and he was uneasy and embarrassed, and yet could not look away. He felt deeply aware of himself standing there, staring, and it seemed he was out of place, lost. He whirled around, catching his breath. He had felt entirely alone for the first time in fifty years.

The next day he decided to call for Father Salmon, the young priest from the neighborhood church Giulio attended. Father Salmon dropped in for friendly chats now and then, and Giulio liked him very much, so much, in fact, that the priest often had to silence him when he got carried away with intimate gossip.

A few days later the priest knocked on the door. He was horse-faced, with thinning hair and rimless glasses, and he was quiet and pleasant.

Giulio was wrapped up in his quilt in the armchair. He did not greet the priest with his usual beam of pleasure; he did not even smile.

"Well, Giulio," the priest said, "how are you feeling? I haven't seen you at church lately."

Giulio said at once, "Father, I'm dying."

"What is the trouble?" the priest asked gently.

"It's my heart," Giulio shot back, his hand scrounging around his shirtfront and fumbling with the buttons until it was clutching his bare chest. He looked as though he were prepared to pull the heart out for inspection. His eyes pleaded with the priest to set it right. The priest sat down next to him.

"What does your doctor say?" he asked.

"Oh, Father," Giulio moaned, "the doctor is a stupid. He never tell me one real thing. In and out and all around, around the bush. He no understand, but *I* understand—this heart, he gonna kill me. You think so, Father? What do you think? You think so?"

"Surely, Giulio," the priest replied, "you must accept the doctor's word. If he says there's no reason to fear . . ."

Giulio looked away, black with melancholy.

The priest sat silently for a moment, then began again. "Giulio, death is as natural as birth. Think of your flowers out there in the garden, how they grow from little seeds and then fade and fall—what could be more natural? God has been with you all your life, and He will not forsake you now . . ."

But Giulio, his eyes shutting tighter and tighter as the priest spoke, got up from his chair and crept into the bedroom, dragging his quilt behind him.

Afterward he said to George, "I no wanna see Father Salmon again."

"Father Salmon is trying to help," George told him.

Giulio shook his head, his fingers rubbing the area of his heart.

What a strange person he is, George thought, looking at him closely. All these years he has been immersed in the church, and now, suddenly, the church means nothing to him. He recalled a conversation he had overheard a few days ago as he was fixing a faulty burner in the second floor kitchen. Two of the students were going down the hall, talking. One had commented on Giulio's bad health. The other had replied, "Don't worry, Aunty Nellie could never do anything so profound as to die."

George had bristled, as he always did whenever anyone made fun of his friend—but it was true that Giulio was not profound. He liked pretty things, and the church gave him its rich symbols; he liked intimate conversation, and the church gave him patient Father Salmon; he liked the idea of an afterlife, and the church gave him that, too. He loved the church, but when you came right down to it, he believed only what he could see with his two eyes, and he could see only his blue lips and wasted face in the mirror. This oddly realistic attitude explained his stinginess toward the saints; they were, after all, only plaster. And yet when Baby had once jumped up on the shrine and relieved himself on St. Francis's foot, Giulio had screamed at the animal until the neighbors hung from the windows.

All these amiable contradictions in Giulio had been known to George for fifty years, and he had always believed that they would sustain his friend through everything. Now the contradictions were gone. All that was left in Giulio was the certainty of death. It made George feel forlorn, on the outside. He sensed that nothing could be set right, that Giulio would live consumed by fear until he died consumed by fear, and the linden tree would not mark two intertwined lives, but forever cast its shadow between two strangers.

They had met for the first time in front of the Minneapolis train station in the first decade of the century. George sat in the driver's seat of a Daimler, in his duster and goggles. His employer had gone inside to meet one Giulio Antonelli, just arrived from Calabria, nephew of the head gardener. When he emerged he had in tow a thin boy of eighteen dressed in a shabby suit and carrying a suitcase that looked like a wicker basket. He wore cherry-colored cigar bands on his fingers, and had a shoot of wilted wild flowers stuck

through the buttonhole of his jacket. His eyes were red-rimmed; apparently he had been crying all the way from Calabria. Delicate and terrified, his cigar bands glittering hectically in the sunlight, he crawled into the Daimler and collapsed in a corner.

George had worked as a chauffeur and handyman on his employer's estate for five years, but was originally from an isolated Finnish farming community where God knows what fates had conspired to bring his parents, a bitter, quarreling, aloof, and extremely poor black couple. George became friends with only one thing native to that cold country, the stones that littered the fields. He could not say what attracted him to them, but he felt a great bond with them. When he was ten he built a wall of the stones. It was only a foot high and not very long, and there was nothing in the world for it to guard there in the middle of the empty field, but he knew he had discovered the proper use of the stones, and all his life he had the feeling he was that wall.

In Minneapolis, on the estate, he kept to himself. He liked the Daimler, which he drove with authority, and the appearance of which on the streets caused people to gawk with admiration. He picked up his employer's speech habits, and this, combined with the Finnish accent he had absorbed, gave a peculiar, unplaceable ring to his words, which he relished, because it was his alone.

The Calabrian boy turned out to be a poor gardener, not because he was listless with homesickness, for that soon passed, but because he made favorites of certain flowers and would have nothing to do with the others. The tulips, for instance, he apparently considered stout and silly-looking, and he made disparaging faces at them. He liked the wild flowers that cropped up in odd corners.

George was fascinated by Giulio, although he did not like him. He reminded him of a woman. Women had never respected George's wall, at least a certain type of woman had not—the bold Finnish farm girls, some of the hired women here on the estate. He was well favored, and maybe there was something in his coloring, too, that attracted women, something tawny, reminiscent of the sun, here, where everyone else looked like a peeled banana. In any case, they were always after him. He was not flattered. He felt they were not interested in him as he knew himself, proud and valuable, but in some small part of him that they wanted for their own use, quickly, in a dark corner.

But Giulio, though girlish, had no boldness in him. He would leave the garden and lean against the garage door where George was polishing the Daimler. *"Bella, bella,"* he would murmur, and his face shone with a kind of radiant simplemindedness. There was no calculation in him—sometimes you could see him cocking his head and singing before the wild flowers in the garden. Watching George, the boy spoke foreign words rich in their tones of admiration, and his quick, glittering fingers—he had bought flashy rings with his pay—seemed anxious to catch the sun and make a present of it to the tall, mute figure in the gloom of the garage.

Two months after his arrival Giulio was fired. George, filled with fear for himself feeling a great chasm opening before him, quit his job, and the two of them, with hardly a word between them, took the train to San Francisco, where Giulio had another uncle. All during the trip George asked himself: "Why am I doing this? Why am I going with him? I don't even like him. He's a silly, ridiculous person; there's something the matter with him."

They got off at the San Francisco depot, and before George was even introduced to the uncle, who stood waiting, he picked up his baggage and, without a word of farewell to Giulio, walked quickly away from him.

First he found odd jobs, and finally he wound up on Rincon Hill with another Daimler. On his half day off each week he would wander around the city, looking at the sights. Whenever he saw a quick, thin figure that reminded him of Giulio his heart would pound, and he would say to himself, "Thank God it's not Giulio, I don't want to see him again." And then he found that what had begun as a casual walk around the city was turning into a passionate weekly search. The day he caught sight of Giulio sadly and ineffectively constructing a pyramid of cabbages in a vegetable market, he had to restrain himself from throwing his arms around him.

Giulio's face had blanched with surprise when he looked up, and then his eyes had filled with a dazzling welcome, and he had extended his hand to his returned friend with a tenderness George never forgot.

They were together from then on. In time they bought a vegetable stand, and as a result of George's frugality and common sense he was able to save in spite of Giulio's extravagances. They worked and invested, and in thirty years they were able to buy, for cash, the old apartment building they now lived in. Life had always been strangely easy for them. They had been incapable of acknowledging affronts, even when they were refused lodgings or openly stared at on the street, and the last twenty years in the security of their own flat had been free from problems, satisfying in all ways.

Now Giulio moaned, "Oh, I gotta pain, I gotta pain."

George would take his hand and say, "I'm here, Giulio, I'm here."

But Giulio would look through him, as though he did not exist.

"Don't we *know* each other?" George finally exploded one day, causing Baby to speed under a table with his ears laid back. "Are we strangers after all these years?"

Giulio closed his eyes, involved with his fear.

George sighed, stroking his friend's hand, thin and waxy as a sliver of soap. "What are you thinking about now, this very minute, Giulio? You must tell me."

"I'm thinking of my dog," Giulio said, after a silence.

"What dog was that?" George asked softly.

"I had him in Nocera."

"And what about him?"

"He died, and my father he dug a hole and put him in." His lips turned down. "I dug him up later, I was lonely for him."

"What a foolish thing to do, my poor Giulio."

"His own mother wouldn'a wanted him. Bones and worms . . ."

"Hush, Giulio."

"Gonna happen to me."

"But your soul . . ."

"What's my soul look like?" Giulio asked quickly.

"Like you, Giulio . . . it's true . . ."

Giulio cast him a look of contempt George would not have thought him capable of.

"The little hole, the bones and worms," Giulio moaned.

"But you've *had* a life!" George suddenly cried with exasperation. "Do you want to live forever?"

Yes, Giulio said simply.

From then on George felt a fury. In the past all Giulio's little fears had been bearable because he, George, could exorcise them, like a stevedore bearing a small load away. But this final cowardice excluded him. And there was nothing, no one he could turn to. He went halfheartedly to church, but got nothing from it. He began making small overtures to his tenants, but his sociability was stiff with rust. He looked with curiosity at the black people on the street, and thought there were more of them than there used to be. When a young black couple stopped him on a corner one day he listened attentively as they talked of civil rights. He accepted a pamphlet from them and read it thoroughly. But afterward he threw it out. He felt no connection with the problems it presented.

He cursed Giulio as he had cursed him fifty years ago when he had walked away from him at the train depot, and he wished for the oneness with himself that he had known in the empty fields of his youth.

In the daytime he was angrily helpful, like a disapproving orderly, but at night as they sat in the small living room with Baby flicking his tail back and forth across the blank television screen, he went to Giulio and mutely pleaded with him. Giulio sighed abstractedly; he seemed far away, deep inside himself, listening to every heartbeat, counting every twinge, with a deep frown line between his eyes.

George moved the twin beds together, and Giulio allowed his hand to be held through the night. From then on they slept that way, hand in hand. George slept lightly, waking often. It was almost as if he wished to be awake to enjoy the only hours of closeness he had with his friend as he held his hand. And also, in the back of his mind was the fear that if he drifted off Giulio would be released into the arms of death. And so he lay quietly, listening to Giulio's breathing, to the wind in the trees.

Then gradually the bedroom window would turn from black to gray, and the breeze that ruffled the curtain carried in the scent of early morning. Dawn brought him sleep; the rising sun gave him a sense of security. Bad things never happened in the daytime—at least one felt that way. And so his fingers grew lax in Giulio's hand as he trusted his friend to the kindness of the dawning day.

But when he awoke later it would be with a sharp sense of foreboding. Quickly he would turn to look at Giulio, his eyes narrowed against the possible shock. But Giulio would be breathing evenly, his bluish lips parted over his gums, his teeth grinning from a water glass on the bureau. Giulio's clothes were neatly laid out, his liver-colored jacket hung over the back of a chair. How lifeless the jacket looked. George would shut his eyes, knowing that the sight of that empty jacket would be unbearable when Giulio was gone. He shook the thought from his head, wondering if life could be more painful than this. Then Giulio's eyes would open, George's face take on a formal nonchalance. And so another night had passed. Their hands parted.

"How do you feel?" George would ask shortly.

Giulio would sigh.

They took their breakfast. The sun shone through the kitchen window with a taunting golden light. George snapped at Giulio. Giulio was unmoved.

One summer morning George persuaded Giulio to sit outside in the backyard. He hoped that watching him work in the garden, Giulio might be persuaded to putter around again. He settled his friend into a chair and picked up the rake, but as the minutes wore on and he moved around the garden in the hot sun, raking the leaves together, Giulio showed no sign of interest. George stopped and put the rake down. Not knowing if he wished to please Giulio or anger him, he suddenly broke off the largest marigold in the garden and held it out.

Giulio shaded his watering eyes with his hand; then his eyes drifted away from the flower like two soap bubbles in the air. George flung the flower to the ground, staring at Giulio, then strode to the shrine and stood there with his hands in fists, blindly determined to do something that would shake his friend open, break him in two if need be. He grabbed the arm of the Virgin Mary and lifted the statue high, and heard Giulio's voice.

"George."

"That's right," George growled, replacing the statue and breathing threateningly through his nostrils, "I would have smashed it to bits!"

"Smash what?" Giulio asked indifferently, and George saw that under the awning of his thin hand his eyes were closed.

"Were your eyes closed?" George thundered. "Didn't you *see* me?"

"You no care that I can't open my eyes— this sun, he hurt them. You *mean*, George, make me sit out here. Too hot. Make me feel sick. I wanna go inside."

"I was going to smash your Virgin Mary!" George cried.

Giulio shrugged. "I wanna go inside."

And then George's shoulders hunched, his face twisted up, and he broke into a storm of tears. Turning his head aside with shame, he made for the back door; then he turned around and hurried back, glancing up at the windows, where he hoped no one stood watching him cry. He put his arm around Giulio and helped him up from his chair, and

the two old men haltingly crossed the garden out of the sun.

"Humiliating," George whispered when they were inside, shaking his head and pressing his eyes with a handkerchief. He slowly folded the handkerchief into a square and replaced it in his pocket. He gave a loud sniff and squared his shoulders, and looked with resignation at his distant friend.

Giulio was settling himself into the armchair, plucking the patchwork quilt around him. "Time for pills," he muttered, reaching next to him, and he poured a glass of water from a decanter and took two capsules, smacking his lips mechanically, like a goldfish. Sitting back, he looked around the room in his usual blank, uninterested way. Then a puzzled expression came into his eyes.

"Why you cry then, George?"

George shook his head silently.

"I do something you no like?"

"You never talk. It's as though we're strangers." And he broke off with a sigh. "I've told you all that before—what's the use?"

"I got big worry, George. No time to talk."

"It would be better than to think and think. What do you think about all day?"

Giulio slowly raised his eyebrows, as though gazing down upon a scene. "Bones and worms."

"Giulio, Giulio."

"Big worry, George."

"You'll drive yourself mad that way."

"I no mad at you. Just him." He lay one thin finger on his heart, lightly as though afraid of rousing it.

"I don't mean angry . . ."

But Giulio was already tired of talking, and was plucking at the quilt again, ill, annoyed, retreating into sleep.

"Giulio, please, you've talked a little. Talk a little more—stay."

With an effort, his eyes sick and distant, Giulio stayed.

But now that he had his attention, George did not know where to begin, what to say. His mind spun; his tongue formed a few tentative words; then, clubbed by an immense fatigue, he sank into a chair with his head in his hands.

"I'm sick man," Giulio explained tonelessly, closing his eyes. After a silence he opened them and looked over at George, painfully, as though from under a crushing weight. "Tonight I hold your hand in bed again, like always. Hold your hand every night, you know that."

"You hold *my* hand?" George asked softly, lifting his head.

"In daytime," Giulio said slowly, his eyes laboriously fixed on George's attentive face, "in daytime only the bones and worms. But in the night . . . in the night, I see other things, too . . ." He was silent for a moment until a twinge had passed, then spoke again. "See you, George. And I hold your hand. Make you feel better . . ." His eyes still fixed on George's face, he gave an apologetic twitch of the lip as his lids closed, and slowly he nodded off to sleep.

Between the Funerals

Ann B. Tracy

Murphy's getting married. Surprise, surprise! We had him pegged for a lifelong bachelor (no rarity in this undermated family) but he was, it seems, just being frugal with his dating money. Now he's fetched a fiancee back from Winnipeg, where he's been doing graduate study, and my mother and I are giddy with the novelty. We haven't added a family member since Murphy himself was born, and now there'll be a whole new relative, bringing along her own story like a character in a hypertext novel. We're delighted with Zirka from the start: she's bright and agreeable and funny, and comes with a bonus of cultural exoticism—she laughs at our struggle to say her name right, while we find her lapses into Ukrainian consonant sounds no end endearing, and she knows how to cook ethnic things we never heard of. She's at first a bit stunned by the skylarking of the family women, having come from a house where nobody whistles or fools around in front of the icons, but she rallies—she's clearly made of the right stuff. Only a few years from now she'll be wearing black leather skirts and driving a vicious bargain in Tibetan bazaars, and nobody will be surprised.

Her family are somewhat stunned too, at having acquired a hairy American. American popularity in Canada is even lower than usual. Murphy not only isn't Ukrainian, he isn't even Catholic, though at least (as a kind aunt points out) the Baptists have a radio program. But the match is made, and in Winnipeg they welcome us to the most exciting wedding we've ever seen, with gold crowns and book-kissing and exhortations in a tongue as mysteriously religious as glossolalia.

In the half day before our plane leaves, my mother and I go shopping at The Bay. By the time we're through at the regional gifts section we've lost our bearings completely, have no idea which way we came in. I stand around vaguely waiting for my mother to lead, as she has, after all, done for my whole life. In a bit it occurs to me that nothing is happening. I look at her, and she's looking at me, clearly waiting for *me* to lead *her* out, this short, white-haired person that I'm suddenly supposed to be responsible for. I'm appalled. I can't believe that a major transition would happen this way, with no discussion. It's not as though one of us had just turned a milestone age. My mother has never announced, "I'm sixty-five now and retiring from management" or "You have now officially entered middle age and become the leader." What is going on in her head and how did she arrive at this point? She just gives me a trustful, dependent look. There's a moment when I can't catch my breath and I want to scream and protest that I'm not ready for this changing of the guard. But what's the use?

"I think it's over this way," I say, and she follows me.

Source: Excerpted from "Between the Funerals" by A. Tracy, 1992. Reprinted with permission of the author.

The Horned Toad

Gerald Haslam

"*Expectoran su sangre!*" exclaimed great-grandma when I showed her the small horned toad I had removed from my breast pocket. I turned toward my mother, who translated: "They spit blood."

"*De los ojos,*" Grandma added. "From their eyes," Mother explained, herself uncomfortable in the presence of the small beast.

I grinned, "Awwwwww."

But my great-grandmother did not smile. "*Son muy toxicos,*" she nodded with finality. Mother moved back an involuntary step, her hands suddenly busy at her breast. "Put that thing down," she ordered.

"His name's John," I said.

"Put John down and not in your pocket, either," my mother nearly shouted. "Those things are very poisonous. Didn't you understand what Grandma said?"

I shook my head.

"Well . . ." Mother looked from one of us to the other—spanning four generations of California, standing three feet apart—and said, "Of course you didn't. Please take him back where you got him, and be careful. We'll all feel better when you do." The tone of her voice told me that the discussion had ended, so I released the little reptile where I'd captured him.

During those years in Oildale, the mid-1940s, I needed only to walk across the street to find a patch of virgin desert. Neighborhood kids called it simply "the vacant lot," less than an acre without houses or sidewalks. Not that we were desperate for desert then, since we could walk into its scorched skin a mere half-mile west, north, and east. To the south, incongruously, flowed the icy Kern River, fresh from the Sierras and surrounded by riparian forest.

Ours was rich soil formed by that same Kern River as it ground Sierra granite and turned it into coarse sand, then carried it down into the valley and deposited it over millenia along its many changes of channels. The ants that built miniature volcanoes on the vacant lot left piles of tiny stones with telltale markings of black on white. Deeper than ants could dig were pools of petroleum that led to many fortunes and lured men like my father from Texas. The dry hills to the east and north sprouted forests of wooden derricks.

Despite the abundance of open land, plus the constant lure of the river where desolation and verdancy met, most kids relied on the vacant lot as their primary playground. Even with its bullheads and stinging insects, we played everything from football to kick-the-can on it. The lot actually resembled my father's head, bare in the middle but full of growth around the edges: weeds, stickers, cactuses, and a few bushes. We played our games on its sandy center, and conducted such sports as ant fights and lizard hunts on its brushy periphery.

That spring, when I discovered the lone horned toad near the back of the lot, had been

Source: "The Horned Toad" by Gerald Haslam, from *Growing Up Chicana/o*, edited by Tiffany Ana López, 1993. New York: Avon Books. Copyright 1993 by Gerald Haslam. Reprinted by permission of the author.

rough on my family. Earlier, there had been quiet, unpleasant tension between Mom and Daddy. He was a silent man, little given to emotional displays. It was difficult for him to show affection and I guess the openness of Mom's family made him uneasy. Daddy had no kin in California and rarely mentioned any in Texas. He couldn't seem to understand my mother's large, intimate family, their constant noisy concern for one another, and I think he was a little jealous of the time she gave everyone, maybe even me.

I heard her talking on the phone to my various aunts and uncles, usually in Spanish. Even though I couldn't understand—Daddy had warned her not to teach me that foreign tongue because it would hurt me in school, and she'd complied—I could sense the stress. I had been afraid they were going to divorce, since she only used Spanish to hide things from me. I'd confronted her with my suspicion, but she comforted me, saying, no, that was not the problem. They were merely deciding when it would be our turn to care for Grandma. I didn't really understand, although I was relieved.

I later learned that my great-grandmother—whom we simply called "Grandma"—had been moving from house to house within the family, trying to find a place she'd accept. She hated the city, and most of the aunts and uncles lived in Los Angeles. Our house in Oildale was much closer to the open country where she'd dwelled all her life. She had wanted to come to our place right away because she had raised my mother from a baby when my own grandmother died. But the old lady seemed unimpressed with Daddy, whom she called *"ese gringo."*

In truth, we had more room, and my dad made more money in the oil patch than almost anyone else in the family. Since my mother was the closest to Grandma, our place was the logical one for her, but Ese Gringo didn't see it that way, I guess, at least not at first. Finally, after much debate, he relented.

In any case, one windy afternoon, my Uncle Manuel and Aunt Toni drove up and deposited four-and-a-half feet of bewigged, bejeweled Spanish spitfire: a square, pale face topped by a tightly-curled black wig that hid a bald head—her hair having been lost to typhoid nearly sixty years before—her small white hands veined with rivers of blue. She walked with a prancing bounce that made her appear half her age, and she barked orders in Spanish from the moment she emerged from Manuel and Toni's car. Later, just before they left, I heard Uncle Manuel tell my dad, "Good luck, Charlie. That old lady's dynamite." Daddy only grunted.

She had been with us only two days when I tried to impress her with my horned toad. In fact, nothing I did seemed to impress her, and she referred to me as *el malcriado,* causing my mother to shake her head. Mom explained to me that Grandma was just old and lonely for Grandpa and uncomfortable in town. Mom told me that Grandma had lived over half a century in the country, away from the noise, away from clutter, away from people. She refused to accompany my mother on shopping trips, or anywhere else. She even refused to climb into a car, and I wondered how Uncle Manuel had managed to load her up in order to bring her to us.

She disliked sidewalks and roads, dancing across them when she had to, then appearing to wipe her feet on earth or grass. Things too civilized simply did not please her. A brother of hers had been killed in the great San Francisco earthquake and that had been the end of her tolerance of cities. Until my great-grandfather died, they lived on a small rancho near Arroyo Cantua, north of Coalinga. Grandpa, who had come north from Sonora as a youth to work as a *vaquero,* had bred horses and cattle, and cowboyed for other ranchers, scraping together enough of a living to raise eleven children.

He had been, until the time of his death, a lean, dark-skinned man with wide shoulders, a large nose, and a sweeping handlebar mustache that was white when I knew him. His Indian blood darkened all his progeny so that not even I was as fair-skinned as my great-grandmother, Ese Gringo for a father or not.

As it turned out, I didn't really understand very much about Grandma at all. She was old, of course, yet in many ways my parents treated her as though she were younger than me, walking her to the bathroom at night and bringing her presents from the store. In other ways—drinking wine at dinner, for example—she was granted adult privileges. Even Daddy didn't drink wine except on special occasions. After Grandma moved in, though, he began to occasionally join her for a glass, sometimes even sitting with her on the porch for a premeal sip.

She held court on our front porch, often gazing toward the desert hills east of us or across the street at kids playing on the lot. Occasionally, she would rise, cross the yard and sidewalk and street, skip over them, sometimes stumbling on the curb, and wipe her feet on the lot's sandy soil, then she would slowly circle the boundary between the open middle and the brushy sides, searching for something, it appeared. I never figured out what.

One afternoon I returned from school and saw Grandma perched on the porch as usual, so I started to walk around the house to avoid her sharp, mostly incomprehensible, tongue. She had already spotted me. *"Venga aqui!"* she ordered, and I understood.

I approached the porch and noticed that Grandma was vigorously chewing something. She held a small white bag in one hand. Saying *"Qué deseas tomar?"* she withdrew a large orange gumdrop from the bag and began slowly chewing it in her toothless mouth, smacking loudly as she did so. I stood below her for a moment trying to remember the word for candy. Then it came to me: *"Dulce,"* I said.

Still chewing, Grandma replied, *"Mande?"*

Knowing she wanted a complete sentence, I again struggled, then came up with *"Deseo dulce."*

She measured me for a moment, before answering in nearly perfect English, "Oh, so you wan' some candy. Go to the store an' buy some."

I don't know if it was the shock of hearing her speak English for the first time, or the way she had denied me a piece of candy, but

I suddenly felt tears warm my cheeks and I sprinted into the house and found Mom, who stood at the kitchen sink. "Grandma just talked English," I burst between light sobs.

"What's wrong?" she asked as she reached out to stroke my head.

"Grandma can talk English," I repeated.

"Of course she can," Mom answered. "What's wrong?"

I wasn't sure what was wrong, but after considering, I told Mom that Grandma had teased me. No sooner had I said that than the old woman appeared at the door and hiked her skirt. Attached to one of her petticoats by safety pins were several small tobacco sacks, the white cloth kind that closed with yellow drawstrings. She carefully unhooked one and opened it, withdrawing a dollar, then handed the money to me. *"Para su dulce,"* she said. Then, to my mother, she asked, "Why does he bawl like a motherless calf?"

"It's nothing," Mother replied.

"Do not weep, little one," the old lady comforted me, "Jesus and the Virgin love you." She smiled and patted my head. To my mother she said as though just realizing it, "Your baby?"

Somehow that day changed everything. I wasn't afraid of my great-grandmother any longer and, once I began spending time with her on the porch, I realized that my father had also begun directing increased attention to the old woman. Almost every evening Ese Gringo was sharing wine with Grandma. They talked out there, but I never did hear a real two-way conversation between them. Usually Grandma rattled on and Daddy nodded. She'd chuckle and pat his hand and he might grin, even grunt a word or two, before she'd begin talking again. Once I saw my mother standing by the front window watching them together, a smile playing across her face.

No more did I sneak around the house to avoid Grandma after school. Instead, she waited for me and discussed my efforts in class gravely, telling Mother that I was a bright boy, *"muy inteligente,"* and that I should be sent to the nuns who would train me. I would make a fine priest. When Ese

Gringo heard that, he smiled and said, "He'd make a fair-to-middlin' Holy Roller preacher, too." Even Mom had to chuckle, and my great-grandmother shook her finger at Ese Gringo. "Oh you debil, Sharlie!" she cackled.

Frequently, I would accompany Grandma to the lot where she would explain that no fodder could grow there. Poor pasture or not, the lot was at least unpaved, and Grandma greeted even the tiniest new cactus or flowering weed with joy. "Look how beautiful," she would croon. "In all this ugliness, it lives." Oildale was my home and it didn't look especially ugly to me, so I could only grin and wonder.

Because she liked the lot and things that grew there, I showed her the horned toad when I captured it a second time. I was determined to keep it, although I did not discuss my plans with anyone. I also wanted to hear more about the bloody eyes, so I thrust the small animal nearly into her face one afternoon. She did not flinch. *"Ola señor sangre de ojos,"* she said with a mischievous grin. *"Qué tal?"* It took me a moment to catch on.

"You were kidding before," I accused.

"Of course," she acknowledged, still grinning.

"But why?"

"Because the little beast belongs with his own kind in his own place, not in your pocket. Give him his freedom, my son."

I had other plans for the horned toad, but I was clever enough not to cross Grandma. "Yes, Ma'am," I replied. That night I placed the reptile in a flower bed cornered by a brick wall Ese Gringo had built the previous summer. It was a spot rich with insects for the toad to eat, and the little wall, only a foot high, must have seemed massive to so squat an animal.

Nonetheless, the next morning, when I searched for the horned toad it was gone. I had no time to explore the yard for it, so I trudged off to school, my belly troubled. How could it have escaped? Classes meant little to me that day. I thought only of my lost pet—I had changed his name to Juan, the same as my great-grandfather—and where I might find him.

I shortened my conversation with Grandma that afternoon so I could search for Juan. "What do you seek?" the old woman asked me as I poked through flower beds beneath the porch. "Praying mantises," I improvised, and she merely nodded, surveying me. But I had eyes only for my lost pet, and I continued pushing through branches and brushing aside leaves. No luck.

Finally, I gave in and turned toward the lot. I found my horned toad nearly across the street, crushed. It had been heading for the miniature desert and had almost made it when an automobile's tire had run over it. One notion immediately swept me: if I had left it on its lot, it would still be alive. I stood rooted there in the street, tears slicking my cheeks, and a car honked its horn as it passed, the driver shouting at me.

Grandma joined me, and stroked my back. "The poor little beast," was all she said, then she bent slowly and scooped up what remained of the horned toad and led me out of the street. "We must return him to his own place," she explained, and we trooped, my eyes still clouded, toward the back of the vacant lot. Carefully, I dug a hole with a piece of wood. Grandma placed Juan in it and covered him. We said an Our Father and a Hail Mary, then Grandma walked me back to the house. "Your little Juan is safe with God, my son," she comforted. We kept the horned toad's death a secret, and we visited his small grave frequently.

Grandma fell just before school ended and summer vacation began. As was her habit, she had walked alone to the vacant lot but this time, on her way back, she tripped over the curb and broke her hip. That following week, when Daddy brought her home from the hospital, she seemed to have shrunken. She sat hunched in a wheelchair on the porch, gazing with faded eyes toward the hills or at the lot, speaking rarely. She still sipped wine every evening with Daddy and even I could tell how concerned he was about her. It got to where he'd look in on her before leaving for work every morning and again at night before turning in. And if Daddy was home, Grandma always wanted him to push her chair when she needed moving, calling, "Sharlie!" until he arrived.

I was tugged from sleep on the night she died by voices drumming through the walls into darkness. I couldn't understand them, but was immediately frightened by the uncommon sounds of words in the night. I struggled from bed and walked into the living room just as Daddy closed the front door and a car pulled away.

Mom was sobbing softly on the couch and Daddy walked to her, stroked her head, then noticed me. "Come here, son," he gently ordered.

I walked to him and, uncharacteristically, he put an arm around me. "What's wrong?" I asked, near tears myself. Mom looked up, but before she could speak, Daddy said, "Grandma died." Then he sighed heavily and stood there with his arms around his weeping wife and son.

The next day my Uncle Manuel and Uncle Arnulfo, plus Aunt Chintia, arrived and over food they discussed with my mother where Grandma should be interred. They argued that it would be too expensive to transport her body home and, besides, they could more easily visit her grave if she was buried in Bakersfield. "They have such a nice, manicured grounds at Greenlawn," Aunt Chintia pointed out. Just when it seemed they had agreed, I could remain silent no longer. "But Grandma has to go home," I burst. "She has to! It's the only thing she really wanted. We can't leave her in the city."

Uncle Arnulfo, who was on the edge, snapped to Mother that I belonged with the other children, not interrupting adult conversation. Mom quietly agreed, but I refused. My

father walked into the room then. "What's wrong?" he asked.

"They're going to bury Grandma in Bakersfield, Daddy. Don't let 'em, please."

"Well, son . . ."

"When my horny toad got killed and she helped me to bury it, she said we had to return him to his place."

"Your horny toad?" Mother asked.

"He got squished and me and Grandma buried him in the lot. She said we had to take him back to his place. Honest she did."

No one spoke for a moment, then my father, Ese Gringo, who stood against the sink, responded: "That's right . . ." he paused, then added, "We'll bury her." I saw a weary smile cross my mother's face. "If she wanted to go back to the ranch then that's where we have to take her," Daddy said.

I hugged him and he, right in front of everyone, hugged back.

No one argued. It seemed, suddenly, as though they had all wanted to do exactly what I had begged for. Grown-ups baffled me. Late that week the entire family, hundreds it seemed, gathered at the little Catholic church in Coalinga for mass, then drove out to Arroyo Cantua and buried Grandma next to Grandpa. She rests there today.

My mother, father, and I drove back to Oildale that afternoon across the scorching westside desert, through sand and tumbleweeds and heat shivers. Quiet and sad, we knew we had done our best. Mom, who usually sat next to the door in the front seat, snuggled close to Daddy, and I heard her whisper to him, "Thank you, Charlie," as she kissed his cheek.

Daddy squeezed her, hesitated as if to clear his throat, then answered, "When you're family, you take care of your own."

34

Elders in Southeast Asian Refugee Families

Barbara W. K. Yee

For the elderly in Southeast Asian refugee families, the experience of aging in America is very different from what they had expected for their second half of life. These elderly Southeast Asian refugees must cope with their rapidly acculturating younger family members, while having to take on different roles and expectations in a frighteningly foreign culture. The gap between the American experience of age, gender, family, and work roles and that of Southeast Asian cultures highlights just a few major differences. Life-course issues such as historical context upon migration, life stage, age at immigration, and acculturation opportunities will have a significant impact upon the adjustment and aging of these immigrants in America. Waves of Southeast Asian refugees who have come to American shores have differed dramatically, for example, in social class or urbanization, and these differences have influenced survival skills and adaptation to American life in predictable ways.

A large majority of middle-aged and elderly Southeast Asian refugees either migrated with their families or joined their relatives through the family reunification program. As a result, there are very few Southeast Asian elders in the United States who have no relatives here. Yet, the large extended family system traditional in Vietnam, has large holes for Southeast Asian families living in America. Family reunification is the major goal for many Southeast Asian families, especially family elders.

As suggested in Gelfand and Yee (1992), the fabric of aging in America will become increasingly complex and diverse. The influences of new cultures will be woven into the American culture by immigrants. These new Americans will, over time, incorporate varying degrees of American culture within themselves and their families. The trend into the year 2000 will be increasing diversity of the aging (Gelfand & Yee, 1992) and general population (Sue, 1991). Our understanding of this diversity will enhance our ability as a society to successfully address the beautiful mosaic of elders in the future.

The purpose of this article is to examine the cultural transformation of the Southeast Asian refugee family as seen from the perspective of the older generation. The story is only beginning to be told. A closer examination of these rapid changes in the Southeast Asian refugee family must be made because they have major implications for elders in these families. Changes in age and gender roles and in intergenerational relationships have occurred within Southeast Asian refugee families after migration to this country. This article will examine the impact of these significant changes on the elder Southeast Asian refugee ("elder" as defined by this cultural group includes both middle-aged and elderly family members).

Source: "Elders in Southeast Asian Refugee Families" by B. W. K. Yee, from *Generations*, Summer 1992, pp. 24-27. Reprinted with permission from *Generations*, 833 Market Street, Suite 512, San Francisco, CA 94103. Copyright 1992, ASA.

Age Roles

Many younger Southeast Asian refugee elders may also find that they are not considered elderly by American society. Migration to a new culture changes the timing and definitions of life stages across the life span. For instance, in the traditional Hmong culture, one can become an elder at 35 years of age when one becomes a grandparent. With grandparent status, these elder Hmong can retire and expect their children to take financial responsibility for the family. Retiring at 35 years of age is not acceptable in this country (Yee, 1989).

There is a strong influence of Confucianism in traditional Vietnamese society (Liem & Kehmeier, 1979). Confucius instituted the Cult of Ancestors, which is reflected in filial piety and respect for the family elders. Age roles within society and the family were hierarchical, with strict rules for social interaction. The child was to have total obedience to the father and to venerate him; the same was true for the relationship between a woman and her father—and later her husband—and for the student/teacher relationship. The major discrepancy for refugee families is between the traditional roles of elders in the homeland and those available to them in the United States (Weinstein-Shr & Henkin, 1991).

Weinstein-Shr and Henkin find that because the older refugees lack facility with the English language and American culture, their credibility is decreased when advising younger family members about important decisions. As youngest family members take on primary roles as family mediators within American institutions—the school or legal system and social service agencies, for example—elders gradually lose some of their leadership roles in the eyes of the family and the larger American society (Yee, in press).

Weinstein-Shr and Henkin also recognize that the older refugees try to maintain their role as transmitters of traditional values and customs, but grandchildren often reject their cultural heritage in order to lessen their cognitive dissonance during acculturation to American ways. The majority of refugee families are still struggling to survive in the work and educational arenas so that they can support dependent family members. This translates into very little time left to show respect toward family elders (Detzner, in press).

Some research in other Asian-American groups, however, shows an increased interest in and appreciation of cultural roots during the adolescent and young adult period by some Asian-Americans (see review in Kitano & Daniels, 1988; D. W. Sue & D. Sue, 1990). A so-called search for cultural roots occurs during critical periods of the life span, when people look for components of their identity. During this phase, the family elders may be called upon to help younger family members explore, discover, and appreciate their cultural heritage and family history.

Although older refugees provide child-care assistance and perform household duties for their families (Detzner, in press), they can no longer offer financial support, land, or other material goods as they would have in the homeland. The refugee process strips away the refugee elders' resources, one of the bases for high status and control of inheritance in the family. What is more important, elderly refugees can no longer provide advice and lend their wisdom: Because their counsel is derived from traditional culture and tied to the homeland, it is too foreign to American ways. Older refugees find that they are increasingly dependent upon their children and grandchildren for help rather than the reverse (see review in Yee, 1989). This role reversal between the elder and young generation has created numerous family conflicts in the Southeast Asian refugee communities (Yee, in press).

Intergenerational Roles

Tran (1991) found that elderly refugees who lived within the nuclear or extended family had a better sense of social adjustment than those living outside the family context. Of elderly living in a family context, those living in overcrowded conditions or in homes including children under the age of 16 experienced a poorer sense of adjustment. The relationship between overcrowding and life satisfaction holds regardless of age and across numerous groups. The relationship between living with younger children and poorer adjustment for the Southeast Asian elderly may be, as Tran speculates, a result of more economic pressures and stressors found in households with younger children. Tran's second speculation is that intergenerational conflicts among three generations living under the same roof create great stress because the younger generations are very Americanized. This acculturation gap leads to greater conflicts among the generations and depresses satisfaction with or adjustment to the refugee elders' new life because their general life satisfaction is closely tied to satisfaction with family relationships (Gelfand, 1982; Yee, in press). The age of these refugees was also inversely related to poorer adjustment. Older refugees have poorer adjustment than their younger counterparts (a finding that has been replicated in other studies) because older refugees experience more losses and fewer gains after coming to America than do their younger family members (Yee & Nguyen, 1987).

In a recent study, Rick and Forward (1992) examined the relationship between level of acculturation and perceived intergenerational differences among high school students from Hmong refugee families. These authors found that students perceived themselves to be more acculturated than their parents. Higher acculturation was associated with higher perceived intergenerational differences. Rick and Forward examined three specific acculturation items concerning the elderly: consulting the elderly on life issues, taking care of the elderly, and respecting the elderly. It appears that values concerning relationships with family elders may be the last to change, if at all, following changes in decisions about timing of marriage, having children, appropriate dress, where to live before marriage, ideal family size, or decisions on marriage.

Gender Roles

Refugee elders must cope with the gender role differences practiced in the homeland versus those in the United States. Even before migration, traditional gender roles were changing in Southeast Asia during the Vietnam war. Men of military age were away fighting the war, and their spouses were solely responsible for tasks normally divided along gender lines. When Vietnamese came to this country, changes in traditional gender roles sped up and became more dramatic. This was especially true for middle-aged and employed refugees. There were more employment opportunities for younger refugees and middle-aged refugee women because their employment expectations often fit with the lower status jobs that were among the few opportunities open to refugees with few English skills and little or non-transferable educational credentials. Age bias against older men and women may be operating as well, and many elders could not find gainful employment outside the home. Many middle-aged women and younger refugees of both sexes became family breadwinners. This was a radical change for the male elders, who had been the major breadwinners of the family.

The body of empirical and anecdotal work on adaptation and adjustment of refugee populations suggests that there might be a gender difference in short- versus long-term adaptation (see review in Yee, 1989). It appears that at least for short-term adaptation, which includes the period soon after migration to as long as 15 years, middle-aged and elderly refugee women adapt to life in the new country in a more positive manner than do men of the same age. Several investigators have attributed this gender difference to the continuity of female roles from the homeland to America (Barresi, 1992; Detzner, in press; Yee, 1989). Female refugee elders perform important but not necessarily honorific roles in the family such as household tasks and childcare, whereas male refugee elders, especially the old men, have less clear functional roles in the family. This latter pattern is especially evident for Cambodian men (Detzner, in press).

The ability of refugees to perform work roles outside the family also shows a gender pattern (see review in Yee, in press). There is an expansion of work roles for both young adults and young middle-aged refugee women, which is especially true for the Vietnamese group. The down side is that both groups must also take on roles and responsibilities they had not anticipated for these periods in the life cycle.

By contrast, there is a constriction of work and family roles for refugee men, especially middle-aged and elderly men. Elderly refugee men experience a significant downward mobility. Migration created the loss of high status work, family, and community roles. Many of these refugee men are not able to recover their former status because their job skills may not be transferable to the United States or employers may be unwilling to hire an older worker. In addition, their lack of facility in English may form an insurmountable barrier to recovering their former job status by passing American credentialing tests (Yee, in press). After struggling for many years, these elderly refugees may resign by putting all their hope in the younger generation and giving the responsibility to achieve their lifelong goals to the next generation.

The pattern for long-term adaptation of refugee elders is yet to be determined empirically, but there are indications that the long-term adaptation of female refugee elders may not be so rosy. Middle-aged and elderly refugee women are integrated within the family in the short term. These elderly women provide household and childcare services in order to free younger family from these responsibilities so that they can work one or two jobs and perhaps go to school to ensure economic survival of the family. While these elderly refugee women are helping younger members of the family succeed in America, they themselves are often isolated at home and not learning new skills, English, or knowledge about American society, with which to cope with the new environment (Tran, 1988). After the family has passed through the stage of meeting basic survival needs, these elderly women may find that they are strangers in their own family and their new country. In other words, their adult children and grandchildren have acculturated to American ways in school and work settings, yet these elderly women have had few opportunities to be exposed to mainstream American culture.

Summary and Conclusions

The elders' place and role in the Southeast Asian family in the years to come are unknown, but there are several indicators that predict increasing difficulty for elderly female refugees. The impact of ethnicity and culture on aging is a dynamic process (Barresi, 1992). It is not unidirectional and unidimensional but bidirectional and multidimensional. The immigrant from another culture is touched and transformed by American culture. This transformation varies across individuals and life contexts. Something not as well recognized, but necessarily true, is that the American culture is forever changed by its association with these new Americans. Our great nation has derived its strength, creativity, and vision from our heritage of immigrants. Let us remember and appreciate this diversity. From within this diversity comes the force that will keep America at the cutting edge in a twenty-first century global society.

References

Barresi, C. M. (1992, Mardi 15). *The impact of ethnicity on aging: A review of theory, research, and issues.* Presentation at the American Society on Aging Annual meeting, San Diego, CA.

Detzner, D. F. (in press). Conflict in Southeast Asian refugee families: A life history approach. In J. Gilgun, K. Daly, & R. Handel (Eds.), *Qualitative methods in family research.* Newbury Park, CA: Sage.

Gelfand, D. E. (1982). *Aging: The ethnic factor.* Boston: Little, Brown.

Gelfand, D., & Yee, B.W.K. (1992). Trends and forces: Influence of immigration, migration, and acculturation on the fabric of aging in America. *Generations, 15*(4), 7-10.

Kitano, H., & Daniels, R. (1988). *Asian Americans.* Englewood Cliffs, NJ: Prentice Hall.

Liem, N. D., & Kehmeier, D. F. (1979). The Vietnamese. In J. R McDermott (Ed.), *Peoples and cultures of Hawaii.* Honolulu: University of Hawaii Press.

Rick, K., & Forward, J. (1992). Acculturation and perceived intergenerational differences among Hmong youth. *Journal of Cross-Cultural Psychology, 23*(1), 85-94.

Sue, D. W., & Sue, D. (1990). *Counseling the culturally different: Theory and practice* (2nd ed.). New York: John Wiley.

Sue, S. (1991). Ethnicity and culture in psychological research and practice. In J. D. Goodchilds (Ed.), *Psychological perspectives on human diversity in America.* Washington, DC: American Psychological Association.

Tran, T. V. (1988). Sex differences in English language acculturation and learning strategies among Vietnamese adults aged 40 and over in the United States. *Sex Roles, 19,* 747-758.

Tran, T. V. (1991). Family living arrangement and social adjustment among three ethnic groups of elderly Indochinese refugees. *International Journal of Aging and Human Development, 32*(2), 91-102.

Weinstein-Shr, G., & Henkin, N. Z. (1991). Continuity and change: Intergenerational relations in Southeast Asian refugee families. *Marriage and Family Review, 16,* 351-367.

Yee, B.W.K. (1989). Loss of one's homeland and culture during the middle years. In R. A. Kalish (Ed.), *Coping with the losses of middle age.* Newbury Park, CA: Sage.

Yee, B.W.K. (in press). Markers of successful aging among Vietnamese refugee women. *Women and Therapy, 12*(2).

Yee, B.W.K., & Nguyen, D. T. (1987). Correlates of drug abuse and abuse among Indochinese refugees: Mental health implications. *Journal of Psychoactive Drugs, 19,* 77-83.

35

Grandparenting Styles: Native American Perspectives

Joan Weibel-Orlando

Grandparental roles among contemporary North American Indians are expressed across a range of activities, purposes, and levels of intensity. The ways these components fit together are so varied as to be identified as distinct grandparenting styles. These five grandparenting styles are identified below as: cultural conservator, custodian, ceremonial, distanced, and fictive.

Freedom of choice in the creation of one's particular brand of grandparenthood is considerable. Some American Indian grandparents petition their children for the privilege of primary care responsibilities for one or more grandchildren with considerable success. When parents are reluctant to relinquish care of a child to its grandparents, individuals who relish continuing child care responsibilities past their childbearing years activate alternative strategies of both traditional and contemporaneous origin. Establishment of fictive kinship, provision of foster parent care, and involvement in cultural restoration programs in the public schools are among the alternative roles available to older American Indians whose grandchildren, either because of distance or parental reluctance, are not immediately accessible to them.

While custodial, fictive, ceremonial, and distanced grandparenting styles are evidenced cross-culturally, I suggest that the cultural conservator grandparenting style, if not particularly North American Indian, is essentially a phenomenon of general ethnic minority-group membership. Fearing loss of identity as a people because of the relentless assimilationist influences of contemporary life, many ethnic minority members view their elders as cultural resources for their children. Grandparents as cultural conservators constitute both a cultural continuity in that responsibility for the enculturation of the youngest generation was traditionally the role of the grandparents across American Indian tribal groups (Amoss, 1981; Schweitzer, 1987). Cognizant of the heady influences which attract their urbanized, educated, and upwardly mobile children away from tribal pursuits, many contemporary American Indian grandparents understand their roles as conservators and exemplars of a world view and ethos that may well disappear if they do not consistently and emphatically impart it to and enact it for their grandchildren.

Grandparenting Styles

What little literature there is on the role of the North American Indian grandparents in

Source: Excerpted from "Grandparenting Styles: Native American Perspectives" by J. Weibel-Orlando from *The Cultural Context of Aging: Worldwide Perspectives,* 1990 (pp. 109-125). New York: Bergin and Garvey, an imprint of Greenwood Publishing Group, Inc., Westport, CT. Reprinted by permission.

the enculturation of their grandchildren during historic times (sixteenth to nineteenth centuries) tends to be sketchy, ambiguous, and highly romanticized. Grandparents are depicted as storytellers (Barnett, 1955, p. 144), mentors to girls about to become socially acknowledged as women (Elmendorf & Kroeber, 1960, p. 439) and to boys old enough to embark upon the first of many vision quests (Amoss, 1981), and caretakers of children left orphaned by disease, war, or famine (Schweitzer, 1987). In all cases the literature depicts Indian grandparents as protective, permissive, affectionate, and tutorial in their interactions with their grandchildren. Only most recently has Pamela Amoss (1986) offered an intriguing analysis of the ambiguous nature of Northwest Coast Native American myths about grandmothers. In these legends the old women have the power both to protect and to destroy their progeny.

The generally acknowledged model of Indian grandparenting presented above fits most closely the cultural conservator and custodial models. In both cases, such grandparenting styles in contemporary American Indian family life spring from the same conditions and concerns that shaped historical grandparenting modes: practical issues of division of labor and the efficacy of freeing younger women so that they can participate more fully in the economic sector of the tribal community; nurturance of unprotected minors so as to maximize the continuance of the tribe as a social entity; and the belief that old age represents the culmination of cultural experience. Elders are thought to be those best equipped to transmit cultural lore across generations, thus ensuring the cultural integrity of the group.

The Cultural Conservator Grandparent

Being raised by one's grandparents is not an enculturative phenomenon unique to either twentieth-century rural or urban American Indian experience. In fact, grandmothers as primary caretakers of first and second grandchildren is a long-established native American child care strategy. Leo Simmons (1945) tells us that "old Crow grandmothers were considered essential elements in the household, engaged in domestic chores" (p. 84) while helping young mothers who were burdened with work. And Marjorie Schweitzer (1987) explains that "within the framework of the extended family a special relationship existed between grandparents and grandchildren which began at birth and lasted a lifetime. Children were cared for by grandparents and, in turn, the family cared for the old when they were feeble" (p. 169).

The cultural conservator role is a contemporary extension of this traditional relationship. Rather than accept an imposed role, the conservator grandparents actively solicit their children to allow the grandchildren to live with them for extended periods of time for the expressed purpose of exposing them to the American Indian way of life. Importantly, the cultural conservator is the modal grandparenting style among the families in this study.

Six families are best described by this term. One Sioux woman, who had two of her grandchildren living with her at the time of the interview, exemplifies the cultural conservator grandparenting style. The enthusiasm about having one or more grandchildren in her home for extended periods of time is tempered by the realization that, for her own children who grew up in an urban environment, the spiritual magnetism of reservation life is essentially lost. She regards their disdain for tribal life with consternation and ironic humor and consciously opts for taking a major role in the early socialization of her grandchildren. She views her children as being just "too far gone" (assimilated) for any attempt at repatriation on her part. Her role as the culture conservator grandmother, then, is doubly important. The grandchildren are her only hope for effecting both personal and cultural continuity: "The second- or third-generation Indian children out [in Los Angeles], most of them never get to see anything like . . . a sun dance or a memorial feast or giveaway or just stuff that Indians do back home. I wanted my children to be involved in them and know what it's all about. So that's the reason that I always try to keep my grandchildren whenever I can" (Sioux woman, sixty-seven, Pine Ridge, South Dakota).

She recognizes the primary caretaking aspects of her grandmotherhood as not only as traditionally American Indian, but also as a particularly Lakota thing to do: "The grandparents always took . . . at least the first grandchild to raise because that's just the way the Lakota did it. They [the grandparents] think that they're more mature and have had more experience and they could teach the children a lot more than the young parents, especially if the parents were young. . . . I'm still trying to carry on that tradition because my grandmother raised me most of the time up until I was nine years old."

She remembers her grandparents' enculturative styles as essentially conservative in the sense that those things they passed on to their grandchildren were taken from traditional Sioux lore. The grandparents rarely commanded or required the grandchild's allegiance to their particular world view. Rather, instruction took the form of suggestions about or presentation of models of exemplary behavior. "Well, my grandfather always told me what a Lakota woman wouldn't do and what they were supposed to do. But he never said I had to do anything." She purposely continues to shape her grandmotherhood on the cultural conservator model of her own grandparents. "I ask [my children] if [their children] could spend the summer with me if there isn't school and go with me to the Indian doings so that they'll know that they're Indian and know the culture and traditions. [I'm] just kind of building memories for them."

Those cultural and traditional aspects of Sioux life to which this grandmother exposes her city-born grandchildren include a wide range of ceremonial and informal activities. The children go everywhere with her. An active participant in village life, she and her grandchildren make continual rounds of American Indian church meetings, senior citizens lunches, tribal chapter hearings, powwows, memorial feasts, sun dances, funerals, giveaways, and rodeos. The children attend a tribe-run elementary school in which classes are taught in both English and Lakota. The children actively participate in the ceremonial life of the reservation, dancing in full regalia at powwows and helping their grandmother distribute gifts at giveaways and food at feasts. Most importantly, those grandchildren who live with her for long periods of time are immersed in the daily ordering of reservation life. Through the grandmother's firm, authoritative tutelage, complemented by their gentle and affectionate grandfather, and through the rough-and-tumble play with rural age-group members who, for the most part, can claim some kinship with the urban-born visitors, they learn, as did nineteenth-century Sioux children (through observation, example, and experimentation), their society's core values and interactional style.

Today, however, presenting one's grandchildren with traditional cultural lore has become a critical issue of cultural survival vis-à-vis a new and insidious enemy. Faced by consuming cultural alternatives and unmotivated or inexperienced children, American Indian grandparents can no longer assume the role of cultural conservator for their grandchildren as practiced historically. Rather, grandparents, concerned with continuity of tribal consciousness, must seize the role and force inculcation of traditional lore upon their grandchildren through a grandparenting style best described as cultural conservation.

References

Amoss, R. (1981). Cultural centrality and prestige for the elderly: The Coast Salish case. In C. Fry (Ed.), *Dimensions: Aging, culture and health* (pp. 47-63). Brooklyn, NY: J. F. Bergin.

Barnett, H. (1955). *The Coast Salish of British Columbia.* Eugene: University of Oregon Press.

Elmendorf, W., & Kroeber, A. (1960). *The structure of Twona culture with notes on Yurok culture.* Pullman: Washington State University Press.

Schweitzer, M. (1987). The elders: Cultural dimensions of aging in two American Indian communities. In J. Sokolovsky (Ed.), *Growing old in different societies.* Acton, MA: Copley.

Simmons, L. (1945). *The role of the aged in primitive society.* New Haven, CT: Yale University Press.

1   bell hooks challenges the idea that motherhood and family are sources of women's oppression. How might Elsa Barkley Brown respond to this argument? What parallels do you see between the image of the adult daughter-older mother relationship described by Brown and that developed by Alice Walker (in "In Search of Our Mothers' Gardens" in Part I)?

2   Official definitions of kin are based on blood and legal ties. How do these official definitions affect the lives of older gay men and lesbians? In what ways, if any, do you think changing attitudes toward homosexuality will produce differences between current cohorts and future cohorts of elderly gay men and lesbians?

3   Ann Tracy's story is told from the standpoint of the adult daughter. How might this account have been different had Tracy told the story from the mother's perspective?

4   The predominance of women as family caregivers of frail elderly should not mask the contributions of men. Male caregivers are most often older husbands caring for their wives. What differences would you predict between older women caring for their husbands and older men caring for their wives? Consider the meaning of care, changes in a couple's daily life, changes in their relationship, and sources of both burden and satisfaction.

5   Project yourself forward in time to the point at which your surviving parent is struggling to maintain independence in the face of increasing frailty. How do you visualize your role as caregiver? What other demands will compete for your time? If you have sisters or brothers, what factors will determine the division of parent care responsibilities among you and your siblings? How will the plans for care you devise be influenced by your social class?

6   Several of the readings in this book illustrate the role of grandparents as cultural conservators as described by Weibel-Orlando (see, for example, Kingsolver and Halsam). What evidence do you see in your own family that the oldest generation fulfills the role of "cultural conservator" or "family historian"?

1 West, D. (1995). *The wedding.* New York: Doubleday.

Dorothy West, a Harlem Renaissance writer now in her eighties, traces the history of an African American family. Her novel vividly illustrates the impact of historical time, changing opportunities, and the intersections of gender, race, and class.

2 Yee, B. (1990, Summer). Gender and family issues in minority groups. *Generations, 14,* 39-41.

A brief overview of empirical work on family and gender issues among elderly Native Americans, Asians and Pacific Islanders, and African Americans.

3 Dilworth-Anderson, P. (1992, Summer). Extended kin networks in black families. *Generations, 16,* 29-32.

This article by Dilworth-Anderson provides additional evidence regarding extended networks of kin and fictive kin among older African American families. She discusses the system of mutual aid characterizing these families and speculates on the role of extended families among future cohorts of elderly African Americans.

4 Bell-Scott, R., Guy-Sheftall, B., Jones Royster, J., Sims-Wood, J., DeCosta-Willis, M., & Fultz, L. (1991). *Double stitch: Black women write about mothers and daughters.* Boston: Beacon.

The editors use quilting as a metaphor for mother-daughter relationships among African American women. The stories, poems, and essays in this anthology elaborate on the material on mothers, daughters, and extended female networks introduced in this part. The editors are members of the editorial collective of *SAGE: A Scholarly Journal on Black Women.*

5 Tan, A. (1989). *The joy luck club.* New York: G. P. Putnam.

In her first novel, Amy Tan explores the bond among four Chinese American women and their adult daughters. Like the central character in the novel, Amy Tan is the daughter of Chinese parents who emigrated to California from China after the Red Army took over China. The stories of these four families bring to life the relationships between two cultures within one family.

6 Erdrich, L. (1984). *Love medicine*. Bloomington: Indiana University Press.

Louise Erdrich's first novel introduces us to an extended Chippewa family in North Dakota. In the nonlinear tradition of Native American writing, we see the Kapshaw family at various times during the 50 years between 1934 and 1984. Louise Erdrich is a Turtle Mountain Chippewa who grew up in North Dakota.

7 Allen, K. R. (1989). *Single women/family ties: Life histories of older women*. Newbury Park, CA: Sage.

As the author explains, women are socialized to structure their lives around an orderly sequence of marital and parental roles. Using a life course perspective, Katherine Allen explores the events and processes that characterize the family lives of never-married, childless women. Her work is based on in-depth, unstructured interviews with 30 women from the 1910 birth cohort.

8 Dwyer, J. W., & Coward, R. T. (Eds.). (1992). *Gender, families and elder care*. Newbury Park, CA: Sage.

This volume explores the gendered nature of family caregiving. In exploring the way gender structures the social context of caregiving, the authors of the 13 chapters explore the structure of specific caregiving relationships (spouse-spouse, parent-child, sibling-sibling), the link between theory and research, and implications for policy and practice.

9 Kimmel, D. C. (1992, Summer). The families of older gay men and lesbians. *Generations, 16,* 37-38.

Kimmel's review of the limited research available illustrates the ways in which older gay men and lesbians maintain family relationships and create networks of close friends that provide the same type of supports we typically associate with families. Kimmel also describes some of the adaptive resources elderly gay men and lesbians have developed in coping with discrimination based on sexual orientation.

10 Coontz, S. (1992). *The way we never were: American families and the nostalgia trap*. New York: Basic Books.

Coontz's historical study of American family life demonstrates that the "traditional nuclear family" was neither traditional nor nuclear. Her demythologizing of American families enriches our understanding of the family contexts in which current cohorts of elderly people grew up and grew old.

11 Gates, H. L., Jr. (1994). *Colored people, a memoir*. New York: Random House.

Described as a story "of a family, of a village, and of a special time and place in American history," Gates's memoir revisits his childhood in Piedmont, West Virginia (population 2,565). His description of a "small, intimate, middle-class colored community" provides a glimpse into the context in which many elderly African Americans experienced their early adulthoods.

PART V

Health and Mortality

Inequalities

Inequalities in Health and Mortality: Gender, Race, and Class

Poor health and disability are among the most feared aspects of old age (National Council on the Aging, 1976). As we get older, the risk of health problems increases. More than 80% of people 65 years of age and older have one or more chronic conditions (National Center for Health Statistics, 1991). Only about 45% of these people report limitations in their desired activities, however, and only about 2% are confined to bed. As with other resources, health is distributed unevenly across the elderly population. People who are disadvantaged by systems of inequality have more chronic conditions, greater disability, and shorter life expectancy than their more privileged counterparts. As we have seen throughout this book, social structure imposes conditions on members of disadvantaged groups that reduce their life chances. These limited opportunities result in inadequate health care and greater exposure to risk factors for disease and mortality at each life stage. The poorer health experienced by disadvantaged people in old age reflects the cumulative effects of a lifetime of blocked opportunities for healthy lifestyles and adequate health care. Here we explore ways in which people's positions on hierarchies based on gender, race, and class affect their health status in old age and the resources available for coping with illness and disability. Our discussion addresses the following questions:

1. How does position on hierarchies based on gender, race, and class influence the likelihood of poor health and mortality?
2. Are disadvantaged elderly people more likely than their privileged counterparts to be exposed to risk factors for disease and death?
3. How do these systems of inequality affect the quantity and quality of health care available to older people?
4. What strategies do people use to manage illness on their own?

How Does Position on Hierarchies Based on Gender, Race, and Class Influence the Likelihood of Poor Health and Mortality?

All three of the systems of inequality we have discussed structure the health status of older people. In most cases, people occupying more privileged positions enjoy better health, less disability, and longer life than their more disadvantaged counterparts. The strongest of these links is between social class and health.

Universally, the poor, the poorly educated, and those on the lower rungs of the occupational ladder are sicker, more functionally limited, and more likely to die earlier than people with higher levels of wealth, income, occupation, and education (Kitagawa & Hauser, 1973; Williams, 1990). Heart disease, cancer, and stroke—the leading causes of death for all elderly people—are more prevalent among people with less than eight years of formal schooling, family incomes below $14,000 a year, and a lifetime of employment in working-class occupations. Social class differences in subjective health assessments are also large. Lower-strata individuals consistently report worse health than their more privileged counterparts. This greater prevalence of illness and disability in the lower strata is not confined to old age. People in the lowest social classes experience poorer health throughout their lives, and they encounter chronic disease and disability earlier in life than people occupying more privileged positions. In fact, health policy experts underscore the importance of equalizing income and occupational and educational opportunities earlier in life so as to equalize the chances for good health in old age (House et al., 1990).

Disadvantaged minority group status is also associated with poor health. This is particularly true of older African American and Native American elderly. African Americans between the ages of 65 and 85 are more likely than whites to die. This difference holds for all three leading causes of death in old age: heart disease, cerebrovascular disease, and cancer. In 1988, heart disease mortality for elderly African Americans was 5% higher than for comparable whites, cancer mortality was 170% higher, and cerebrovascular mortality was 24% higher (National Center for Health Statistics, 1991). Elderly African Americans also experience more difficulties with activities of daily living (e.g., eating, bathing, dressing, using the toilet, getting in and out of a bed or chair, walking, and getting outside) and with instrumental activities of daily living (e.g., preparing meals, shopping for personal items, managing money, using the telephone, and doing housework). Not a surprise, given these differences in disease and disability, African Americans are about twice as likely as whites to assess their health as poor. Native Americans also encounter higher rates of disease and disability across the life course. They are more likely than the general population to die from influenza, pneumonia, diabetes, alcoholism, suicide, and homicide. A lifetime of poverty translates into poor nutrition, substandard living conditions, and inadequate medical care, all of which undermine the likelihood of living to old age. In fact, only one in three Native Americans can expect to reach age 65 (Kart, 1990).

Despite greater functional limitations, older African Americans at almost all ages are much less likely than older whites to be living in nursing or personal care homes. Under age 75, whites are slightly less likely than African Americans to be living in nursing and personal care homes, but the percentage of whites who are institutionalized is larger than the percentage of African Americans after age 75. Whites between 75 and 84 years are about one and one half times more likely than African Americans that age to be institutionalized. At ages 85 and over, whites are almost twice as likely to be institutionalized, with the ratio increasing to whites being about four times as likely after age 100 (Gibson & Jackson, 1992). What accounts for these increasingly large race disparities in successively older age groups? Slower rates of decline in health status for very old African Americans than for very old whites? Poverty that increases more with age among older African Americans than older whites? Race differences in family values on institutionalization? More support in the community for African Americans with functional disabilities? Or racial discrimination in nursing homes? Gerontologists have not yet learned the answers to these questions.

Although it is true that up to about age 85, African Americans are more likely than nonminority elders to have poorer objective and subjective health, more functional limitations, and a higher probability of death, something very curious happens at about age 85. When people 65 years and older are disaggregated by age, health and mortality differentials appear that do not always favor white Americans. The black disadvantage in health and mortality observed in younger age groups of the elderly population narrows, disappears, or even turns into a minority group advantage among the oldest old. This trend is evident in morbidity data and in both all-cause and cause-specific mortality data. For example, death rates from heart and cerebrovascular disease are consistently higher for African Americans than for whites from ages 65 to 84, but become lower for African Americans at about age 85 (Gibson, 1994). Thus the relationship between race and health is more complicated than it first appears.

Gender is also related to health status and risk of mortality, but the relationship between privilege and positive outcome is less clear cut. Men in all age groups over 65 are more likely than women to die (Van Nostrand, Furner, & Suzman, 1993). This gender difference holds for two of the three leading causes of death in old age: heart disease and cancer. The exception to female advantage in mortality occurs with cerebrovascular disease: The death rate for women 85 years and older for cerebrovascular disease is higher than it is for men. Despite their lower likelihood of dying, women report more non-life-threatening chronic conditions and more functional limitations than men (Verbrugge, 1984). Elderly women in all age groups are more likely than older men to report difficulties with both activities of daily living and instrumental activities of daily living.

Women over 65 years old are also more likely than men to be living in nursing homes. This disparity increases with age until, by age 85 and over, women are almost twice as likely to be living in nursing homes than men. Part of this gender difference might reflect the fact that women have more non-life-threatening conditions that cause disability (Van Nostrand et al., 1993). Inability to function in the community is a significant predictor of institutionalization. Another reason for higher rates of institutionalization among older women might be that they are more likely to be living alone. As we saw in Part IV on family, women are more likely than men to be widowed in old age. Having a spouse who can serve as caregiver is an important deterrent to nursing home entry among disabled older people. One of the following readings illustrates the nursing home placement decision faced by a woman living alone. Anzia Yezierska's story "A Window Full of Sky" presents the dilemma of a poor woman who confronts fewer options when she questions her ability to live independently.

In summary, although women are more advantaged than men in terms of life expectancy, they are more disadvantaged in terms of non-life-threatening chronic diseases that limit their functioning. Some gerontologists have captured this phenomenon with the idea that "women get sick but men die." Perhaps because women are advantaged on measures of mortality and men are advantaged on measures of functional capacity, there are no gender differences in subjective health. Women and men are about equally likely to rate their health as excellent or poor throughout old age.

Although gender, race, and social class are each linked with health status in old age, the three systems of inequality often interlock to produce more complicated patterns of disease, disability, and death. For example, it is not just men who live shorter lives, but African American men in particular. It is not just women who are likely to live out their final days in institutions, but white women in particular. It is not just those in lower strata who are sicker and who die sooner but, in particular, lower-strata African Americans. In understanding the health status of older people, it is important to be aware not only of the individual effects of class, race, and gender but of their interlocking effects as well. The selection by Jan Mutchler and Jeffrey Burr explores the intersection between two of these hierarchies in explaining health differences among older people.

Are Disadvantaged Elderly People More Likely Than Their Privileged Counterparts to Be Exposed to Risk Factors for Disease and Death?

One explanation for the uneven distribution of disease, disability, and death within the elderly population is differences in exposure to risk factors across the life course. The greater prevalence of risk factors for disease and mortality among people who are disadvantaged in systems of inequality is related to the social structure. The disadvantaged respond to the reduced life chances imposed by the social conditions under which they have lived. These lifestyle responses of the disadvantaged contribute in large part to their mortality rates. The U.S. Surgeon General, in fact, estimated that only 20% of mortality can be attributed to genetic factors, only 20% to environmental factors, and only 10% to inadequate medical care, but fully 50% can be attributed to individual health behaviors and lifestyles (Williams, 1990).

Health researchers classify risk factors into three broad categories: biomedical, social, and psychological. Diabetes and hypertension are two conditions that illustrate the distribution of biomedical risk factors along systems of inequality. Diabetes is associated with vascular changes involving many organ systems, including eyes, kidneys, peripheral nervous system, and the heart. Hypertension is an important risk factor for coronary heart and cerebrovascular disease (National Center for Health Statistics, 1991). Among people 65 and older, both diabetes and hypertension are more prevalent among women, African Americans, and those in lower socioeconomic strata (National Center for Health Statistics, 1991). Native Americans also exhibit high rates of diabetes. But this is only part of the story. Race and gender interact with both diabetes and hypertension. Although white women are less likely than white men to have diabetes, black women are more likely than black men to develop this disease. In fact, elderly black women are the most likely of these four race-gender groups to have diabetes.

A similar interaction pattern occurs with hypertension. Hypertension is more prevalent among elderly white than among elderly African American men but more prevalent among older African American women than among older white women. African American women are the most likely among these groups to have hypertension. Once again, we see how looking at one hierarchy at a time presents an overly simplistic picture. To get a valid picture of biomedical risk factors for disease and dying among the older population, it is important to examine the interrelationships among systems of inequality.

The second class of risk factors for disease and mortality are social. Social risks include both environmental stress and lifestyles that lead to nonhealthful behaviors. Environmental stress includes greater lifetime exposure to crime, air and water pollutants, accidents, hazardous wastes, pesticides, and industrial chemicals. People living in inner-city neighborhoods face greater exposure to many of these risk factors. Others are related to a lifetime of dangerous occupational conditions. High mortality rates from motor vehicle accidents among Native Americans have been attributed to the greater need for automobiles in areas of low population density, poor road conditions on rural reservations, and high rates of alcohol use (Carr & Lee, 1978).

Lifestyles that lead to nonhealthful behaviors are another type of social risk factor that is more prevalent among disadvantaged elders. Obesity, smoking, and alcohol abuse illustrate this category of behavioral risks. Being severely overweight is associated with increased risks of hypertension, non-insulin-dependent diabetes, and certain cancers (National Center for Health Statistics, 1991). Excess weight is more prevalent among women, among people in lower socioeconomic strata, and among disadvantaged minorities, particularly Mexican Americans, Puerto Rican Americans, and African Americans. Again, however, there is a race-gender interaction. Among disadvantaged minorities, excess weight is more prevalent among women than men. Among nonminorities, the pattern is reversed. As with interactions among biomedical risk factors, elderly African American women are the category of people most likely to be overweight (National Center for Health Statistics, 1991).

Thousands of people die each year from the consequences of smoking. Smoking is a major risk factor for lung cancer, cardiovascular disease, and chronic obstructive lung disease. Gender, race, and class differences in mortality from these diseases reflect lifelong smoking patterns in the older population. Cigarette smoking has been more prevalent among today's older African Americans, Native Americans, and Puerto Rican Americans than among whites; more prevalent among whites than among Asian Americans; more prevalent in the lower than middle classes; and more prevalent among men than among women. Once again, however, an interaction emerges between gender and social class. Men with lower education, income, and occupational status are more likely to smoke than higher-status men. Among women, however, the opposite pattern has been documented. Women with higher levels of education, income, and occupational status were more likely to smoke than lower-status women; women who were employed outside the home were more likely to smoke than women who were full-time homemakers (Kurtz & Chalfant, 1984). Some of these patterns may change with future cohorts of elderly people, however, if people with higher levels of education stop smoking at higher rates than people with lower levels of education.

Alcohol consumption also varies along dimensions of gender, race, and class. George Maddox (1988), who studied use of alcohol among older people, estimated that about 5% of older Americans can be classified as problem drinkers. However, alcohol problems are distributed unevenly across systems of inequality. Men are about four times as likely as women to report problem drinking. Alcohol-related problems are also inversely related to social class (Maddox, 1988). A number of researchers have emphasized problems of alcohol abuse among Native Americans (Markides & Mindel, 1987).

The third set of risk factors are more psychological in nature: high stress, weak feelings of personal control and mastery, and weak perceived or actual social ties. All three of these psychological risk factors are more prevalent among people disadvantaged along hierarchies based on race and class. High levels of stress are associated with a number of disease outcomes (Williams, 1990). Older people disadvantaged by race and class have been exposed to more stressors throughout their lives than their more privileged counterparts. They are more likely to experience divorce, unemployment, and the death of someone close to them. They more often struggle with substandard housing and unpaid bills and report being more troubled by the everyday annoyances researchers call "daily hassles." As we saw in Part I, "The Life Course Perspective," surviving in a racist society is another source of chronic stress. African Americans have learned to live "in a react mode" (White, 1991, p. 190). Harriet McAdoo described this type of stress as a "mundane extreme environment," highlighting the pervasiveness of coping with racism as a daily reality. White Americans rarely think about the consequences of being white. In fact, part of race privilege is the luxury of ignoring the implications of race in one's daily life (McIntosh, 1988).

Several types of adaptive resources can buffer the effects of stress. Strong feelings of personal control, in contrast to feelings of powerlessness, seem to enhance health and soften the impact of stress. A sense of control is molded by the conditions under which people live and work. For example, corporate executives and professionals have more opportunities to exercise their authority, to use their expertise to solve problems, and to control the pace of their work than do industrial workers on an assembly line. The accumulation of these experiences over the work life contributes to a sense of control over one's life. Men, particularly in today's cohorts of older people, have had more decision-making power in families. Constantina Safilios-Rothschild (1970) argued that husbands had more orchestration power, which involves making infrequent but important decisions that determine family situation and lifestyle, whereas wives had more implementation power, which involves making frequent, routine decisions about daily life. "Spouses with 'orchestration' power set the limits within which the spouses with 'implementation' power exercise discretion" (Davidson & Gordon, 1979, p. 50). Once again, however, it is important to recognize the impact of interlocking hierarchies, as privilege along one dimension can sometimes buffer the impact of disadvantage along another. Affluent women have more opportunities to exert control over their environments than poor women. For example, as we saw in Part IV, "Family," upper-class women had more resources to help their children overcome problems in school than did poor or working-class mothers, who often exhibit very limited feelings of personal control.

Strong social ties are another resource that often predicts better health and lower mortality (House et al., 1990; Kasl & Berkman, 1985; Rowe & Kahn, 1987). Social ties can enhance health status in several ways. Close friends and relatives can provide emotional support and advice in times of trouble. Social networks can also help shape healthy lifestyles, link members to formal health services, and affirm people's self-esteem. People sometimes assume that extended kin networks of poor and minority elders mean that they enjoy an advantage over more privileged groups in social support resources. But social ties and social support are not necessarily equivalent. Sometimes networks lack the resources to provide support to members. Relationships with other people can be sources of stress as well as sources of support. Older parents can be upset, for example, by an adult child's divorce or loss of a job. Problems of alcoholism and drug addiction reverberate throughout a family. Given the higher prevalence of negative life events among more disadvantaged segments of the population, the conclusion that social networks of poor and minority elders provide stress and support in roughly equal doses should come as no surprise (Williams, 1990).

How Do Systems of Inequality Affect the Quantity and Quality of Health Care Available to Older People?

Another reason older people who are disadvantaged in systems of inequality experience more disease, disability, and mortality than their more privileged counterparts is that they receive poorer health care. Although Medicare and Medicaid have increased the quantity of health care for the elderly and the poor, it is less clear that the quality of that care has increased.

Health care quantity is most often measured by number of contacts with the health care system. Currently, the number of physician contacts per person does not differ by gender, race, or social class (Van Nostrand et al., 1993). Health care quality is assessed using several types of indicators, including use of services aimed at disease prevention, accessibility of care, availability of health care resources, and the doctor-patient relationship. People who are more disadvantaged in systems of inequality are less likely to have full access to the health care system, less likely to receive preventive services, more likely to have problems paying for health care, and less likely to enjoy high-quality relationships with physicians.

The health care received by disadvantaged elders is more oriented toward treatment of existing disease than toward prevention of future problems. Disadvantaged elders enter the medical care system later and are sicker upon diagnosis than more privileged elders. For example, once hospitalized, average lengths of stay are longer for elderly African Americans and for elderly people with incomes less than $14,000 per year than they are for other older people.

Restricted access to high-quality medical care results from a range of both perceived and actual barriers. Limited financial resources limit access for many near-poor and working-class elderly people. Without private insurance, they have difficulty paying for Medicare deductibles and copayments and for costs not covered by Medicare, such as medications, dental checkups, and nursing home care. Many people also have difficulty paying the premiums for

Medicare's Supplemental Medical Insurance (Part B), which reimburses some physician and related services. Coverage under Medicaid, the program of medical assistance designed for the poor, has also decreased over the past decade as states have attempted to control rising costs by limiting services and restricting eligibility. As a result, only one third of the elderly poor are covered by Medicaid (Nathan, 1990).

More affluent elderly can afford to purchase private "medicap" insurance to supplement Medicare coverage. Older people who were employed in jobs in the primary labor market are also more likely to have access to health plans that extend coverage to retired workers (Davis & Rowland, 1991). As we saw in Part III, "Productive Activity," older workers of color are less likely to have found employment in the primary labor market, so they are less likely to have access to these benefits. Older women are also less likely to have worked in primary labor market jobs, but women married to affluent men are often covered through spousal benefits. This provides yet another example of the interface of privilege and disadvantage. As with other financial resources in late life, a lifetime of limited financial benefits translates into limited medical coverage in old age. This situation is compounded by minority status. Among low-income elderly, fully one third of ethnic minorities but only one quarter of whites rely exclusively on Medicare for paying for health care (Nathan, 1990).

Finding a source of medical care can also be difficult. Some physicians will not accept Medicaid patients. The availability of physicians also varies by geographic setting. The ratio of physicians to patients is lower in low-income and minority areas, and the cost and difficulty of travel can reduce access, particularly for people with mobility problems. The mismatch of patient characteristics with the values of a predominantly white middle-class health care system further limits access to quality medical care. This gap can create psychological barriers that undermine the quality of health care for minority and poor elderly, barriers that include fear of loss of personal control and self-esteem and fear of class, gender, or racial discrimination. Discriminatory practices of practitioners and medical institutions often make encounters with the medical system a dehumanizing experience for lower-class and for minority elders (Bullough & Bullough, 1972; Williams, 1990). The selection by Zora Neale Hurston titled "My Most Humiliating Jim Crow Experience" illustrates such discriminatory treatment of a woman of color by a white physician.

The doctor-patient relationship is likely to be of poorer quality for disadvantaged individuals. Systematic and regular visits to private physicians' offices result in more thorough delivery of care and foster better patient-physician relationships. Encounters with physicians, however, are less systematic and regular in disadvantaged groups. For example, minority elders and elders with annual incomes below $25,000 have longer intervals between physician visits than do whites and people with higher incomes. Where the physician contact takes place also differs by minority and socioeconomic status. Whites and people with family incomes above $14,000 per year are more likely to see physicians in their offices, whereas African Americans and people with lower incomes are more likely to see physicians in hospital outpatient departments, emergency rooms, and nonhospital clinics (National Center for Health Statistics, 1991). In these settings, there is small likelihood of seeing the same physician over time, and patients have limited choice in who provides their care.

What Strategies Do People Use to Manage Illness on Their Own?

Physicians are not the only source of information for managing symptoms of illness. Health surveys suggest that the majority of symptoms are evaluated and treated outside the formal medical care system and that a large proportion of people who seek medical care have treated themselves before seeking medical advice. Lay treatment strategies include use of medications, including both over-the-counter medications purchased on their own or prescription medications prescribed previously for managing ongoing chronic conditions; use of appliances such as thermometers, enemas, heating pads; use of homemade preparations such as certain foods, herb teas, salves, and gargles; changes in activity such as bed rest or changes in exercise level; avoidance behaviors such as not stooping or lifting, not smoking or drinking, avoiding stressful situations, avoiding drafts; or changes in diet such as increasing fluids or increasing bulk. Katherine Dean's (1986) review of the research literature on self-care strategies used by older people led her to conclude that self-care decisions are generally appropriate and self-treatment generally helpful.

As with family care of frail elderly relatives, women are most often the providers of lay health care. Women are more likely than men to serve as lay consultants in matters of health and illness (Stoller, 1993). They are more likely to practice health-enhancing behaviors, to exhibit more knowledge about health matters, and to monitor their own health (Waldrun, 1988). Spouses reportedly talk about most health problems, but these discussions focus more frequently on the husband's health than on the wife's (Dean, 1986). Debra Umberson (1992) found that wives are more likely than husbands to try to modify their spouses' behavior to reduce their chance of illness.

Some of the health-related information shared within these informal networks parallels current medical care practices. People develop lay understandings of disease from multiple sources. These repertoires of lay knowledge and beliefs are created from people's own experience with illness, the vicarious experience of other people shared through the telling and retelling of personal illness narratives, observation of specific cases of disease in both personal networks and the public arena, and information gained over the years from professional practitioners and from the media (Davison, Frankel, & Smith, 1992; Segall & Goldstein, 1989; Stoller, Forster, & Pollow, 1994). Some of these beliefs and practices are based on traditional or folk medical practices that are part of ethnic or regional cultures. Doris Wilkinson (1987) defines *folk medicine* as "the health maintenance wisdom of family elders and associated customs." Wilkinson attributes the duration of folk medicine and indigenous healing customs to several factors: (a) repeated success with particular treatments, (b) limited economic resources and the escalating costs of formal medical care, (c) distrust of modern medical technology and of doctors, (d) lack of immediate access to treatment facilities in rural and isolated communities, and (e) traditional helping patterns.

Wilkinson studied folk medicine among Native Americans, Appalachian whites, African Americans, and Mexican Americans. In all of these groups, she stressed the role of elders, particularly older women, as lay healers. In his novel *Bless Me, Ultima*, Rudolfo Anaya describes the character La Grande as a *curandera*, or healer, "a woman who knew the herbs and remedies of the ancients, a miracle-worker who could heal the sick." Curanderas treat illness with food and herbs, massages and manipulations of the body, and use of religious or magical objects (Twaddle & Hessler, 1987). These practices reflect beliefs about causation that emphasize imbalances between hot and cold within the body, dislocation of bodily organs, emotional disturbances, and magic or witchcraft. The narrator in Anaya's novel alludes to beliefs in magic within traditional Mexican healing systems when he refers to La Grande's power "to lift the curses laid by brujas [witches]." In this part, the Mexican curandera in Gonzales's story, Doña Toña, also exhibits beliefs in magic to cure disease.

Native American healers also mix medications and mechanical interventions with the use of religious symbols and spiritual interventions. Native American practitioners developed stimulants, anesthetics, astringents, cathartics, emetics, antibiotics, and herbal contraceptives, many of which were borrowed by Western practitioners (Twaddle & Hessler, 1987). They also employed sweat baths, poultices, surgery, and quarantines. These physical interventions were supplemented with incantations, singing, and use of symbols, including ceremonial masks, rattles, drums, and pipes. Healing practices reflect Native American beliefs that emphasize harmony or balance among everything in the universe.

Wilkinson (1987) documented a number of traditional therapies among the groups she studied:

> One long-standing folk remedy for the common cold is a mixture of honey, lemon, and liquor. The effectiveness of this preparation is enhanced by the Vitamin C . . . and potassium content of

lemons. Other examples include the use of cranberries and juniper berries to treat fluid retention, ginger to soothe gastric discomfort, and poke root for the glandular system and for regulating the liver. (p. 72)

Use of lay or folk remedies is not limited to ethnic minorities. In a study of a predominantly white sample of older people in upstate New York, Stoller et al. (1993) identified a range of lay treatments, including cranberry drinks for urinary problems; heating pads and liniments for joint or muscle pain; camphor oil, mustard plasters, and various gargles (water with salt, baking soda, vinegar, or whiskey) for sore throats; and leisure activities and prayer for depression.

The extent to which lay understandings of disease coincide with medical explanations used by health care professionals remains an empirical question, but available literature suggests that the fit is less than perfect. The discrepancy between lay and professional understandings of disease is most clearly evident when lay theories of disease are grounded in ethnic or rural subcultures. For example, rural blacks and poor whites in Appalachia complain of "high blood," "sugar," "fallin' out," and "nerves." But even explanations couched in medical terms do not always reflect tenets of scientific medicine. Hypertension is the most widely cited example. Although hypertension is an asymptomatic condition, patients often believe that they can monitor their own blood pressure by referring to their body's signs or symptoms. For example, one study found that 80% of a sample of patients in treatment for hypertension agreed that people in general cannot tell when their blood pressure was elevated, but 90% of the same set of patients believed they themselves could tell when their pressure went up. This type of misinterpretation can have detrimental effects on adherence to treatment regimens, because differences in disease representations suggest different treatment goals. As the health psychologist Howard Leventhal explains, "Successful treatment for patients meant the amelioration of symptoms, while for physicians it meant lowering the blood pressure reading. Thus, the physicians were asking the patients to begin and sustain a treatment which basically made no sense from the patient's perspective" (Leventhal, Dieffenbach, & Leventhal, 1992, p. 156). Not surprisingly, Leventhal and his colleagues found that patients who believed they could monitor their own blood pressure were less likely to follow prescribed treatments.

The anthropologist Suzanne Heurtin-Roberts, who studied lay understandings of hypertension among lower-class elderly African American women, discovered that her subjects were experiencing two chronic folk illnesses ("high-pertension" and "high blood") rather than the biomedical condition "hypertension." "High-pertension" is understood as primarily a disease of the "nerves." "High blood," a condition in which excessively "hot," "thick," or "rich" blood rises up in body, is most often caused by salty, highly seasoned or greasy foods but can also be exacerbated by heredity, hot temperatures, or stress. This confusion has strong implications for treatment. If hypertension is considered a disease stemming from nervousness (as in "high-pertension"), adherence to a medication or dietary regimen designed to improve cardiovascular fitness may be seen as irrelevant. The readings in this part include an excerpt from Heurtin-Roberts's research.

Key Issues

This discussion and the following readings illustrate several key points:

1. How hierarchies based on gender, race or ethnicity, and class influence the meaning and distribution of disease, disability, and mortality
2. The distribution of risk factors among people occupying different positions in systems of inequality
3. How systems of inequality affect the quantity and quality of health care available to older people
4. Use of lay care strategies and folk medicine among older people and the role of women as lay providers of health care

The Readings

The following readings provide several illustrations of the ways in which interlocking hierarchies structure the experience and interpretation of disease, disability, and mortality. In the Introduction to this book, we emphasized differences in the meanings people attach to old age. Maya Angelou's poem "On Aging" returns to this theme by reminding us that the same symptoms or disabilities can be interpreted very differently by different people. Angelou's narrator acknowledges the physical changes that often accompany old age: stiff and aching bones, loss of hair, "a lot less lungs and much less wind." But she cautions against interpreting these changes within the context of negative stereotypes. She may have changed in physical appearance and physical abilities, but she's still "the same person I was back then." Angelou's poem thus stresses continuity over the life course: The physical losses that people experience in late life do not erase or diminish the essence of who they are.

For some people, age-related decrements challenge their understanding of quality of life. Older people and their families sometimes confront this dilemma near the end of life when deciding whether or not to use complicated surgical techniques or life support systems to extend the life of a terminally ill patient. The older couple in Arna Bontemps's story "A Summer Tragedy" face a similar decision far from the high-tech environment of a hospital ICU. The Pattons were poor black sharecroppers in the rural South, who were living independently when the story begins. But their ability to maintain this independence is threatened by poor health and minimal resources, and they plan to wrest control over their future in one of the few ways open to them.

Other choices regarding health care also require us to evaluate what gives meaning to life. The story by Anzia Yezierska provides a window on decisions about nursing home placements for older women. The focus on women is appropriate, because women are more likely than men to be institutionalized in old age. The older woman in Yezierska's story confronts nursing home placement with fewer resources and fewer options than do more affluent women. Yezierska's narrator does not have the luxury of weighing dining room access against therapy programs. Her only option is an old people's home she calls "The Isle of the Dead, . . . that house of doom from which I had fled with uncontrollable aversion for years." She faces her decision alone, guided only by her contacts with Miss Adcock, the admissions director, and Mr. Rader, the "Welfare man." Yezierska doesn't tell us whether her narrator ultimately chose the coffinlike room in the nursing home or the rooming house with her few possessions and "a window full of sky."

Yezierska's story also illustrates the impact that the attitudes and behaviors of health and social workers can have on the experience of receiving services. Miss Adcock's smile "helped me start talking." When she visited the rooming house, her comments made the narrator feel "that she saw something special in my room that no one else had ever seen." In contrast, Mr. Rader's behavior caused the narrator to mumble, "unable to conceal my fright. . . . Guilt and confusion made me feel like a doddering idiot."

The selection "My Most Humiliating Jim Crow Experience" also illustrates how poor patient-physician relationships are brought about by discriminatory practices of practitioners and how both perceived and actual discriminatory treatment can dampen the patient's enthusiasm for seeking future medical care. This selection also illustrates the interlocking nature of systems of inequality. Zora Neale Hurston was an African American woman who completed graduate study in anthropology at Columbia University, but this class advantage was not sufficient to deflect the racist response of the white physician.

Hierarchies based on race, class, and gender are reflected in the organization of the medical care system as well as in the performance of individual practitioners. The percentage of health workers who are women and people of color increases as we move down the medical hierarchy from highly paid physicians and administrators, most of whom are white men, to lowly paid aides and assistants. From the consumer's perspective, affluent patients receive the best care that money can buy, whereas poor and minority patients have disproportionately served the medical care system as teaching and research material (Waitzkin, 1974). Perhaps nowhere has this bias been more dramatically illustrated than in the 40-year Tuskegee Syphilis Study described in the selection by Stephen Thomas and Sandra Quinn. Under the guise of medical research, the African American men in this study, many poor men who welcomed the government's offer of free medical checkups and burial insurance, were denied treatment without their permission for a curable yet ultimately fatal disease.

The excerpt from Suzanne Heurtin-Roberts's article, "High-Pertension—The Uses of a Chronic Folk Illness for Personal Adaptation," illustrates the construction of lay understandings of disease that blend scientific medicine with folk models. Heurtin-Roberts also illustrates the ways in which people can modify professional explanations of disease to produce lay models that are both "logical to them in terms of their everyday thinking and, most importantly, useful in terms of their everyday needs" (Hunt, Jordan, & Irwin, 1989, p. 954). For some of her subjects, reinterpreting "hypertension" as "high-pertension" is instrumental in adapting to worries and negative life experiences. The women in this study were African American and of lower status, illustrating how gender, race, and class interact to influence health—in this case, the use of chronic illness as an adaptive resource.

Louie the Foot Gonzalez's story "Doña Toña of Nineteenth Street" also illustrates the ways in which different positions on systems of inequality influence the strategies people use to manage illness outside the formal medical care system. The Mexican American *curandera* in his story uses traditional Mexican folk medicine—magic objects, herbs, and massage—to treat illness after other healing techniques have failed. The curandera is a shamanistic wise woman who is revered and respected but also feared because of her powers and associations with the supernatural.

Nicholasa Mohr's story of a Puerto Rican family, "A Time With a Future," illustrates three of the key issues in this part: how hierarchies based on ethnicity, gender, and class influence the distribution of disease, disability, and mortality; how the distribution of risk factors for poor health and mortality differ by position in these hierarchies; and how membership in systems of inequality affects the quantity and quality of health care. This reading also illustrates how women are usually nominated as lifelong caregivers and how that role influences attitudes of women in old age. It was Carmela who longed to be near her young son's bedside when he died, and it was Carmela who cared for her husband during his final illness. After Benjamin died, it was Carmela's two daughters who assumed the role of caregiver for their elderly mother.

Taken together, these readings provide several examples of how interlocking hierarchies structure the experience and interpretation of disease, disability, and mortality. The final selection explores these interrelationships in a more formal way. Jan Mutchler and

Jeffrey Burr report on a statistical analysis of how race and class combine to affect health status. Their analysis of the interrelated effects of these two hierarchies provides a more telling picture of inequality in health status than would separate analyses of race or class alone. Their analyses reveal that some differences between elderly African Americans and elderly whites reflect the fact that African Americans are more likely than whites to be concentrated in lower socioeconomic strata. But they also show that "pure" racial differences persist. Elderly African Americans assess their health more negatively and report fewer annual visits to health care providers, even after the effects of social class differences are removed.

On Aging

Maya Angelou

When you see me sitting quietly,
Like a sack left on the shelf,
Don't think I need your chattering.
I'm listening to myself.
Hold! Stop! Don't pity me!
Hold! Stop your sympathy!
Understanding if you got it,
Otherwise I'll do without it!

When my bones are stiff and aching
And my feet won't climb the stair,
I will only ask one favor:
Don't bring me no rocking chair.

When you see me walking, stumbling,
Don't study and get it wrong
'Cause tired don't mean lazy
And every goodbye ain't gone.
I'm the same person I was back then,
A little less hair, a little less chin,
A lot less lungs and much less wind.
But ain't I lucky I can still breathe in.

Source: From *And Still I Rise* by M. Angelou. Copyright
© 1978 by Maya Angelou. Reprinted by permission of
Random House, Inc.

A Summer Tragedy

Arna Bontemps

Old Jeff Patton, the black share farmer, fumbled with his bow tie. His fingers trembled and the high stiff collar pinched his throat. A fellow loses his hand for such vanities after thirty or forty years of simple life. Once a year, or maybe twice if there's a wedding among his kinfolks, he may spruce up; but generally fancy clothes do nothing but adorn the wall of the big room and feed the moths. That had been Jeff Patton's experience. He had not worn his stiff-bosomed shirt more than a dozen times in all his married life. His swallow-tailed coat lay on the bed beside him, freshly brushed and pressed, but it was as full of holes as the overalls in which he worked on weekdays. The moths had used it badly. Jeff twisted his mouth into a hideous toothless grimace as he contended with the obstinate bow. He stamped his good foot and decided to give up the struggle.

"Jennie," he called.

"What's that, Jeff?" His wife's shrunken voice came out of the adjoining room like an echo. It was hardly bigger than a whisper.

"I reckon you'll have to he'p me wid this heah bow tie, baby," he said meekly. "Dog if I can hitch it up."

Her answer was not strong enough to reach him, but presently the old woman came to the door, feeling her way with a stick. She had a wasted, dead-leaf appearance. Her body, as scrawny and gnarled as a string bean, seemed less than nothing in the ocean of frayed and faded petticoats that surrounded her. These hung an inch or two above the tops of her heavy unlaced shoes and showed little grotesque piles where the stockings had fallen down from her negligible legs.

"You oughta could do a heap mo' wid a thing like that'n me—beingst as you got yo' good sight."

"Looks like I oughta could," he admitted. "But ma fingers is gone democrat on me. I get all mixed up in the looking glass an' can't tell wicha way to twist the devilish thing."

Jennie sat on the side of the bed and old Jeff Patton got down on one knee while she tied the bow knot. It was a slow and painful ordeal for each of them in this position. Jeff's bones cracked, his knee ached, and it was only after a half dozen attempts that Jennie worked a semblance of a bow into the tie.

"I got to dress maseff now," the old woman whispered. "These is ma old shoes an' stockings, and I ain't so much as unwrapped ma dress."

"Well, don't worry 'bout me no mo', baby," Jeff said. "That 'bout finishes me. All I gotta do now is slip on that old coat 'n ves' an' I'll be fixed to leave."

Jennie disappeared again through the dim passage into the shed room. Being blind was no handicap to her in that black hole. Jeff heard the cane placed against the wall beside the door and knew that his wife was on easy ground. He put on his coat, took a battered top hat from the bedpost and hobbled to the front door. He was ready to travel. As soon as

Source: "A Summer Tragedy" by A. Bontemps. Copyright 1933 by Arna Bontemps, renewed. Reprinted by permission of Harold Ober Associates Incorporated.

Jennie could get on her Sunday shoes and her old black silk dress, they would start.

Outside the tiny log house, the day was warm and mellow with sunshine. A host of wasps were humming with busy excitement in the trunk of a dead sycamore. Gray squirrels were searching through the grass for hickory nuts and blue jays were in the trees, hopping from branch to branch. Pine woods stretched away to the left like a black sea. Among them were scattered scores of log houses like Jeff's, houses of black share farmers. Cows and pigs wandered freely among the trees. There was no danger of loss. Each farmer knew his own stock and knew his neighbor's as well as he knew his neighbor's children.

Down the slope to the right were the cultivated acres on which the colored folks worked. They extended to the river, more than two miles away, and they were today green with the unmade cotton crop. A tiny thread of a road, which passed directly in front of Jeff's place, ran through these green fields like a pencil mark.

Jeff, standing outside the door, with his absurd hat in his left hand, surveyed the wide scene tenderly. He had been forty-five years on these acres. He loved them with the unexplained affection that others have for the countries to which they belong.

The sun was hot on his head, his collar still pinched his throat, and the Sunday clothes were intolerably hot. Jeff transferred the hat to his right hand and began fanning with it. Suddenly the whisper that was Jennie's voice came out of the shed room.

"You can bring the car round front whilst you's waitin'," it said feebly. There was a tired pause; then it added, "I'll soon be fixed to go."

"A'right, baby," Jeff answered. "I'll get it in a minute."

But he didn't move. A thought struck him that made his mouth fall open. The mention of the car brought to his mind, with new intensity, the trip he and Jennie were about to take. Fear came into his eyes; excitement took his breath. Lord, Jesus!

"Jeff . . . O Jeff," the old woman's whisper called.

He awakened with a jolt. "Hunh, baby?"
"What you doin'?"
"Nuthin. Jes studyin'. I jes been turnin' things round'n round in ma mind."
"You could be gettin' the car," she said.
"Oh yes, right away, baby."

He started round to the shed, limping heavily on his bad leg. There were three frizzly chickens in the yard. All his other chickens had been killed or stolen recently. But the frizzly chickens had been saved somehow. That was fortunate indeed, for these curious creatures had a way of devouring "Poison" from the yard and in that way protecting against conjure and black luck and spells. But even the frizzly chickens seemed now to be in a stupor. Jeff thought they had some ailment; he expected all three of them to die shortly.

The shed in which the old T-model Ford stood was only a grass roof held up by four corner poles. It had been built by tremulous hands at a time when the little rattletrap car had been regarded as a peculiar treasure. And, miraculously, despite wind and downpour it still stood.

Jeff adjusted the crank and put his weight upon it. The engine came to life with a sputter and bang that rattled the old car from radiator to taillight. Jeff hopped into the seat and put his foot on the accelerator. The sputtering and banging increased. The rattling became more violent. That was good. It was good banging, good sputtering and rattling, and it meant that the aged car was still in running condition. She could be depended on for this trip.

Again, Jeff's thought halted as if paralyzed. The suggestion of the trip fell into the machinery of his mind like a wrench. He felt dazed and weak. He swung the car out into the yard, made a half turn and drove around to the front door. When he took his hands off the wheel, he noticed that he was trembling violently. He cut off the motor and climbed to the ground to wait for Jennie.

A few minutes later she was at the window, her voice rattling against the pane like a broken shutter.

"I'm ready, Jeff."

He did not answer, but limped into the house and took her by the arm. He led her slowly through the big room, down the step and across the yard.

"You reckon I'd oughta lock the do'?" he asked softly.

They stopped and Jennie weighed the question. Finally she shook her head.

"Ne' mind the do'," she said. "I don't see no cause to lock up things."

"You right," Jeff agreed. "No cause to lock up."

Jeff opened the door and helped his wife into the car. A quick shudder passed over him. Jesus! Again he trembled.

"How come you shaking so?" Jennie whispered.

"I don't know," he said.

"You mus' be scairt, Jeff."

"No, baby, I ain't scairt."

He slammed the door after her and went around to crank up again. The motor started easily. Jeff wished that it had not been so responsive. He would have liked a few more minutes in which to turn things around in his head. As it was, with Jennie chiding him about being afraid, he had to keep going. He swung the car into the little pencil-mark road and started off toward the river, driving very slowly, very cautiously.

Chugging across the green countryside, the small battered Ford seemed tiny indeed. Jeff felt a familiar excitement, a thrill, as they came down the first slope to the immense levels on which the cotton was growing. He could not help reflecting that the crops were good. He knew what that meant, too; he had made forty-five of them with his own hands. It was true that he had worn out nearly a dozen mules, but that was the fault of old man Stevenson, the owner of the land. Major Stevenson had the odd notion that one mule was all a share farmer needed to work a thirty-acre plot. It was an expensive notion, the way it killed mules from overwork, but the old man held to it. Jeff thought it killed a good many share farmers as well as mules, but he had no sympathy for them. He had always been strong, and he had been taught to have no patience with weakness in men. Women or children might be tolerated if they were puny, but a weak man was a curse. Of course, his own children—

Jeff's thought halted there. He and Jennie never mentioned their dead children any more. And naturally he did not wish to dwell upon them in his mind. Before he knew it, some remark would slip out of his mouth and that would make Jennie feel blue. Perhaps she would cry. A woman like Jennie could not easily throw off the grief that comes from losing five grown children within two years. Even Jeff was still staggered by the blow. His memory had not been much good recently. He frequently talked to himself. And, although he had kept it a secret, he knew that his courage had left him. He was terrified by the least unfamiliar sound at night. He was reluctant to venture far from home in the daytime. And that habit of trembling when he felt fearful was now far beyond his control. Sometimes he became afraid and trembled without knowing what had frightened him. The feeling would just come over him like a chill.

The car rattled slowly over the dusty road. Jennie sat erect and silent, with a little absurd hat pinned to her hair. Her useless eyes seemed very large, very white in their deep sockets. Suddenly Jeff heard her voice, and he inclined his head to catch the words.

"Is we passed Delia Moore's house yet?" she asked.

"Not yet," he said.

"You must be drivin' mighty slow, Jeff."

"We might just as well take our time, baby."

There was a pause. A little puff of steam was coming out of the radiator of the car. Heat wavered above the hood. Delia Moore's house was nearly half a mile away. After a moment Jennie spoke again.

"You ain't really scairt, is you, Jeff?"

"Nah, baby, I ain't scairt."

"You know how we agreed—we gotta keep on goin'."

Jewels of perspiration appeared on Jeff's forehead. His eyes rounded, blinked, became fixed on the road.

"I don't know," he said with a shiver. "I reckon it's the only thing to do."

"Hm."

A flock of guinea fowls, pecking in the road, were scattered by the passing car. Some of them took to their wings; others hid under bushes. A blue jay, swaying on a leafy twig, was annoying a roadside squirrel. Jeff held an even speed till he came near Delia's place. Then he slowed down noticeably.

Delia's house was really no house at all, but an abandoned store building converted into a dwelling. It sat near a crossroads, beneath a single black cedar tree. There Delia, a cattish old creature of Jennie's age, lived alone. She had been there more years than anybody could remember, and long ago had won the disfavor of such women as Jennie. For in her young days Delia had been gayer, yellower and saucier than seemed proper in those parts. Her ways with menfolks had been dark and suspicious. And the fact that she had had as many husbands as children did not help her reputation.

"Yonder's old Delia," Jeff said as they passed.

"What she doin'?"

"Jes sittin' in the do'," he said.

"She see us?"

"Hm," Jeff said. "Musta did."

That relieved Jennie. It strengthened her to know that her old enemy had seen her pass in her best clothes. That would give the old she-devil something to chew her gums and fret about, Jennie thought. Wouldn't she have a fit if she didn't find out? Old evil Delia! This would be just the thing for her. It would pay her back for being so evil. It would also pay her, Jennie thought, for the way she used to grin at Jeff—long ago when her teeth were good.

The road became smooth and red, and Jeff could tell by the smell of the air that they were nearing the river. He could see the rise where the road turned and ran along parallel to the stream. The car chugged on monotonously. After a long silent spell, Jennie leaned against Jeff and spoke.

"How many bale o' cotton you think we got standin'?" she said.

Jeff wrinkled his forehead as he calculated.

"'Bout twenty-five, I reckon."

"How many you make las' year?"

"Twenty-eight," he said, "How come you ask that?"

"I's jes thinkin'," Jennie said quietly.

"It don't make a speck o' difference though," Jeff reflected. "If we get much or if we get little, we still gonna be in debt to old man Stevenson when he gets through counting up agin us. It's took us a long time to learn that."

Jennie was not listening to these words. She had fallen into a trance-like meditation. Her lips twitched. She chewed her gums and rubbed her gnarled hands nervously. Suddenly she leaned forward, buried her face in the nervous hands and burst into tears. She cried aloud in a dry cracked voice that suggested the rattle of fodder on dead stalks. She cried aloud like a child, for she had never learned to suppress a genuine sob. Her slight old frame shook heavily and seemed hardly able to sustain such violent grief.

"What's the matter, baby?" Jeff asked awkwardly. "Why you cryin' like all that?"

"I's jes thinkin'," she said.

"So you the one what's scairt now, hunh?"

"I ain't scairt, Jeff. I's jes thinkin' 'bout leavin' eve'thing like this—eve'thing we been used to. It's right sad-like."

Jeff did not answer, and presently Jennie buried her face again and cried.

The sun was almost overhead. It beat down furiously on the dusty wagon-path road, on the parched roadside grass and the tiny battered car. Jeff's hands, gripping the wheel, became wet with perspiration; his forehead sparkled. Jeff's lips parted. His mouth shaped a hideous grimace. His face suggested the face of a man being burned. But the torture passed and his expression softened again.

"You mustn't cry, baby," he said to his wife. "We gotta be strong. We can't break down."

Jennie waited a few seconds, then said, "You reckon we oughta do it, Jeff? You reckon we oughta go 'head an' do it, really?"

Jeff's voice choked; his eyes blurred. He was terrified to hear Jennie say the thing that had been in his mind all morning. She had egged him on when he had wanted more than anything in the world to wait, to reconsider, to think things over a little longer. Now she was getting cold feet. Actually there was no need of thinking the question through again. It would only end in making the same painful decision once more. Jeff knew that. There was no need of fooling around longer.

"We jes as well to do like we planned," he said. "They ain't nothin' else for us now—it's the bes' thing."

Jeff thought of the handicaps, the near impossibility, of making another crop with his leg bothering him more and more each week. Then there was always the chance that he would have another stroke, like the one that had made him lame. Another one might kill him. The least it could do would be to leave him helpless. Jeff gasped—Lord, Jesus! He could not bear to think of being helpless, like a baby, on Jennie's hands. Frail, blind Jennie.

The little pounding motor of the car worked harder and harder. The puff of steam from the cracked radiator became larger. Jeff realized that they were climbing a little rise. A moment later the road turned abruptly and he looked down upon the face of the river.

"Jeff."

"Hunh?"

"Is that the water I hear?"

"Hm. Tha's it."

"Well, which way you goin' now?"

"Down this-a way," he said. "The road runs 'long 'side o' the water a lil piece."

She waited a while calmly. Then she said, "Drive faster."

"A'right, baby," Jeff said.

The water roared in the bed of the river. It was fifty or sixty feet below the level of the road. Between the road and the water there was a long smooth slope, sharply inclined. The slope was dry, the clay hardened by prolonged summer heat. The water below, roaring in a narrow channel, was noisy and wild.

"Jeff."

"Hunh?"

"How far you goin'?"

"Jes a lil piece down the road."

"You ain't scairt, is you, Jeff?"

"Nah, baby," he said trembling. "I ain't scairt."

"Remember how we planned it, Jeff. We gotta do it like we said. Brave-like."

"Hm."

Jeff's brain darkened. Things suddenly seemed unreal, like figures in a dream. Thoughts swam in his mind foolishly, hysterically, like little blind fish in a pool within a dense cave. They rushed, crossed one another, jostled, collided, retreated and rushed again. Jeff soon became dizzy. He shuddered violently and turned to his wife.

"Jennie, I can't do it. I can't." His voice broke pitifully.

She did not appear to be listening. All the grief had gone from her face. She sat erect, her unseeing eyes wide open, strained and frightful. Her glossy black skin had become dull. She seemed as thin, as sharp and bony, as a starved bird. Now, having suffered and endured the sadness of tearing herself away from beloved things, she showed no anguish. She was absorbed with her own thoughts, and she didn't even hear Jeff's voice shouting in her ear.

Jeff said nothing more. For an instant there was light in his cavernous brain. The great chamber was, for less than a second, peopled by characters he knew and loved. They were simple, healthy creatures, and they behaved in a manner that he could understand. They had quality. But since he had already taken leave of them long ago, the remembrance did not break his heart again. Young Jeff Patton was among them, the Jeff Patton of fifty years ago who went down to New Orleans with a crowd of country boys to the Mardi Gras doings. The gay young crowd, boys with candy-striped shirts and rouged-down girls in noisy silks, was like a picture in his head. Yet it did not make him sad. On that very trip Slim Burns had killed Joe Beasley—the crowd had been broken up. Since then Jeff Patton's world had been the Greenbriar Plantation. If there had been other Mardi Gras carnivals, he had not heard of them. Since then there had been no time; the years had fallen on him like waves. Now he was old, worn out. Another paralytic stroke (like the one he had already suffered) would put him on his back for keeps. In that condition, with a frail blind woman to look after him, he would be worse off than if he were dead.

Suddenly Jeff's hands became steady. He actually felt brave. He slowed down the motor of the car and carefully pulled off the road. Below, the water of the stream boomed, a soft thunder in the deep channel. Jeff ran the car onto the clay slope, pointed it directly toward the stream and put his foot heavily on the accelerator. The little car leaped furiously down the steep incline toward the water. The movement was nearly as swift and direct as a fall. The two old black folks, sitting quietly side by side, showed no excitement. In another instant the car hit the water and dropped immediately out of sight.

A little later it lodged in the mud of a shallow place. One wheel of the crushed and upturned little Ford became visible above the rushing water.

A Window Full of Sky

Anzia Yezierska

A few blocks away from the roominghouse where I live is an old people's home. "Isle of the Dead," I used to call it. But one day, after a severe attack of neuritis, I took a taxi to that house of doom from which I had fled with uncontrollable aversion for years. Cripples in wheelchairs and old men and women on benches stared into vacancy—joyless and griefless, dead to rapture and despair. With averted eyes I swept past these old people, sunning themselves like the timbers of some unmourned shipwreck.

The hallman pointed out a door marked "Miss Adcock, Admissions." I rapped impatiently. Almost as though someone had been waiting, the door opened, and there was Miss Adcock trimly tailored with not a hair out of place. Just looking at her made me conscious of my shabbiness, my unbrushed hair escaping from under my crumpled hat, the frayed elbows of my old coat. She pulled out a chair near her desk. Even her posture made me acutely aware of my bent old age.

The conflict, days and nights, whether to seek admission to the home or to die alone in my room, choked speech. A thin thread of saliva ran down from the corner of my mouth. I tried to wipe it away with my fingers. Miss Adcock handed me a Kleenex with a smile that helped me start talking.

Source: "A Window Full of Sky" from *The Open Cage* by Anzia Yezierska. Copyright © 1979 by Louise Levitas Henriksen. Reprinted by permission of Persea Books, Inc.

"I've been old for a long, long time," I began, "but I never felt old before. I think I've come to the end of myself."

"How old are you?"

"Old enough to come here."

"When were you born?"

"It's such a long time ago. I don't remember dates."

Miss Adcock looked at me without speaking. After a short pause she resumed her probing.

"Where do you live?"

"I live in a roominghouse. Can anyone be more alone than a roomer in a roominghouse?" I tried to look into her eyes, but she looked through me and somehow above me.

"How do you support yourself?"

"I have a hundred dollars a month, in Social Security."

"You know our minimum rate is $280 a month."

"I've been paying taxes all my life. I understood that my Social Security would be enough to get me in here. . . ."

"It can be processed through Welfare."

I stood up, insulted and injured: "Welfare is charity. Why surrender self-respect to end up on charity?"

"Welfare is government assistance, and government assistance is not charity," Miss Adcock calmly replied. "I would like to explain this more fully when I have more time. But right now I have another appointment. May I come to see you tomorrow?"

I looked at Miss Adcock and it seemed to me that her offer to visit me was the hand-clasp of a friend. I was hungry for hope. Hope even made me forget my neuritis. I dismissed the thought of a taxi back to the roominghouse. I now had courage to attempt hobbling back with the aid of my cane. I had to pause to get my breath and rest on the stoops here and there, but in a way hope had cured me.

The prospect of Miss Adcock's visit gave me the strength to clean my room. Twenty years ago, when I began to feel the pinch of forced retirement, I had found this top-floor room. It was in need of paint and plumbing repairs. But the afternoon sun that flooded the room and the view across the wide expanse of tenement roofs to the Hudson and the Palisades beyond made me blind to the dirty walls and dilapidated furniture. Year after year the landlord had refused to make any repairs, and so the room grew dingier and more than ever in need of paint.

During my illness I had been too depressed to look at the view. But now I returned to it as one turns back to cherished music or poetry. The sky above the river, my nourishment in solitude, filled the room with such a great sense of space and light that my spirits soared in anticipation of sharing it with Miss Adcock.

When Miss Adcock walked into my room, she exclaimed: "What a nice place you have!" She made me feel that she saw something special in my room that no one else had ever seen. She walked to the window. "What a wonderful view you have here. I wonder if it will be hard for you to adjust to group living—eating, sleeping, and always being with others."

"I can no longer function alone," I told her. "At my age people need people. I know I have a lot to learn, but I am still capable of learning. And I feel the Home is what I need."

As if to dispel my anxiety, she said, "If you feel you can adjust to living with others, then of course the Home is the place for you. We must complete your application and arrange for a medical examination as soon as possible. By the way, wouldn't you like to see the room we have available right now? There are many applicants waiting for it."

"I don't have to see the room," I said in a rush.

She pressed my hand and was gone.

About two weeks later, Miss Adcock telephoned that I had passed the medical examination and the psychiatrist's interview. "And now," she said, "all that is necessary is to establish your eligibility for Welfare."

"Oh, thank you," I mumbled, unable to conceal my fright. "But what do you mean by eligibility? I thought I was eligible. Didn't you say . . . ?"

In her calm voice, she interrupted: "We have our own Welfare man. He comes to the Home every day. I'll send him to see you next Monday morning. As soon as I can receive his report, we can go ahead."

The Welfare man arrived at the appointed time.

"I'm Mr. Rader," he announced. "I am here to find out a few things to complete your application for the Home." The light seemed to go out of the room as he took possession of the chair. He was a thin little man, but puffed up, it seemed to me, with his power to give or withhold "eligibility." He put his attaché case reverently on the table, opened it, and spread out one closely printed sheet. "Everything you say," he cautioned, "will of course be checked by the authorities." He had two fountain pens in his breast pocket, one red and one black. He selected the black one. "How long have you lived here?"

"Twenty years."

"Show me the receipts." He leaned back in his chair and looked around the room with prying eyes. He watched me ruffling through my papers.

"I must have last month's receipt somewhere. But I don't bother with receipts. I pay the rent . . . they know me," I stammered. I saw him make rapid, decisive notations on his form.

"What are your assets?" he continued.

My lips moved but no words came out.

"Have you any stocks or bonds? Any insurance? Do you have any valuable jewelry?"

I tried to laugh away my panic. "If I had valuable jewelry, would I apply to get into the Home?"

"What are your savings? Let me see your bankbook." I stopped looking for the rent receipts and ransacked the top of my bureau. I handed him the bankbook. "Is that all your savings?" he asked. "Have you any more tucked away somewhere?" He looked intently at me. "This is only for the last few years. You must have had a bank account before this."

"I don't remember."

"You don't remember?"

Guilt and confusion made me feel like a doddering idiot. "I never remember where I put my glasses. And when I go to the store, I have to write a list or I forget what I came to buy."

"Have you any family or friends who can help you?" He glanced at his watch, wound it a little, and lit a cigarette, puffing impatiently. "Have you any professional diplomas? Do you go to a church or synagogue?"

I saw him making quick notes of my answers. His eyes took in every corner of the room and fixed on the telephone. He tapped it accusingly.

"That's quite an expense, isn't it?"

"I know it's a luxury," I said, "but for me it's a necessity."

He leaned forward. "You say you have no friends and no relatives. Who pays for it? Can you afford it?"

"I use some of my savings to pay for it. But I have to have it."

"Why do you have to have it?"

"I do have a few friends," I said impulsively, "but I'm terribly economical. Usually my friends call me."

I could feel my heart pounding. My "eligibility," my last stand for shelter, was at stake. It was a fight for life.

"Mr. Rader," I demanded, "haven't people on Social Security a burial allowance of $250? I don't want a funeral. I have already donated my body to a hospital for research. I claim the

right to use that $250 while I am alive. The telephone keeps me alive."

He stood up and stared out the window; then he turned to me, his forehead wrinkling: "I never handled a case like this before. I'll have to consult my superiors."

He wrote hastily for a few minutes, then closed the attaché case. "Please don't phone me. The decision rests in the hands of my superiors."

When the door closed, there was neither thought nor feeling left in me. How could Miss Adcock have sent this unseeing, unfeeling creature? But why blame Miss Adcock? Was she responsible for Welfare? She had given me all she had to give.

To calm the waiting time, I decided to visit the Home. The woman in charge took great pride in showing me the spacious reception hall, used on social occasions for the residents. But the room I was to live in was a narrow coffin, with a little light coming from a small window.

"I do not merely sleep in my room," I blurted out. "I have to live in it. How could I live without my things?"

She smiled and told me, "We have plenty of storage room in the house, and I'll assign space for all your things in one of the closets." "In one of the closets! What earthly good will they do me there?" I suddenly realized that it would be hopeless to go on. Perhaps the coffin-like room and the darkness were part of the preparation I needed.

Back in my own place, the sky burst in upon me from the window and I was reminded of a long-forgotten passage in *War and Peace*. Napoleon, walking through the battlefield, sees a dying soldier and, holding up the flag of France, declaims: "Do you know, my noble hero, that you have given your life for your country?"

"Please! Please!" the soldier cries. "You are blotting out the sky."

My Most Humiliating Jim Crow Experience

Zora Neale Hurston

My most humiliating Jim Crow experience came in New York instead of the South as one would have expected. It was in 1931 when Mrs. R. Osgood Mason was financing my researches in anthropology. I returned to New York from the Bahama Islands ill with some disturbances of the digestive tract.

Godmother (Mrs. Mason liked for me to call her Godmother) became concerned about my condition and suggested a certain white specialist at her expense. His office was in Brooklyn.

Mr. Paul Chapin called up and made the appointment for me. The doctor told the wealthy and prominent Paul Chapin that I would get the best of care.

So two days later I journeyed to Brooklyn to submit myself to the care of the great specialist.

His reception room was more than swanky, with a magnificent hammered copper door and other decor on the same plane as the door.

But his receptionist was obviously embarrassed when I showed up. I mentioned the appointment and got inside the door. She went into the private office and stayed a few minutes, then the doctor appeared in the door all in white, looking very important, and also very unhappy from behind his rotund stomach.

He did not approach me at all, but told one of his nurses to take me into a private examination room.

The room was private all right, but I would not rate it highly as an examination room. Under any other circumstances, I would have sworn it was a closet where the soiled towels and uniforms were tossed until called for by the laundry. But I will say this for it, there was a chair in there wedged in between the wall and the pile of soiled linen.

The nurse took me in there, closed the door quickly and disappeared. The doctor came in immediately and began in a desultory manner to ask me about my symptoms. It was evident he meant to get me off the premises as quickly as possible. Being the sort of objective person I am, I did not get up and sweep out angrily as I was first disposed to do. I stayed to see just what would happen and further to torture him more. He went through some motions, stuck a tube down my throat to extract some bile from my gall bladder, wrote a prescription and asked for twenty dollars as fee.

I got up, set my hat at a reckless angle and walked out, telling him that I would send him a check, which I never did. I went away feeling the pathos of Anglo-Saxon civilization.

And I still mean pathos, for I know that anything with such a false foundation cannot last. Whom the gods would destroy, they first made mad.

Source: "My Most Humiliating Jim Crow Experience" by Zora Neale Hurston, reprinted in *I Love Myself When I Am Laughing: A Zora Neale Hurston Reader*, edited by Alice Walker. Oldwestbury, NY: The Feminist Press, 1979.

Public Health Then and Now:
The Tuskegee Syphilis Study, 1932 to 1972

Stephen B. Thomas
Sandra Crouse Quinn

How Did It Go on for So Long?

The Tuskegee study of untreated syphilis in the Negro male is the longest nontherapeutic experiment on human beings in medical history. Numerous factors contributed to the continuation of this experiment over a period of 40 years. However, almost from the outset, its scientific merit was questionable.

The Alabama state health officer and the Macon County Board of Health extracted a promise from the PHS that all who were tested and found to be positive for syphilis, including those selected for the study, would receive treatment. It was understood by all, except the subjects, that the treatment given was less than the amount recommended by the PHS to cure syphilis. By the late 1930s some physicians began to raise concerns regarding the scientific merit of a study about untreated syphilis when it was clear that some subjects had received some form of treatment. In 1938, removal of these men from the experiment was briefly considered, but it was decided that in the interest of maintain-

ing esprit de corps among the participants and in order to avoid suspicion, those men who had received minimal treatment would remain in the experimental group.

The ultimate tragedy of the Tuskegee experiment was exemplified by the extraordinary measures taken to ensure that subjects in the experimental group did not receive effective treatment. During World War II, approximately 50 of the syphilitic cases received letters from the local draft board ordering them to take treatment. At the request of the PHS, the draft board agreed to exclude the men in the study from its list of draftees needing treatment. According to Jones:

[Preventing] the men from receiving treatment had always been a violation of Alabama's public health statutes requiring public reporting and prompt treatment of venereal diseases.... Under the auspices of the law health officials conducted the largest state-level testing and treatment program in the history of the nation [but] state and local health officials continued to cooperate with the study. (p. 178)

In 1943, the PHS began to administer penicillin to syphilitic patients in selected treatment clinics across the nation. The men of the Tuskegee Syphilis Study were excluded from this treatment for the same reason other drugs had been withheld since the beginning

Source: Excerpted from "The Tuskegee Syphilis Study, 1932 to 1972: Implications for HIV Education and AIDS Risk Education Programs in the Black Community," by S. Thomas and S. Quinn, excerpted from *American Journal of Public Health,* November 1991, *81*(11). Copyright © 1991 American Public Health Association. Reprinted by permission.

of the study in 1932—treatment would end the study. Once penicillin became the standard of treatment for syphilis in 1951, the PHS insisted that it was all the more urgent for the Tuskegee study to continue because "it made the experiment a never-again-to-be-repeated opportunity" (p. 179).

In 1952, in an effort to reach subjects who had moved out of Macon County, the PHS utilized its entire national network of state and local health departments for the first time in its history in order to bring subjects in for examination. Over the next 20 years, state and local health departments cooperated in keeping the men in the study, yet denying treatment.

According to Jones, the ultimate reason why the Tuskegee Syphilis Study went on for 40 years was a minimal sense of personal responsibility and ethical concern among the small group of men within the PHS who controlled the study. This attitude was reflected in a 1976 interview conducted by Jones with Dr. John Heller, Director of Venereal Diseases at the PHS from 1943 to 1948, who stated, "The men's status did not warrant ethical debate. They were subjects, not patients; clinical material, not sick people" (p. 179).

Jones details the following chronology of events leading to the end of the Tuskegee Syphilis Study:

- November 1966. Peter Buxtun, a venereal disease interviewer and investigator with the PHS in San Francisco, sent a letter to Dr. William Brown, Director of the Division of Venereal Diseases, to express his moral concerns about the experiment. He inquired whether any of the men had been treated properly and whether any had been told the nature of the study.

- November 1968. Buxtun wrote Dr. Brown a second letter, in which he described the current racial unrest prevalent in the nation. Buxtun made the point that "the racial composition of the study group [100% Negro] supported the thinking of Negro militants that Negroes have long been used for medical experiments and teaching cases in the emergency wards of county hospitals . . ." (p. 193). Dr. Brown showed this letter to the Director of the Centers for Disease Control. For the first time, health officials saw the experiment as a public relations problem that could have severe political repercussions.

- February 1969. The CDC convened a blue-ribbon panel to discuss the Tuskegee study. The group reviewed all aspects of the experiment and decided against treating the men. This decision ended debate on the Tuskegee study's future: It would continue until "end point." The committee also recommended that a major thrust be made to upgrade the study scientifically.

In the final analysis, it was Peter Buxtun who stopped the Tuskegee Syphilis Study by telling his story to a reporter with the Associated Press. On July 25, 1972, the *Washington Star* ran a front-page story about the experiment. It is important to note that the PHS was still conducting the experiment on the day when the story broke.

41

High-Pertension: The Uses of a Chronic Folk Illness for Personal Adaptation

Suzanne Heurtin-Roberts

Chronic illness exerts a lasting and pervasive influence on personal experience of the world. It is commonly viewed as a phenomenon to be coped with, requiring an adaptive response on the part of an individual. Chronic illness, however, is a culturally-influenced tool which in itself can be used to organize and implement an adaptive response to personal experience. Employing Hallowell's concept of the self in the behavioral environment, the uses of a chronic folk illness, 'high-pertension', for personal adaptation are discussed.

Data from research on health beliefs about hypertension and illness behavior in a sample of 60 older African-American women in New Orleans are presented. 'High-pertension', a chronic folk illness related to the biomedical 'hypertension', and involving blood and 'nerves', is described. Health beliefs and illness behavior associated with high-pertension are considered as part of an individual's total effort at adaptation within the behavioral environment.

These points are made: (1) Chronic illness can be used as a means to express one's self in relation to the behavioral environment. (2) Chronic illness can be used to manipulate and manage the relation of self to environment.

Source: "High-Pertension: The Uses of a Chronic Folk Illness for Personal Adaptation" by S. Heurtin-Roberts, *Social Science & Medicine* 37(3), 285–294. Copyright © 1993 Elsevier Science Ltd. Reprinted by permission.

(3) Chronic illness can be used to legitimize and announce role change. These uses are available to the individual by virtue of social interaction, cultural precedent and the chronicity and meaning of the illness itself. For persons in a severely stressed, constrained, and disadvantaged social position, as are many older African-American women, chronic illness offers one of the few means of controlling the behavioral environment available to the individual. Although in anthropology and biology we speak of adaptation in terms of human groups, we are ultimately considering person-environment fit, that is, personal adaptation. Chronic illness can be a part of a culturally-influenced adaptive response.

In the health and social sciences, chronic illness frequently has been conceived as a phenomenon alien to the behavioral environment requiring an adaptive response, and coping strategies [1, 2]. However, chronic illness can be viewed conversely, as a phenomenon having adaptive worth. The illness itself can be used to organize and implement a personal adaptive response to the behavioral environment.

In this paper I will explore how a group of African-American women in New Orleans draw on their own mythic world of health and illness to formulate a chronic folk illness, 'high-pertension', and individual explanatory models of the folk illness for themselves. The paper describes the significance of 'high-pertension' for the self within the behavioral environment, and efforts to manage the illness as part of an individual's personal adaptive effort. The data come from a study of essential hypertension, health beliefs and compliance with treatment in older African-American women in New Orleans [16].

Chronic hypertension can be defined as the persistent unfavorable ratio between cardiac output and total peripheral vascular resistance, so that the cardiovascular system operates at excessively high pressure [17]. Over time this can result in vascular damage and secondary pathology such as heart disease, kidney disease, stroke and blindness. Consequently, from the biomedical perspective, careful monitoring and treatment are extremely important.

From the perspective of many of the study's participants, however, two chronic folk illnesses, 'high-pertension' and 'high blood', actually are being experienced rather than the biomedical condition, 'hypertension'. While both illnesses involve the placement and behavior of blood in the body, they differ in that 'high-pertension' is primarily a disease of the 'nerves' whereas 'high blood' is more strictly a physical malady. The meaning that 'high-pertension' has for individual adaptation within the context of a socioculturally constructed behavioral environment is explored here.

Illness Models

The general terms 'pressure' or 'pressure trouble' were used by informants to describe their condition. Many women said they simply used the term 'high blood' for 'high blood pressure', but discriminated between 'high blood/high blood pressure' and 'hypertension' (or 'high-pertension', as discussed below). Over half ($n = 32$, or 53%) said that these were two different conditions. Of those who felt there was no difference, six women said they were aware that some people differentiate between the two. This suggests a fairly widely recognized belief within the population.

Individual explanatory models did vary among individuals. This is to be expected since an explanatory model is an individual assessment of one's illness experience. Two basic folk illness models, however, did emerge from analysis of the interview data, 'high blood' and 'high-pertension' [18]. Both illnesses will briefly be described and then the 'uses' of high-pertension, a chronic folk illness, for personal adaptation will be discussed.

Both illnesses operated on what can be called a 'thermometer' model of cardiovascular physiology [19]. Participants described normal blood as being 'at rest' or 'quiet', wherein the blood is lower in the body. When 'pressure trouble' occurs, the blood rises in the body towards the head. This can occur for various reasons and in different ways, but, regardless of how or why, this is considered dangerous and bad for one's health and well-being. Both high blood and high-pertension are considered serious illnesses. The two illnesses differ markedly in other respects.

In order to facilitate comparison of the two chronic folk illnesses, semantic networks of 'high blood' and 'high-pertension' are provided. Semantic networks are visual representations of terms associated with a central term, and the links among the terms [20]. In this case the central terms are the folk illnesses high blood and high-pertension. The associated terms are the causal and exacerbating factors for each illness. Numbers refer to the number of times a factor was cited by informants as causing or exacerbating the illness in question. Arrows refer to the relationships of factors to the central terms as described by participants in their interviews. Please see the semantic networks of the two illnesses (Figs 1 and 2) for comparison.

Causal and exacerbating factors were differentiated from each other by informants during the interviews. A factor which might be viewed as influential enough to exacerbate a pre-existing condition might not be viewed as influential enough to cause that condition. For example, as the semantic network of high-pertension indicates, 19 informants thought that 'anger' would exacerbate high-

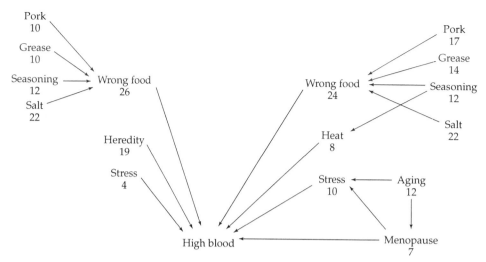

Figure 1. Semantic network of high blood, N = 32. Positive responses.

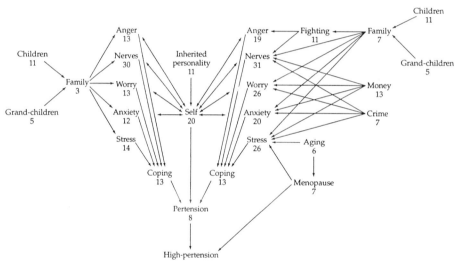

Figure 2. Semantic network of high-pertension, N = 32. Positive responses.

pertension. Only 13 informants thought that 'anger' would be powerful enough to cause high-pertension. "It'll definitely make it [high-pertension] worse. I don't know that it's enough to cause it though," said an informant.

It must be emphasized that semantic networks are not meant to be precise renderings of cultural or cognitive structure in any manner. They are simply useful devices for visually representing the general meanings associated with a term under question. If a network is

not internally logical or consistent, it is because neither are cultural beliefs necessarily logical or consistent.

High Blood

High blood is said to be a 'disease of the blood and heart'. In high blood, excessively 'hot', 'thick' or 'rich' blood rises up in the body, clogs, and remains there (it is said to be 'elevated'). Participants say their blood can remain elevated for months at a time: 'it stays high'. The illness is said to 'work on the heart too hard'.

For 'high blood', both causal and exacerbating factors are almost exclusively physical in nature, with 'wrong food', by far, the single most important factor. Participants considered the most harmful foods to be pork (fresh or salt), salt, 'seasoning', and 'grease'. High blood is also caused or exacerbated by heredity, heat (weather and body temperature, which make the blood hotter and thicker) and stress. Worry and anger were not important problems nor were 'nerves'.

Most of the participants thought appropriate treatment for high blood included medically prescribed antihypertensive drugs, dietary control, and less importantly weight loss. Home remedies such as garlic, lemon, or vinegar to 'thin and cool' the blood and draw it away from the head were also viewed as useful supplements to biomedical care, but not as substitutes. High blood is not considered curable but it is thought to be controllable with proper treatment.

High-Pertension

In contrast to high blood, high-pertension is a 'disease of the nerves' [21]. In high-pertension the blood is usually 'at rest'. At times of intense emotion, the blood shoots up suddenly to the head, but then goes back down. In high-pertension, the blood tends to go up higher, all the way to the head, and more rapidly than in high blood, which can cause instant death. It is said to 'accelerate' in high-pertension, whereas in high blood it only 'elevates'. One informant said it 'shoots up to my head and rings like a bell'. High-pertension is caused by 'bad nerves', stress, worry, and anger. This is said to stem from an excitable, emotional self interacting with one's social milieu.

Medication was not thought particularly useful in managing high-pertension. Of those who thought medications might help, some women said these should be 'nerve pills', or some other medication to cause relaxation and sleep. Neither dietary control nor weight loss were considered effective in high-pertension management. Most important for high-pertension was that the individual avoid worrying, relax, rest, stay quiet, and get away from people.

High-pertension is thought to be extremely unpredictable and episodic, since the blood only goes up when someone is very upset emotionally and this is not easily foreseen. Because it is unpredictable, sudden, and the blood goes up higher than in high blood, high-pertension is thought to be more dangerous.

Hysterectomy and menopause were considered by some women to exacerbate both high blood and high-pertension. According to informants, when the menstrual flow is stopped, excess blood goes up to the head, aggravating one's 'pressure troubles'. As one woman phrased it "there's no place for all that waste blood to go so it backs up into your head."

In sum, high-pertension is an episodic chronic illness caused by temperament and emotional arousal. It causes the blood's position in the body to fluctuate dangerously, shooting towards the head and possibly causing death. Appropriate treatment is rest, relaxation, control of one's self and control of the social milieu.

Illness as an Expressive Form: Distress in the Behavioral Environment

High-pertension is an idiom in which to express problems in the interaction of the self and its behavioral environment, particularly in the social area. The following informants' statements illustrate how these problems are formulated and expressed in terms of African-American women's mythic world of health and illness in New Orleans. (All informants' names are pseudonyms.)

High-pertension is because of your personality. You the kind of person that get real mad and excited. . . . I might get to the point where the high blood pressure will go away, and I can stop taking my medicine, but I'll always have high-pertension, because that's just the way I am. [T. Coleman]

My problem is pertension, too much pertension. My pertension is real high . . . it means you're high tempered and your blood goes up . . . high-pertension is from the nerves that's got you high strung. [A. Tureaud]

My blood just boils, and you don't know what's making it happen. You can't help it. I can't control it. I'm the kind of person who just can't keep my mouth shut for nothing. That pertension can hit you at any time . . . it's higher and stronger than with pressure. If you have pressure your blood is up, but not as high as with pertension. [O. Porche]

Blood is of great importance in the African-American woman's mythic world, and this is expressed in high-pertension. One's blood rises with the problems of the world, at times it boils up and almost spills over. One's worries, fears, angers and frustrations accumulate as does one's perceived inability to cope with them, damaging the body and ultimately resulting in death.

The sources of distress in the environment are problems representative of many African-American women in American society. This is especially true of older African-American women who often find themselves in central roles of responsibility for large networks of kin and others. They have greatly important roles in child-rearing, of their own children, and, frequently, grandchildren, nieces and nephews as well as fictive kin. The burden of responsibility for holding one's family together, for safety and survival in a world of endless work, insufficient resources, and threats from crime and drugs is expressed by one's blood.

The situations of the next women illustrate this. Johnnie Johnson is a 51 year old woman who lives with her daughter in a dangerous neighborhood with a thriving drug trade. She lacks the finances to move, even

though the neighborhood has taken its toll on her family. Ms. Johnson's grief, loss anxiety and pain are expressed by her high-pertension. Ms. Johnson discussed her condition:

High-pertension is when you're thinking on something real hard or you worry real hard. I had a lot of pertension. I think high-pertension comes from worry and grief. My family thinks I worry too much; they try to keep worry from me. In 1971, I had a 21 year old daughter that was murdered and left a 4 year old child. I had a 18 year old boy killed in 1976. All that had come into it, I guess. They never knew who did it, they just found him, shot with a bullet in his neck.

I've been doing better though. I had a hysterectomy that made my blood go up some but I'm not worried, it only makes things worse. It doesn't worry me now; it worried me at one time. My granddaughter was dying with sickle cell a few years ago; that was pretty bad. It took a long time . . . but after that was over I been feeling better.

It's just when you get older, high-pertension's when you get older. It might go away if I keep myself strong and try not to think back . . . for high-pertension there's no medicine.

Amy Washington is a 56 year old woman with high-pertension. She has never married and has one child living away from home. She works as an aide at a public nursing home on New Orleans' West Bank, across the Mississippi river from the main part of the city, Charity Hospital, and other public health care. She lives in a rather out-of-the-way West Bank neighborhood, accessible by only one through street and far from public transportation.

There's a lot of high blood pressure in my family. I'm the only one with high-pertension though. High blood is something you inherit, but high-pertension come from nerves. It got bad as I got older. I guess you have more problems as you get older.

. . . my sister says to rest. Well she can. She's got a house and a husband. She stays in bed late and watches her stories. She gets up when she wants. Me, I'm pulling double shifts trying to pay the rent on this piece of shit [her apartment]. I tell you I am tired. I got my brother's baby girl staying with me, and my boy is in college in Michigan. I don't know when I'm gonna be laid off. They're talking about closing us all down. Now where's them old people gonna go? . . . I don't know what the hell my pressure is. I can't keep running to Charity, they won't let me off work, not for that long. That car out there stopped running. My brother's supposed to look at it, but I ain't seen his face yet. I got to take three buses to get there and I got to walk all the way to General De Gaulle [avenue—a little over a mile away] to catch one. I'd be gone all day and dead by the time I got there.

I got to be careful, you can't stir things up too much cause they's always got people watching, waiting to complain and next thing you know I'll be the next to go [be laid off]. Sister [a Catholic nun who was also a physician] had her clinic over here . . . but they closed her down. Now we all got to go across the river. You know, I guess my blood would be down too if I could stay in bed all morning.

Ms. Washington relates her rising blood and 'high-pertension' to her 'nerves' brought about by the hardships she experiences simply in trying to manage her day-to-day life.

High-pertension serves as an idiom for the symbolic expression of negative emotion: to say one has the illness is to say one is anxious, angry, or grieving. The illness also affords African-American women an acceptable means for the behavioral expression of this emotion. The idealized mother and wife should be loving, strong, optimistic, and solicitous of her family's well-being. Uncontrollable anger, anxiety and sadness are not highly valued traits in a mother.

Also, according to some studies, the expression of negative emotion has been a problem for African Americans in post-colonial America, due both to psychology and the realities of social organization [23-25]. High-pertension allows the legitimate expression of negative emotion which would otherwise be negatively sanctioned by virtue of one's ethnicity, gender and social role. Since illness is the source of negative behavior, personal responsibility on the overt level (no matter what is believed on the covert level) is absolved. For women who are tired of holding their feelings in, or anxious about letting them go, high-pertension provides an outlet of personal expression.

Illness as Life Passage: The Changing Self in the Behavioral Environment

High-pertension can also be viewed as a marker, a milestone of life passage. The biomedical illness, hypertension, is likely to occur later in life. So is the appearance of high-pertension which frequently occurs after pregnancy or childbearing. Menopause and hysterectomy are also implicated in general 'pressure trouble' such as high-pertension and high blood. At one level this is simply because there is no outlet for menstrual blood and this contributes to excessive blood volume [26]. Menopause and hysterectomy are also, however, indicative of a life passage; menopause is commonly called a 'change of life'.

This sense of change is reflected in feelings about high-pertension. Twenty women said they noted a change in themselves and their life since developing high-pertension. They try to worry less and rest more. The following statements are examples of successfully negotiated change.

The high-pertension's not as bad as when it first started. . . . When you have a lot of children the problems get really bad and you take it all on yourself. But now that they're older I let it rest on them. If they still want to be with their problems bothering them, keep having all that foolishness, then there's nothing I can do about it. . . . I don't let it bother me as much as before because I can't. [R. Bell]

I used to worry about my kitchen and always be in the kitchen, but now the doctor told me not to worry . . . about the house and I just sort of let the house go. And that's what you have to do if you got high-pertension. . . . My grandchildren don't bother me at all, cause now I make 'em go home. They used to be always in the house all the time, but I finally put an end to that. [L. Jeanne-marie]

Nope, I ain't gonna worry about it no more. I put in my share on this earth. I ain't gonna make myself sick no more, that ain't right. I did my best for 'em when I could, but now it's their turn. That what you have children for. Now they can take care of me. [A. Cantrelle]

I try to get more rest now. I try to walk and sew. Maybe I need to rest more. I try not to worry because if I worry too much I'll get sick. Maybe you should talk about what's bothering you more. I used to hold it in, but I changed and now my mouth's too big. [O. Marshall]

The change expressed in these statements is one which offers release from social norms which would govern a younger woman in good health. By virtue of high-pertension, a woman is given increased freedom and power to act.

Later life change in Western industrial society is commonly viewed as a clearly demarcated 'retirement', passing from work to leisure. For persons with a less clearly defined, formal work history, however, such as many women and members of ethnic minority groups, this concept is less applicable [27]. A more useful perspective on later life change is to examine changes in behavior, social identity and sense of self.

Gutmann has addressed such change in a comparative cross-cultural analysis of the developmental psychology of aging [28]. He notes among older women a detachment from socially ordained strictures and norms. This is not disengagement as discussed by

Cummings and Henry [29], which describes a withdrawal from active life and the human arena in passive to active mastery of life and the environment. Gutmann says of this change in women: "Across cultures and with age, they seem to become more domineering, more agentic and less willing to trade submission for security . . . looking across cultures at actual behavior, we do find mid and late life 'women's liberation', even where this development is not given formal recognition" [28].

The data suggest that high-pertension may serve to provide this recognition, phrased in a socioculturally acceptable manner. High-pertension marks and legitimizes a change from one phase of life to another. It legitimizes role change and change in social identity to coincide with an emergent sense of self which is freer and more powerful. One cannot legitimately say one is tired of being a mother, especially in a culture where motherhood is so highly valued (if also exceedingly demanding). But one can say that sickness makes former role-specific behavior dangerous and, therefore, impossible. High-pertension is a culturally stylized illness which allows behavioral change that would otherwise be frowned upon.

Illness as Instrument:
Managing the Behavioral Environment

High-pertension is not only expressive of the problems and distress encountered in the daily life of many African-American women in New Orleans, but it is also instrumental in offering a way out. By marking a life passage, it allows change from a high to relatively lower pressured status. It allows women to at least partially put the role of the caregiver behind, and to acknowledge personal needs for care and to legitimately tend to one's own well being. Furthermore, high-pertension offers a means by which to defuse conflict and manage immediate social interaction. High-pertension can be used as a tool for managing the social milieu. This is readily apparent. High-pertension is a dangerous, possibly fatal illness, which is volatile, episodic and unpredictable. Because episodes are triggered by emotional upheaval, it is necessary to control the emotional tone of personal interaction and manage social proceedings. The following case illustrates this.

Elnora Perez's house was always noisy. She usually had a window fan running, soap operas on television, Mahalia Jackson spirituals playing, and two small grandchildren running in and out giggling, all of which the author had come to expect in her visits there. One particular day the two grandchildren were running through and arguing over a transistor radio that belonged to Terrell, Ms. Perez's 20 year old son. He came running after them to retrieve it, and whacked one on the bottom when she refused to give it up. The child began to wail and her mother, Wanda (Terrell's sister), came in and asked what the hell did he think he was doing hitting her child. He laughed at her and began to walk away. She punched him in the back; he swung around and punched her in the arm. They were in a deadlock; pulling each other's hair and screaming. Until then Ms. Perez (and the author) had tried to ignore them, but this was too much. "Get out of here with your fighting, get out," she yelled, standing up and flailing at them with a handful of papers. "What do you think you're doing acting like that with the nurse [sic] here? Y'all gonna run my pressure up for sure. You giving me a headache, you want me to have a stroke?" She turned to the researcher, "Take my pressure and see what it is." She turned to her children "You want to have to take me to Charity? [hospital]" The children initially reacted to their mother's anger with laughter, but when the researcher began to take her blood pressure everyone, including the grandchildren, settled down into silence. As would be expected, her blood pressure was indeed high, and the rest of the visit proceeded in peace and quiet.

Some families have stories of family members who died suddenly from high-pertension induced by family discord. One story is presented here.

It's like with my sister, my sister got upset with her children. She kept telling 'em to stop.

They kept running around and telling on one another and bothering her. She got all upset and her face got all twisted. Right before that happened she put her hands up to her head, stood up and said 'you see what you're gonna do—you're gonna do that to me' and then she had a stroke and died right there. Upset will do it quicker than anything. It's with the nerves. Now how do you think them children felt? Her face got all twisted and upset. It killed her right on the spot. [A. Tureaud]

This is a powerful threat with which to control family and friends who behave improperly. Rather they are enjoined to cultivate a peaceful milieu for the high-pertensive relative, to refrain from any action that would make her angry, worried, or excited. Efforts at personal adaptation are made through improved management of the behavioral environment.

Anita Leonard had high blood. She was concerned about her teenage son's behavior; he had been staying out late, she suspected he was involved with drugs, and disapproved of the company he was keeping. One day the author was at her house for an interview while her son was present. The interview did not go well. Ms. Leonard spoke little and there was considerable tension in the atmosphere. It did seem that Ms. Leonard and her son had been arguing earlier. The author asked if she suffered with her nerves. She said "I didn't used to, but now, with this one [she nodded to her son], I'm getting bad nerves, I think I might be going into high-pertension, now he's going to give me high-pertension" [30]. He mumbled something unintelligible, got up and left, apparently angry. The interview continued, but her attention was not focused on it.

Ms. Leonard believed that disruptions in the behavioral environment might result in the development of a serious illness. This illness, however, could provide her a means to effectively manage these disruptions. Certainly, this is the use of illness for secondary gain. It is, however, more than that. High-pertension is a culturally formulated expression of a problem which also contains built-in stratagems for the management of the problem. Because the illness is chronic, the illness is incorporated as a tool into everyday life on a long-term basis. Illness creates the need to re-organize one's life but because one has a chronic illness, one is able to reorganize one's life. The difference is subtle but important. On the one hand, a chronic illness poses a problem, on the other, it offers a solution to that problem.

In sum, individuals sharing certain culturally influenced views of illness discuss their experiences in terms of these beliefs. They try to make sense of and organize their health experiences by fitting them in with what their own 'mythic world' of health suggests as well as what is learned from biomedicine, personal experience and social interaction; all part of the behavioral environment. In an ongoing process of everyday life, these chronically ill individuals attempt to manage their person-environment fit, to achieve a more satisfactory adaptation of self by whatever means are at hand. A chronic folk illness such as high-pertension is the product.

These considerations have implications for health education and illness management. If certain beliefs about an illness have adaptive worth, persons may be loathe to relinquish them, limiting the prospects for successful biomedical health education. There may be also reluctance to manage illness to the point that it is not threatening, because the ill person then loses what little control is possessed over the environment [32]. If so, manipulation of the social environment may be a necessary condition for optimal illness management. Illness will not get better unless everyday life does.

To say that these women use their illness is not to say that they want high blood pressure any more than they might want diabetes or cancer. However, given that a chronic physical malady exists, it is reasonable to make use of the illness in a way that is culturally allowed and guided. People tend to maximize their options in personal adaptation as best they can, using whatever tools are available to them. I suggest that this is true to some extent of all illness, whether chronic or not, and debilitating or not. When an illness

is chronic and serious, an individual has that much more leverage.

Farmer, discussing blood illnesses in Haiti, cautioned against ignoring the "social origins of much—if not most—illness and distress" [19, p. 80]. In the case of a chronic folk illness such as high-pertension, we should turn toward the behavioral environment's social and cultural areas for solutions as well as origins. The cultural and social areas of the behavioral environment hold substantial resources for personal adaptation. Aging minority women are master strategists in developing psychosocial and cultural strengths and using scarce resources for coping with the problems of everyday life [33]. A chronic folk illness can be one of those resources.

References

1. Corbin J. M. and Strauss A. *Unending Work and Care: Managing Chronic Illness at Home.* Jossey-Bass, San Francisco, 1988.
2. Heurtin-Roberts S. *Managing a chronic illness: Self, culture and experience.* Paper presented at the 86th Annual Meetings of the American Anthropological Association. Chicago, Illinois, 1988.
16. Heurtin-Roberts S. and Reisin E. Folk models of hypertension among black women: Problems in illness management. In *Anthropology and Primary Health Care* (Edited by Coreil J. and Mull J. D.), pp. 222-250. Westview, Boulder, 1990.
17. Lund-Johansen P. The hemodynamics of essential hypertension. In *The Handbook of Hypertension*, Vol. 1. (Edited by Robertson J.), pp. 151-173. Elsevier Science, Amsterdam, 1983.
18. Eight informants explicitly used the term 'high-pertension.' They said it meant one had too much 'pertension,' a general term to describe stress, 'nerves' and worry. More informants than eight may have been saying 'high-pertension' but, because they did not specifically mention 'pertension', I misunderstood, and thought they were saying 'hypertension', a homonym of 'high-pertension.' In this report, 'high-pertension' will be used to distinguish it from the biomedical 'hypertension' and

Blumhagen's 'hyper-tension.' See Blumhagen D. Hypertension: A folk illness with a medical name. *Cult. Med. Psychol. 4,* 197, 1980. 'High-pertension' will be used in direct quotations only for those informants who explicitly distinguished between 'high blood' and 'high-pertension' in their interviews.

19. Farmer, in discussing blood-related folk illnesses of Haitians, likens the blood to a moral 'barometer,' reflecting the well-being of one's social self and milieu. See Farmer P. Bad blood, spoiled milk: Bodily fluids as moral barometers in rural Haiti. *Am. Ethnol.* 62-83, 1988. It is interesting that I conceptualized the folk cardiovascular model of New Orleans African-Americans as a thermometer before having read Farmer's article. This coincidence speaks to the compelling nature of an African-American tendency to view one's physical being, especially one's blood, as reflecting one's social and emotional situation.

20. Good B. The heart of what's the matter: The semantics of illness in Iran. *Cult. Med. Psychol. 1,* 25-58, 1977.

21. This dichotomy of physical (high blood) vs. nervous (high-pertension) disease is similar to that described by Blumhagen. His predominantly Anglo-American, middle-class sample considered hypertension (Blumhagen called it hyper-tension) to mean an individual was very nervous and under considerable stress. High blood pressure denoted the biomedically recognized illness involving impaired cardiovascular functioning. See Blumhagen D. The meaning of hypertension. In *Clinically Applied Anthropology* (Edited by Chrisman N. J. and Maretzki N. J.), pp. 297-323. D. Reidel, Dordrecht, 1980. Elements of New Orleans 'high-blood' and also 'high-pertension' show strong similarities to the folk illness 'high blood' described by Snow (1974) and Weidman (1978). They both involve blood which travels upward in the body. This is unlike Blumhagen's 'hyper-tension' which

does not involve a folk cardiovascular model. See Snow L. F. Folk medical beliefs and their implications for care of patients. *Ann. Int. Med. 81,* 82-96, 1974. See also Weidman H. H. *The Miami Health Ecology Report: A Statement of Ethnicity and Health,* Vol. I. Department of Psychiatry, University of Miami School of Medicine, Miami, 1978.

23. Grier W. H. and Cobbs P. M. *Black Rage.* Basic Books, New York, 1968.

24. Kardiner A. and Ovesey L. *The Mark of Oppression: A Psychosocial Study of the American Negro.* W. W. Norton, New York, 1951.

25. Powdermaker H. The channeling of negro aggression by the cultural process. *Am. J. Sociol. 48,* 750-758, 1943.

26. Weidman also noted this in Southern Blacks and Haitians in Miami. (See Ref. [21]).

27. Gibson, R. C. Reconceptualizing retirement for black Americans. *The Gerontologist 27,* 691, 1987.

28. Gutmann D. The cross-cultural perspective: Notes toward a comparative psychology of aging. In *Handbook of the Psychology of Aging* (Edited by Birren J. E. and Schaie K. W.), pp. 302-326. Van Nostrand Reinhold, New York, 1977.

29. Cummings E. and Henry W. *Growing Old: The Process of Disengagement.* Basic Books, New York, 1961.

30. One can have both folk illnesses at the same time, although they do not have to both begin at the same time. Furthermore, one illness can go away and the other begin. Each illness requires its own appropriate strategy for management, even when occurring at the same time.

32. In fact, poor compliance with treatment was found associated with a self diagnosis of high-pertension (see Ref. [16]).

33. Padgett D. Aging minority women: Issues in research and health policy. In *Women in the Later Years: Health, Social and Cultural Perspectives* (Edited by Grau L.), p. 213, Haworth, Binghamton, NY, 1989.

42

Doña Toña of Nineteenth Street

Louie the Foot González

Her name was Doña Toña and I can't help but remember the fear I had of the old lady. Maybe it was the way all the younger kids talked about her:

"Ya, man. I saw her out one night and she was pulling some weeds near the railroad tracks and her cat was meowing away like it was ready to fight that big black dog and, man, she looked just like a witch, like the Llorona trying to dig up her children."

"Martin's tellin' everybody that she was dancin' aroun' real slow and singin' some witch songs in her backyard when it was dark and everybody was asleep."

Doña Toña was always walking somewhere . . . anywhere . . . even when she had no particular place to go. When she walked, it was as though she were making a great effort because her right leg was kind of funny. It dragged a little and it made her look as if her foot were made of solid metal.

Her face was the color of lightly creamed coffee. The wrinkles around her forehead and eyes were like the rings of a very old tree. They gave her age as being somewhere around seventy-five years old, but as I was to discover later, she was really eighty-nine. Even though her eyes attracted much attention, they always gave way to her mouth.

Source: "Doña Toña of Nineteeth Street" by Louie the Foot González, from *Growing Up Chicana/o*, edited by Tiffany Ana López, 1993. New York: Avon Books. Copyright © 1993 Elsevier Science Ltd. Reprinted by permission.

Most of the people that I had observed looking at her directed their gaze at her mouth. Doña Toña had only one tooth to her name and it was the strangest tooth I had ever seen. It was exceptionally long and it stuck out from her upper gum at a forty-five degree angle. What made it even stranger was that it was also twisted. She at one time probably had an overabundance of teeth, until they began to push against each other, twisting themselves, until she had only one last tooth left. It was the toughest of them all, the king of the hill, 'el mero chingón.'

Doña Toña was born in 1885 in one of the innumerable little towns of México. The Mexican Revolution of 1910 drove her from her little-town home when she was twenty-seven years old. She escaped the mass bloodshed of the Revolution by crossing the border into the United States and living in countless towns from Los Angeles to Sacramento, where she became the most familiar sight in Barrio Cinco. She was one of the barrio's landmarks; when you saw her, you knew that you were in the barrio. She had been there longer than anyone else and yet no one, except perhaps her daughter Maria, knew very much about her. Some people said that was the way she wanted it. But as far as I could see, she didn't show signs of wanting to be alone.

Whenever Doña Toña caught someone watching her during one of her never-ending strolls, she would stop walking and look at that person head-on. No one could keep staring at her once she had started to stare back. There was something in Doña Toña's stare that could make anybody feel like a child. Her crow-black eyes could hypnotize almost anybody. She could have probably put an owl to sleep with her stare.

* * *

Doña Toña was Little Feo's grandmother. She lived with her daughter, Maria, who was Little Feo's mother. All of Little Feo's ten years of life had passed without the outward lovingness that grandmothers are supposed to show. But the reason for it was Little Feo's own choice.

Whenever Little Feo, who was smaller, thinner, and darker than the rest of the barrio ten years olds, was running around with us (Danny, Fat Charlie, Bighead, Joe Nuts, and a few other guys that lived close by) nobody would say anything about his "abuelita." Before, whenever anybody used to make fun of her or use her for the punchline of a joke, Little Feo would get very quiet; his fists would begin to tighten and his face would turn a darker shade as all his blood rushed to his brain. One time when Fat Charlie said something like, "What's black and flies at night? Why . . . it's Feo's granny," Little Feo pounced on him faster than I had ever seen anybody pounce on someone before. Fat Charlie kicked the hell out of Little Feo, but he never cracked another joke like that again, at least not about Doña Toña.

Doña Toña was not taken very seriously by very many people until someone in the barrio got sick. Visits to Doctor Herida when someone got sick were common even though few people liked to go to him because he would just look at the patient and then scribble something on a prescription form and tell the sick one to take it next door to McAnaws Pharmacy to have it filled. Herida and the pharmacist had a racket going. When the medicine Herida prescribed didn't have the desired effect, the word was sent out in the barrio that Doña Toña was needed some-

where. Sometimes it was at the Osorio house, where Jaime was having trouble breathing, or the Canaguas place, where what's-her-name was gaining a lot of weight. Regardless of the illness, Doña Toña would always show up, even if she had to drag herself across the barrio to get to where she was needed and, many times, that's exactly what she did. Once at the place of need, she did whatever it was she had to and then she left asking nothing of anyone. Usually, within a short time of her visit—hours (if the illness were a natural one) or a day or two (if it were supernatural)—the patient would show signs of improvement.

Doña Toña was never bothered about not receiving any credit for her efforts.

"You see, comadre, I tol' you the medicina would estar' to work."

"Ándale, didn't I tell you that Doctor Herida knew what he was doing?"

"I didn't know what that stupid old lady thought she was going to accomplish by doing all the hocus-pocus with those useless herbs and plants of hers. Everybody knows that an old witch's magic is no match for a doctor's medicine. That crazy old WITCH."

And that's how it was. Doña Toña didn't seem to mind that they called on her to help them and, after she had done what she could, they proceeded to badmouth her. But that's the way it was and she didn't seem to mind.

I remember, perhaps best of all, the time my mother got sick. She was very pale and her whole body was sore. She went to see Doctor Herida and all he did was ask *her* what was wrong and, without even examining her, he prescribed something that she bought at McAnaws. When all the little blue pills were gone the soreness of her bones and the paleness of her skin remained. Not wanting to go back to Herida's, my mother asked me to go get Doña Toña. I would have never gone to get the old lady, but I had never before seen my mother so sick. So I went.

On the way to Little Feo's house, which was only three blocks from my own, I saw Doña Toña walking towards me. When she was close enough to hear me, I began to speak but she cut me off, saying that she knew my mother was sick and had asked for her. I got a little scared because there was no way that she could have known that my mother had asked for her, yet she knew. My head was bombarded with thoughts that perhaps she might be a witch after all. I had the urge to run away from her but I didn't. I began to think that if she were a witch, why was she always helping people? Witches were bad people. And Doña Toña wasn't. It was at this point that my fear of her disappeared and, in its place, sprouted an intense curiosity.

Doña Toña and I reached my house and we climbed the ten steps that led to the front door. I opened the door and waited for her to step in first, but she motioned with her hand to me to lead the way.

Doña Toña looked like a little moving shadow as we walked through the narrow hallway that ended at my mother's room. Her leg dragged across the old faded linoleum floor making a dull scraping sound. I reached the room and opened the door. My mother was half-asleep on the bed as Doña Toña entered. I walked in after her because I wanted to see what kind of magic she was going to have to perform in order to save my mother; but as soon as Doña Toña began taking some candles from her sack, my mother looked at me and told me to go outside to play with the other kids.

I left the room but had no intentions of going outside to play. My mother's bedroom was next to the bathroom and there was a door that connected both of them. The bathroom could be locked only from the inside, so my mother usually left it unlocked in case some unexpected emergency came up. I went into the bathroom and, without turning on the light, looked through the crack of the slightly open door.

My mother was sprawled on the bed, face down. Her night gown was open exposing her shoulder blades and back. Doña Toña melted the bottoms of two candles and then placed one between the shoulder blades and the other at the base of the spine. Doña Toña began to pray as she pinched the area around the candles. Her movements were almost imperceptible. The candlelight made her old brown hands shine and her eyes looked like little moons. Doña Toña's voice got louder as her hands moved faster across my mother's back. The words she prayed were indecipherable even with the increase in volume. The scene reminded me of a priest praying in Latin during Mass, asking God to save us from damnation while no one knew what he was saying. The wax from the candles slid down onto my mother's back and shoulder blades, forming what looked like roots. It looked as though there were two trees of wax growing out of her back.

About a half an hour went by before the candles had burned themselves into oblivion, spreading wax all over my mother's back. Doña Toña stopped praying and scraped the wax away. She reached into the sack and pulled out a little baby food jar half-filled with something that resembled lard. She scooped some of the stuff out with her hand and rubbed it over the areas that had been covered by the wax. Next, she took from the sack a coffee can filled with an herb that looked like oregano. She sprinkled the herb over the lardlike substance and began rubbing it into the skin.

When she was almost finished, Doña Toña looked around the room and stared straight into the dark opening of the bathroom. I felt that she knew I was behind the door but I stayed there anyway. She turned back to face my mother, bent down, and whispered something in her ear.

Doña Toña picked up all her paraphernalia and returned it to its place in the sack. As she started to leave, she headed for the bathroom door. The heart in my chest almost exploded before I heard my mother's voice tell Doña Toña that she was leaving through the wrong door.

I hurried from the bathroom and ran through the other rooms in the house so that I could catch Doña Toña to show her the way out. I reached her as she was closing the door to my mother's room and led her to the front of the house. As she was making her way down the stairs I heard her mumble something about "learning the secrets" then she looked up at me and smiled. I couldn't help but smile back because her face looked like a brown jack-o-lantern with only one strange tooth carved into it. Doña Toña turned to walk down the remaining four stairs. I was going to ask her what she had said, but by the time I had the words formed in my mind, she had reached the street and was on her way home.

I went back inside the house and looked in on my mother. She was asleep. I knew that she was going to be all right and that it was not going to be because the "medicina" was beginning to work or because Doctor Herida knew what he was doing.

43

A Time With a Future

Nicholasa Mohr

(Carmela)

"A whole lifetime together, imagine! And now it's over." Edna spoke, holding back her tears. "I don't know what I would do if I were Mama, honest."

"Poor Mama," murmured Mary, "she's had such a hard time of it. I'm glad that in these last few years they had each other. Papa was her whole life." Mary stopped and began to sob quietly. Edna put her arms around Mary, who buried her head in her sister's bosom.

"Oh Edna, it's so sad to see it all come to an end. The end of something so special."

"Come on, Mary." Edna very gently pushed Mary away from her. "Let's not get like this. Think of Ma. If she sees us crying, it'll be worse for her. We all have to figure this thing out calmly and rationally."

"I know." Mary wiped her eyes and swallowed. "It's . . . the finality of it that's so hard for me to bear, you know? But you're right, we're all Mom's got now, so it's up to us to decide what's best. At her age, it's like you say, she can't be left alone."

"That's more like it, and we can't stay here day after day indefinitely like this. I don't know how long Joe's mother is going to hold out with my kids. How about you? Exactly how long do you think Mark's gonna come home from work to take care of your three

and do housework? That's why, when Roberto gets here, I'll discuss what Joe and I have agreed to. Then all three of us have to sit down and decide Mama's future."

Carmela had left her daughters seated in the kitchen, entered the small bedroom of her four room flat and closed the door, shutting out their voices. She was sick of her daughters' tear-stained faces, their wailing, crying and self-pity. Grown women, with families, acting like children. Carmela shook her head; it was all too much. Her whole body was tired; every bone, every muscle ached. She pulled back the bedspread, kicked off her shoes and lay down.

They had buried Benjamin two days ago, but her daughters had insisted on remaining with her both nights. And that meant Carmela had to make the daybed in the other room, share her own bed with one of her daughters, find more sheets, towels, dishes and all the extra work that was part of caring for others. She had not been able to rest; not as she should, by herself, alone with her private grief and deep sense of relief. There had been too many people at the funeral. Benjamin's friends from the union, neighbors and people she had not seen in years. Carmela felt her eyelids closing with a heaviness from lack of sleep. She had not really slept peacefully in over a week and, before that, for what had seemed like a timeless battle, she had hardly known sleep at all.

Her mind was still filled with him, with Benjamin. When they had laid Benjamin out in the casket, they had pinned a bright scarlet

Source: "A Time With a Future" from *Rituals of Survival* by N. Mohr. Copyright © 1986 by Nicholasa Mohr. Reprinted by permission of Arte Publico Press, University of Houston.

carnation on the lapel on his best suit. The rich red color of the flower contrasted sharply with the dry greyness of his skin and accentuated the dark purple lines of pain that the long illness had etched in his face. Carmela had asked the morticians to replace the red carnation with a white one; this change had made it easier to look at him.

She remembered her Freddie all too vividly. There are things one never forgets, always feels. Like my Freddie, Carmela nodded. His small casket had been laden with flowers. They had placed a bright red rose in his hands which were cupped together as if in prayer. For him, this had been the right color, matching his full red mouth which was fixed in a serene smile. He appeared to be sleeping and, for one long moment, Carmela had actually believed that Freddie would look up, his dark eyes smiling, and question her. "Where am I, Mami? What am I doing here?" And she would respond, "A bad dream, my baby. Freddie, you and me, we are both having a bad dream."

But it was no dream. Freddie's illness had been unexpected, swift and real. In a matter of days she had lost him. Not like Benjamin; more than a year of waiting patiently for him to die. . . .

As soon as Benjamin came home from work, Carmela returned, staying by Freddie's side for the better part of two days. Freddie was not improving, but he had not gotten worse. When he was awake, he smiled at her from under the oxygen tent and she smiled back, telling him all about the things she would get for him after he got well again.

When on the third day she had made her brief visit home to check on the others, Benjamin complained.

"Two days! Two days! I can't stay out another day. Woman, what am I gonna do for money to buy food, pay rent . . . when they dock me? I must get back to work. Freddie's all right now. He's in the best place, in the hospital with the doctors who know better than you what to do." This time Carmela fought back. "But if something should happen to him, I want to be there at his side. Freddie mustn't be alone." Benjamin was un-

shaken. "I can't be here with the kids, cooking, washing and doing your housework . . . just in case something happens! There's plenty men out there looking for jobs. I'll lose my job . . . woman! If you want to go when I'm not here, call in a neighbor or get a friend. How about Sara, you've done her plenty of favors, eh?" Carmela resisted. "What friends? When do I have time to make friends? Neighbors can't be staying here all day with our kids, and neither can Sara. Besides, she's alone with her own children and worse off than us. There's only you; nobody else can stay here except you. Ben . . . maybe you can ask for part-time work just a few more days until Freddie is over the crisis . . . maybe . . . " Benjamin shouted, "Stop it!" Full of his own fears, his mind raced with memories of his childhood in a time where death and starvation had dictated his existence. And for two days now, the words to a song he had not heard since he was a small boy would not leave his mind; they played on his lips over and over.

First the tremors,
then the typhoid

follows hunger with every breath
we pray for joy, for better times
but the only relief is the promise of death!

The peasants of his tiny rural village would sing this song during the typhoid epidemic. Benjamin had lost his father, two older brothers and baby sister, leaving only his mother, older sister and younger brother. He was nine when he became head of the household. Sometimes he would get work at the fields or at the sugar refinery, working from sun-up to sundown, bringing home twenty-five, maybe thirty cents a day, depending on the work to be done. Other days he would work chopping wood, running errands and cleaning the hog pens, to be paid in food; usually leftovers, but enough so that they wouldn't starve at home. At thirteen, when his mother died, his sister found work as a domestic and he and his younger brother set out on their own.

"Absolutely not, woman! There's a god-dam depression out there. Do you think I'm gonna let us all starve? I ain't selling apples or shoelaces in the street, not when I got a job to go to. And we don't take charity in this family. I go back to work tomorrow and you . . . you can do what the hell you want!" Carmela kept silent. Benjamin had a strong will and his fears justified his reasoning. She understood she could not persuade him.

Carmela had not wanted Freddie to die alone in the hospital, but that's how it had happened. For the next three days, she had only been able to be with him for a few hours, and always with the thought of the others that she left at home, unattended for the most part. That evening when Mr. Cooper, owner of the candy store, sent a message that the hospital had called on the public phone asking her to come right away, Carmela guessed what it was they would tell her.

"Too late. We did everything we possibly could." The young doctor was compassionate and visibly upset. "Double pneumonia . . . there was nothing we could give him. All of us did the best we could. We are all very, very sorry. Mrs. Puig, Freddie was a wonderful little boy."

That was in another lifetime, the time of the Great Depression, before the Second World War, before penicillin, antibiotics and miracle drugs. Today it would have been different; children don't have to die from that illness anymore. Medicine, in this lifetime, knows no limits. Look at an old man like Benjamin, eh? Kept alive, full of disease and tortured by pain beyond human endurance. And for what? No future, no hope, only the knowledge that each day he remained alive would be a torment for both of them.

Carmela opened her eyes and yawned, stretching her body. There was no sense in expecting sleep to come, take over and soothe away her weariness. Too much was still happening inside, repeating itself. The past was still the present and the present was not yet real.

When the doctor told her about Benjamin, she had insisted he be told as well. It was too much for her at this time; no longer did she have that kind of strength for others. Besides, Benjamin was a proud man, and it was only right. He had already suspected what the doctors confirmed; he was frightened, but not shocked. Calmly, Benjamin had told her he was resigned to the inevitable, but wanted to ask her for one last favor. And that request stirred and brought to the surface those deep and private feelings of hatred and revenge that can only be felt by one human being for another when they have been as close as Benjamin and Carmela. Then, as he spoke, Carmela felt herself spinning with rage.

"Carmela, no matter how sick I get, don't send me away. Let me die here in my own bed, Carmelita, here with you, by your side."

A tirade of words she had been nurturing, rehearsing and storing away for that day when she would leave him, walk out, walk out for good, choked Carmela. "Remember Freddie? Remember our son, Benjamin? How he died alone? In a strange place, in a strange bed. Without me by his side. I owed him at least as much as you ask of me. A baby, four years old with no one to comfort him from the fear of death, to guide him gently into the unknown. It all happened thirty-eight years ago, but I remember. And now, today, now . . . you want the right to die here, safe and secure in my arms. I didn't give birth to you! You selfish, hateful man, how well I know you!"

They had looked at each other silently. He, waiting for her to answer. She, unable to speak, afraid of that explosion of terrible words that would vent her rage. Now it was so easy to hurt him, to make him suffer as she had suffered the death and loss of her child. She couldn't speak, not one word left her lips. Carmela saw him old and tired, bracing himself against death, preparing himself and seeking her help. He spoke again, this time pleading.

"Promise, Carmela, that's all I ask of you. Just this favor and never will I ask you for another thing; I give you my word . . . just don't, don't send me away; no matter what, let me die at home."

Carmela had hidden her resentment and put aside her hatred. Instead, she responded as always, to the unspoken bond that existed between them, that dependency on each other.

And she had promised, "It'll be all right, Benjamin, you can remain at home. No matter how sick you get. Don't worry, I won't let them take you away. You can stay here with me . . . until it's over."

This pact, built on survival, was what held them together; it was what had cemented them to a lifetime of sharing without so much as a day's voluntary separation. That security, that dependency, was the foundation of their marriage; solid and tough, like a boulder of impenetrable granite.

For a full year she had nursed him, giving him medicine, caring for him as he got weaker, almost every minute of the day and night. In time, she had to bathe him, give him the bedpan and finally spoon-feed him. His body, at first, was still strong and straight. They had not slept together for many years and so Carmela had been amazed by his supple body, the muscular limbs and tightness of skin that was unusual for a man as old as Benjamin. But, as he got sicker and lost weight, his body became frail and bent; his skin hung loosely as if lightly tacked onto his bones.

The sleepless nights, when he called out to her for comfort not once, but constantly . . . the three flights she had to climb, loaded with bundles, began to rip Carmela apart. The burden of his illness gave her no time to rest. Completely exhausted, she decided to speak to him about her promise.

"Benjamin, maybe it's better for you in the hospital. Listen, think about it, please. They can care for you better there, give you stronger medicine, maybe, eh? Look, Benjamin, I'm so tired, because there's nothing more I can do for you. Please, I don't know how long I can hold out . . . please think about it. I promise, I'll be out to see you every day; every single day I'll be by your side at the hospital, I swear . . ."

"No, you promised me! And now you talk about sending me out! You said I could stay. Carmela, you've become hard-hearted to say this to me. No!" His eyes had filled with tears. Like a child, he clung desperately to her, grabbing her hands, groping at her body. "Please, in the name of God . . . please don't send me away. Let me die here, with you . . . you promised!" Carmela had pushed him away, tearing at his fingers, shoving and struggling, unable to free herself from his fierce grip. "You promised! Now that I'm dying, I don't matter anymore . . . you can't send me away . . . you can't . . . ."

"Selfish man, you deserve to die alone, just like my dead baby! It would be justice to send you away . . . away from me."

Again the words remained unspoken, instead, she said "All right, stop it! Stop! For God's sake, you can stay, I promise you. But I'm getting some help. I can't do it all alone. All right, I said you can stay!" Only then, after she had reassured him, had Benjamin released her.

Carmela had run away to the other side of the apartment and had put her hands over her ears to shut out his crying. But she still heard his loud sobbing and screaming.

"Carmela, Carmelita, you are a good woman!"

Carmela was able to get some help, a practical nurse came three times a week and later, every day. Benjamin journeyed each day on a long painful road that would lead to death. The kind of merciless journey that comes with cancer. The cancer had started in his lower intestines and finally ran rampant through the body, leaving him helpless, barely able to move. But still he clung to life, determined to put up a battle; fighting to survive was all he knew.

He would call out "Carmela . . . get me some water, Carmela, I don't want the nurse, tell her to leave. Do something for this pain! Carmela, give me something. Don't leave me, Carmela." And she would hope and pray that before he could utter her name once more, he would stop breathing.

Then, at last, he lapsed into a coma, feebly clinging to life. He would utter sounds and sentences which were, for the most part, unintelligible. Sometimes he screamed out the names of his own parents, brothers and sisters. Events of his childhood, memories of back home filled his mind and escaped from his lips. He spoke mostly in Spanish, laughing, crying and asking questions. No one knew what he wanted and, after two days, no one listened except Carmela. Maybe at this time, Carmela hoped, he would say something about their dead child, but in all his tangled words and gibberish, Freddie's name was never mentioned.

Her children had been at the apartment since the father's latest turn for the worse. That day, they all sat in the kitchen, drinking coffee and hot chocolate, waiting for him to die. They shared the vigil, taking turns at Benjamin's bedside. Late that evening, Roberto called his mother and when she returned, they found Benjamin staring blankly, not breathing. A look of peace spread over his face, as if the pain had finally disappeared. Gently, Carmela closed his eyes and mouth, kissed his dry lips and covered his face with the sheet.

Again, thoughts about the funeral, the people, the flowers and Freddie crowded Carmela's thoughts. It was as if her thinking pattern were following a cycle, winding up always with Benjamin's death.

Perhaps she was avoiding this latest part of the whole business? Carmela knew she had to deal with her children, grown-ups who still insisted on that relationship of mother and child. Now they felt themselves to be in charge. Carmela sighed, almost out of patience. She heard the front door and voices. That would be Roberto, and now her children would begin another discussion about her future.

She had been through their weddings, the birth of their children, marital disputes from time to time; always she had listened and given her support. What they wanted now, and what they might ask of her, created an anxiety that drained Carmela's energy. In a few minutes she would get up and speak to them. Sooner or later they had to talk.

"Mama can come home with me, we'll find the room; Suzie and Gigi can double up . . ." Mary looked at her brother and sister nervously, then continued, "Mark won't mind, honest."

"No," Edna responded, "I think it's better if she comes with me; after all, we have the big house. Nobody will be put out for space."

"I wish I could say it's all right at my house, but the way things are with me and Gloria, well . . ." Roberto hesitated.

"We understand, don't worry," Edna said. "Besides, it's better for Mama to be with her own daughter."

"Financially, I can always help out, you know that," Roberto smiled.

"She's got Papa's pension and some savings; she's all right as far as that goes," Edna said, "but if we need anything more, I'll let you know."

"There's only one thing about her going with you," Mary said. "She's not gonna want to go way out to Long Island, Port Jefferson is too far away from everything for her."

"She'll get used to it. It'll take a little time, that's all. Anyway, you're far way yourself, Mary. Mount Vernon isn't around the corner! And your apartment isn't big enough for another person. Where are you gonna put her?"

"You know what I think? I don't think we are gonna get Mama out of this old apartment, period." Roberto nodded emphatically. "She's too attached to it. Remember the time they took a trip to Puerto Rico, back to Papa's town, to see about retiring there? Ma said she couldn't stand it. She missed the city, her friends, everything. How long have they been living here in this place? Twenty six years or something like that, right?"

"It'll be better for her to leave here. Personally, I don't know how anybody can live here, in this city, if they can get out . . ." Edna shook her head. "The noise, the pollution, the crime! Oh, I know I wouldn't want my kids here. When we were kids, maybe it was different . . . it just seems worse today . . ."

"Mama said it's not too bad since they put up all the new middle-income buildings. She says it's better than ever with new shops and all kinds of interesting people around. Ma says she can go right to Broadway and buy anything she wants at any time of the day or . . ."

"Stop being so naive . . ." Edna interrupted. "Mary, how long can Mama stay by herself? She's sixty-six. In a few years, when she can't cope, then what? It'll be a lot worse to get her out of here. I'm not going to be commuting back and forth. And I know you, Mary . . . you too, Roberto, especially the way your marriage is going, who knows where you'll be, eh? No, we have to make a decision between us and stick to it. Now, listen to what Joe and I have planned . . ." Edna paused, making sure her brother and sister were listening. "Mama has a fairly good income from Papa's pension, so she won't be a financial burden to anyone. She's in good health, except for some arthritis now and then, but nobody ever hears her complain. And, she has some savings . . . all right, then. With a little more than half her savings we can convert the playroom area on the lower level of my house into living quarters for Mama. Like a kind of efficiency apartment, with her own kitchenette and half bath. She won't need much more because she will have the rest of the house as well. This is necessary because we will know how independent Mama is. After that initial investment, I won't charge her rent or anything. She can live there as long as she wants . . . I mean, for the rest of her days."

Roberto opened his mouth to speak, but thought better of it. Instead, he shrugged and smiled, looking at Mary. She smiled back. After a long silence, Mary said, "It sounds pretty good . . . what do you think, Roberto?" "Well, so far it's the best plan, and also the only plan. There's only one thing, like I said, Ma's gotta go for it." "She will," Edna said, "but it's up to us to convince her. The two of you better back me on this. Understand? We have to be united in this thing? Well?" Mary and Robert nodded in agreement. "Good," Edna continued, "now, what to do with this place? Mama's got all kinds of pots and pans . . . look at all of this furniture and junk. I suppose she'll want to take some of this with her . . . let's see . . ."

Carmela sat up, put on her shoes and placed the bedspread neatly back on her bed.

She heard the voices of her children. Well, she might as well get it over with. Carmela opened a bureau drawer, removed a small grey metal box and opened it. She searched among her valuable papers; the will she and Benjamin had made, the life insurance policy she had taken out on herself many years ago and still faithfully paid every month, some very old photographs, letters from her children as youngsters and from her grandchildren. Finally, she found the large manila envelope with all the material she was looking for. She closed the box and put it back. Then she walked into the kitchen where her children were waiting.

"Ma, how you feeling?" Roberto kissed his mother lightly on the forehead.

"How about something to eat, Ma?" Edna asked. "Some tea? Or a little hot broth?"

"No," Carmela sat, holding the envelope in her hands. "I'm fine; I'm not hungry."

"Mama, you should eat more, you're getting too thin . . . it's not good for you. You should eat regularly, it could affect your . . ."

"Ma . . ." interrupted Edna, ignoring Mary, "we have to have a serious talk."

"I wasn't finished," snapped Mary.

"Mama's not hungry!" Edna looked directly at Mary. "All right?"

"Listen . . ." Roberto spoke. "Why don't I go out and get us all something to eat. Chinese or Cuban . . . so nobody has to cook."

"Sit down, Roberto," Edna then continued in a quiet, calm voice, "We have all the food we need here . . ." Turning to Carmela, she went on, "Mama, now that Papa isn't here anymore . . . we want you to know that you have us and you don't have to be alone. You are our responsibility now, just as if you had Papa. We all know this . . . don't we?" She turned to Mary and Roberto.

"Yes."

"Oh yes, Mama."

"We've all discussed this a great deal, just between ourselves. And, we've decided on a plan that we know you'll like. Of course, we want to talk it over with your first, so that we have your approval. But, I'm certain that when you hear what it is, you'll be pleased."

"Oh yes, Mama, wait until you hear what Edna . . . what we . . . oh, go ahead, Edna, tell her . . ." Mary smiled.

"Joe and I agreed and thought this out carefully. You . . . are coming to live with us, Mama. With me, Joe and the kids. We are the ones with a big house. Mary's in an apartment and Roberto doesn't exactly know where he's gonna settle, not the way things are right now. I know how proud you are and how independent, so you'll want to contribute something. Here's what we think . . . you know my house is a split level and there's room for expansion, right?"

Carmela felt an urge to open the envelope at that moment and tell them, so that Edna could stop talking nonsense. But instead, she listened, trying to hide her impatience.

". . . so that your savings, or part anyway, can pay for your private apartment. Of course, as I said, you don't need such a big area, because you can share the house with the rest of us. Outside, you can take a section of the lot, Mama, if you want to have a vegetable garden or flowers. The kids would love it, and of course Joe and I won't take a cent, you can live the rest of your days rent free. You know Joe's pleased, he wants you to feel welcome in our home." Edna was almost out of breath. "Well, there, I've said my piece . . . now what do you think, Mama."

All three waited for Carmela to respond. She held out the envelope.

"I've got something to show all of you." Carefully she removed its contents and spread several sheets of paper out on the kitchen table. "I suppose I should have said something before this, but with your father's illness and everything else . . ." Carmela gestured that they come closer. "Here we are . . . take a look. It's a co-op. The building's only been up about three years. Everything is brand new. My apartment is on the sixteenth floor, on the northwest corner, just like I wanted, with lots of windows and it's got a terrace! Imagine, a terrace . . . I'm gonna feel rich . . . that's what. Look . . . kids, here are the floor plans, see? I got one bedroom, a living room-dining room, a brand new kitchen. Oh, and here's an incin-erator for garbage. They've got one on every floor and a community room with all kinds of activities. I heard from some of the people who live there, that there are some well-known experts, lecturers, coming in to speak about all kinds of subjects. The best part is that it's right here, around the corner, on Amsterdam Avenue. On the premises we have a drugstore, stationery and delicatessen. You know, I put my name down for this with a deposit right after Papa got sick. He hadn't wanted us to move, but once I knew how things would be, I went ahead. They called me just before Benjamin died, when he was almost in a coma, and asked if I could move in around the first of the month. I took a chance . . . I knew he couldn't last much longer, and said yes. That's in two weeks!" Carmela was busy tracing the floor plans with her fingers showing them the closets and cabinet space. "Here? See, I've paid the purchase, my savings covered the amount. You are all welcome to come and sit on the terrace . . . wait until you see how beautiful it is . . ."

"Mama . . ." Edna's voice was sharp, "what about what I just said? I finished explaining to you . . . a very important plan concerning your future. What about it?"

"I'm moving the first of the month, Edna," Carmela continued to look at floor plans. "But, I thank you and your husband for thinking of me."

"Is that it, Mama?"

"Yes, Edna."

"You already signed the lease, paid the money and everything?"

"Yes, all I have to do is move in, Edna."

"Well . . . I'm glad to see you figured it all out, Mama." Edna looked at Mary and Roberto; they avoided her eyes. "There's just one thing, eh? Who is gonna look after you when you can't . . .? You are sixty-six, ma! Sixty-six!"

"Not you, Edna." Carmela looked at her children. "Or you, Mary, or you, Roberto."

"Mama, I don't think you are being practical. Now, I'm too far away to be here if anything happens! If you get sick . . . and so is Mary. And as far as Roberto is concerned . . ."

"I'll manage."

"Manage? Please, Mama. Mary, Roberto, what do you have to say? Don't you think Mama should have asked us first about this? Mama, you should have spoken to us! After all, we are your children."

"I didn't ask any of you to come here when Papa was so sick, did I? I never called or bothered you. I took care of all of you once, and I took care of him . . . now, I want the privilege of taking care of myself!" There was a long silence and Carmela continued. "Thank you Edna, Mary, Roberto, you are all good children. But I can take care of myself; I've done it all my life."

"If that's the way you see it, Mama, I'm with you." Roberto said. "Right, Mary?"

"Okay . . . I guess . . ." Mary smiled weakly at Edna.

"All right, Mama." Edna stood up. "Go ahead . . . but remember, I tried my best to work something out for you. When something happens, you won't have anybody near you."

"I appreciate your good intentions, Edna, but it's all settled."

"When are you moving in, Mama?" asked Mary.

"I hope on the first, but since the landlord here knows me so well after twenty six years, and we always paid our rent, I might be able to stay a few days extra, if things are not ready at the new place. I've already arranged everything with the movers and with the super of the new building . . ."

They spoke for a while and Carmela talked excitedly about her new apartment.

"I feel better now that you all know . . . in fact," a feeling of drowsiness overcame her, "I think I might take a nap."

"Mama," Edna said, "we are all gonna have to leave soon, you know, get back to our families. But if you need us, please call."

"Good," Carmela smiled, "we should all get back to our own business of living, eh? The dead are at peace, after all. You were all a great help. Your husbands and children need you, and you too, Roberto . . . Gloria and the kids would like to see you, I'm sure."

"Go on, Mama, take your nap. Edna and I will cook something light, and then I think I'll call Mark to pick me up."

Carmela put everything back into her envelope and left. She closed her door and lay down, a sweet twilight state embraced her; it seemed to promise a deep sleep.

The two sisters began to open the refrigerator and pantry to prepare the evening meal. Mary turned to Edna, who was still sobbing quietly.

"What's the matter now?"

"I . . . wish she would be sorry . . ."

Carmela stood on the small terrace of her new apartment. She looked down at the city laid out before her. In between and over some of the buildings she could see the Hudson River and part of the George Washington Bridge. The river was dotted with sailboats and small craft that slipped in and out of sight. Overhead she had a view of a wide blue sky, changing clouds competing with the bright sun. Flocks of birds were returning home now that winter was over. Carmela took a deep breath. There was a warmth in the air; spring was almost here. In a couple of weeks she could bring out her new folding chair, lounger and snack table. Soon she would bring out her plants. New buds would begin to sprout, growing strong and healthy with the abundant sunlight and fresh air.

Carmela missed no one in particular. From time to time her children and grandchildren visited. She was pleased to see them for a short while and then was even happier when they left. In a few days it would be a whole year since Benjamin's death. It seemed like yesterday sometimes, and sometimes it was like it never happened.

She rarely thought about Benjamin. Memories of her days as a young girl became frequent, clear and at times quite vivid. Before Carmela had married at sixteen, she had dreamed of traveling to all the many places she had seen in her geography book. After school she would often go with her brothers to the docks of San Juan just to watch the freighters and big ships.

"When I grow up I'm going to work and travel on those ships." "Carmelita, don't be silly, you can't. Girls can't join the navy or the merchant marine."

How she had wished she had been born a boy, to be able to travel anywhere, to be part of that world. Carmela loved the water; ocean, sea, river, all gave her a feeling of freedom.

She looked out from her terrace at the river, and a sense of peace filled her whole being. Carmela recognized it was the same exhilarating happiness she had experienced as a young girl, when each day would be a day for her to reckon with, all her own, a time with a future.

44

Racial Differences in Health and Health Care Service Utilization in Later Life: The Effect of Socioeconomic Status

Jan E. Mutchler
Jeffrey A. Burr

Reasons for the observed health differences between Blacks and Whites are not entirely clear. One of the more compelling arguments traces both morbidity and mortality experiences of Blacks and Whites to differences in socioeconomic status. This argument is plausible because socioeconomic status conditions many factors that relate to health, ranging from knowledge of health care practices and nutrition to ability to purchase medical care. Indeed, studies that have addressed socioeconomic determinants of health show conclusively that individuals with more education and income are in better health (Antonovsky, 1967; Syme & Berkman, 1981; Victor, 1989). Because the trajectories of both health and socioeconomic accumulation converge in later life, the study of the association between health and socioeconomic status is particularly important for the older population.

The primary goal of this study is to consider the association between socioeconomic status and health among Blacks and Whites in later life. The study begins with a descriptive review of health-related differences be-

Source: Excerpted from "Racial Differences in Health and Health Care Service Utilization in Later Life: The Effect of Socioeconomic Status" by Jan E. Mutchler and Jeffrey A. Burr, *Journal of Health and Social Behavior* 32(December 1991), 342-356. Reprinted by permission.

tween Blacks and Whites age 55 and over. This is followed by a multivariate analysis of health status and health care service utilization in later life that emphasizes socioeconomic explanations. This analysis extends previous work in the area by considering multiple indicators of health as well as multiple dimensions of socioeconomic status, in order to provide a more comprehensive assessment of the ways in which socioeconomic status and race interact to shape patterns of health in later life. The empirical analysis is undertaken using the third and fourth waves of the 1984 panel of the Survey of Income and Program Participation, a nationally representative survey of the household population. The goal of this analysis is to examine the degree to which health differences between Blacks and Whites can be explained by socioeconomic status. If race effects are eliminated when socioeconomic status is controlled, we may conclude that class differences between Blacks and Whites have largely replaced those based on race per se. However, inequality based on race alone may have shifted out of the economic sphere but still be present in other settings (Wilson, 1978). Thus, racial inequality and racism could continue to affect health through stress associated with minority group status.

Some of the Health Status Findings

In summary, it appears that some share of the association between race and health status is a function of socioeconomic characteristics. Consistent with other research, one of the reasons that Blacks are in poorer health than Whites in later life is because they are less advantaged in terms of income, wealth, access to health care, and the like. However, even controlling for many of these differences, race retains a significant effect for the most subjective measure of health.

Some of the Health Care Service Utilization Findings

These results indicate that Blacks have more visits to health care professionals than do Whites, and that this pattern persists even net of socioeconomic status. Those with private insurance have more visits, as do those with more education and those with more income. A comparison of the independent contributions of each socioeconomic measure to overall fit of the model indicates that those most directly associated with affordability—income and private insurance coverage—are most important in explaining variation in the nights spent in the hospital within this population. As would be expected, most of the health status measures are also positively associated with number of visits to a health care professional. The sole exception is number of limitations in daily activities. This variable, while having only a small effect, is negatively related to health care visits.

The second utilization variable considers the number of nights spent in a hospital over the year prior to interview. Once again, all health care status measures are positively associated with hospital stays except the activities of daily living measure, which is not significant. Although the race variable is initially associated with fewer nights spent in the hospital, this coefficient loses significance when socioeconomic status is introduced. Indeed, hospital stays appear to be determined largely by health and affordability (in terms of income and insurance coverage), with age and sex playing an ancillary role. Once again,

comparisons of the independent contributions of each measure of socioeconomic status to the overall fit of the model suggests that income and private insurance coverage are the most important socioeconomic characteristics explaining hospital use.

Interactive Models of Health Status and Utilization

To consider the possibility that the health of Blacks and Whites is differentially related to the other variables in the model, a final model was generated for each health care utilization measure including interaction terms for each socioeconomic status indicator with race. These models include the main effect terms plus interaction terms for race with private insurance coverage, education, net worth, and income.

Considering self-ratings first, several significant differences between Blacks and Whites in the effects of socioeconomic indicators are noted. First, the effect of private insurance on self-rated health is significantly stronger for Blacks than for Whites. Further, while education and net worth are significantly negative for Whites, they appear to have smaller effects for Blacks. Only the negative effect for income is not significantly different between the two race groups. These results suggest that the accumulation of education and net worth over the life course does not provide an equivalent level of good health for Blacks as it does for Whites, and that having private insurance may be particularly important to the perceived health of Blacks.

Important Black/White differences in effects of net worth and private insurance on the physical mobility index are noted. The effects of private insurance on mobility are significantly more negative for Blacks than for Whites, while the effects of net worth are substantially smaller for Blacks. The effects of education and income are negative for both groups and not significantly different. While most of the effects of socioeconomic status on activities of daily living and number of bed days are consistent for Blacks and Whites, some significant differences in coefficients occur. The effect of education on activities of daily living is negative for Whites but essentially zero for Blacks. Similarly, the effect of net worth on number of bed days is negative for Whites but very small for Blacks.

Taken as a whole, these results suggest that Black and White health in later life is conditioned by income in similar ways. However, socioeconomic characteristics that may be most reflective of life-long patterns of inequality—that is, net worth and education—do interact with race in producing health differences. Further, private insurance also tends to be more important in determining good health among Blacks than among Whites.

No significant differences between Blacks and Whites were identified for annual number of visits to a health care professional, although most of the coefficients appeared to be smaller in magnitude for Blacks. Thus, once health status is considered, the association between other characteristics and visits to health care professionals is quite similar for Blacks and Whites, although Blacks make more visits. The analysis of nights spent in the hospital during the previous year indicates that a significant difference between Blacks and Whites is observed in the effect of income. While higher income is associated with more nights spent in the hospital for Whites, the effect for Blacks is much smaller and negative in direction.

Discussion

The purpose of this paper was to examine differences between older Blacks and Whites on a range of indicators of health status and health care service utilization. Our goal was to assess these differences in the context of the uneven distribution of socioeconomic status and resources across these racial groups. Although older Blacks report poorer health than similar Whites, our results indicate that for most measures of health status, Blacks and Whites have similar levels of health once socioeconomic differences are taken into account. Importantly, our results show that the socioeconomic factors most critical in health differ-

entials are education and net worth—features related to the earlier life course. The analysis of health care service utilization measures indicates that Blacks make more visits to health care professionals, but spend fewer nights in the hospital. In contrast to the analysis of health status, the most important dimensions of socioeconomic status for health care utilization are those conditioning affordability (i.e., income and private insurance coverage). Additional analyses illustrate that similar levels of resources are deferentially associated with health for Blacks and Whites, for several of the indicators examined here.

These results are consistent with other studies showing that health status and health care service utilization levels are strongly associated with socioeconomic status. Indeed, most theoretical statements on the association between race and health highlight socioeconomic status as the critical intervening factor between race and health (Cockerham, 1989; Susser, Watson, & Hopper, 1985). While our results suggest that the health differential among individuals in these race groups would dissipate if Blacks and Whites became more similar in socioeconomic standing, this conclusion must be drawn with caution. Other characteristics, such as lifestyle, health practices, diet, and stress associated with racism and various forms of discrimination, are correlated with, but distinct from, socioeconomic status, and may be reflected in the health differences observed here (Mechanic & Aiken, 1989). If this were the case, closing the socioeconomic gap between Blacks and Whites might not narrow the health gap. As an alternative solution, Black-White health differences might be resolved in large part through the equalization of, access to, and utilization of health care services, even in the absence of other socioeconomic remedies. The overall importance of private health insurance coverage, and the relatively larger effect of this resource for Blacks than for Whites, suggests that this solution may have some effect. However, based on our analysis we are confident that no simple solution will adequately remedy the health differences observed here.

More likely, widespread changes in the social structure including but not limited to the equalization of access to and utilization of health care services throughout the life course are required.

Two important findings of our study further support this generalization. First, the effect of race on the self-assessment of health remains significant in the expanded model that controls for socioeconomic differences. This means that even after socioeconomic characteristics are considered, Blacks report significantly poorer self-rated health than Whites. Consistent with this result, Blacks report more visits to a health care professional during the year prior to interview, even after controlling for socioeconomic characteristics. Thus, in terms of self-rated health and some associated health-related behaviors, older Blacks appear to have poorer health than Whites regardless of socioeconomic status. These indicators, perhaps more than the others, suggest that above and beyond the socioeconomic costs of being Black, the stress associated with minority group status may take a toll on perceived health among older Blacks. Again, the resolution of this stress would require changes in our society beyond what the equalization of earnings might provide.

In conclusion, we have documented important differences between Blacks and Whites along several dimensions of health and health care service utilization. While part of this differential appears to be associated with socioeconomic status, an effect of race persists for self-assessed health and annual visits to a health care provider. The extent to which these effects reflect life-long inequalities in health and health care access, cultural differences between Blacks and Whites, or stress associated with minority group status, are topics for future study. To resolve this issue, more research is needed on the association between socioeconomic status and health for Blacks and Whites, especially research on longitudinal and cohort changes in health, resources, and service utilization of individuals over extended periods of time.

References

Antonovsky, A. (1967). Social class, life expectancy and overall mortality. *Milbank Memorial Fund Quarterly, 45*, 31-73.

Cockerham, W. C. (1989). *Medical sociology* (4th ed.). Englewood Cliffs, NJ: Prentice Hall.

Mechanic, D., & Aiken, L. H. (1989). Access to health care and use of medical care services. In H. Freeman & S. Levine (Eds.), *Handbook of medical sociology* (4th ed., pp. 166-184). Englewood Cliffs, NJ: Prentice Hall.

Susser, M., Watson, W., & Hopper, K. (1985). *Sociology in medicine* (3rd ed.). New York: Oxford University Press.

Syme, S. L., & Berkman, L. F. (1981). Social class susceptibility and sickness. In P. Conrad & R. Kern (Eds.), *The sociology of health and illness: Critical perspectives* (pp. 35-44). New York: St. Martin's.

Victor, C. R. (1989). Inequalities in health in later life. *Age and Aging, 18*, 387-391.

Wilson, W. J. (1978). *The declining significance of race.* Chicago: University of Chicago Press.

1 Mutchler and Burr found that once socioeconomic status was controlled, African Americans still assessed their health more negatively than whites. Other differences "disappeared" once the effects of social class were removed. Which differences disappeared? What do these results suggest? What explanations can you develop for Mutchler and Burr's results?

2 How might the meaning of illness and dying be different for Jennie and Jeff Patton than for an urban, more affluent couple? How might exposure to social and psychological risk factors for disease have shaped the situation the Pattons are facing in Bontemps's story?

3 Imagine that you are attending a conference in which a physician in private practice presents a paper lamenting the tendency of elderly African Americans to delay seeking medical care and their low rates of compliance with recommended treatment. How might you use a life course perspective to respond to this physician?

4 Yezierksa does not tell us whether or not the narrator in her story "A Window Full of Sky" chose to enter the "old folks' home" or to stay in her rooming house. What decision do you think she made? If you were Miss Adcock, how might you have advised her? What factors should she consider in her decision? How does Maya Angelou's poem "On Aging" guide your advice?

5 Heurtin-Roberts's article illustrates lay models of chronic disease among African American women. This part provided other examples of lay health care that varies by membership in systems of inequality. How might such beliefs and practices interfere with healthful behaviors and with seeking appropriate medical care? Do you think it is important for health care professionals to understand lay models of disease and lay treatment strategies? Why or why not?

6 Imagine that the president invites you to join a task force charged with minimizing risks of disease and disability in future cohorts of elderly Americans. Outline a plan of action that not only would reduce average levels of disease and disability but would also reduce gaps based on gender, race, and social class.

1   Williams, D. R. (1990). Socioeconomic differentials in health: A review and redirection. *Social Psychology Quarterly, 53*(2), 81-99.

This article explores the relationship between social class and health, with special emphasis on exposure to risk factors. Lower socioeconomic status is systematically associated with nonhealthful behaviors, greater stress, and weaker social ties. Greater prevalence of these psychosocial risk factors across the life course accounts for the poorer health status of people disadvantaged by social class.

2   Belgrave, L. (1990). The relevance of chronic illness in the everyday lives of elderly women. *Journal of Aging and Health, 2*(4), 475-500.

This qualitative study explores the experience of chronic illness in the everyday lives of 29 elderly women suffering from chronic health problems. Belgrave's analysis provides insight into what it is like to live with chronic illness. She explores the ways older women talk about their illness, its impact on their self-concept, and its effect on lifestyle and relationships with others.

3   Krause, N., & Wray, L. A. (1992). Psychosocial correlates of health and illness among minority elders. In E. P. Stanford & F. M. Torres-Gil (Eds.), *Diversity: New approaches to ethnic minority aging* (pp. 41-52). Amityville, NY: Baywood.

This article explores differences in health status among elderly African Americans and elderly Hispanic Americans. The authors document uneven distribution of risk factors for health: biomedical, access to health care, and social support. Policy implications of current patterns are also discussed.

4   Jones, J. (1991). *Bad blood: The Tuskegee Syphilis Experiment.* New York: Free Press.

A detailed history of the infamous experiment in which 399 African American men with syphilis were denied treatment for "science's sake." Begun in the 1930s, the experiment continued for 40 years.

5   Wilkinson, D. (1987). Traditional medicine in American families: Reliance on the wisdom of elders. *Culture, Medicine, and Psychiatry, 11,* 65-76.

Wilkinson discusses the social history and prevalence of folk medicine among Native Americans, Appalachian whites, African Americans, and Mexican Americans. Mothers and grandmothers have played central roles as traditional healers within African American, Mexican American, and Appalachian white communities. Wilkinson concludes with a discussion of the relationships between traditional and Western scientific medicine.

6   Naylor, G. (1989). *Mama Day*. New York: Vintage.

This novel is set on a sea island off the coast of South Carolina and Georgia. Although health care and traditional medicine are not the focus of her story, the title character is Mama Day, a family matriarch and traditional healer. Naylor illustrates the relationship between traditional and Western scientific medicine in this community, where people still practice herbal medicine and honor ancestors brought from Africa as slaves.

7   National Resource Center on Health Promotion and Aging and AARP Health Advocacy Services. (1990). *Healthy aging: Model health promotion programs for minority elders* [½-in. videocassette/ 46 min./color]. (Distributed by National Resource Center on Health Promotion and Aging and AARP, Washington, DC, 202-434-2277)

This video illustrates five specially tailored programs for elderly target populations: Hispanic Americans, Pacific/Asian Americans, Native Americans, African Americans, and multicultural groups. The programs are designed on the premise that each group has its own set of health characteristics and issues. All groups face barriers of discrimination, oppression, and social and economic inequities. Thus the best health promotion efforts for minorities should emphasize advocacy, assertiveness, affirmative action, and the rights of individuals as both citizens and patients.

8   Seltzer, J. (1987). A place for mother. In S. Martz (Ed.), *When I am an old woman I shall wear purple*. Watsonville, CA: Papier-Mache.

A series of 10 poems illustrate the nursing home decisions of two generations of women in a middle-class family.

Bibliography

Abbott, J. (1977). Socioeconomic characteristics of the elderly: Some black/white differences. *Social Security Bulletin, 40,* 16-42.

Abbott, J. (1980). Work experience and earnings of middle-aged black and white men, 1965-1971. *Social Security Bulletin, 43,* 16-34.

Abel, E. (1986). Adult daughters and care for the elderly. *Feminist Studies, 12,* 479-497.

Abel, E. (1989). Family care of the frail elderly: Framing an agenda for change. *Women's Studies Quarterly, 1-2,* 75-86.

Acker, J. (1990). Hierarchies, jobs, bodies: A theory of gendered organizations. *Gender and Society, 4,* 139-158.

Aging Health Policy Center. (1985). *The homeless mentally ill elderly* (Working paper). San Francisco: University of California.

Allen, K. R. (1989). *Single women/family ties: Life histories of older women.* Newbury Park, CA: Sage.

Allen, K. R., & Chin-Sang, V. (1990). A lifetime of work: The context and meanings of leisure for aging black women. *The Gerontologist, 30,* 734-740.

Amoss, R. (1981). Cultural centrality and prestige for the elderly: The Coast Salish case. In C. Fry (Ed.), *Dimensions: Aging, culture and health* (pp. 47-63). Brooklyn, NY: J. F. Bergin.

Amoss, P. (1986). *Northwest coast grandmother myths.* Paper presented at the 84th Annual Meeting of the American Anthropological Association, Philadelphia.

Anaya, R. (1982). Uno. In *Bless me, Ultima: A novel.* Berkeley, CA: Tonatiuh International.

Andersen, M. L. (1983). *Thinking about women: Sociological and feminist perspectives.* New York: Macmillan.

Andersen, M. L. (1993). *Thinking about women: Sociological perspectives on sex and gender* (3rd ed.). New York: Macmillan.

Andersen, M. L., & Collins, P. H. (1992). *Race, class, and gender: An anthology.* Belmont, CA: Wadsworth.

Anderson, B. E., & Cottingham, D. H. (1981). The elusive quest for economic equality. *Daedalus, 110,* 257-274.

Angel, R., & Thoits, R. (1987). The impact of culture on the cognitive structure of illness. *Culture, Medicine, and Psychiatry, 11,* 465-494.

Angelou, M. (1969). *I know why the caged bird sings.* New York: Random House.

Angelou, M. (1992). On aging. In M. W. Secundy (Ed.), *Trials, tribulations and celebrations: African-American perspectives on health, illness, aging and loss* (p. 150). Yarmouth, ME: Intercultural Press.

Antonovsky, A. (1967). Social class, life expectancy and overall mortality. *Milbank Memorial Fund Quarterly, 45,* 31-73.

Archbold, P. G. (1983). The impact of parent-caring on women. *Family Relations, 32,* 39-45.

Arendell, T., & Estes, C. L. (1991). Older women in the post-Reagan era. *International Journal of Health Services, 21,* 59-73.

Aronson, J. (1992). Women's sense of responsibility for the care of old people: But who else is going to do it? *Gender and Society, 6*, 8-29.

Atchley, R. C. (1976). *The sociology of retirement.* New York: Schenkman.

Atchley, R. C. (1979). Issues in retirement research. *The Gerontologist, 19*, 44-54.

Atchley, R. C. (1991). *The social forces in later life: An introduction to social gerontology* (6th ed.). Belmont, CA: Wadsworth.

Bahr, H. M., & Caplow, T. (1973). *Old men drunk and sober.* New York: New York University Press.

Bandura, A. (1977). Self-efficacy: Toward a unifying theory of behavioral change. *Psychological Review, 84*, 191-215.

Banner, L. (1983). *American beauty.* New York: Knopf.

Barnett, H. (1955). *The Coast Salish of British Columbia.* Eugene: University of Oregon Press.

Baron, H. M. (1985). Racism transformed: The implications of the 1960s. *Review of Radical Political Economics, 17*, 10-33.

Barresi, C. M. (1992, March 15). *The impact of ethnicity on aging: A review of theory, research and issues.* Paper presented at the American Society on Aging Annual Meeting, San Diego, CA.

Bassuk, E. L. (1984). The homelessness problem. *Scientific American, 251*, 40-45.

Baxandall, R., Gordon, L., & Reverby, S. (1976). *Factory girls: America's working women: A documentary history 1600 to the present.* New York: Vintage.

Beck, E. M., Horan, R. M., & Tolbert, C. M. (1980, December). Industrial segregation and labor market discrimination. *Social Problems, 28*(2), 113-130.

Becker, G. (1985). Human capital, effort, and the sexual division of labor. *Journal of Labor Economics, 3*, S33-S58.

Belgrave, L. (1990). The relevance of chronic illness in the everyday lives of elderly women. *Journal of Aging and Health, 2*(4), 475-500.

Bell, L. P. (1989). The double standard: Age. In J. Freeman (Ed.), *Women: A feminist perspective* (4th ed., pp. 236-244). Mountain View, CA: Northfield.

Bell-Scott, P. (1982). Debunking sapphire: Toward a non-racist and non-sexist social science. In G. T. Hull, P. Bell-Scott, & B. Smith (Eds.), *But some of us are brave.* Old Westbury, NY: Feminist Press.

Bell-Scott, P., Guy-Sheftall, B., Jones Royster, J., Sims-Wood, J., DeCosta-Willis, M., & Fultz, L. (1991). *Double stitch: Black women write about mothers and daughters.* Boston: Beacon.

Bengston, V. L., Cutler, N., Mangen, D. J., & Marshall, V. W. (1985). Generations, cohorts, and relations between age groups. In R. H. Binstock & E. Shanas (Eds.), *Handbook of aging and the social sciences* (2nd ed., pp. 304-338). New York: Van Nostrand Reinhold.

Berg, R. R., & Cassells, J. S. (Eds.). (1990). *The second fifty years: Promoting health and preventing disability.* Washington, DC: National Academy Press.

Berger, R. L. (1990). Nazi science: The Dachau hypothermia experiments. *New England Journal of Medicine, 322*(20), 1435-1440.

Bergmann, B. (1986). *The economic emergence of women.* New York: Basic Books.

Berkman, L., Singer, B., & Manton, K. (1989). Black/white differences in health status and mortality among the elderly. *Demography, 26*, 661-678.

Biddle, B., & Thomas, E. (Eds.). (1966). *Role theory: Concepts and research.* New York: John Wiley.

Biesanz, M. H. (1992). Growing up in a Finnish community. In A. Jarvenpa (Ed.), *In two cultures: The stories of second generation Finnish-Americans*. St. Cloud, MN: North Star.

Blaxter, M. (1976). *The meaning of disability*. London: Heinemann.

Blumberg, L., Shipley, T. E., & Shandler, I. W. (1973). *Skid row and its alternatives*. Philadelphia: Temple University Press.

Bogue, D. J. (1983). *Skid row in American cities*. Chicago: University of Chicago Press.

Bohrnstedt, G. W. (1969). Observations on the measurement of change. In E. F. Borgatta (Ed.), *Sociological methodology*. San Francisco: Jossey-Bass.

Bontemps, A. (1992). A summer tragedy. In M. W. Secundy (Ed.), *Trials, tribulations, and celebrations: African-American perspectives on health, illness, aging and loss* (pp. 153-161). Yarmouth, ME: Intercultural Press. (Original work published 1933)

Bowlby, J. (1980). *Loss: Sadness and depression* (Vol. 3). New York: Basic Books.

Brenner, M. H. (1973). *Mental illness and the economy*. Cambridge, MA: Harvard University Press.

Breslau, N., Salkever, D., & Staruch, K. S. (1982). Women's labor force participation and responsibilities for disabled dependents: A study of families with disabled children. *Journal of Health and Social Behavior, 23*, 169-183.

Brickner, P. W. (1985). Health issues in the care of the homeless. In P. W. Brickner, L. K. Schaner, B. Conanan, A. Elvy, & M. Savarese (Eds.), *Health care of homeless people*. New York: Springer.

Brody, E. M. (1985). Parent care as a normative stress. *Gerontologist, 25*, 19-29.

Brody, E. M. (1990). *Women in the middle: Their parent-care years*. New York: Springer.

Brody, E. M., Johnson, R., Fulcomer, M., & Lang, A. (1983). Women's changing roles and help to elderly parents: Attitudes of three generations of women. *Journal of Gerontology, 38*, 597-607.

Brody, E. M., Kleman, M. H., Johnston, P. T., Hoffman, C., & Schoonover, C. B. (1987). Work status and parent care: A comparison of four groups of women. *The Gerontologist, 27*, 201-208.

Brooks, G. (1953). At the Burns-Cooper's. In *Maud Martha*. New York: Harper.

Brown, E. B. (1991). Mothers of mind. In P. Bell-Scott, B. Guy-Sheftall, J. Jones Royster, J. Sims-Wood, M. DeCosta-Willis, & L. Fultz (Eds.), *Double stitch: Black women write about mothers and daughters* (pp. 74-93). Boston: Beacon.

Brubaker, E., & Brubaker, T. (1992). The context of retired women as caregivers. In M. Szinovacz, D. Ekerdt, & B. Vinick (Eds.), *Families and retirement* (pp. 222-235). Newbury Park, CA: Sage.

Bullard, S. (1993). Free at last. In V. Cyrus (Ed.), *Experiencing race, class and gender in the United States* (pp. 269-272). Mountain View, CA: Mayfield. (Original work published 1989)

Bullough, B., & Bullough, V. (1972). *Poverty, ethnic identity and health care*. New York: Appleton-Century-Crofts.

Burnham, L. (1985). Has poverty been feminized in black America? *Black Scholar, 16*, 14-24.

Burr, J. A. (1990). Race/sex comparisons of elderly living arrangements: Factors influencing the institutionalization of the unmarried. *Research on Aging, 12*, 507-530.

Burton, L., Dilworth-Anderson, P., & Bengtson, V. (1991, Fall-Winter). Creating culturally relevant ways of thinking about diversity and aging. *Generations, 15,* 67-72.

Butler, R. N. (1975). *Why survive? Being old in America.* New York: Harper & Row.

Byerly, V. (1986). *Hard times cotton mill girls: Personal histories of womanhood and poverty in the South.* Ithaca, NY: ILR.

Cain, G. G. (1976). The challenge of segmented labor market theories to orthodox theory: A survey. *Journal of Economic Literature, 14,* 1215-1257.

Calasanti, T. M., & Bailey, C. (1991). Gender inequality and the division of labor in the United States and Sweden. *Social Problems, 38*(1), 34-53.

Calasanti, T. M., & Bonanno, A. (1992). Working overtime: Economic restructuring and retirement of a class. *Sociological Quarterly, 33*(1), 135-152.

Campbell, B. M. (1992). *Your blues ain't like mine.* New York: G. P. Putnam.

Cantor, M. H. (1979). Neighbors and friends: An overlooked resource in the informal support system. *Research on Aging, 1,* 434-463.

Carr, B. A., & Lee, E. S. (1978). Navajo tribe mortality: A life table analysis of the leading causes of death. *Social Biology, 24,* 279-287.

CBS Fox Video. (1990). *Come see the paradise* [Film]. New York.

Cheung, M. (1989). Elderly Chinese living in the United States: Assimilation or adjustment? *Social Work, 14,* 457-461.

Chirikos, T., & Nestel, G. (1983). *Economic aspects of self-reported work disability.* Columbus: Ohio State University, Center for Human Resource Research.

Chodorow, N. (1978). *The reproduction of mothering: Psychoanalyses and the sociology of gender.* Berkeley: University of California Press.

Clausen, J. A. (1993). *American lives.* New York: Free Press.

Clive, A. (1987). The home front and the household: Women, work and family in Detroit. In N. A. Hewitt (Ed.), *Women, families and communities: Readings in American history* (Vol. 2, pp. 188-203). Glenview, IL: Scott, Foresman/Little, Brown.

Coalition for the Homeless. (1984). *Crowded out: Homelessness and the elderly poor in New York City.* New York: Author.

Cockerham, W. C. (1989). *Medical sociology* (4th ed.). Englewood Cliffs, NJ: Prentice Hall.

Cohen, C. I., Teresi, J., Holmes, D., & Roth, E. (1988). Survival strategies of older homeless men. *The Gerontologist, 28*(1), 58-65.

Cohn, R. M. (1978). The effect of employment status on self-attitudes. *Social Psychology Quarterly, 41,* 81-93.

Cole, J. (1986). *All American woman: Lives that divide, ties that bind.* New York: Free Press.

Collins, P. H. (1990). *Black feminist thought: Knowledge, consciousness, and the politics of empowerment.* Boston: Unwin Hyman.

Collins, R. H. (1991). The meaning of motherhood in black culture and black mother-daughter relationships. In P. Bell-Scott, B. Guy-Sheftall, J. Jones Royster, J. Sims-Wood, M. DeCosta-Willis, & L. Fultz (Eds.), *Double stitch: Black women write about mothers and daughters* (pp. 42-60). Boston: Beacon.

Collins, S. M. (1983). The making of the black middle class. *Social Problems, 30,* 369-382.

Commonwealth Fund Commission on Elderly People Living Alone. (1987). *Medicare's poor.* Washington, DC: Author.

Congressional Budget Office. (1988). *Trends in family income: 1970-1986.* Washington, DC: Government Printing Office.

Cool, L. E. (1980). Ethnicity and aging: Continuity through change for elderly Corsicans. In C. Fry (Ed.), *Aging in culture and society* (pp. 149-169). New York: Praeger.

Coontz, S. (1992). *The way we never were: American families and the nostalgia trap.* New York: Basic Books.

Corbin, J. M., & Strauss, A. (1988). *Unending work and care: Managing chronic illness at home.* San Francisco: Jossey-Bass.

Corcoran, M., & Duncan, G. J. (1978). A summary of part l findings. In G. J. Duncan & J. N. Morgan (Eds.), *Five thousand American families* (Vol. 5). Ann Arbor: University of Michigan, Institute for Social Research.

Coverman, S. (1983). Gender, domestic labor time and wage inequality. *American Sociological Review, 48,* 623-637.

Coward, R. T., & Dwyer, J. W. (1990). The association of gender, sibling network composition, and patterns of parent care by adult children. *Research on Aging, 12,* 158-181.

Coward, R. T., Horne, C., & Dwyer, J. W. (1992). Demographic perspectives on gender and family caregiving. In J. W. Dwyer & R. T. Coward (Eds.), *Gender, families, and elder care.* Newbury Park, CA: Sage.

Cowgill, D. O. (1986). Economic systems and economic roles of the aged: Ascendancy and continuity. In *Aging around the world* (pp. 108-119). Belmont, CA: Wadsworth.

Cummings, E., & Henry, W. (1961). *Growing old: The process of disengagement.* New York: Basic Books.

Crystal, S., & Shea, D. (1990). Cumulative advantage, cumulative disadvantage, and inequality among elderly people. *The Gerontologist, 30,* 437-443.

Crystal, S., Shea, D., & Krishnaswami, S. (1992). Educational attainment, occupational history, and stratification: Determinants of later life economic outcomes. *Journal of Gerontology: Social Sciences, 47,* S213-S221.

Cyrus, V. (Ed.). (1993). *Experiencing race, class, and gender in the United States.* Mountain View, CA: Mayfield.

Danigelis, N., & Cutler, S. (1991). An inter-cohort comparison of change in racial attitudes. *Research on Aging, 13*(3), 383-404.

D'Augelli, A., & Hart, M. M. (1987). Gay women, men and families in rural settings: Toward the development of helping communities. *American Journal of Community Psychology, 15*(1), 79-93.

Davidson, L., & Gordon, L. K. (1979). *The sociology of gender.* Chicago: Rand McNally.

Davis, A. (1981). *Women, race and class.* New York: Vintage.

Davis, K., & Rowland, D. (1991). Old and poor: Policy challenges in the 1990s. *Journal of Aging: Social Policy, 2,* 37-59.

Davison, C., Frankel, S., & Smith, G. D. (1992). The limits of lifestyle: Reassessing "fatalism" in the popular culture of illness prevention. *Social Science and Medicine, 34,* 675-685.

Dean, K. (1986). Lay care in illness. *Social Science and Medicine, 22,* 275-284.

Delany, S., & Delany, E. (with A. H. Heart). (1993). *Having our say: The Delany sisters' first 100 years.* New York: Kodansha America.

Detzner, D. F. (in press). Conflict in southeast Asian refugee families: A life history approach. In J. Gilgun, K. Daly, & F. Handel (Eds.), *Qualitative methods in family research.* Newbury Park, CA: Sage.

DeViney, S., & O'Rand, A. (1988). Gender-cohort succession and retirement among older men and women, 1951-1984. *Sociological Quarterly, 29,* 525-540.

Diao, N. (1987). From homemaker to housing advocate: An interview with Mrs. Chang Jok Lee. *Signs: Journal of Women in Culture and Society, 12,* 440-453.

Dill, B. T. (1979). The dialectics of black womanhood. *Signs: Journal of Women in Culture and Society, 4,* 543-555.

Dill, B. T. (1983). Race, class, and gender: Prospects for an all-inclusive sisterhood. *Feminist Studies, 9,* 131-150.

Dilworth, A. R. (1992, Summer). Extended kin networks in black families. *Generations, 16,* 29-32.

Dorris, M. (1987). *A yellow raft in blue water.* New York: Warner.

Dowd, J. J. (1980). *Stratification among the aged.* Monterey, CA: Brooks/Cole.

Dressel, P. (1986). Civil rights, affirmative action, and the aged of the future: Will life chances be different for blacks, Hispanics, and women? An overview of the issues. *The Gerontologist, 26,* 128-131.

Dressel, P. L. (1988). Gender, race, and class: Beyond the feminization of poverty in later life. *The Gerontologist, 28*(2), 177-180.

Duncan, G., & Morgan, J. (1980). The incidence and some consequences of major life events. In G. Duncan & J. Morgan (Eds.), *Five thousand American families* (Vol. 8, pp. 183-240). Ann Arbor: University of Michigan, Institute for Social Research.

Dunker, B. (1987). Aging lesbians: Observations and speculations. In Boston Lesbian Psychologies Collective (Ed.), *Lesbian psychologies* (pp. 72-88). Urbana: University of Illinois Press.

Dwyer, J., & Coward, R. T. (Eds.). (1992). *Gender, families and elder care.* Newbury Park, CA: Sage.

Ehrenreich, B., & Piven, F. F. (1984). The feminization of poverty. *Dissent, 31,* 162-170.

Ehrenreich, B., & Stallard, K. (1982). The nouveau poor. *Ms., 11,* 217-224.

Elder, G. H., Jr. (1974). *Children of the Great Depression.* Chicago: University of Chicago Press.

Elder, G. H., Jr. (1985). Perspectives on the life course. In *Life course dynamics: Trajectories and transitions, 1968-1980* (pp. 23-27). Ithaca, NY: Cornell University Press.

Elder, G. H., Jr., & Liker, J. K. (1982). Hard times in women's lives: Historical influences across forty years. *American Journal of Sociology, 88*(2), 241-269.

Elder, G. H., Jr., & Rockwell, R. C. (1978). Economic depression and postwar opportunity: A study of life patterns and health. In R. A. Simmons (Ed.), *Research in community and mental health* (pp. 249-303). Greenwich, CT: JAI.

Ellison, D. L. (1968). Work, retirement and the sick role. *The Gerontologist, 8,* 189-192.

Ellison, R. (1952). *Invisible man.* New York: Random House.

Elmendorf, W., & Kroeber, A. (1960). *The structure of Twona culture with notes on Yurok culture.* Pullman: Washington State University Press.

Erdrich, L. (1984). *Love medicine.* Bloomington: Indiana University Press.

Esping-Anderson, G. (1989). The three political economics of the welfare state. *Canadian Review of Sociology and Anthropology, 26*(1), 10-36.

Farley, R., & Allen, W. R. (1987). *The color line and the quality of life in America.* New York: Russell Sage.

Featherman, D. (1983). Lifespan perspectives in social science research. In P. Baltes & O. G. Brim (Eds.), *Lifespan development and behavior* (Vol. 5, pp. 621-648). New York: Academic Press.

Ferraro, K. F. (1987). Double jeopardy to health for black older adults? *Journal of Gerontology: Social Sciences, 42,* 528-533.

Fillenbaum, G., George, L., & Palmore, E. (1985). Determinants and consequences of retirement among men of different races and economic levels. *Journal of Gerontology, 40,* 85-95.

Fischer, L. R., & Hoffman, C. (1984). Who cares for the elderly: The dilemma of family support. In M. Lewis & J. Miller (Eds.), *Research in social problems and public policy, a research annual* (Vol. 3, pp. 169-215). Greenwich, CT: JAI.

Fischer, P. J., Breakey, W. R., Shapiro, S., & Kramer, M. (1986). Baltimore mission users: Social networks, morbidity, and employment. *Psychosocial Rehabilitation Journal, 9,* 51-63.

Fischer, R. J., Shapiro, S., Breakey, W. R., Anthony, J. C., & Kramer, M. (1986). Mental health and social characteristics of the homeless: A survey of mission users. *American Journal of Public Health, 76,* 519-524.

Foner, A. (1986). *Aging and old age: New perspective.* Englewood Cliffs, NJ: Prentice Hall.

Ford, A., Haug, M. R., Jones, R. K., Roy, A. W., & Folman, S. J. (1990). Race-related differences among elderly urban residents: A cohort study, 1975-1984. *Journal of Gerontology: Social Sciences, 45,* S163-S171.

Friedan, B. (1964). *The feminine mystique.* New York: Norton.

Galarza, E. (1971). On the edge of the barrio. In *Barrio boy.* Notre Dame, IN: University of Notre Dame Press. (Original work published 1905)

Garrow, D. (1987). The origins of the Montgomery bus boycott. In N. A. Hewitt (Ed.), *Women, families and communities: Readings in American history* (Vol. 2, pp. 225-234). Glenview, IL: Scott, Foresman/Little, Brown. (First published in 1985)

Gates, H. L., Jr. (1989, November 12). TV's black world turns—but stays unreal. *New York Times,* sec. II, pp. 1 ff.

Gates, H. L., Jr. (Ed.). (1991). *Bearing witness: Selections from African-American autobiography in the twentieth century.* New York: Pantheon.

Gates, H. L., Jr. (1994). *Colored people, a memoir.* New York: Random House.

Gelfand, D. E. (1982). *Aging: The ethnic factor.* Boston: Little, Brown.

Gelfand, D. E., & Yee, B. (1992). Trends and forces: Influence of immigration, migration, and acculturation on the fabric of aging in America. *Generations, 15*(4), 7-10.

George, L. K. (1993). Sociological perspectives on life transitions. *Annual Review of Sociology, 19,* 353-373.

Gibson, R. C. (1983). Work patterns of older black and white and male and female heads of household. *Journal of Minority Aging, 8*(1-2), 1-16.

Gibson, R. C. (1987). Reconceptualizing retirement for black Americans. *The Gerontologist, 27*(6), 691-698.

Gibson, R. C. (1994). The age-by-race gap in health and mortality in the older population. *The Gerontologist, 34*(4), 454-462.

Gibson, R. C., & Jackson, J. S. (1992). The black oldest old. In R. Suzman, K. Manton, & D. Willis (Eds.), *The oldest old* (pp. 321-340). New York: Oxford University Press.

Gibson, R. C., Jackson, J. S., & Antonucci, T. C. (1993). *Race differences in productive activity.* Unpublished manuscript, University of Michigan, Institute for Social Research.

Giddings, P. (1984). *When and where I enter: The impact of black women on race and sex in America.* New York: Bantam.

Gilkes, C. T. (1985). Together and in harness: Women's traditions in the sanctified church. *Signs: Journal of Women in Culture and Society, 10,* 678-699.

Gilligan, C. (1982). *In a different voice: Psychological theory and women's development.* Cambridge, MA: Harvard University Press.

Goings, K. W. (1993). Memorabilia that have perpetuated stereotypes about African Americans. In V. Cyrus (Ed.), *Experiencing race, class and gender in the United States* (pp. 165-167). Mountain View, CA: Mayfield.

Good, B. (1977). The heart of what's the matter: The semantics of illness in Iran. *Culture, Medicine, and Psychology, 1,* 25-58.

Gordon, H. A., Hamilton, C. A., & Tipps, H. C. (1982). *Unemployment and underemployment among blacks, Hispanics, and women* (U.S. Commission on Civil Rights Clearinghouse Publication No. 74). Washington, DC: Government Printing Office.

Gornick, M., Howell, E., & McMillan, A. (1985). Twenty years of Medicare and Medicaid: Covered populations, use of benefits, and program expenditures. *Health Care Financing Review* (Annual Suppl.), pp. 13-59.

Graham, H. (1985). Providers, negotiators and mediators: Women as the hidden carers. In E. Lewin & V. Oleson (Eds.), *Women, health and healing* (pp. 25-52). London: Tavistock.

Gramlick, E. M., & Laren, D. S. (1984). How widespread are income losses in a recession? In D. L. Bawden (Ed.), *The social contract revisited: Aims and outcomes of President Reagan's social welfare policy.* Washington, DC: Urban Institute Press.

Grant, J. (1982). Black women and the church. In G. T. Hull, R. Bell-Scott, & B. Smith (Eds.), *But some of us are brave: Black women's studies* (pp. 141-152). Old Westbury, NY: Feminist Press.

Greenberg, J. (1978). *The Old Age Survivors and Disability Insurance (OASDI) system: A general overview of the social problem* (HS 7094, U.S. Report No. 78-200 EPW). Washington, DC: Government Printing Office.

Grier, W. H., & Cobbs, P. M. (1968). *Black rage.* New York: Basic Books.

Guberman, N. (1988). The family, women and caring: Who cares for the carers? *New Feminist Research, 17*(2), 37-41.

Guemple, L. (1983). Growing old in Inuit society. In J. Sokolovsky (Ed.), *Growing old in different cultures* (pp. 24-28). Belmont, CA: Wadsworth.

Gutmann, D. (1977). The cross-cultural perspective: Notes toward a comparative psychology of aging. In J. E. Birren & K. W. Schaie (Eds.), *Handbook of the psychology of aging* (pp. 302-326). New York: Van Nostrand Reinhold.

Guy-Sheftall, B. (1991). Piecing blocks: Identities—introduction. In R. Bell-Scott, B. Guy-Sheftall, J. Jones Royster, J. Sims-Wood, M. DeCosta-Willis, & L. Fultz (Eds.), *Double stitch: Black women write about mothers and daughters* (pp. 61-63). Boston: Beacon.

Gwaltney, J. L. (Ed.). (1980). *Drylongso: A self-portrait of black America.* New York: Random House.

Hacker, A. (1992). *Two nations: Black and white, separate, hostile, unequal.* New York: Scribner.

Harvest Moon Eyes. (1992). The day the crows stopped talking. In C. Trafzer (Ed.), *Earth song, sky spirit: Short stories of the contemporary Native American experience.* New York: Doubleday.

Haslam, G. (1993). The horned toad. In T. A. López (Ed.), *Growing up Chicana/o*. New York: Avon Books.

Hatch, L. R., & Thompson, A. (1992). Family responsibilities and women's retirement. In M. Szinovacz, D. J. Ekerdt, & B. Binick (Eds.), *Families and retirement* (pp. 99-113). Newbury Park, CA: Sage.

Hatfield, L. (1989, June 30). Gays say life getting better. *San Francisco Examiner*, p. A15.

Hayes, H. (1973). Voices: An epilogue. In P. O'Brian (Ed.), *The woman alone*. New York: Quadruple/New York Times Book Co. Reprinted (1991) in M. Fowler & P. McCutcheon (Eds.), *Songs of experience: An anthology of literature on growing old* (pp. 278-283). New York: Ballantine.

Healey, S. (1986). Growing to be an old woman: Aging and ageism. In J. Alexander, D. Berrow, L. Domitrovich, M. Donnelly, & C. McLean (Eds.), *Women and aging: An anthology by women* (pp. 58-62). Corvallis, OR: Calyx.

Herz, D. (1988). Employment characteristics of older women, 1987. *Monthly Labor Review, 3*(9), 3-12.

Herzog, A. R., Kahn, R. L., Morgan, J. N., Jackson, J. S., & Antonucci, T. C. (1989). Age differences in productive activities. *Journal of Gerontology, 44*(4), 129-138.

Hess, B. (1990). Beyond dichotomy: Drawing distinctions and embracing differences. *Sociological Forum, 5*(1), 75-93.

Heurtin-Roberts, S. (1988). *Managing a chronic illness: Self, culture and experience.* Paper presented at the 86th Annual Meetings of the American Anthropological Association, Chicago.

Heurtin-Roberts, S. (1993). High-pertension: The uses of a chronic folk illness for personal adaptation. *Social Science & Medicine, 37*(3), 285-294.

Heurtin-Roberts, S., & Reisin, E. (1990). Folk models of hypertension among black women: Problems in illness management. In J. Coreil & J. D. Mull (Eds.), *Anthropology and primary health care* (pp. 222-250). Westview, CO: Boulder.

Heyck, D. L. D. (1994). *Barrios and borderlands: Cultures of Latins and Latinas in the United States.* New York: Routledge.

Higginbotham, E. (1989). *Privilege and the inclusive curriculum.* Paper presented at the annual meeting of the American Sociological Society, San Francisco.

Hill, L., Colby, A., & Phelps, E. (1983). *Coping and adaptation to aging in a sample of black women leaders.* Unpublished manuscript, Cambridge, MA.

Hill, M. S. (1981, January). *Trends in the economic situation of U.S. families and children: 1970-1980.* Paper presented at the Conference of Families and the Economy, Washington, DC.

Himes, C. B. (1975). Headwaiter. In *Black on black: Baby sister and selected writings* (pp. 144-160). London: Joseph.

Himes, C. B. (1975). Pork chop paradise. In *Black on black: Baby sister and selected writings* (pp. 161-175). London: Joseph.

Hines, R. N., Garcia-Preto, M., McGoldrick, R. A., & Weltman, S. (1992). Intergenerational relationships across cultures. *Families in Society: The Journal of Contemporary Human Services* (CEU Article No. 23), pp. 323-338.

Hochschild, A. (1989). *The second shift: Working parents and the revolution at home.* New York: Viking Penguin.

Hogan, L. (1984). *Principles of black political economy.* Boston: Routledge & Kegan Paul.

Holden, C. (1986). Homelessness: Experts differ on root causes. *Science, 232,* 569-570.

Holm, S. T. (1992). Facing two worlds. In A. Jarvenpa (Ed.), *In two cultures: The stories of second generation Finnish-Americans* (pp. 13-17). St. Cloud, MN: North Star.

Hong, M. (Ed.). (1993). *Growing up Asian American: An anthology.* New York: William Morrow.

hooks, b. (1981). *Ain't I a woman: Black women and feminism.* Boston: South End Press.

hooks, b. (1984). *Feminist theory from margin to center.* Boston: South End Press.

Hooyman, A. (1989). *Caregiving and equity: A feminist perspective.* Invited presentation at the annual program meeting of the Council on Social Work Education.

Horowitz, A. (1985). Family caregiving to the frail elderly. In M. P. Lawton & G. L. Maddox (Eds.), *Annual Review of Gerontology and Geriatrics, 5,* 194-256.

Hospital, C. (Ed.). (1988). *Cuban American writers: Los atrevidos.* London: Lane.

House, J. S., Kessler, R. C., Herzog, A. R., Mero, R., Kinney, A., & Breslow, M. (1990). Age, socioeconomic status, and health. *Millbank Quarterly, 68*(3), 383-406.

House, J. S., Landis, K. R., & Umberson, D. (1988). Social relationships and health. *Science, 241,* 540-544.

Hughes, L. (1926). Mother to son. In *Selected poems of Langston Hughes.* New York: Knopf. Reprinted (1991) in M. H. Washington (Ed.), *Memory of kin: Stories about family by black writers* (p. 165). New York: Anchor.

Hunt, L., Jordan, B. & Irwin, S. (1989). Views of what's wrong: Diagnosis and Patients' Concepts of Illness. *Social Science and Medicine, 28,* 945-956.

Hurd, M. D. (1989). The economic status of the elderly. *Science, 244,* 659-664.

Hurston, Z. N. (1992). How it feels to be colored me. In C. Schuster & W. Van Pelt (Eds.), *Speculations: Readings in culture, identity and values.* Englewood Cliffs, NJ: Prentice Hall.

Hurston, Z. N. (1992). My most humiliating Jim Crow experience. In M. G. Secundy (Ed.), *Trials, tribulations and celebrations: African-American perspectives on health, illness, aging and loss.* Yarmouth, ME: Intercultural Press. Reprinted in A. Walker (Ed.), *I love myself when I am laughing: A Zora Neale Hurston reader* (pp. 163-164). Old Westbury, NY: Feminist Press.

Irelan, L. M., & Bell, D. B. (1972). Understanding subjectively defined retirement: A pilot analysis. *The Gerontologist, 12,* 354-356.

Jackson, J. J. (1988, May-June). Aging black women and public policies. *Black Scholar,* pp. 31-43.

Jackson, J. S. (1989). Race, ethnicity and psychological theory and research. *Journal of Gerontology: Psychological Sciences, 41*(1), P1-P2.

Jackson, J. S., Antonucci, T. C., & Gibson, R. C. (1993). Cultural and ethnic contexts of aging productively over the lifecourse: An economic network framework. In S. A. Bass, F. G. Caro, & Y. Chen (Eds.), *Achieving a productive aging society* (pp. 249-268). Westport, CN: Auburn House.

Jackson, J. S., & Gibson, R. C. (1985). Work and retirement among the black elderly. In Z. Blau (Ed.), *Current perspectives on aging and the life cycle* (pp. 193-221). Greenwich, CT: JAI.

Jackson, J. S., McCullough, W., Gurin, G., & Broman, C. (1991). Race identity. In J. S. Jackson (Ed.), *Life in black America* (pp. 238-253). Newbury Park, CA: Sage.

Jacobs, J., & Slawsky, N. (1984). Seniority vs. minority. *Atlanta Journal and Constitution, 35*, 1D, 7D.

James, W. (1950). *The principles of psychology.* New York: Dover.

Jen, G. (1991). *Typical American.* Boston: Houghton Mifflin.

Johnson, C. L., & Barer, B. M. (1990). Families and networks among older inner-city blacks. *The Gerontologist, 39*(6), 726-733.

Johnson, C. L., & Catalano, D. (1983). A longitudinal study of family supports to impaired elderly. *The Gerontologist, 23*, 612-618.

Jones, J. (1991). *Bad blood: The Tuskegee syphilis experiment.* New York: Free Press.

Jones, S. W. (1983). Esse quam videri. In E. H. Wilson (Ed.), *Hope and dignity: Older black women of the South* (pp. 59-65). Philadelphia: Temple University Press.

Jöreskog, K. G., & Sörbom, D. (1978). *LISREL IV: Analysis of linear structural relationships by the method of maximum likelihood.* Chicago: International Educational Services.

Jöreskog, K. G., & Sörbom, D. (Eds.). (1979). *Advances in factor analysis and structural equation models.* Cambridge, MA: Abt.

Joseph, J. (1987). Warning. In S. Martz (Ed.), *When I am an old woman I shall wear purple.* Watsonville, CA: Papier-Mache.

Juster, F. T. (1965). *Time, goods and well-being.* Ann Arbor: University of Michigan, Survey Research Institute, Institute for Social Research.

Juster, F. T. (1986). A note on recent changes in time use. In F. T. Juster & F. Stafford (Eds.), *Studies in the measurement of time allocation.* Ann Arbor: University of Michigan, Institute for Social Research.

Kammerman, S., & Kahn, A. (1987). *The responsive workplace: Employers and a changing labor force.* New York: Columbia University Press.

Kaplan, B. H., Cassel, J. C., & Gore, S. (1977). Social support and health. *Medical Care, 15*(5), 47-58.

Kardiner, A., & Ovesey, L. (1951). *The mark of oppression: A psychosocial study of the American Negro.* New York: Norton.

Kart, C. S. (1990). *The realities of aging: An introduction to gerontology* (3rd ed.). Boston: Allyn & Bacon.

Kasl, S. V. (1979). Changes in mental health status associated with job loss and retirement. In American Psychopathological Association (Ed.), *Stress and mental disorder* (pp. 179-200). New York: Raven.

Kasl, S. V., & Berkman, L. F. (1985). Some psychosocial influences on the health status of the elderly: The perspective of social epidemiology. In J. L. McGaugh & S. B. Kiesler (Eds.), *Aging: Biology and behavior* (pp. 345-385). New York: Academic Press.

Kaufman, S. R. (1986). *The ageless self.* Madison: University of Wisconsin Press.

Keith, J. (1995). The aging experience: Diversity and commonality across cultures. In C. Fry (Ed.), *Aging.* Thousand Oaks, CA: Sage.

Kim, K. C., Kim, S., & Hurh, W. M. (1991). Filial piety and intergenerational relationship in Korean immigrant families. *International Journal of Aging and Human Development, 33*(3), 233-245.

Kimmel, D. C. (1977). Psychotherapy and the older gay man. Psychotherapy: Theory. *Research and Practice, 14*, 386-393.

Kimmel, D. C. (1978). Adult development and aging: A gay perspective. *Journal of Social Issues, 34*(3), 113-130.

Kimmel, D. C. (1992, Summer). The families of older gay men and lesbians. *Generations, 16*, 37-38.

Kingsolver, B. (1989). Homeland. In *Homeland and other stories*. New York: Harper & Row.

Kingson, E. (1988). Generational equity and intergenerational policies. *The Gerontologist, 28*(6), 765-772.

Kitagawa, E. M., & Hauser, P. M. (1973). *Differential mortality in the United States: A study in socioeconomic epidemiology*. Cambridge, MA: Harvard University Press.

Kitano, H., & Daniels, R. (1988). *Asian Americans*. Englewood Cliffs, NJ: Prentice Hall.

Kivett, V., & Learner, R. M. (1980). Perspectives on the childless rural elderly: A comparative analysis. *The Gerontologist, 20*, 708-716.

Kohn, M. L. (1972). Class, family and schizophrenia: A reformulation. *Social Forces, 50*, 295-304.

Kohn, M. L. (1977). *Class and conformity*. Chicago: University of Chicago Press.

Kohn, M., Donley, C., & Wear, D. (Eds.). (1992). *Literature and aging*. Kent, OH: Kent State University Press.

Krause, N., & Wray, L. A. (1992). Psychosocial correlates of health and illness among minority elders. In E. P. Stanford & R. M. Torres-Gil (Eds.), *Diversity: New approaches to ethnic minority aging* (pp. 41-52). Amityville, NY: Baywood.

Kurdek, L. A., & Schmitt, J. P. (1986). Relationship quality of partners in heterosexual married, heterosexual cohabiting, and gay and lesbian relationships. *Journal of Personality and Social Psychology, 51*, 711-720.

Kurtz, R., & Chalfant, H. P. (1984). *The sociology of medicine and illness*. Newton, MA: Allyn & Bacon.

Lacayo, C. G. (1980). *A national study to assess the service needs of the Hispanic elderly* (Final report). Los Angeles: Asociacion Nacional Pro Personas Mayores.

Lamb, H. R., & Rogawski, A. S. (1978). Supplemental security income and the sick role. *American Journal of Psychiatry, 135,* 1221-1224.

Langner, T. S., & Michael, S. T. (1963). *Life stress and mental health*. New York: Free Press.

Lee, G. (1988, March). *Family caregiving for the rural elderly*. Paper presented at the conference, "The Rural Elderly in 1988: A National Perspective," sponsored by the U.S. Department of Agriculture and the University of Arizona, San Diego, CA.

Lee, G. (1992). Gender differences in family caregiving: A fact in search of a theory. In J. W. Dwyer & R. T. Coward (Eds.), *Gender, families, and elder care*. Newbury Park, CA: Sage.

Leffland, E. (1992). The linden tree. In *Last courtesies and other stories*. New York: Harper Collins.

Lerner, G. (1973). *Black women in white America*. New York: Vintage.

Leventhal, H., Dieffenback, M., & Leventhal, E. (1992). Illness cognition: Using common sense to understand treatment adherence and affect cognition interactions. *Cognitive Therapy and Research, 16*(2), 143-163.

Lewis, J. (1986). *The caring process: Mothers and daughters at home*. Albany, NY: Rockefeller Foundation. Reprinted (1988) in J. Lewis & B. Meredith, *Daughters who care: Daughters caring for mothers at home*. London: Routledge & Kegan Paul.

Liem, N. D., & Kehmeier, D. (1979). The Vietnamese. In J. R. McDermott (Ed.), *Peoples and cultures of Hawaii*. Honolulu: University of Hawaii Press.

Linn, M. W., Hunter, K. I., & Linn, B. S. (1980). Self-assessed health, impairment and disability in Anglo, black and Cuban elderly. *Medical Care, 43,* 282-288.

Lipman, A. (1986). Homosexual relationships. *Generations, 10*(4), 51-54.

The long walk home [Film]. (1991). Van Nuys, CA: Live Home Video.

Lowe, P. (1943). Father cures a presidential fever. *In Father and glorious descendant.* Boston: Little, Brown. Reprinted (1993) in M. Hong (Ed.), *Growing up Asian American: An anthology.* New York: Morrow.

Ludwig, A. (1981). The disabled society? *American Journal of Psychotherapy, 35,* 5-15.

Lund-Johansen, P. (1983). The hemodynamics of essential hypertension. In J. Robertson (Ed.), *The handbook of hypertension* (Vol. 1, pp. 151-173). Amsterdam: Elsevier Science.

Maas, H. S., & Kuypers, J. A. (1974). *From thirty to seventy: A forty-year? Longitudinal study of adult life styles and personality.* San Francisco: Jossey-Bass.

Macfarlane, J. W. (1938). Studies in child guidance: I. Methodology of data collection and organization. *Monographs of the Society for Research in Child Development, 3,* 1-254.

Maddox, G. (1988). Aging, drinking, and alcohol abuse. *Generations, 12*(4), 14-16.

Malbin-Glazer, N. (1976). Housework. *Signs, 1,* 905-922.

Manton, K. G., Patrick, C. H., & Johnson, K. W. (1987). Health differences between blacks and whites: Recent trends in mortality and morbidity. *Milbank Quarterly, 65,* 129-199.

Marable, M. (1983). *How capitalism underdeveloped black America.* Boston: South End Press.

Markides, K. S. (1978). Reasons for retirement and adaptation to retirement by elderly Mexican Americans. In E. P. Stanford (Ed.), *Retirement: Concepts and realities of minority elders.* San Diego: San Diego State University.

Markides, K. S. (1989). Consequences of gender differentials in life expectancy for black and Hispanic Americans. *International Journal of Aging and Human Development, 29*(2), 95-102.

Markides, K. S., & Martin, H. W. (with E. Gomez). (1983). *Older Mexican Americans: A study in an urban barrio* (Monograph of the Center for Mexican American Studies). Austin: University of Texas Press.

Markides, K. S., & Mindel, C. H. (1987). *Aging and ethnicity.* Newbury Park, CA: Sage.

Martz, S. H. (Ed.). (1987). *When I am an old woman I shall wear purple.* Watsonville, CA: Papier-Mache.

Martz, S. H. (Ed.). (1992). *If I had my life to live over, I would pick more daisies.* Watsonville, CA: Papier-Mache.

Matthews, S. H. (1988). The burden of parent care: A critical assessment of the recent literature. *Journal of Aging Studies, 2,* 158-165.

McAdoo, H. (1986). Societal stress: The black family. In J. Cole (Ed.), *All American women: Lines that divide, ties that bind* (pp. 187-197). New York: Free Press.

McIntosh, P. (1988). *White privilege and male privilege: A personal account of coming to see correspondences through work in women's studies* (Working paper). Wellesley, MA: Wellesley College Center for Research on Women.

McLaughlin, D., & Jensen, L. (1993). Poverty among older Americans: The plight of nonmetropolitan elders. *Journal of Gerontology: Social Sciences, 48*(2), S44-S54.

Mechanic, D. (1972). Social class and schizophrenia: Some requirements for a plausible theory of social influence. *Social Forces, 50,* 305-309.

Mechanic, D., & Aiken, L. H. (1989). Access to health care and use of medical care services. In H. Freeman & S. Levine (Eds.), *Handbook of medical sociology* (4th ed., pp. 166-184). Englewood Cliffs, NJ: Prentice Hall.

Meier, E. (1986, December). Employment experience and income of older women. *AARP Bulletin* (No. 8608; Washington, DC).

Meyer, M., & Quadagno, J. (1990). The dilemma of poverty-based long term care. In S. Stahl (Ed.), *The legacy of longevity* (pp. 255-269). Newbury Park, CA: Sage.

Mills, C. W. (1959). *The sociological imagination.* New York: Oxford University Press.

Minkler, M. (1989). Gold in gray: Reflections on business; discovery of the elderly market. *The Gerontologist, 29*(1), 17-23.

Minkler, M., & Stone, R. (1985). The feminization of poverty and older women. *The Gerontologist, 25,* 351-357.

Mitchell, L. (1940, May 5). Slave markets typify exploitation of domestics. *The Daily Worker.* Reprinted (1973) in G. Lerner (Ed.), *Black women in white America* (pp. 275-281). New York: Vintage.

Moen, P. (1989). *Working parents: Transformations in gender roles and public policies in Sweden.* Madison: University of Wisconsin Press.

Moen, P. (1992). *Women's two roles: A contemporary dilemma.* New York: Auburn House.

Moen, P., Dempster-McClain, D., & Williams, R. M., Jr. (1989). Social integration and longevity: An event history analysis of women's roles and resilience. *American Sociological Review, 54,* 635-647.

Moen, P., Dempster-McClain, D., & Williams, R. M., Jr. (1992). Successful aging: A life course perspective on women's multiple roles and health. *American Journal of Sociology, 97,* 1612-1638.

Moen, P., Downey, G., & Bolger, N. (1990). Labor-force re-entry among U.S. homemakers in midlife: A life-course analysis. *Gender and Society, 4,* 230-243.

Moen, P., Robison, J., & Fields, V. (1994). Women's work and caregiving roles: A life course approach. *Journal of Gerontology: Social Sciences, 49*(4), S176-S186.

Mohr, N. (1986). A time with a future In R. Barrzca (Ed.), *Woman of the century: Thirty modern short stories.* New York: St. Martin's.

Montagna, P. D. (1977). *Occupations and society: Toward a sociology of the labor market.* New York: John Wiley.

Montgomery, R. J. V., & Kamo, Y. (1989). Parent care by sons and daughters. In J. A. Mancini (Ed.), *Aging parents and adult children* (pp. 213-230). Lexington, MA: Lexington Books.

Morgan, J. N. (1980). Retirement in prospect and retrospect. In G. Duncan & J. Morgan (Eds.), *Five thousand American families: Patterns of economic progress* (Vol. 8). Ann Arbor: University of Michigan, Institute for Social Research.

Moses, Y. (1992). *Diversity in the undergraduate curriculum.* Plenary address at "Rethinking the Major," conference sponsored by the Association of American Colleges, Philadelphia.

Moynihan, D. P. (1965). *The Negro family: The case for national action.* Washington, DC: Government Printing Office.

Munnell, A. H. (1978, January-February). The economic experience of blacks, 1964-1974. *New England Economic Review,* pp. 5-18.

Murray, J. (1979). Subjective retirement. *Social Security Bulletin, 42,* 20-25, 43.

Mutchler, J. E., & Burr, J. A. (1991, December). Racial differences in health and health care service utilization in later life: The effect of socioeconomic status. *Journal of Health and Social Behavior, 32,* 342-356.

Myerhoff, B. (1978). *Number our days.* New York: Simon & Schuster.

Myers, G. (1990). Demography of aging. In R. Binstock & L. K. George (Eds.), *Handbook of aging and the social sciences* (3rd ed., pp. 19-34). San Diego, CA: Academic Press.

Nathan, J. (1990). Public policy issues and the minority elder. In *Minority aging.* Washington, DC: U.S. Public Health Services.

National Center for Health Statistics. (1991). *Health, United States, 1990.* Hyattsville, MD: Public Health Service.

National Council on the Aging. (1976). *The myth and reality of aging in America.* Washington, DC: Author.

National Film Board of Canada. (1991). *Strangers in good company* [Film]. Burbank, CA: Buena Vista Home Video.

National Resource Center on Health Promotion and Aging and AARP Health Advocacy Services. (1990). *Healthy aging: Model health promotion programs for minority elders* [½-in. videocassette/46 min./color]. (Distributed by National Resource Center on Health Promotion and Aging and AARP, Washington, DC, 202-434-2277)

Naylor, G. (1989). *Mama Day.* New York: Vintage.

Neal, M. B., Chapman, N. J., Ingersoll-Dayton, B., & Emlen, A. C. (1993). *Balancing work and caregiving for children, adults and elders.* Newbury Park, CA: Sage.

Neugarten, B. L. (1970). Dynamics of transition of middle age to old age: Adaptation and the life cycle. *Journal of Geriatric Psychiatry, 4,* 71-89.

New York City Human Resources Administration. (1983). *Project future: Focusing, understanding, targeting, and utilizing resources for homeless mentally ill, older persons, youth and employables.* New York: Author.

Nordisk, S. S. (1984). *Social security in the Nordic countries: Scope, expenditure and financing.* Copenhagen: Statistical Reports of the Nordic Countries.

Novas, H. (1994). *Everything you need to know about Latino history.* New York: Penguin.

Oakley, A. (1974). *The sociology of housework.* Oxford: Martin Robertson.

O'Connor, J. (1973). *The fiscal crisis of the state.* New York: St. Martin's.

Older Women's League. (1986). *Report on the status of midlife and older women.* Washington, DC: Author.

Oliver, J. (1983). The caring wife. In J. Finch & D. Groves (Eds.), *A labour of love: Women, work and caring* (pp. 72-88). London: Routledge & Kegan Paul.

Oliver, M. L., & Glick, M. A. (1982). An analysis of the new orthodoxy on black mobility. *Social Problems, 29,* 511-523.

Olsen [Lerner], T. (1934, March). I want you women up north to know. *Partisan, 1.* Reprinted (1990) in J. Zandy (Ed.), *Calling home: Working-class women's writings, an anthology.* New Brunswick, NJ: Rutgers University Press; and in D. Rosenfelt (1981), From the thirties: Tillie Olsen and the radical tradition. *Feminist Studies, 7*(3), 367-369.

Olsen, T. (1971). I stand here ironing. In *Tell me a riddle.* New York: Dell.

Olson, L. K. (1982). *The political economy of aging.* New York: Columbia University Press.

O'Rand, A. (1984). Women. In E. Palmore (Ed.), *Handbook of the aged in the U.S.* Westport, CT: Greenwood.

O'Rand, A., & Henretta, J. (1982a, June). Delayed career entry, industrial pension structure and early retirement in a cohort of unmarried women. *American Sociological Review, 47,* 365-373.

O'Rand, A., & Henretta, J. (1982b). Midlife work history and retirement income. In M. Szinovacz (Ed.), *Women's retirement: Policy implications of recent research* (pp. 25-44). Beverly Hills, CA: Sage.

Ostrander, S. (1984). Community volunteer. In *Women of the upper class* (pp. 111-139). Philadelphia: Temple University Press.

Packard, M. D. (1987). Income of new disabled-worker beneficiaries and their families: Findings from the new survey. *Social Security Bulletin, 50,* 5-23.

Padgett, D. (1989). Aging minority women: Issues in research and health policy. In L. Grau (Ed.), *Women in the later years: Health, social and cultural perspectives.* Binghamton, NY: Haworth.

Palley, H. A., & Otkay, J. S. (1983). The chronically limited elderly: The case for a national policy for in-home and supportive community-based services. *Home Health Care Services Quarterly, 2*(2), 3-141.

Palmore, E. B. (1971). Why do people retire? *Aging and Human Development, 2,* 169-283.

Palmore, E. B. (1984). The retired. In E. B. Palmore (Ed.), *Handbook on the aged in the United States.* Westport, CT: Greenwood.

Palmore, E. B., Fillenbaum, G. G., & George, L. K. (1984). Consequences of retirement. *Journal of Gerontology, 39,* 109-116.

Palmore, E. B., & Manton, K. (1973). Ageism compared to racism and sexism. *Journal of Gerontology, 28,* 363-369.

Parker, P. (1970). *A view from the Bowery.* Unpublished manuscript.

Parnes, H., & Nestel, G. (1981). The retirement experience. In H. Parnes (Ed.), *Work and retirement: A national longitudinal study of men* (pp. 155-197). Cambridge: MIT Press.

Parsons, T. (1955). The American family: Its relations to personality and the social structure. In T. Parsons & R. Bales (Eds.), *Family socialization and interaction process* (pp. 3-21). Glencoe, IL: Free Press.

Passuth, R., & Bengtson, V. (1988). Emergent theories of aging. In J. E. Birren & V. L. Bengston (Eds.), *Sociological theories of aging: Current perspectives and future directions* (pp. 333-355). New York: Springer.

Pearce, D. (1978). The feminization of poverty: Women, work, and welfare. *Urban and Social Change Review, 11,* 28-36.

Pearlin, L. I., & Johnson, J. S. (1977). Marital status, life strains, and depression. *American Sociological Review, 42,* 704-715.

Peplau, L. A. (1991). Lesbian and gay relationships. In J. C. Gonsiorek & J. D. Weinrich (Eds.), *Homosexuality: Research implications for public policy.* Newbury Park, CA: Sage.

Peplau, L. A., Padesky, C., & Hamilton, M. (1982). Satisfaction in lesbian relations. *Journal of Homosexuality, 8,* 23-35.

Peterson, C. (1980, October 5-6). *The sense of control over one's life: A review of recent literature.* Paper prepared for the Social Science Research Council Meeting, "Self and Personal Control Over the Life Span," New York.

Phillips, D. (1965). Self-reliance and the inclination to adopt the sick role. *Social Forces, 43,* 555-563.

Pittman, D. J., & Gordon, T. W. (1958). *Revolving door: A study of the chronic police case inebriate.* Glencoe, IL: Free Press.

Powdermaker, H. (1943). The channeling of Negro aggression by the cultural process. *American Journal of Sociology, 48,* 750-758.

Prince, E. (1978). Welfare status, illness and subjective health definition. *American Journal of Public Health, 68,* 865-871.

Quadagno, J. (1988). Women's access to pensions and the structure of eligibility rules: Systems of production and reproduction. *Sociological Quarterly, 29*(4), 541-558.

Quadagno, J., & Meyer, M. H. (1990). Gender and public policy. *Generations, 14*(3), 64-66.

Rainwater, L., & Yancey, W. (1967). *The Moynihan Report and the politics of controversy.* Cambridge: MIT Press.

Reskin, B., & Hartmann, H. (1986). *Women's work and men's work: Sex segregation on the job.* Washington, DC: National Academy of Sciences Press.

Rick, K., & Forward, J. (1992). Acculturation and perceived intergenerational differences among youth. *Journal of Cross-Cultural Psychology, 23*(1), 85-94.

Riley, M. W., & Riley, J. W., Jr. (1989). The lives of olde people and changing social roles. *Annals of the American Academy of Political and Social Science, 503,* 14-28.

Rimmer, L. (1983). The economics of work and caring. In J. Finch & D. Groves (Eds.), *A labour of love* (pp. 131-147). London: Routledge & Kegan Paul.

Rodeheaver, D., & Stohs, J. (1991). The adaptive misperception of age in older women: Sociocultural images and psychological mechanisms of control. *Educational Gerontology, 17,* 141-156.

Rollins, J. (1985). *Between women: Domestics and their employers.* Philadelphia: Temple University Press.

Rosenthal, C. J. (1985). Kinkeeping in the familial division of labor. *Journal of Marriage and the Family, 47,* 965-974.

Rowe, J. W., & Kahn, R. L. (1987). Human aging: Usual and successful. *Science, 237,* 143-149.

Safilios-Rothschild, C. (1970). The study of family power structures. *Journal of Marriage and the Family, 38,* 629-640.

Sainsbury, D. (1989, April). *Welfare state variations, women and equality: On varieties of the welfare state and their implications for women.* Paper presented at the ECPR Workshop, "Equality Principles and Gender Politics," Paris.

Sarbin, T., & Allen, V. (1968). Role theory. In G. Lindzey & E. Aronson (Eds.), *Handbook of social psychology.* Reading, MA: Addison-Wesley.

Scharlach, A., & Boyd, S. (1989). Caregiving and employment: Results of an employee survey. *The Gerontologist, 27,* 627-631.

Schecter, S. (Producer & director). (1985). *The homefront* [Film]. PBS.

Schmidt, D., & Boland, S. (1986). Structure of perceptions of older adults: Evidence for multiple stereotypes. *Psychology and Aging, 1,* 255-260.

Schulz, J. H. (1985). *The economics of aging* (3rd ed.). Belmont, CA: Wadsworth.

Schulz, J. H. (1988). *The economics of aging* (4th ed.). Belmont, CA: Wadsworth.

Schuman, H., & Scott, J. (1989). Generations and collective memories. *American Sociological Review, 54,* 359-381.

Schweitzer, M. (1987). The elders: Cultural dimensions of aging in two American Indian communities. In J. Sokolovsky (Ed.), *Growing old in different societies.* Acton, MA: Copley.

Scott, P. B. (1982). Debunking Sapphire: Toward a non-racist and non-sexist social science. In G. T. Hull, P. B. Scott, & B. Smith (Eds.), *But some of us are brave*. Old Westburg, NY: Feminist Press.

Scott, R., Gaskell, R. G., & Morrell, D. C. (1966). Patients who reside in common lodging-houses. *British Medical Journal, 2*, 1561-1564.

Seccombe, K. (1992). Employment, the family, and employer-based policies. In J. W. Dwyer & R. T. Coward (Eds.), *Gender, families, and elder care*. Newbury Park, CA: Sage.

Segall, A., & Goldstein, J. (1989). Exploring the correlates of self-provided health care behavior. *Social Science and Medicine, 29*(2), 153-161.

Seltzer, J. (1987). A place for mother. In S. Martz (Ed.), *When I am an old woman I shall wear purple*. Watsonville, CA: Papier Mache.

Shurkin, J. N. (1992). *Terman's kids: The groundbreaking study of how the gifted grow up*. Boston: Little, Brown.

Sieber, S. (1981). *Fatal remedies: The ironies of social intervention*. New York: Plenum.

Silko, L. M. (1981). Lullaby. In *The storyteller*. New York: Seaver. Reprinted (1991) in B. R. Rico & S. Mano (Eds.), *American mosaic: Multicultural readings in context* (pp. 587-594). Boston: Houghton Mifflin.

Simmons, L. (1945). *The role of the aged in primitive society*. New Haven, CT: Yale University Press.

Singer, I. B. (1988). The hotel. In *The death of Methuselah and other stories*. New York: Farrar, Straus & Giroux. Reprinted (1991) in M. Fowler & P. McCutcheon (Eds.), *Songs of experience: An anthology of literature on growing old* (pp. 165-175). New York: Ballantine.

Skolnick, A. (1991). Changes of heart: Family dynamics in historical perspective. In P. Cowan, D. Field, D. Hansen, A. Skolnick, & G. Swanson (Eds.), *Family, self and society: Towards a new agenda for family research*. Hillsdale, NJ: Lawrence Erlbaum.

Smith, B. (Ed.). (1983). *Home girls: A black feminist anthology*. Albany, NY: Kitchen Table.

Smith, D. E. (1987). *The everyday world as problematic: A feminist sociology*. Toronto: University of Toronto Press.

Sokolovsky, J., Cohen, C. I., Teresi, J., & Holmes, D. (1986). Gender, networks, and adaptation among an inner-city elderly population. *The Gerontologist, 26* (Special Issue 247A).

Sone, M. (1953). Pearl Harbor echoes in Seattle. In *Nisei daughter*. Boston: Little, Brown. Reprinted (1991) in B. R. Rico & S. Mano (Eds.), *American mosaic: Multicultural readings in context* (pp. 335-346). Boston: Houghton Mifflin.

Spadley, J. P. (1970). *You owe yourself a drunk*. Boston: Little, Brown.

Srole, L. (1978). *Mental health in the metropolis: The midtown Manhattan study* (rev. and enlarged ed.). New York: New York University Press.

Stacey, M. (1981). The division of labor revisited or overcoming the two Adams: The special problem of people work. In P. Abrams, R. Deen, J. Finch, & R. Rock (Eds.), *Practice and progress: British sociology, 1950–1980* (pp. 172-204). London: George Allen & Unwin.

Stack, C. (1974). *All our kin*. New York: Harper & Row.

Stair, N. (1992). If I had my life to live over. In S. Martz (Ed.), *If I had my life to live over, I would pick more daisies*. Watsonville, CA: Papier-Mache.

Stanford, E. P., Peddecord, M., & Lockery, S. (1990). Variations among the elderly in black, Hispanic, and white families. In T. Brubaker (Ed.), *Family relations in later life* (2nd ed.). Newbury Park, CA: Sage.

Stanford, E. P., & Yee, D. (1991, Fall-Winter). Gerontology and the relevance of diversity. *Generations, 15,* 11-14.

Steinitz, L. Y. (1981). The local church as support for the elderly. *Journal of Gerontological Social Work, 4,* 43-53.

Steuve, A., & O'Donnell, L. (1989). Interactions between women and their elderly parents: Constraints of daughters' employment. *Research on Aging, 11,* 331-353.

Stoller, E. P. (1983). Parental caregiving by adult children. *Journal of Marriage and the Family, 45,* 851-858.

Stoller, E. (1990). Males as helpers: The role of sons, relatives, and friends. *The Gerontologist, 30,* 228-235.

Stoller, E. (1993). Why women care: Gender and the organization of lay care. *Journal of Aging Studies, 7*(2), 151-170.

Stoller, E., & Cutler, S. J. (1992). The impact of gender on configurations of care among elderly couples. *Research on Aging, 14*(3), 313-330.

Stoller, E., Forster, L., & Pollow, R. (1994). Older people's recommendations for treating symptoms: Repertoires of lay knowledge about disease. *Medical Care, 32*(8), 847-862.

Stoller, E., Forster, L., & Portugal, S. (1993). Self-care responses to symptoms by older people. *Medical Care, 30,* 24-42.

Stoller, E., Pugliesi, K., & Gilbert, M. (1992). *Informal support networks of the rural elderly: A panel study* (Technical Report to the National Institute on Aging, Washington, DC).

Stone, R. I. (1989, Spring & Summer). The feminization of poverty among the elderly. *Women's Studies Quarterly, 17,* 20-34.

Stone, R. I., Cafferata, G., & Sangl, J. (1987). Caregivers of the frail elderly: A national profile. *The Gerontologist, 27,* 616-626.

Stone, R. I., & Short, P. F. (1990). The competing demands of employment and informal caregiving to disabled elders. *Medical Care, 28,* 513-526.

Strauss, R. (1946). Alcohol and the homeless man. *Quarterly Journal of Studies of Alcohol, 7,* 360-404.

Streib, G., & Schneider, G. (1971). *Retirement in American society.* Ithaca, NY: Cornell University Press.

Stryker, S. (1968). Identity salience and role performance: The relevance of symbolic interaction theory for family research. *Journal of Marriage and the Family, 30,* 558-562.

Sudarkasa, N. (1980, November-December). African and Afro-American family structure: A comparison. *Black Scholar,* pp. 43-44.

Sudarkasa, N. (1981). Interpreting the African heritage in Afro-American family organizations. In H. McAdoo (Ed.), *Black families* (pp. 37-53). Beverly Hills, CA: Sage.

Sue, S. (1991). Ethnicity and culture in psychological research and practice. In J. D. Gbodchilds (Ed.), *Psychological perspectives on human diversity in America* (pp. 51-85). Washington, DC: American Psychological Association.

Sue, D. W., & Sue, D. (1990). *Counselling the culturally different: Theory and practice* (2nd ed.). New York: John Wiley.

Susser, M., Watson, W., & Hopper, K. (1985). *Sociology in medicine* (3rd ed.). New York: Oxford University Press.

Syme, S. L., & Berkman, L. F. (1981). Social class: Susceptibility and sickness. In R. Conrad & R. Kern (Eds.), *The sociology of health and illness: Critical perspectives* (pp. 35-44). New York: St. Martin's.

Tan, A. (1989). *The joy luck club.* New York: G. P. Putnam.

Taylor, R. J., & Chatters, L. M. (1986). Church-based informal support among elderly blacks. *The Gerontologist, 26*(6), 637-642.

Taylor, S. (1982). Religion as a coping mechanism for older black women. *Quarterly Contact, 5*(4), 2-3.

Terkel, S. (1974). Mike LeFevre. In *Working: People talk about the work they do all day and how they feel about what they do*. New York: Pantheon. Reprinted (1992) in C. Schuster & W. Van Pelt (Eds.), *Speculations: Readings in culture, identify and values* (pp. 520-524). Englewood Cliffs, NJ: Prentice Hall.

Terkel, S. (1980). *American dreams: Lost and found*. New York: Pantheon.

Terkel, S. (1992). *Race: How blacks and whites think and feel about the American obsession*. New York: Doubleday.

Terkel, S. (1995). *Coming of age*. New York: The New Press.

Terrell, M. C. (1973). What it means to be colored in the capital of the United States. In G. Lerner (Ed.), *Black women in white America*. New York: Vintage.

Thomas, E. M. (1959). *The harmless people*. New York: Knopf.

Thomas, R. (1967). Puerto Rican paradise. In *Down these mean streets* (pp. 268-272). New York: Knopf.

Thomas, S. B., & Quinn, S. C. (1991, November). The Tuskegee syphilis study, 1932-1972: Implications for HIV education and AIDS risk education programs in the black community. *American Journal of Public Health, 81*, (11).

Thone, R. R. (1992). *Women and aging: Celebrating ourselves*. New York: Haworth.

Thurlow, H. J. (1971). Illness in relation to life situation and sick role tendency. *Journal of Psychosomatic Research, 15*, 73-88.

Toomer, J. (1923). *Cane*. New York: Boni and Livenright.

Torres-Gil, F. M., & Hyde, J. C. (1990). The impact of minorities on long-term care policy in California. In P. Kiebig & W. Lammers (Eds.), *California policy choices for long-term care* (pp. 31-52). Los Angeles: University of Southern California Press.

Tracy, A. (1992). *Between the funerals: Measuring*. Unpublished manuscript.

Tran, T. V. (1988). Sex differences in English language acculturation and learning strategies among Vietnamese adults aged 40 and over in the United States. *Sex Roles, 19*, 747-758.

Tran, T. V. (1991). Family living arrangement and social adjustment among three ethnic groups of elderly Indochinese refugees. *International Journal of Aging and Human Development, 32*(2), 91-102.

Treas, J. (1977). Family support systems for the aged: Some social and demographic considerations. *The Gerontologist, 17*, 486-491.

Twaddle, C. A., & Hessler, R. (1987). *A sociology of health* (2nd ed.). New York: Macmillan.

Twigg, J. (1989). Models of carers: How do social care agencies conceptualize their relationship with informal carers? *Journal of Social Policy, 18*(1), 53-66.

Umberson, D. (1992). Gender, marital status and the social control of health behavior. *Social Science and Medicine, 34*, 907-917.

U.S. Bureau of the Census. (1980). The social and economic status of the black population in the United States 1790-1978. *Current Population Reports* (Special Studies Series P-23, No. 80). Washington, DC: Government Printing Office.

U.S. Bureau of the Census. (1987). Pensions: Worker coverage and retirement income. *Current Population Reports* (Series P-70, No. 12). Washington, DC: Government Printing Office.

U.S. Bureau of the Census. (1989). Projections of the population of the United States, by age, sex, and race: 1988 to 2080. *Current Population Reports* (Series 25, no. 1018). Washington, DC: Government Printing Office.

U.S. Commission on Civil Rights. (1981). *Civil rights: A national, not a special interest.* Washington, DC: Author.

U.S. Commission on Civil Rights. (1982). *Unemployment and under-employment among blacks, Hispanics, and women* (Clearinghouse Publication 74). Washington, DC: Author.

U.S. Department of Health and Human Services. (1985). 1982 new beneficiary survey: No. 4. Women and social security. *Social Security Bulletin, 48*(2), 17-26.

U.S. Senate Special Committee on Aging. (1988, February 29). *Developments in aging: The long-term care challenge* (Vol. 3). Washington, DC: Author.

Van Nostrand, J. F., Furner, S., & Suzman, R. (Eds.). (1993). Health data on older Americans: United States, 1992. *Vital Health Statistics, 3*(77). Hyattsville, MD: National Center for Health Statistics.

Verbrugge, L. (1984). A health profile of older women with comparisons to older men. *Research on Aging, 6*(3), 291-322.

Victor, C. R. (1989). Inequalities in health in later life. *Age and Aging, 18*, 387-391.

Waitzkin, H. (1974). *The exploitation of illness in capitalist society.* Indianapolis, IN: Bobbs-Merrill.

Waldrun, I. (1988). Gender and health-related behavior. In D. S. Gochman (Ed.), *Health behavior: Emerging perspectives* (pp. 193-208). New York: Plenum.

Walker, A. (1983). In search of our mothers' gardens. In *In search of our mothers' gardens: Womanist prose* (pp. 231-243). San Diego, CA: Harcourt Brace Jovanovich.

Wallace, S. (1965). *Skid row as a way of life.* Totowa, NJ: Bedminister.

Walls, C. T., & Zarit, S. H. (1991). Informal support from black churches and the well-being of elderly blacks. *The Gerontologist, 32*(4), 490-495.

Walser, A. (1986). I didn't have no family before I was married. In V. Byerly (Ed.), *Hard times cotton mill girls: Personal histories of womanhood and poverty in the South.* Ithaca, NY: ILR. Reprinted (1990) in J. Zandy (Ed.), *Calling home: Working-class women's writings, an anthology* (pp. 21-26). New Brunswick, NJ: Rutgers University Press.

Weibel-Orlando, J. (1989). Elders and elderlies: Well-being in Indian Old Age. *American Indian Culture and Research Journal, 13*(3-4), 149-170.

Weibel-Orlando, J. (1990). Grandparenting styles: Native American perspectives. In J. Sokolovsky (Ed.), *The cultural context of aging: Worldwide perspectives* (pp. 109-125). New York: Bergin and Garvey.

Weinstein-Shr, G., & Henkin, N. Z. (1991). Continuity and change: Intergenerational relations in southeast Asian refugee families. *Marriage and Family Review, 16*, 351-367.

Westat, Inc. (1989). *A survey of elderly Hispanics* (Final report). Baltimore: Commonwealth Fund Commission on Elderly People Living Alone.

White, A. J. (1991). Dyad/triad. In P. Bell-Scott, B. Guy-Sheftall, J. Royster, J. Sims-Wood, M. DeCosta-Willis, & L. Fultz (Eds.), *Double stitch: Black women write about mothers and daughters* (pp. 188-195). Boston: Beacon.

Wilkinson, D. (1987). Traditional medicine in American families: Reliance on the wisdom of elders. *Culture, Medicine, and Psychiatry, 11,* 65-76.

Williams, D. R. (1990). Socioeconomic differentials in health: A review and redirection. *Social Psychology Quarterly, 53*(2), 81-99.

Wilson, E. H., & Mullalley, S. (Eds.). (1983). *Hope and dignity: Older black women of the South.* Philadelphia: Temple University Press.

Wilson, W. J. (1978). *The declining significance of race.* Chicago: University of Chicago Press.

Wolinsky, F. D. (1980). *The sociology of health: Principles, professions, and issues.* Boston: Little, Brown.

Woo, D. (1989). The gap between striving and achieving: The case of Asian American women. In Asian Women United of California (Eds.), *Making waves: An anthology of writings by and about Asian American women* (pp. 185-194). Boston: Beacon.

Wray, L. (1991). Public policy implications of an ethnically diverse elderly population. *Journal of Cross-Cultural Gerontology, 6,* 243-257.

Wright, R. (1991). The ethics of living Jim Crow. In H. L. Gates, Jr. (Ed.), *Bearing witness: Selections from African-American autobiography in the twentieth century.* New York: Pantheon. (Original work published 1937)

Wu, C. (1989). *Making waves: The world of our grandmothers.* Boston: Beacon.

Yee, B. W. K. (1989). Loss of one's homeland and culture during the middle years. In R. A. Kalish (Ed.), *Coping with the losses of middle age* (pp. 281-300). Newbury Park, CA: Sage.

Yee, B. W. K. (1990, Summer). Gender and family issues in minority groups. *Generations, 14,* 39-41.

Yee, B. W. K. (1992, Summer). Elders in southeast Asian refugee families. *Generations,* pp. 24-27.

Yee, B. W. K. (in press). Markers of successful aging among Vietnamese refugee women. *Women and Therapy, 12*(2).

Yee, B. W. K., & Nguyen, D. (1987). Correlates of drug abuse and abuse among Indochinese refugees: Mental health implications. *Journal of Psychoactive Drugs, 19,* 77-83.

Yezierska, A. (1991). A window full of sky. In M. Fowler & P. McCutcheon (Eds.), *Songs of experience: An anthology of literature on growing old* (pp. 284-288). New York: Ballantine.

Zinn, M. B., Cannon, L. W., Higginbotham, E., & Dill, B. T. (1986). The costs of exclusionary practices in women's studies. *Signs, 11,* 290-303.

Zsembik, B. A., & Singer, A. (1990). The problem of defining retirement among minorities: The Mexican Americans. *Gerontologist, 30*(6), 749-757.

Zuckerman, M. (1987). After sixty. In P. Doress & D. Ziegel (Eds.), *Ourselves, growing older.* New York: Simon & Schuster.

Index

Of special interest from

RESEARCH ON AGING
A Quarterly of Social Gerontology and Adult Development
Editor: Rhonda J.V. Montgomery, *University of Kansas*
. . . a journal of interdisciplinary research on current issues, and methodological
and research problems in the study of the aged.
Quarterly: March, June, September, December
Yearly rates: Institution $180 / Individual $57

JOURNAL OF APPLIED GERONTOLOGY
The Official Journal of the Southern Gerontological Society
Editor: Graham D. Rowles, *University of Kentucky*
. . . strives to consistently publish articles in all subdisciplines of aging whose findings,
conclusions, or suggestions have clear and sometimes immediate applicability to the
problems encountered by older persons.
Quarterly: March, June, September, December
Yearly rates: Institution $166 / Individual $56

JOURNAL OF AGING AND HEALTH
Editor: Kyriakos S. Markides, *University of Texas Medical Branch, Galveston*
. . . deals with social and behavioral factors related to aging and health, emphasizing
health and quality of life.
Quarterly: February, May, August, November
Yearly rates: Institution $153 / Individual $58

ABSTRACTS IN SOCIAL GERONTOLOGY:
Current Literature on Aging
Published in Cooperation with The National Council on the Aging, Inc.
. . . provides abstracts and bibliographies of major articles, books, reports, and other
materials on all aspects of social gerontology: including demography, economics, family
relations, government policy, health, institutional care, physiology, psychiatric
dysfunctions, psychology, societal attitudes, work and retirement.
Quarterly: March, June, September, December
Yearly rates: Institution $186 / Individual $86

ORDER TODAY!
Sage Customer Service: 805-499-9774   ☐   Sage FaxLine: 805-499-0871

SAGE PUBLICATIONS, INC. | SAGE PUBLICATIONS LTD | SAGE PUBLICATIONS INDIA PVT. LTD
2455 Teller Road | 6 Bonhill Street | M-32 Market, Greater Kailash I
Thousand Oaks, CA 91320 | London EC2A 4PU, England | New Delhi 110 048, India

⑤SAGE Periodicals Press